# Modeling Socioeconomic Evolution and Continuity in Ancient Egypt

## The value and limitations of zooarchaeological analyses

Carol Yokell

BAR International Series 1315
2004

Published in 2016 by
BAR Publishing, Oxford

BAR International Series 1315

*Modeling Socioeconomic Evolution and Continuity in Ancient Egypt*

ISBN 978 1 84171 664 0



BAR Publishing is the trading name of British Archaeological Reports (Oxford) Ltd. British Archaeological Reports was first incorporated in 1974 to publish the BAR Series, International and British. In 1992 Hadrian Books Ltd became part of the BAR group. This volume was originally published by Archaeopress in conjunction with British Archaeological Reports (Oxford) Ltd / Hadrian Books Ltd, the Series principal publisher, in 2004. This present volume is published by BAR Publishing, 2016.

Printed in England

BAR
PUBLISHING

BAR titles are available from:

BAR Publishing
122 Banbury Rd, Oxford, OX2 7BP, UK
EMAIL info@barpublishing.com
PHONE +44 (0)1865 310431
FAX +44 (0)1865 316916
www.barpublishing.com

# CONTENTS

# List of Figures

# List of Tables

# ABSTRACT

The present thesis examined patterns of taxonomic utilization from a wide range of sites from different geographic regions and through several thousand years in order to contribute to an eventual understanding of the mechanisms by which disparate regional societies were subsumed into the unified Egyptian 'state.' An examination of the relative adaptability of cattle, sheep, goat, and pigs was fundamental to understanding the choices by humans for exploiting a particular species or its products in a given area. A predictive model was developed based on issues of economic and social production among modern societies utilizing these same domesticated taxa under similar environmental conditions. Five strategies were identified: nomadic pastoralism, semi-nomadic pastoralism, transhumance, agro-pastoralism, and ranching. Contrary to previous interpretations, pigs were shown to be well adapted to utilization by sedentary populations in both the southern Valley and northern Delta regions.

The methods for the investigation of alternatives of social and economic production and intensification were closely linked to zooarchaeological analysis. However, it was necessary to supplement faunal inferences with evidence such as artistic depictions, Egyptian texts, and literature.

# 1. INTRODUCTION

## RESEARCH GOALS AND FOCUS

Much of the research in Egyptian archaeology has focused on the location, date and development of the state-level society by which later centuries are characterized. The shift to state society in Egypt has been viewed as a progression from a somewhat simpler to more complex society, and rightly so. What is often ignored, however, is the continuity between the Predynastic and Dynastic periods. In this study, evolutionary ecology, and to a lesser extent economic, theories are applied to ethnographic and archaeological data in an attempt to further our current understanding of the development, adoption and perpetuation of alternative food production strategies in ancient Egypt, and how those strategies also influence other aspects of Egyptian society. A methodology is developed for applying evolutionary theory—in the Darwinian sense rather than the cultural evolutionary sense (e.g., Sahlins and Service [1960])—to an eventual understanding of why human food production patterns took the forms they did, and by what means they were maintained within Dynastic Egyptian society.

Following the appropriation of animals from their natural environment into a "human-constructed" environment, changes occurred in animal morphology, behavior, growth, development, reproduction, body composition, productivity, and physiology, and most were reflected in the gene pool. Some scholars have hypothesized that because humans are animals and are subject to natural selection as well, evolutionary changes in animals have corresponding changes in human genetic structures. While the ability of humans to alter (rather than merely adapt to) their environment renders the identification of coevolutionary changes in humans and animals extremely difficult, such changes are likely. However, social and behavioral changes are more readily apparent in archaeological human populations than genetic changes. The formation of new social institutions to handle the increasing numbers of animals needed to feed the society, to direct processing and distribution of new products, or resulting from the adoption of social traits characteristic of societies from whom one population obtained domesticates or trade goods, are only a few examples.

The research and analysis presented here are significant because they represent a new application of zoo-archaeological[1] techniques to a wide range of ancient Egyptian assemblages. The majority of faunal reports are of limited scope, usually restricted to a single site or a comparison of a few sites within a small geographic region. With such a narrow focus, it is tempting to attribute unexpected patterns to unique conditions in that area and as a result regional or cultural variations remain invisible. Site-specific reports are a necessary first step to expanding accumulated databases, but few syntheses or generalizing interpretations have been attempted (for exceptions, see Brewer et al. 1994; Hecker 1982; Redding 1991). The anthropological perspective utilized by Brewer (1986) was the first time such an approach had been used to interpret Egyptian zooarchaeological data, and the current research is the first time this perspective is applied on a large scale to the understanding of the development of complex Egyptian societies. To begin to investigate the mutually beneficial relationship between humans and their domesticated animals, a synthesis of the existing data is presented, and attempts are made to address several specific questions, such as:

1. What was the distribution of domesticated taxa across Egypt? How did the distribution change through time? Are there areas where certain taxa predominated? (see chapters six and seven)
2. What is the evidence for the evolution of domestic breeds and what purposes underlie their development? (see chapter seven)
3. What economic functions are discernible? Did a site's occupants raise domesticates for trade with other areas, or rely on different resources depending on social class? (see chapters six and seven)
4. How is the reliance on domesticated animals reflected in religious practices? Why were there taboos/proscriptions against certain foods in particular regions or social classes? (see chapters six and seven)

Each of these questions is complex, and it is not possible at present to answer each to the same degree, because of biases in the archaeological record, scarce or missing textual data, and so on, but they may be answered more completely with future research. In order to obtain information concerning the effects of domestication on Egyptian society in particular, the data were most effectively gathered and analyzed in a three-stage process: (1) development of faunal and cultural expectations through examination of ethnographic literature, (2) identification and quantification of recovered faunal remains, and (3) corroboration of zooarchaeologically based inferences through correlation with other lines of evidence, such as art historical and Egyptological sources, including translated Egyptian texts and literature.[2] The approach is strongly ecological and for this reason the temporal boundaries include several millennia of prehistory in which the development of the precursors to classic Egyptian society can be traced, as well as three millennia of historical time. The methods are necessarily interdisciplinary, and make use

[1] The study of the osteological remains of animals recovered from archaeological sites.

[2] 'Texts' are public inscriptions, government documents or decrees, all are subject to exaggeration or use in propaganda. 'Literature' refers primarily to private documents: personal letters, poetry, etc., and are more rare. A discussion of the dates of appearance is presented in chapter two.

of the wealth of documentation provided by classical authors and the ancient Egyptians themselves through reconstructions by modern archaeologists and Egyptologists.

The focus here is not to examine the *transition* to the reliance on domesticated animals, but rather the concomitant *repercussions* of that adoption throughout a society. Egypt is a good testing ground for this type of study because the geographical and environmental conditions render it a relatively simple case study of the dramatic changes in the social structure and of the roles of the domesticated animal complex within that developing human society. Also, Egypt has received intense study by scholars from a variety of scientific disciplines, and it is the only place at present in which the archaeological, faunal, textual, and pictographic evidence of social and religious ramifications of integration can be evaluated from the same time period (and the same site in rare instances) rendering it particularly attractive for the present research. Additionally, the process of social change is expected to have occurred more quickly in Egypt, because several of the domesticated taxa were imported from other regions such as southwest Asia.

The addition of detailed knowledge of this ancient culture's history contributes to an eventual understanding of the initial integration of Upper and Lower Egyptian societies, and is also important in a larger research context. Comparison of other early complex societies with Egyptian traits may reveal the most basic requirements under which a state-level society may form (Brewer 1992). In this way, future research can concentrate on *how* those stimuli lead to state development. Thus it is possible to trace the development of domesticates and social complexity in Egypt in order to identify the processes and ramifications of that development likely to have occurred in other areas.

## Organization and Synopsis

The development of domesticates—whether plant or animal—has traditionally been attributed to environmental and climatic shifts during the Holocene. The tending or sowing of plants and the keeping or breeding of stock were viewed as deliberate attempts by prehistoric humans to produce a more dependable food supply in the semi-arid regions where domestication is presumed to have taken place (e.g., Flannery 1969:77; Redding 1981:90). This certainly appears to have been a possibility in ancient Egypt, where resources were subject to unpredictable inconsistencies in Nile floods. The idea of ruminants as 'converters' of the plentiful but unusable grasses and shrubbery into a higher quality resource—meat—is still common as the idea of mobile food storage or the 'walking larder' (Clutton-Brock 1989), a particularly attractive option in more marginal environments not suitable for crops. The basic thesis in this study is that significant advances in the understanding of the development of complex societies are unlikely unless human–(plant)–animal relationships are investigated within the context of general theories which address the underlying principles affecting both subsistence and social behaviors. This theme is elaborated in chapters two and five.

The variables comprising the process of identifying changes in the economy, politics, religion and daily life following the shift to domesticate-based subsistence are also defined in chapter two. Such variables and concepts must not only be described for the present research, but must be placed within a solid anthropological framework for any systematic cross-cultural comparisons to be made in the future. Previous perspectives on the evolution and adoption of domesticates—primarily animals—are also summarized; see Appendix A for a detailed discussion of theories and methods for the identification of the origins of domesticated animals. These concepts provide a necessary foundation on which much of the faunal data are based, but are not central to the main thesis. For example, it is imperative to examine the reliability and validity of the criteria by which animal remains are classified as 'wild' or 'domestic' in order to determine the earliest occurrences of the domesticate complex, after which the social, economic, religious and political changes begin to appear. Similarly, examination of research concerning the spread of domesticated animals is useful because such investigations have emphasized questions of social interactions among populations with different subsistence strategies, and will provide needed ethnographic and linguistic data for model-building and -testing.

The regional environment of ancient Egypt during and following the Holocene is presented in some detail, in order to identify likely areas of reliance on domesticated taxa, seasonal resource scheduling, and ecological change (chapter three). This reconstruction includes climatic factors such as seasonality of rainfall or flooding, and the predictability, abundance and density of resources available to animal and human inhabitants of those regions. The presentation of climatic change is somewhat limited, but gives an indication of when or where the predictability of domesticates would have rendered them an attractive economic pursuit of the ancient Egyptians. The different non-biotic properties (e.g., climate, geography, geology) of Upper Egypt, the Delta and the deserts supported different floras and faunas; thus different modes of subsistence would expectedly have developed in each of the different regions.

The taxa of the Egyptian complex to be studied here are cattle, sheep, goat, and pig. Because of the difficulties in distinguishing sheep and goat osteologically, and given that they were often part of the same herd (Redding 1981), the roles of these two species will be examined together in some instances. These four taxa are the most abundant, easily preserved and recognized archaeologically, and are well-known throughout the

Middle East as a 'triad' in much the same way as the corn/bean/squash triad of MesoAmerica. Pgs have received the least attention because of erroneous, often implicit, assumptions of their minor contribution to prehistoric diet or economy. The physiology and productivity of the four taxa are compared (chapter four) in order to determine which species was best adapted to particular habitats and human exploitation, and indicate that pigs were actually ideal resources under certain conditions. It is readily apparent that the desert-tolerant taxa which allow renewable resource harvest from living animals (such as milk, blood or wool), would be preferable over less tolerant taxa or those which provide resources only after death (such as meat and hides). Such an understanding allows predictions of where certain taxa would likely have been utilized in the past.

Definitions of pastoral strategies vary widely, and it was necessary to construct generalized models of several strategies from examination of ethnographic and development studies of modern indigenous African pastoral populations (chapter five). Ethnographies demonstrate the intimate relationship existing in the traditional patterns of African agriculture between the human populations and their stock and food plants. These models effectively represent a human-constructed environment in which social and economic factors influence the survival of the four domestic taxa, in much the same way that factors of the natural environment do. Perhaps more importantly, these models suggest that the relative abundances of various taxa are dictated less by purely factors of ecological tolerance than by how the products of several species complement one another. Additionally, these models provide the basis of reconstruction and beginning to understand the complex and dynamic interactions between various pastoral and agricultural segments of Egyptian society.

The purpose of the modeling chapter is to present—against the background of a review of earlier uses of such concepts—a classificatory model which arranges them along a continuum of human/animal interaction (e.g., Harris and Hillman 1989 for human/plan interactions). That is, each group in the model represents a place along the continuum, or stages of control over animals (i.e., increased input of human energy) and also reflects the availability and quality of land. While based on ecological and evolutionary principles, the model is not unidirectional or deterministic. Rather, the aim is to present a descriptive—not explanatory—model for a series of animal exploitative activities and associated ecological and social effects, tested and documented by ancient Egyptian archaeological, faunal, and Egyptological evidence.

In brief, the continuum classifies four patterns of exploitation. Nomadic pastoralists represent the least amount of human control over animals or land and are characterized by relatively small human populations with family-ownership or individual responsibility for the herds. These populations relocate periodically in order to obtain fresh water or pasture, and often travel considerable distances in a superficially random pattern (i.e., the pattern reflects the availability of resources, and is not truly random). In some areas, gardens or small plots of plants can be cultivated as a seasonal addition to the diet, but the majority of effort is still devoted to animal husbandry; these are known as semi-nomadic pastoralists. Both of these groups are usually found in fairly marginal environments (such as the desert regions in Egypt) which cannot support extensive agriculture or large, dense concentrations of inhabitants.

Further along this continuum is a transhumant mode of subsistence, in which a population—or a portion of a fully sedentary population—moves seasonally across the landscape in order to obtain needed resources. This may entail a fully mobile society which relocates along a prescribed or traditional path at specific seasons, or merely the driving of herds to expanses of pasture during times of seasonal environmental stress. Such groups are generally larger and travel shorter distances within a 'home range' in a comparatively more favorable habitat.

Sedentary strategies require more control over the animals and the landscape because the animals' movements are restricted and fodder is generally provided to some degree. Two types of sedentary strategies are discussed here: Agro-pastoralism and ranching, in which animals are penned, food is provided, etc. (note that ranching may have seasonally mobile aspects). Ranching represents a considerable shift in focus from previous strategies, in that the goal is profit in a market-based economy. Thus, while the goal of herders practicing other strategies is to maintain a herd that provides adequate resources year-round and that can rebound after environmental stress, the goal of ranching is to maximize the output or off-take from the herd, leaving only the minimum number of animals needed to rejuvenate the herd.

Correlating the ancient Egyptian environment with the physiological or biological needs of the four animal taxa permitted definition of the areas where different species would have thrived or faltered. The identification of expected fauna in a given habitat and the means by which modern human populations utilize them formed the basis of the models to be tested. The origins of the Egyptian domesticated animal complex are presented through examination of the zooarchaeological—and to a less extent artistic and linguistic—evidence. Reconstruction of the direction of spread of those taxa into Egypt encourages identification of cultural traits that may have been transmitted as well. The level of social complexity in each ecological zone during the period that domesticated animals appear is also presented as a "base-line" by which subsequent modifications can be judged.

The dominance of a taxon archaeologically in a given site or region was then attributed to either natural or cultural factors. By recognizing the geographic and environmental (especially taphonomic) constraints on identified faunal samples, differences between assemblages could be more reliably attributed to cultural preferences and practices of the evolving society. However, the zooarchaeological record alone is insufficient to provide unequivocal evidence of regional cultural preferences or to interpret the cultural significance of these patterns. Therefore, "it is necessary to use multiple lines of evidence and to identify trends through time and compare data between sites, avoiding the use of information from a single assemblage to exemplify the whole" (Meadow 1992:267; similarly, Grayson 1984).

In the last phase of research, the models were tested through comparisons with other archaeological artifact classes and historical sources. This phase relies on the qualitative, rather than quantitative, analysis of these sources. By combining several sources of data, it is possible to construct a picture of social interaction and pastoral land use that reflects concerns for the environment and the choice of animals best suited to it. The goal is to justify how or why several different modes of subsistence were adopted into a state-level society, and what modifications were made in order to survive as part of a different, and clearly more complex, sociopolitical organization. For example, the low productivity of the deserts necessitated at least a seasonal reliance on or access to delta pastures during the drier climatic periods.

Tests of the models with specific Egyptian faunal data sets are presented in chapter seven, and the interpretation of these results and the application to significant research questions are presented in chapters six and seven. The utility of the domestic complex in Egypt is tested by evaluating the 'fit' or 'error' of the Egyptian complex to the expectations outlined by the ethnographic-based models. The available data are, of course, subject to the biases of the recovered archaeological record. Our knowledge about the social and economic organization of ancient Egypt comes mainly from texts, and what little archaeological information we have comes primarily from ceremonial sites are larger settlements (Wenke 1986:19-20). That is, with the exception of Putters attempt at a pan-Egyptian Predynastic ceramic sequence, the majority of research has emphasized community-level organization (i.e., site-specific research).

Recently, a detailed, large-scale survey conducted in the eastern Delta concerning settlement and subsistence patterns (van den Brink 1988), and on-going investigations at Mendes (Brewer and Wenke 1992) have added significantly to the understanding of the economic and political aspects of late Predynastic and early Dynastic Egypt. By roughly 5700 B.C. in the deserts, 4100 B.C. in Lower Egypt and 3800 B.C. in Upper Egypt (see Table 1.1 for chronology), foragers had shifted from a generalized subsistence strategy to a more specialized one emphasizing crops and livestock. Evidence indicates that the broad food base of earlier times had narrowed and, although wild products were still used, they only supplemented the domesticates (e.g., Boessneck and von den Driesch 1985; Gautier 1976c; Yokell in prep).

The pre- and proto-historic cultures of the three regions were uniquely different and yet complementary to the eventual unification (ca. 3100 B.C.). The Predynastic was characterized by a 'typical' North African neolithic model of subsistence which included some pastoral-based groups and some sedentary agriculturalists; members of these groups were certainly interacting (and I argue, interacting symbiotically).

Table 1.1. Generalized Chronology of Ancient Egypt (after Hoffman 1991:15-16, Tables I, II; Quirke 1992:186; Brewer and Yokell 1996). Dates before 664 B.C. are approximate.

| Date (B.C.) | Upper Egypt | Lower Egypt |
|---|---|---|
| A.D. 323-642 | Byzantine | |
| 332 B.C.-A.D. 323 | Greco-Roman (dynasty 32) | |
| 525-332 | Late Period (dynasties 27-31) | |
| 664-525 | Saïte Period (dynasty 26) | |
| 1070-664 | - - - -Third Intermediate Period- - - - | |
| 1570-1070 | New Kingdom (dynasties 18-20) | |
| 1782-1570 | - - - -Second Intermediate Period- - - - | |
| 2040-1782 | Middle Kingdom (dynasties 11b-12) | |
| 2181-2040 | - - - -First Intermediate Period- - - - | |
| 2684-2181 | Old Kingdom (dynasties 3-6) | |
| 3050-2700 | Archaic or Early Dynastic (dynasties 1 & 2) | |
| 3300-3050 | Proto-dynastic | Proto-dynastic |
| 3650-3300 | Early Gerzean (Naqada II) | Ma'adian/Omari B? |
| 3900-3650 | Amration (Naqada I) | Omari A? |
| 4000-3900 | Badarian | Merimden/Fayum A |

The Dynastic period was the result of many significant changes in subsistence, economy, religion, etc., but it is of the utmost importance to recognize that the 'simpler' lifeways of the Predynastic were not eliminated or replaced, but were maintain and even expanded upon by the government of the unified Egyptian state.

Finally, in chapter eight, the organizing principles are reiterated and major aspects of the results in this research are summarized. This is done to assess the success and significance of this new application of zooarchaeological data using an anthropological approach. The theoretical approach adopted here generates useful bodies of quantitative and qualitative data, brings into question previously held interpretive assumptions, and suggests several new directions for substantive research. Further, the utility of the approach used here for addressing issues of early food production expands the range of potential applications and tests of domesticated animal-based models which can contribute to explanations of subsistence behavior in a wide variety of human situations and environments, well beyond Egypt's borders.

# 2. Evolutionary and Social Perspectives of Food Production

## Introduction

During the many years of early research directed at identifying the spatial and temporal origins of food production, scholars focused on the complex environmental and behavioral processes that presumably led to the transition from forager to food producer. Accepting that in general, human behavior has evolved in response to changes in the natural (physical) and cultural (social) environments, these scholars have variously isolated habitat, climatic variation, innovation, demographic movements, and population growth as factors significant in the development of food production strategies (e.g., Binford and Binford 1968; Childe 1936; Clark 1976; Cohen 1977; Flannery 1969, 1973; Harris 1977; Reed 1969; Wright 1968, 1976, 1977).

Although substantive enquiry into the origins of food production has been underway for only about a half a century, volumes of bioarchaeological evidence have been accumulated, and ethnographic and historical research have contributed immensely to its interpretation. Often the debates have centered around definitions of terms, the validity or reliability of variables and the ability to measure them archaeologically (see Appendix A). These debates are not mere philosophical discussions, because the meanings attributed to general concepts directly affect research design and the interpretation of evidence.

## The Evolution and Adoption of Food Producing Strategies: Previous Research

Widely cited by proponents of the "secondary products revolution," Sherratt argued that all herd species were first exploited for meat production, while milk and other products were not exploited until millennia later (1981, 1983). More recently, opposition to this position has gained in popularity. Thus, some authors attempt to demonstrate that milk production was an essential element of the domestication process of goats and cattle (e.g., Banks 1984; Hafez 1968a,b,c; Raish 1992; Rosen 1988; Wendorf and Schild 1980; Zeuner 1963), while others suggest that wild species generally only produce enough milk for their own young. Thus, increased milk production and dairying were the result of post-domestication selective breeding (e.g., Bőkőnyi 1976; Brewer et al. 1994; Harris 1977; Herre 1969, 1970; Hole 1984; Ingold 1980; Watson 1979). Russell (1988:24–32) convincingly argues that the hypothesis of milk production as a fundamental element of the domestication process for some taxa is supported by extensive data, and that the idea of the exploitation of milk/products only millennia after domestication remains largely unsubstantiated.

The most frequently-cited factor against the importance of dairying in early pastoralist strategies is adult hypolactasia, or lactose intolerance. Simoons (1971) is attributed by Blumler and Byrne (1991:26, fn 8) with the only proven example of domestication as a co-evolutionary process, describing the evolution of lactose tolerance in pastoralist groups that practiced milking. Coevolution designates genetic change in both animals and humans. While human behavior certainly changed as a result of adopting domesticates, genetic changes in humans may have been minimal, because as much as 10% of populations without a prior history of dairying appear to be lactose absorbers (see Russell 1988:31, and references cited there). The co-evolutionary change is not in the *appearance* of lactose tolerance following domestication, but in the *increase* in the proportion of the population with that genetic tolerance (i.e., the much higher prevalence of the genetic tolerance for lactose among populations with long histories of milk consumption may perhaps be evidence of a selective advantage by those who are able to digest lactose).

The question then becomes why or how lactose-intolerant individuals were able to overcome this disadvantage. Russell discusses several means available to reduce or eliminate the ill-effects of lactose intolerance (1988:31–32). The simplest method is merely diluting milk with water, thereby reducing the osmotic action in the large intestine from which many of the symptoms of intolerance arise. Perhaps the most common practice in modern societies is the production of fermented milk products such as soured milk, yogurt, cultured buttermilk, and cheeses. Documented among modern pastoralists as a means of preserving otherwise perishable but highly nutritious milk resources, it seems highly likely that prehistoric pastoralists would have practiced fermentation processing activities as well. Examination of pottery cooking vessels in the Negev suggests that they were used to process perishable milk into storable milk products (Haiman and Goren 1992), and Meadow proposes this class of artifacts as an archaeologically testable means of documenting the processing of secondary animal products in much the same way that spindle whorls can provide insight into other animal-based activities (1992:266, and citing Gouin 1990 for the Indus valley). This avenue remains untested in Egypt.

Another "secondary product" which may have been an indirect factor in species selection for domestication is wool. Ryder (1983:45) believes that sheep could not have been selectively bred for wool production "until shears suitable for clipping the fleece had been invented...in the Iron Age." However, he has previously noted that both wild and domesticated sheep often rub a shedding fleece against branches or rock outcrops, forming long strands of wool (Ryder 1964), which could have been easily collected well prior to any attempts at selective breeding. Perhaps most surprising is the assumption that no existing tool could have been used to remove the fleece of early domesticated sheep; surely lithic tools sharp enough to slice through sinew and tendons could have been used for this purpose. Nomadic pastoralists in eastern Sudan keep primarily hairy sheep, with "some hair being removed for use with a knife" (Ryder 1983:570). While Ryder is probably correct that sheep (or goats) were not selectively bred for wool as a *primary* means of their domestication, this does not negate the possibility that early herders made use of the product nonetheless, and may have kept higher numbers of (castrated) males than in milk-or meat-oriented strategies in order to maximize wool production (cf. Payne 1973).

Others attribute the domestication of browsing species to the need to protect crops, and there is increasing evidence that agriculture preceded or developed contemporaneously with animal domestication (see Stemler 1984; Ucko and Dimbleby 1969; Wetterstrom 1993). A symposium dedicated to causes and consequences of African food production, included in the 1978 Annual Meeting of the American Anthropological Association, represents the first time that international specialists engaged in the study of both African plant *and* animal domesticates had met, and a strong correlation between the geographic spread of domesticated plants and animals was noted (Clark and Brandt 1984:1). It now appears that in some areas, pastoral strategies may have evolved prior to the agricultural exploitation of *marginal* dry-farming lands. Pastoralism was eventually marginalized relative to cultivation in *optimal* agricultural areas, but not to agricultural strategies in general (see Russell 1988). This is an important distinction often overlooked in the popular statements that pastoralism developed in areas where agriculture was not feasible.

However, neither the correlation of plant with animal domestication nor the hypothesis of protecting crops by domesticating browsers explains why deer or other browsers failed to be domesticated anywhere in the world. Heiser believed that the reason "other animals which might have been domesticated were not is probably due in part to a geographic and historical accident...[p]eople for the most part have tried to adapt the same animals to new habitats rather than to exploit new species..." (1990:34). While this seems plausible in the Egyptian case, Zeuner's (1963) comments concerning the gregarious social structure of potential domesticates are more widely applicable. Further research has identified an 'ideal' progenitor of a domesticated herbivore as non-territorial, living in large, wide-ranging herds of mixed sexes, organized in hierarchies, having a wide tolerance of different food plants, a short flight distance, and a relatively slow response to danger (Clutton-Brock 1987, 1994; Garrad 1984; Hale 1962:28). The dominant members of the domesticate complex in Egypt (cattle, sheep, goats, and pigs) share all of these characteristics. The social behavior of gazelles, addax and oryx are different and perhaps explains why—although some evidence suggests that Egyptians attempted to domestic them ca. 3000 B.C. (Smith 1969)—they were never brought fully under human control.

Additionally, it demonstrates that while many scholars view the process of domestication as unidirectional, when it is not. The capture and maintaining of animals can be the first stage in domestication as Bőkőnyi (1969) and Ingold (1980, 1987) propose, but it need not necessarily result in human control of breeding. Animal keeping is indeed a proving ground that precedes domestication, but not all penned species come under full control of humans. Although Smith's (1969) work concentrated on identifying Egyptian animal cults, it is important for demonstrating that prehistoric humans had to employ trial and error to find suitable domesticates. Reed attributed the increased environmental control achieved by humans through the more intense utilization of animal resources to have been a process of trial and error, and he assumed an ability on the part of prehistoric humans to predict the end result of their efforts (1969:361–362).

Members of several scholarly fields concur that the more stable food supply provided by herding allowed sedentism, eventually resulting in sufficient population pressure that agriculture became the only viable subsistence alternative. Traditional models appeal to 'optimal foraging strategies' utilized by ecologists (see Pyke 1984) and by anthropologists—whether among hunger-gatherers (e.g., Winterhalder and Smith 1981) or among food producers (e.g., Hastorf 1980; Johnson and Behrens 1982; Keegan 1986; Hardesty 1977). Appealing to ecological theories that the most efficient means of obtaining foods will be utilized, the goal of subsistence behavior is identified as maximization of energy yield per unit of expenditure; these approaches are clearly based in evolutionary theory. Animal domestication does permit sedentism is some habitats, and sedentism has been shown to result in population increases (Hasson 1988; Wilmsen 1982).

Regardless of ecological conditions, however, human control of animals need not result in the formation of permanent settlements, and certainly not force a reliance on agriculture, or there would be no mobile pastoral groups today. Different responses to the adoption of domesticated animals are dependent upon the evolutionary trajectory established by previous selective pressures (discussed in more detail in chapter five). The development of food production marked a qualitative change in human subsistence behavior that had far-reaching consequences for cultural evolution. Investigations have been aimed largely at the causes and consequences (for animals) of the domestication process itself (e.g., Clutton-Brock 1970; Epstein 1971; Flannery 1973; Harlan et al. 1976; Matolsçi 1976; Redding 1981; Reed 1977; Siegel 1976), and yet the social consequences for the human populations have received comparatively little scientific attention. The interpretations that have been proposed clearly vary considerably in their complexity, theoretical sophistication, and intended generality (Redding 1988:58). Most focus on the *development* of food production and thus describe some precedent and antecedent changes in human subsistence behavior (e.g., Christenson 1980; Cohen 1977; Earle 1989; Flannery 1968, 1969). Generally, the attempts to explain why some plants or animals in an area were domesticated and others were not resulted in region-specific explanations essentially based on geographic distributions of potential domesticates. This approach is too limited for building a generalized predictive model. Optimization models have been criticized on theoretical grounds (see for example Reed 1977; Rindos 1984). The problems of *in situ* domestication, the diffusion of domesticates or food-producing populations, and social changes are, however, separate issues that optimization theory is not designed to directly explain, and should not be criticized on such grounds (see Redding 1981). These processes are discussed separately below.

### *Means of Acquisition*

The origins of domesticated animals in an area can be subdivided into three means of acquisition: (1) independent invention of the idea or methods for domesticating animals, (2) 'stimulus' diffusion, whereby one culture develops its own domesticates following exposure to another culture, and (3) 'demic' diffusion resulting from direct exposure to immigrating human populations relying on domesticates. Research on the topic of the origins of domesticated animals is clearly dominated by attempts to locate examples of the former, i.e., the *earliest* occurrences or loci of incipient domestication. This is done in order to determine the underlying causes or stimuli for undertaking the control of certain animal species. The major stumbling block for determining the true origin of a domesticated species has been that the archaeological evidence of domestication typically represents *later* stages of the process; changes in the morphological characters, for example, do not usually appear in the first few generations. Also, some characteristics (such as changes in the internal structures of bone) can occur in penned wild animals, and need not necessarily indicate human control of breeding, or true domestication. Fortunately, when different research methods and the criteria given above are applied to the same assemblage, more primitive domesticates can be recognized and the reliability of such identifications is much improved.

More recently, zooarchaeological and archaeological research have been gradually moving away from the emphasis on locating 'the' earliest occurrences, because doing so provides the mistaken impression that domestication occurs as a recognizable cultural *event* rather than as a convoluted and archaeologically problematic *process*.[1] As the centers or loci of initial domestication become more securely established through constant revision and addition to the regional chronology, it becomes possible to attempt to trace the spread of those domesticates. For the purposes here, however, the ultimate location of 'the first' domesticated animals is essentially irrelevant, because the goal is to explore the changes in Egyptian society *after* adopting domesticates. Principles of Darwinian evolution provide the necessary theoretical framework.

## The Potential of an Evolutionary Perspective

While most scientists readily accept the Darwinian theory that organisms evolve through a process of adaptation under natural selection, anthropology has sought to justify humans (or at least human behavior) as largely exempt from this process through an appreciation of the role given to culture. Human culture, when viewed as a means whereby humans consciously and intentionally adapt to a multitude of environments, effectively removes humans from the natural selection of heritable variation—because culture is far too variable and too subject to change through learning to be explained in genetic terms through natural selection (see Sahlins 1976). However, Richard Alexander, and more recently David Rindos and others, have been outspoken proponents for the applicability of natural selection in addressing the evolution of human behavior (Alexander 1978a, b, 1979; Rindos 1980, 1984, 1985).

Darwinian evolution has three components: variation, transmission, and differential persistence (Dunnell 1980; Larson et al. 1996; Smith and Winterhalder 1992). *Variation* is simply that phenotypes (in the present case, human phenotypes) vary. Information can be *transmitted* or inherited either through natural (i.e., genetic) or phenotypic (i.e., behavioral or cultural) systems. Finally, *differential persistence* incorporates the previous two ideas operating in concert and resulting in different 'fitness'. Phenotypic variability leads to different levels of success at transmission of genetic and cultural information through each inheritance system; this results in greater or lesser fitness (Larson et al. 1996:220). Following Darwinian principles, characteristics of 'more fit' individuals will increase in frequency over time.

Simply put, the variation in human culture is not merely the result of totally random processes of genetic mutation

[1] Excavation and dating techniques rarely permit determination of precise age, and contemporaneity between site areas cannot always assumed. The result is a "loss of understanding of short-term process, and changes can look dramatic and sudden..." Archaeologists must view "process as a punctuated series of configurations of material remains or 'events,' whether or not it was actually so" (Meadow 1992:265–266). While accelerator radiocarbon dating and various corrective measures yield finer and more accurate resolution, the nature of the record is such that critical transformational periods may be inadequately preserved or accessible for these types of studies.

or recombination, but has some meaning. Variation likely also reflects processes of innovation, learning and memory. Ethnographic analyses and comparative studies have demonstrated that specific cultural variants frequently show a fit to the environment. For example, human ecological studies have shown strong correlations between resource predictability and/or abundance, and the size, mobility, and structure of human populations in those areas (e.g., Ambrose and Lorenz 1987; Dyson-Hudson and Smith 1978; Wilmsen 1973). Stated using evolutionary terms

> the cultural pattern found in a given environment includes information (behaviors or beliefs as described in the most general terms) that apparently matches information (opportunities or problems) within that environment. [Rindos 1985:65]

Thus culture is, at least to some degree, adaptive and its variant forms result in part from causal processes integrating culture and environment. This tie between culture and environment and the ethnographic basis for expecting small, mobile, acephalous, communal-property groups in marginal areas but larger sedentary, hierarchically-organized groups in areas of greater resource predictability or abundance suggests that similar processes would have operated on the developing societies in ancient Egypt.

## The Secondary Spread of Domesticates

The diffusion of ideas, technology, or objects typically occurs through direct or intermediate contact, or by stimulus diffusion. Even by the Predynastic period, the exposure of Egyptians to new ideas is undisputed, considering the degree of interaction and trade between Egypt and southwest Asia—including house styles assumed to be foreign (e.g., as at Ma'adi [Menghin and Amer 1932]). Unfortunately, the diffusion of an idea may be indistinguishable archaeo-logically from synchronous but independent invention because of imprecision in dating, and biases or lack of data. Both the North African invention or adoption from other parts of southern Europe and/or southwestern Asia remain plausible explanations for the appearance of domesticated cattle in Egypt.

In cases of direct contact, the idea or object itself is transmitted, and examples appear in the new area rapidly. With intermediate contact, the exposure occurs through contact with a third party. For example, the mobility of desert populations is the most likely means for the early introduction of domesticated sheep and goat, whose wild predecessors do not occur in Africa.[2] Following the direct contact between Egyptian desert populations and southwest Asians with domesticates, the Valley and Delta Egyptians adopted domesticates through intermediate contact—through their desert neighbors.

In stimulus diffusion, a local population is exposed to the idea of domestication through contact with other groups (who may or may not move into the area), and the local group applies the idea to indigenous species. This would occur at a rapid pace (archaeologically) but should include transitional forms. This may apply to non-food domesticates in Egypt, such as the cat (*Felis sylvestris*).

Another means of acquisition is the actual immigration of populations with the idea, technology or object into a new area. In this instance, the spread would appear to occur more slowly, as populations move across the landscape over a period of generations. This has been proposed, for example, for a "village-by-village" introduction of domesticated pigs into Egypt (Zeuner 1963:260).

The intermediate interdisciplinary approach emerging from recent archaeological investigations has broadened the foundation on which the analysis of the origins and spread of domesticated animals is based. This perspective combines aspects of both biological and cultural extremes, and incorporates geologic and environmental stimuli. It is somewhat easier to trace the spread—rather than the origins—of domesticated animals for several reasons.

Generally, the spread of such taxa relies on additional criteria as well as those described above for identifying newly domesticated animals. First, the archaeological remains of fully domesticated species are more easily recognizable as domesticated, in contrast to the often ambiguous or contradictory evidence provided by assemblages in the early stages of domestication. Second, these remains typically appear without any developmental precursors or failed attempts. Third, in many regions the spread of domesticates occurred sufficiently late that oral traditions or other historical sources of information are available. For example, chickens (*Gallus gallus*) are not native to Africa, but appear abruptly and fully domesticated in Egyptian art during the New Kingdom, and textual evidence from Mesopotamia suggests that the bird had been obtained through trading contacts from India by the Third Dynasty of Ur (ca. 2213–2006; Houlihan 1986:81, see also fn 436). This is in contrast to the much earlier and more complicated developmental history of domesticated cattle, for example, which is addressed in chapter six.

It must be noted that each form of diffusion occurs as a *selective*—rather than automatic—process; members of one society do not accept *in toto* the culture of members of other societies with whom they have contact. Rather, they may reject items and practices that do not satisfy (or conflict with) some psychological, social, cultural needs or traditions. Further, although people, animals or the techniques used to control them may spread to new areas through diffusion, the structures of production that relate

[2] Although the Barbary sheep does occur in the wild in Egypt, it is only a distant relative of domesticated sheep. Similarly, the ibex is a variety of wild goat which is only remotely related to domesticated forms of goat. Also see chapter 6.

these elements together evolve under their own internal dynamic. That is

> Diffusion, along with innovation and modification, is channeled within an underlying structural matrix whose transformations are evolutionary in nature. Every conjunction of social and ecological relations will define a set of functional prerequisites that condition the acceptability or non-acceptability of particular animals or techniques, and that thereby constrain their diffusion. But conversely, an animal or technique, adopted within the context of a given structure of production, may simultaneously introduce the preconditions for the evolutionary transformation of that structure. [Ingold 1980:110–111]

There were several options available to local groups exposed to pastoral societies (e.g., Barth 1956, 1969; Clutton-Brock 1989; Khazanov 1984; Ingold 1980, 1984):

(1) Ingore or refuse to participate in the new society, although there is strong evidence that the more mobile populations would have been pushed into increasingly marginal habitats by agriculture-based societies;
(2) Develop symbiotic relationships with the new group as compensation for the partial loss of territory and/or access to resources and modes of production, although pastoral societies are usually incorporated into a lower socio-economic level when the dominant group is agro-pastoral;
(3) Diversify their subsistence base by adopting some aspects of the immigrating society while maintaining the majority of their traditional lifestyle;
(4) Give up their former way of life and shift to a domesticate-based subsistence strategy.

In the vast expanse of geography which is Africa, each of these potential outcomes occurred at some point in the past, and to some degree continue today among the few remaining indigenous societies. In Egypt, for example, all four responses are recorded throughout later prehistory and the Dynastic period, and are addressed in detail in subsequent chapters (six and seven).

The utility of merely documenting the spread of domesticates is somewhat limited with regard to the present work. For example, there is currently insufficient evidence to determine if North African herders were indeed 'the first' to domesticate cattle and it is apparent that they were already experimenting with potential domesticates contemporaneously with herders outside Africa. Therefore, the effects of the adoption from outside of North Africa should have been minimal and would be difficult to separate archaeologically from independent domestication. However, the lines of evidence used to trace the spread of domesticates provide needed data concerning the nature and degree of interactions between populations, political control of subsistence and the development of animal cults, etc. For example, the study of the spread of domesticated animals across the landscape emphasizes historical sources such as artistic depiction, governmental and private documentation of ownership, taxation and offerings, as well as the developing data on the linguistic correlations between North African populations with domesticates. These sources of information are valuable in tracing the development of domesticate-based societies throughout Egypt, and for proposing possible explanations or means by which they were incorporated into the unified Dynastic society.

**Research Area**

The Nile is Egypt's most important natural feature and encouraged both the ancient Egyptians and modern archaeologists to view Egypt as three distinct regions: Upper Egypt, the Delta, and the deserts. Upper Egypt is the southern two-thirds of the country where the Nile flows as a single stream within a narrow convex floodplain bounded by steep cliffs. The broad, flat, alluvial plain in the north is correspondingly known as Lower Egypt or the Delta. The desert regions extend to the Red Sea in the east and into the eastern Sahara in the west. The developmental trajectories of human cultures in each area were influenced to varying degrees by the differing environmental conditions. The reconstruction of the society in each region is restricted to the available archaeological and Egyptological[3] data, which differ according to the nature of investigations carried out as well as preservational factors in each region.

## *Overview of Cultural and Historical Events*

Following the political and economic unification at approximately 2700 B.C., Egypt entered the Old Kingdom, which lasted until nearly 2180 B.C.. The 'florescence' of Egyptian literature, art, architecture, mortuary cults, divine kingship and Dynastic succession, and numerous other aspects of culture during this period are well-documented (See Trigger et al. 1983; Kemp 1989). Although significant gaps in the data still exist, convincing arguments have been presented that the continuation of developmental trends begun in the Predynastic render differences between these two time periods qualitative rather than substantive (see especially Wenke 1991).

The economic structure during Dynastic Egypt was organized on the principle of redistribution; surpluses from rural households were collected by the two tiers of authority (the state and temples), and redistributed among different sections of the society (e.g., officials, priests, corvée laborers, etc.). According to Janssen (1982:253), this complexly interwoven system was

> concentrated in the cities and towns, [and] rested as a superstructure upon a 'peasant society' consisting of households that were largely self-sufficient as far as

[3] Used in its strictest sense to denote studies of the ancient language and writing, and thus distinguish it from archaeological and other investigations within Egypt.

> the necessities of life were concerned. Those goods which they did not produce themselves (e.g., salt, copper, particular types of trinkets, and other luxuries), or which did not come to them through redistribution, they acquired either by direct barter from their neighbors or, to a minor extent, on the market. ...A third way by which commodities were acquired—particularly the relatively large amounts of food needed for festive occasions in the household or services for exception activities such as the building of a new house—was reciprocal gift-giving. Actual profit-motivated trade hardly touched the peasant household.

Domesticated animals were key components of this redistributive economy, serving not only as food and beasts of burden at the local level, but also as items of payment or barter at the regional and country levels. Too often, however, archaeological research problems and explanations have been confined to local or, at best, regional areas. Such particularlistic explanations do not aid an understanding of general cultural processes. Archaeological investigations have great potential to contribute to this understanding when the data are analyzed from a wider perspective, particularly faunal remains themselves. Preservational factors such as the deflation of desert sites, inaccessibility of deeply buried Predynastic and earlier sites, and the bias for recovery of more durable cultural remains such as stone or pottery are common reasons that interpretations are restricted in scope. Preservational biases are exacerbated by the dominance of scientific effort at certain types of sites. Mortuary and royal sites have received the most attention, and comparatively little is known about other aspects of Egyptian society. For example, only a few settlements

> of the crucial periods of evolving cultural complexity in Egypt have been excavated in even a preliminary fashion (e.g., 1982; Hassan 1984; Mills 1984; Wenke and Redding 1985). Egypt's rich documentary record compensates to some extent for these data deficiencies (Baier 1960; Kaplony 1982; Goedicke 1967), but by themselves, these documents do not provide reliable statistical evidence about the demographic, economic and political factors that are central to historical analyses. [Wenke 1986:15]

Even as little as fifteen years ago, the faunal data "published for the dynastic and later periods consist mainly of reports on individual specimens recovered from tombs..." (Redding 1984:39). House chapels and religious material from other domestic contexts promise to yield valuable insight in the future into sacred uses of particular species at the household level. Because house chapels are a surplus or luxury construction, investigations of such remains should provide insight into the activities of the wealthier non-royal component of ancient Egyptian society, but not the average population. However, data from such ritual deposits are of little use for reconstructing herd management or economic strategies because these assemblages represent only a portion of the off-take from unknown herds. The complex redistributive network also complicates to some degree interpreting faunal samples recovered from settlements because of the possibility of provisioning sites by herds maintained at some distance. Thus, the nature of the site or faunal sample is crucial to interpreting the assemblage. The level of detail and interpretability of course varies between samples from various sites, but considerably larger assemblages have undergone intensive analysis and publication since Redding's statement. Testing these varied sources of data against models constructed in reference to modern ethnographic societies allows more robust and reliable interpretations of the available archaeological data.

As indicated, however, the scarce and biased archaeological data make it difficult to analyze Egyptian cultural evolution. In fact, so little archaeological evidence exists that it is impractical at this time to thoroughly test complicated hypotheses and models concerning the rise of the Egyptian state. A preliminary step in the analysis of complex Egyptian societies must, therefore, focus on the general ecological and cultural context in which these societies evolved (Wenke 1986:16; 1989). With the goal in mind of understanding initial state formation, the ecology, level of subsistence and economy, settlement patterns, and extent of religious control are only a few of the many factors that must be considered. Comprehensive studies in which these types of archaeological data can be evaluated are needed. As demonstrated in this work, zooarchaeology can yield valuable information on such aspects of society (see also Brewer 1986, 1989a; Brewer and Friedman 1989).

Like any set of objects, however, a faunal assemblage can be analyzed in numerous ways, and why types of data are chosen to be collected, measured and reported are contingency bound (Brewer 1992). That is, the archaeological research problems dictate the type of data needed, and unfortunately, previous zooarchaeological research has been limited to investigation of questions of basic subsistence and initial domestication—not the diversity of management, breeding, production and distribution of livestock in different regions or in different institutional or social contexts. The interdependence between human societies and domesticated animals is one of the most significant innovations in human history, creating a need for complex networks of interactions and the establishment of a resource base capable of supporting the large populations characteristic of early developing states (Brewer et al. 1994).

Two levels of analysis are required for this monograph. First, the ecological constraints are determined, and what strategies—social, technological, and physical—are required to function within or to overcome them. This aspect of the analysis, in the form of environmental description, ethnographic modeling, and the tracing of the development and spread of the domesticate complex in Egypt, is presented in chapters three through six. Second, questions concerning the pathways to complexity via strategies of intensification, or means of incorporating groups of different levels of complexity into a single cohesive society via religion and politics, are presented in chapters six and seven.

The approach used here is strongly ecological in that the economic/social behavior of the ancient Egyptians is assessed against the environmental background within which they functioned (similar to Clark 1952, 1957), an approach which is at variance with the culture-history paradigm underlying similar research in other regions. A distinction is drawn between the *biome*, which includes the totality of living organisms in a particular vegetative zone, and the *habitat*, which describes the critical factors of soil and climate. To some degree, then, the ecology of a region limits the types and numbers of human and non-human populations which can survive successfully there. Further, a semantic distinction is maintained between *subsistence* and *economy*: the former being *what* resources people utilized for survival, the latter referring to the *management* and *mobilization* of those resources (after Barker and Gamble 1985:5, emphasis added).

Environmental archaeology (including zooarchaeology as a subdiscipline) has made great strides in developing analytical techniques to answer questions concerning diet and subsistence from the fragmentary and biased archaeological record. There has been surprisingly little attempt before now, however, to develop a methodology specifically for a comparative approach to the study of the economic management of past societies and the role of basic subsistence resources in the processes of social change. Paleo-economic data (such as can be deduced from zooarchaeological and botanical remains) are essential for establishing comparative measurements of past systems at a variety of spatial scales, from the individual site to regional environmental zones. Although the habitat may impose constraints on subsistence and limit the production of certain resources (and thereby give rise to very different institutions and social formations despite the use of the same set of animal and plant resources), it is imperative to remember that environments never assume active roles in determining what sort of society will inhabit them. Rather, the social system is dominant over the ecological system: the set of social relations consolidated within the institutions, roles and organization of a society determine how any landscape is to be exploited (Ingold 1980). In other words, the ecological system imposes constraints on the types of resources that can be utilized, but does not determine the degree of reliance on those resources by the human population, nor does it determine what is done with those resources. In Egypt, for example, the three geographic or habitat regions imposed limitations on which animal species could best survive there and influenced the density of human populations, but certainly did not determine how the ancient Egyptians would incorporate those animals into their economic, political or cosmological systems.

Following Clark (1957:174), it is useful to "construct a model of the various aspects of social life, show how these are interrelated, and consider how a study of each may contribute to an understanding of the whole." In particular, the various modes of Egyptian subsistence (e.g., nomadic pastoralism, seasonal transhumance, and sedentary strategies) represent increasing control by humans over both animals and land, yet should not be viewed—as they often are—from an evolutionary perspective. Several works by archaeologists have correlated ecological context with particular modes of subsistence (Ambrose 1984; Clark and Brandt 1984; S. Smith 1980) and indirectly with degrees of social complexity, contradicting earlier anthropological debate that pastoralism is a branch off the mainstream of social evolution (Barth 1969; Cohen 1974; Isaac 1971). That ecological context affects the viability of herding in an area is true, but the variety of socio-economic responses to habitats documented among modern groups has not been widely applied to pastoral societies known only through the archaeological record. These strategies were once independent and largely self-sufficient in different habitat zones of Egypt, and the means by which they were incorporated into a single, cohesive society must have been complex.

## *Methods of Analysis*

To investigate what subsistence strategies were utilized in Egypt, and how they were maintained in the unified society, models of ethnographic animal uses were constructed by comparison of numerous modern societies in environments similar to those of ancient Egypt. These models were compared with the available archaeological data.

Briefly, zooarchaeological analyses were conducted following standardprocedures of identification and quantification. Bone fragments were identified to the most specific taxonomic level possible, often relying on comparative specimens and reference texts (e.g., Amorosi 1989; Boessneck 1963; von den Driesch 1976; Walker 1985). The accepted criteria for species identification vary substantially between analysts and preservational factors affect each assemblage differently. To assure consistency, metrical analyses based on von den Driesch (1976) or Walker (1985) were used to distinguish species of similar size (e.g., sheep and goat). In many instances, however, a more generalized combined category was required (e.g., ovicaprid [sheep/goat]). See Appendix B for more detail on measurement techniques and Appendix D for raw data from sites personally examined by this author.

Quantification was carried out using the NISP or **N**umber of **I**dentified **Sp**ecimens, rather than calculating the MNI or **M**inimum **N**umber of **I**ndividuals (see Appendix B). This portion of the analysis resulted in nominal-level data from which the geographic distribution of domesticated taxa was discerned. Recognition of changes in distribution through time was possible through the examination of faunal data from temporally varied sites.

Several assemblages (e.g., Merimde Beni-Salâme and Ma'adi) were reported before many taphonomic and statistical biases were understood; these were reevaluated using current techniques of analysis of ordinal level data (see especially Lyman 1984, 1985; Grayson 1984, 1988). The remains from each site were tabulated to determine the distribution of relative abundances (rather than simply presence/absence) of various taxa, and the results were compared geographically. The potential for breeding centers, restrictions of taxa to particular social classes, etc., were identified through quantitative analysis.

By recognizing the geographic and environmental (i.e., taphonomic) constraints on identified faunal samples, variability between assemblages could then be more reliably attributed to cultural preferences and practices. In other words, sufficient data on ecological history, economy and sociopolitical configurations within the various regions of Egypt may answer questions of why some populations adopted agricultural and others pastoral lifeways, and how food production relates to social complexity. However, the utility and reliability of the zooarchaeological record alone is insufficient to interpret the cultural significance of these patterns. For example, it is difficult (if not impossible) to distinguish breeds solely on osteological evidence; it was necessary to rely on artistic representations, textual evidence and other historic sources. Egyptological sources must be used with caution and a brief discussion of the dates of appearance and interpretive limits of these sources is important. In the formative Predynastic period, sources are restricted to artifact classes such as burial goods and recovered skeletal remains. Beginning in the early Dynastic period, funerary depictions (and more rarely, written documents) can be used to trace sociopolitical and religious development. Not only are technological innovations resulting from the reliance on domesticates often represented, but inferences can be made concerning secular and ritual roles played by particular domesticated breeds.

Personal names, titles, offering formulae and 'autobiographies' (tomb inscriptions typical of members of the upper classes) span the full range of periods since the advent of writing, although they are more abundant in the later periods. Continuity or change over time may be discernible through comparison between time periods and sources of evidence (e.g., Breasted 1906). They also can corroborate suggestive evidence in one source with stronger evidence in others, providing multiple lines of evidence and lending additional credence to a particular interpretation. Caution is warranted with interpretations based on offering formulae and 'autobiographies' because of the tendency for self-aggrandizement or exaggeration (Quirke 1992).

Legal papyri referring to temples are rare before 600–700 B.C. with the exception of the abundant Ramesside documents. Oracle texts may be useful, but are known only after approximately 1450 B.C. (Quirke 1992:10). Letters are an excellent source of information because they are private documents, and are unaffected by constraints of the ideal versus the actual. These sources can yield personal opinions or observations, and are helpful for ascertaining widespread attitudes (e.g., Wente 1990; Lichtheim 1973, 1976, 1980). Baines has suggested that such sources are more indicative of actual practice because they are less subject to omission due to the "system of decorum" restricting topics in more formally regulated sources such as the offering formulae and 'autobiographies' in tombs (1987:82).[4] They are known primarily from the 2nd millennium B.C., but occur rarely in the 1st millennium B.C. as well. With these caveats in mind, the available data provide considerable information on Egyptian society.

## Conclusions

Investigations of the origin and development of food production in general have occupied a prominent position in archaeology for decades. Efforts have been aimed primarily at specific causes and immediate consequences of the domestication process itself (Clutton-Brock 1970; Epstein 1971; Flannery 1973; Harlan et al. 1976; Matolsçi 1976; Redding 1988; Reed 1977; Siegel 1976), and conducted in areas of primary occurrence (such as southwest Asia and Mesoamerica), where various plant and animal species were domesticated by and incorporated into societies that for some time afterward continued to include substantial quantities of wild plants and animals in their diet. However, there has recently been an upsurge in interest in the secondary spread of domesticated forms, particularly in sub-Sarahan African. Here, the shift from hunting and gathering to food production involved the importation of domesticated taxa from societies that were already substantially committed to agricultural, pastoral or agro-pastoral means of sustenance (Bower 1988; Klein 1986; Klein and Cruz-Uribe 1989; Phillipson 1977, 1984; A. Smith 1992a).

Since the secondary spread of such species has little, if any, potential for shedding light on the process of domestication, investigations have emphasized questions of social interaction (i.e., exchange and its effects on intergroup relations, the direction and rate of diffusion, etc.). However, questions of ecology and sociocultural transformation resulting from the shift to food production—whether primary or secondary—have not been ignored (Bower 1991; Clark and Brandt 1984). Information gathered from investigations of the primary and secondary links between the management of this mobile food resource and human populations are applied here to better understand the concomitant transformations and means for maintaining institutions within the process of social change and reproduction.

[4] This system defines in hierarchical terms what may be depicted or written in what context, as well as restricting negativity from representation or discussion. Although the concept was defined for iconographic phenomena, Baines argues that it can be extended to textual mentions (1987:82, fn. 11).

As archaeological and other techniques for identifying domesticates and tested, refined or replaced, and earlier sites discovered, excavated and interpreted, the resultant pattern of the origin and spread of domesticated species naturally reflects these changes. Despite statements recognizing the importance of the effects by humans on the animals, the discipline has largely ignored questions of long-term change in the *human society* resulting from the reliance on domesticated animals. That is, while the links between the management of animal resources and human populations are now being made, the transformation and maintenance of institutions within the process of social change and reproduction—such as the dramatic changes in the social structure, size and complexity of the society—have not been thoroughly studied in Egypt. It is these sorts of changes which are of interest here.

Beyond the studies of the origins of domesticated animals, past research endeavors related to domesticates have emphasized horticultural aspects of human subsistence—particularly the impetus for the shift to food production—and occasionally, the effects of domestication on a single species. As a result, the important roles played by animal husbandry (as a complex rather than a single species), have received little scientific attention. And, despite the strong tie of the spread of domesticated animals with that of plants, the social consequences of this shift have received little investigative attention. Traditional hypotheses concerning the effects of the adoption of domesticates (when attempted) have gone only so far as to predict population growth, with minimal or no consideration of the dramatic changes in social structure, economy, religious, or political aspects of that society. Thererore, the important roles played by a complex of domesticated animals in a developing human society remain poorly understood. In a summary of the work to date concerning the late Paleolithic and early Neolithic in Egypt, Wetterstrom noted that "...perhaps the most intriguing question posed...is not *why* or *how* domesticates were originally adopted, but *what happened* to subsistence strategies once domesticates were added to the food base" (1993:225, emphasis added). Modern ethnographic research demonstrates the intimate relationship existing in the traditional patterns of African agriculture between the human populations and their stock and food plants (Clark and Brandt 1984:2). Further work along this avenue of research is needed to more fully understand the impact of the domesticated animal complex on various aspects of prehistoric society.

# 3. CLIMATIC AND VEGATATIONAL SETTINGS IN ANCIENT EGYPT

## Introduction

The specific environment and climate of an area limit the population density and subsistence alternatives available to its inhabitants, without *actively* determining the nature of human exploitation. In much the same way that the environmental parameters of an area influence the survival of various animal species, human settlement and subsistence patterns must be responsive to similar factors, given the population's level of technology. To understand the nature of human settlement and subsistence—including the appearance and spread of domesticates—in Egypt during and following the Holocene Wet Phase,[1] it is necessary to understand the environmental conditions faced by both human and animal populations during these periods, and those factors that would have made animal-keeping attractive as an economic pursuit. Potential areas of occupation are defined below based on the type, density, predictability, and seasonality of resources in various habitats found in the three major geographic regions of Egypt. In the following chapter, the physiological tolerances and adaptations of the four domesticated species are described with reference to the habitats available in ancient Egypt in order to determine which species, or complement of species, would have been best adapted to survival and exploitation.

## Holocene and Recent Environmental Contexts

The existence of a biome or ecosystem is actually a complicated interaction between both non-biotic and biotic factors. Non-biotic factors include: (a) the climate, composed of sunlight, temperature variations, rainfall and wind; (b) geography, or the physical features of the land such as mountains, plains and rivers; and (c) geology, the distribution of various parent rock types which eventually form the soil. Examples of biotic factors include the overall productivity and general habitat structure of the region (including seasonal reproduction patterns and variations in density); and the living community (producers, herbivorous or carnivorous consumers, and decomposers). The complexity of the interaction between these (and other) variables, makes the identification of a *single* ecosystem somewhat arbitrary; wherever the boundaries are drawn, there will be connections across them.

Precisely defining a single valley, delta or desert ecosystem in Egypt is impossible, because in reality each general ecosystem takes several forms, each has specific non-biotic characteristics and particular assemblages of floral and faunal communities (the latter of which may move seasonally into other ecosystems). The level of detail needed to distinguish fully between such ecosystems is lacking at present, and may never be accessible archaeologically. Moreover, human populations do not interact directly with their entire environment or complete biomes, but with selected, well-defined species and components. These components may be termed 'habitats' and can be distinguished according to soil, vegetation, climate, and a definite and well-characterized animal community (Ellen 1989:81). Unfortunately, the terms 'biome' and 'habitat' are often misapplied as synonyms.

Traditionally, Egypt is viewed as composed of three ecological zones, based largely on the gross geomorphology of each region: the Nile Valley, the Delta, and the Deserts. The latter is usually subdivided into the Eastern and Western Deserts. The habitat descriptions of each of these major regions are generalized in order to define where in Egypt the domesticated taxa could survive (noting again that this may differ seasonally) and help to explain why human and animal populations occupied the land where and how they did.

### *Nile Valley*

As a reminder that the Nile River itself begins well to the south of the modern Egyptian border and that this river is therefore tied to other habitats, it has been described as

> A giant lotus, with its roots planted in the heart of Africa...[f]rom Khartoum the sap rises along a thin stem, which pushes into Egypt at Wadi Halfa and shows green at Aswan. Near Beni Suef, it bears a single leaf, the Faiyum; it flowers at Cairo, and spreads in a great head of blossom on the Rosetta and Damietta branches, until it touches the Mediterranean... [Ayrout 1963:1]

The Egyptian Nile Valley north of Asyut is hemmed in by 200 m precipitous limestone scarps which run to Qena (Figure 3.1). South of Qena, the west bank is a high, continuous scarp while the eastern bank is formed by isolated crests which rise abruptly from the gravel plateau or lower clay hills (Hume 1925:8). South of Luxor, the western cliff trends away from the modern riverbed as low gravel ridges, and the eastern scarps are of sandstone. Between Idfou and Aswan the river narrows and forms rapids because of the difficulty of carving through the granites and other igneous rocks. Within the Nubian

[1] Throughout the central Sahara, two general humid phases (the Great Wet Phases [10,050-5550 b.c.] and the Neolithic Wet Phase [4450-2550 b.c.]) are characterized by different rainfall patterns separated by an extended arid interval; these are interpreted as three distinct climatic periods. However, in the eastern Saraha, topographical relief was insufficient to affect air circulation, to create local depressions or to affect sources of rainfall (Banks 1984:2). The result was a series of major playa transgressions within a single, overall stable period, and is therefore referred to in the singular.

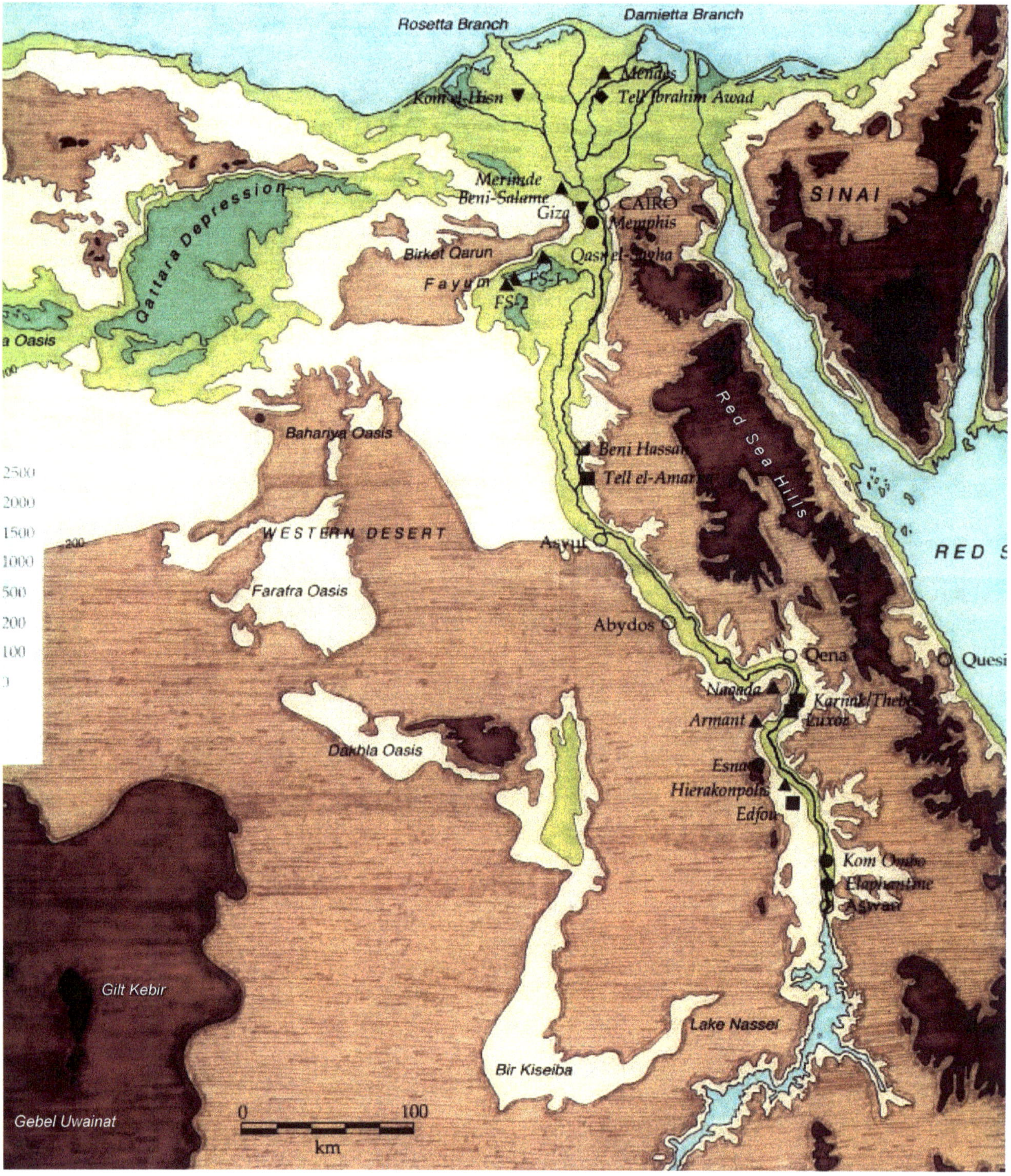


Figure 3.1. The Egyptian Nile Valley

Valley, the western scarps are lower and broken into isolated hills, with the wind-carved hollows filled with the typical golden-yellow sand. The eastern bank resumes the precipitous cliff, often rising more than 300 m directly from the water's edge. Soils along this region of the Nile are characterized as 'toic'. The high clay content causes poor internal drainage and moisture-holding capacity; thus the region easily floods but becomes extremely hard and "virtually impossible to cultivate during the dry season" (Bontkes 1991:14). These soils produce a high vegetation biomass (predominantly grasses), and are north of even the northernmost extent of tsetse fly infestation (Barbour 1961:237; Andrews 1948; cited in A. Smith 1992a:132), which would have precluded cattle herding.

North of the Qena bend, the Nile swerves eastward in the direction of the Red Sea and the valley broadens appreciably. The average width of the alluvial floor of the valley between Aswan and Cairo is about 10 km, and that of the river itself about 0.75 km (Butzer 1976, from Said 1990). It is significant that throughout its entire course, the Nile tends to occupy the eastern side of the valley so that the cultivable lands to the west of the river are generally much wider than those to the east. In some places, the stream almost washes the eastern boundary cliffs (Said 1981), clearly limiting or even prohibiting settlements. Areas of cultivable land were "often small and separated from each other by stretches of rock reaching right down to the river" (Rowly-Conwy 1991:204). The potential for foraging, and eventually farming, varied markedly throughout the river valley.

The Nile Valley is filled with alluvial sediments divisible into five units, each corresponding to the main stages of development of the river. Work in the last two decades in Egypt (Wendorf and Schild 1986; Hassan 1986b; Paulissen and Vermeersch 1987) has resulted in significant revision of these units, particularly the youngest deposits, which are of interest here. Evidence from this work indicates that the connection of the Nile with its African sources began only during the Middle Pleistocene. Further, the interfingering of dune sands with the silts and channel gravels beginning approximately 8,000 B.C. is interpreted by Said as indicating a depositional cycle within an arid climatic region (1990:491). Currently, the Nile provides Egypt with 98% of its water supply (Said 1981:4).

In arid and semi-arid regions, rainfall is typically restricted to a particular season of the year, apparently during the winter months in ancient Egypt (as it is today). If the Mediterannean rain belts had moved southward, Upper Egypt would have experienced only a few centimeters of rain during the early winter months (Butzer 1959, 1975). This single season of rain would have rendered the summer months very dry, particularly after the floods had receded. It also has important implications for the seasonal nature of plants and animals available to the prehistoric inhabitants of the outlying regions of the Valley.

During the moist phases, however, summer rains may have fallen as far north as Qena (Wetterstrom 1993), although probably never exceeding 300 mm in the south (Hassan 1986a:493–4, 1986b:66–7; Hassan and Gross 1987:91). Wadi activity on the east bank of the Nile is interpreted as evidence of run-off of winter rains in the Red Sea Hills (Butzer 1980:273–5; Vermeersch 1978:146). Wetterstrom concludes that the limited vegetation available in the wadis would have provided additional grazing lands (1993:183).

The seasonally inundated river plain within the Nile Valley had a typical "convex" cross-section (Butzer 1976), as it does today. Suspended silty and clay sediments are sorted and deposited through breeches in natural levees, such that the largest grains and thickest accumulations are closest to the main channel, tapering off in size and thickness toward the outer margins of the valley (see Figure 3.2). The natural levees rise between one and three meters above the lowest alluvial basins, which are themselves cross-crossed with abandoned secondary and eroded older Nile channels and levees (Butzer 1959, 1076; Said 1993:61). The end result is a complicated braided stream pattern with numerous islands, oxbow lakes and marshy hollows, offering a variety of microhabitats for humans and animals to exploit.

The tendency for the river to flow along the eastern portion of its floodplain throughout the Valley, and the low relief of the floodplain itself resulted in dramatic differences in the amount of flooded land following even small variations in flood height (see Bell 1970). The valley was composed of numerous, discrete natural basins, averaging approximately 100 sq km, which could have been utilized and controlled by relatively small groups of people (Butzer 1976:17, *contra* Wittfogel 1957). Thus, while sites located at the floodplain and desert margins had access to several habitats, resource abundance was still principally affected by floods.

Ideally, the flooding would crest in southern Egypt by mid-August, spreading out through various overflow channels and levee breeches to flood successive basins, with the northernmost basins filling with water and sediment four to six weeks later (Butzer 1976; Willcocks and Craig 1913:306). During this season, rainfall was scant, the wadis remained dry, and vegetation on the hills was thin and scarce (Hassan 1984:60). Annual floods prevented occupation on the majority of the floodplain for part of the year, although higher elevations would have remained a few meters above water and inhabitable. In response to a combination of falling river levels, soil infiltration, evaporation and dropping groundwater due to natural drainage back the main channel, the southernmost alluvial flats would emerge and dry by early October, with the northernmost reaches drained by late November (Butzer 1976:18; Said 1981:89). Wide and deep cracks would form on the exposed floodplain and in fallow fields, effectively aerating the soils.

Studies of relict vegetation on islands in the Nile suggest that much of the alluvial flats would have been covered by *Cyperus–Panicum* meadows (el-Hadidi and Springuel 1978, 1989; Springuell 1981; Wetterstrom 1993:183). These reports specify only nut- and cyperus-grasses, and although not specifically mentioned, these meadows should include papyrus (*C. papyrus*; Wetterstrom personal communication). Papyrus has been shown to be among the most productive plants in terms of annual biomass, and is higher in protein than similarly digestible grasses (Muthuri and Kinyamario 1989:28). Wetterstrom (1993:177) noted that the starchy rhizomes may have been processed for human consumption, as Hillman et al. (1989:217–226) have suggested at Wadi Kubbanyia in Upper Egypt. Several classical authors noted that the plant's lower portion was prepared in a variety of ways and eaten, especially by children (see Darby et al. 1977:645–647). This would have been most common in

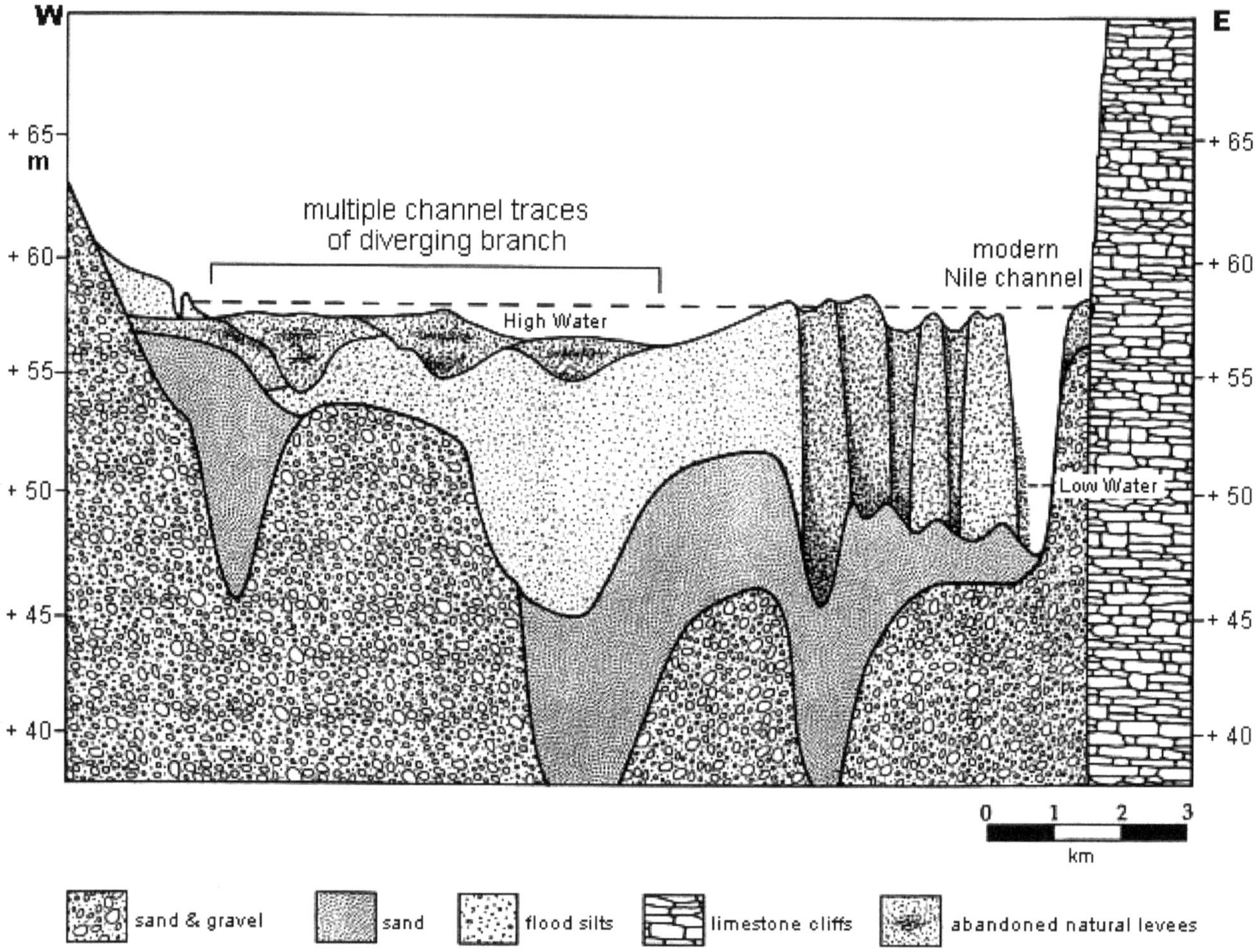


Figure 3.2. Schematic Cross-Section of the Nile Flood Plain (After Butzer 1976).

the spring, at the Nile's lowest levels. The remainder could always be cropped and bundled by herdsmen for feed. In the Middle and New Kingdom when most arable land was under cultivation, papyrus would have offered an important supplement to the diet of the vast [cattle] herds reported to pasture in Egypt. [Brewer et al. 1994:40–41]

This has important implications for seasonal fodder consumption in ancient Egypt as a means to reduce competition for land between human and animal plant foods (see chapter five). Under natural conditions, papyrus is rarely utilized by wild herbivores, probably because few of them are adapted to the unstable swamp substrate (Muthuri and Kinyamario 1989). However, Hakanen (1984) reportedly noted that in other areas of Lake Victoria and the upper Nile basin, cattle graze on papyrus and other sedges, especially during the dry season when other plant species are scarce or of low quality. When chopped up, papyrus is voluntarily eaten by penned cattle (Hakanen 1984). However, it is unknown whether the high value attached to papyrus—for its uses in medicine and paper—would have prohibited its use as animal fodder in ancient Egypt.

Grains such as *Panicum* and *Pennisetum* (both millets) are generally associated with wadi and Nile silts (Wetterstrom 1993), and even by the Upper Paleolithic, southern Egyptians were already relying on sorghum and millets, perhaps cultivating these plants (Wendorf et al. 1992). Marshes would have been found in the lower areas of the valley margins and in oxbow lakes of abandoned channels (Butzer 1976), while "acacias, palms and other trees and shrubs may have formed a savanna woodland on active and old levees which were rarely inundated" (Wetterstrom 1993:183). Also, Hassan proposed that *Tamarix* and acacia would have been present in areas with deep wadi fill where surface run-off water accumulated (1980). The northward movement and intensification of the monsoons during the early Holocene were sufficient to shift the savanna boundary 600–700 km northwards into southern Egypt (Clark 1984). Today, the northern boundary occurs just north of the latitude of Khartoum in central Sudan, and generally coincides with the 100 m isohyet (Harlan 1975). This is important for cattle domestication, as well as the resource potential of deserts.

Acacia is, and presumably was, an important resource

both for humans and their livestock. For example, el-Hadidi and Boutos (1988:32) note that it is one of the most popular shade trees in rural areas and would have provided needed respite from the intense sun. The foliage and pods are eaten by livestock, and the seeds are highly nutritious. The bark and seed pods have a high tannin content, and were used for tanning leather (especially goat hides) or dyeing cloth (el-Hadidi and Boutos 1988). The hardwood is often used in carpentry or making charcoal; the resin content allows it to resist water and insects, making it ideal for use in boats. In contrast, tamarisk is a less prized resource. The young branches of this evergreen are grazed by herd species and the older wood is sometimes used for charcoal; it is only rarely used in (inferior) carpentry (el-Hadidi and Boutos 1988:114). Both genera flower during the summer months; those of the acacia are used in perfumes, cosmetics or in medicines.

## *Delta*

Although Herodotus first applied the term 'delta' nearly 2500 years ago to the northern Egyptian plain because of its resemblance to the shape of the Greek letter, the geological history and internal morphology of the Nile Delta have received comparatively less attention in the published literature than several other deltas. Said (1962, 1981, 1990, 1993) has contributed the most complete treatment of the evolution of the river and its delta. It is unique in that it has a core of sand and gravel overlain by a comparatively thin layer of mud, rather than formed entirely of silt (Said 1993:78). This core renders the region less subject to compaction or subsidence than other deltas, and thus it is not dependent upon sediment supply to sustain itself.

North of Cairo, the Nile continues in a northwesterly direction for approximately 20 km before dividing into the two modern deltaic branches, the Rosetta and the Damietta, and an intricate mesh of canals and drains. Throughout recorded history, the network of deltaic tributaries varied considerably and many fossil branches are recognized. Classical authors (e.g., Herodotus, Strabos and Ptolemy) verified seven or eight major distributaries, and more recent geological analyses indicate that these evolved only during the third and second millennia B.C. as the southern delta plain expanded (Butzer 1976; Said 1981:82–3). The Egyptians themselves used distributaries as geographical markers at least by the First Intermediate Period, and probably well before, for example delineating the southern boundary of the western Delta as the "Two-Fish Channel" or (*śnʿmśd·t*), the southern most part of the Canopic branch of the Nile (Lichtheim 1973:107, fn 10).

Throughout the delta, divergence of the flood waters over multiple distributaries produced lower flood crests, and correspondingly lower levees relative to the Nile Valley. Along the Mediterranean coast is a belt of salt marshes interspersed with a number of lagoons. Known as the *Berari*, this region would have been of comparatively little economic value to the ancient Egyptians (although marsh hunting was a well-documented sport of the rulers).

While rapid Nile alluviation was depositing a thick sheet of mud over the Delta, the Mediterranean Sea rose between 6500–5500 B.C., and the northern third of the Delta was reduced to a vast swamp and lagoon (Stanley and Warne 1993a,b). However, circa 4000 B.C. the Mediterranean Sea had retreated sufficiently that the Delta had reached its present dimensions (Butzer 1976:23). With this combination of erosion and alluviation, debate continues concerning whether the region was uninhabitable (cf. Holmes 1993; Stanley and Warne 1993a, b), or if the earlier archaeological record was washed away or lies buried under extensive deposits of Nile sediments (cf. Butzer 1976; Hoffman 1991; van den Brink 1998, 1992; Wetterstrom 1993).

Much of the western reaches of the delta are designated 'transitional delta to desert' depositional environments, and only narrow areas around distributary branches were sufficiently drained for use as pasture and farmland (Stanley and Warne 1993a: Figures 5, 6; Holmes 1993). Butzer's work supports the contention that while the bulk of the delta was marshy, there were numerous elevated hillocks in the central and southern reaches (1959; 1976).

The northeastern tectonic tilt of the delta has resulted in the rapid burial and preservation of deposits to the east of the major Nile branches (Stanley and Warne 1993a). Millennia of annual deposition of sediments have rendered archaeological recognition and excavation of such sites slow and expensive; the sites of Buto (western delta) and Mendes (east central delta) remain the only two known sites with predynastic levels with the potential for recovery. A survey in the eastern delta region provided a 'trait list' for settlement location in the delta, and demonstrates that the levees here were utilized in much the same way as in Upper Egypt, as were exposed Pleistocene sand 'turtleback' islands or *geziras* (van den Brink 1988). A more recent survey in the central delta confirming the use of *geziras* as settlement foundations complements the earlier findings (Wenke and Brewer 1996).

Thus, the considerably lower slope of the Damietta branch relative to the Rosetta results in "the gradual silting up of the former…explaining the greater thickness [of] agricultural clay layers" here (Said 1981:81). Further, water retention along the Damietta is posited to be at a minimum. The implications for this are not clear, but it may indicate a relatively more productive agricultural area without the aid of human-made irrigation.

Only 170 km in length and 258 km at its widest, the delta incorporates twice the area of Upper Egypt, and ranges from sea level to approximately 100 m above (Hume 1925). The moister climate during the Predynastic encouraged a more lush concentration of plant and animal life than in the rest of Egypt, and the Egyptians themselves referred to the Delta as *Mḥw* or *T3-mḥ* which

Goedicke (1988:165) interpreted as "aquatic plants" or "flooded land." In an analysis of more than 3500 petrological samples, Stanley and Warne (1993b:438) noted that rising base level and decreasing river gradient resulted in a meandering distributary system, and during floods "deposited large volumes of fine-grained deposits, forming a broadening fertile floodplain...which retained enough moisture for longer periods during the year to allow plants to flourish." These core sections contain abundant grasses and other plants which indicate that Nile delta silts—even during periods of aridity—could sustain grazing and cultivation without artificial irrigation (Stanley and Warne 1993a, b; Butzer 1976).

The same *Panicum* and *Cyperus* meadows proposed for the seasonally flooded areas of the Valley would have covered much wider areas of the Delta, owing to the larger floodplain. Marshes or other partially submerged ground were found to include plants such as *Phragmites, Polygonum,* and *Cyperus* (Schild and Wendorf 1989:97; see also Hayes 1965:119; Zohary and Hopf 1988:189). The area was abundant in animal resources as well, including a variety of fishes, hippopotamus, crocodiles, turtles, and antelopes (von den Driesch and Boessneck 1985; von den Driesch 1986:6; Gautier 1987:175; Yokell in prep A).

Shrubs and trees thrive on occasionally submerged sandy deposits, and would have been restricted to hillocks scattered throughout the delta, or along dunefields at its outer margins. Tamarisk groves are considered by botanists to represent the natural climax vegetation in well-watered wadis, and as many as 22 separate plant species have been identified in similar habitats where annual rainfall was well below five centimeters (Kassas 1952; cited in Hoffman 1991:161). As with margins of the Valley proper, these marginal Delta areas provided human inhabitants access to both aquatic- and desert-adapted animals. The Delta as a whole remained a favorite hunting ground (especially for hippopotamus and crocodile, but also for numerous birds and fishes) throughout the Dynastic period; scenes recounting such activities are considered standard components of tomb decoration.

Rather than being distributed fairly evenly—as along the restricted floodplain in the Valley—settlements in the north would have been irregularly distributed because of the varying sizes of Delta flood basins. This may have made communication and travel between villages more difficult than in the Valley because overland travel may have been unpredictable, and following meandering distributaries would have increased distances. Predynastic delta villages were essentially economically independent, and some argue that resource abundances allowed or encouraged dwellers to delay shifting to a heavy reliance on domesticates.

The Fayum Depression is an oasis that lies approximately 60 km southwest of the apex of the Delta (Figure 3.3.). During the Holocene, it was a freshwater lake—Lake Mœris—replenished by an influx of floodwaters through the Bahr Yousef (Hassan 1986a:493). The connection to the Nile is thought to have been maintained until about the first millennium B.C. (Hassan 1986a:495). All that remains of Lake Mœris today is a comparatively small, shallow, saline lake (Birket Qarun) in the northeast corner of the depression. Because floodwaters had to reach the sill-level of the Nile–Fayum divide, the water supply would have been effectively cut off during some low floods, and the very high evapotranspiration rate would have caused the level to drop rapidly (Hassan 1986a). Hassan proposed that the lake could have disappeared in as little as 40–100 years without influx from the Nile (1986a). With the exception of groundwater seepage, the only drainage was through the Hawara channel, and it is thought that the level could have risen suddenly with high floods, remaining submerged longer than the Valley floodplain (Wetterstrom 1993:187). The combination of a minimum flood height to feed the depression and the single outflow channel led Wendorf and Schild to conclude that the Fayum was probably more susceptible to flood level fluctuations than the Nile Valley proper (1976a:311).

The lake reached its highest levels at the peak of the flood in early autumn, and most of the depression was probably covered by vast marshes. Nearly all of the bird and dominant fish taxa (catfishes) preferred shallow-water habitats (Brewer 1989a:150), and all of the identified plant remains were of moist or wetland species (Wetterstrom 1993:187). Although never dense, trees—and more abundantly shrubs and acacia—lined the margins of the lake (el-Hadidi and Springuel 1978). For this reason, the Fayum is grouped here with the Delta. Beyond this may have been a narrow band of grasses, ending abruptly in a landscape nearly devoid of vegetation (Hassan 1986a:494). Desert- adapted animal species would have come to the lake during and following the flood; their remains have been documented in all excavated sites in the area (Brewer 1989a:111; Gautier 1976a, b, c; Wenke et al. 1988:42). Thus, a variety of resources would have been available in the immediate environs of the Fayum Depression, although they would have been highly seasonal, and somewhat less predictable than valley resources due to the nature of Fayum hydraulics.

### *Deserts*

The perennial stream of the Nile divides Egypt into two different desert regions: the Eastern dissected plateau and the flat expanse of the Western (or Libyan) desert (see Figure 3.1). In the eastern region, the desert is further divided into the Eastern Desert proper and the Peninsula of the Sinai, separated by the Gulf of Suez. Although the Sinai is not discussed in detail here, it is important to note that since the area was far less of a desert during the Holocene than it is today, emigration of livestock from Asia to Africa would have provided no problem (Reed 1969:372, fn 59). Unfortunately, the deserts are sites of intense erosion, and most of the Quaternary sediments are

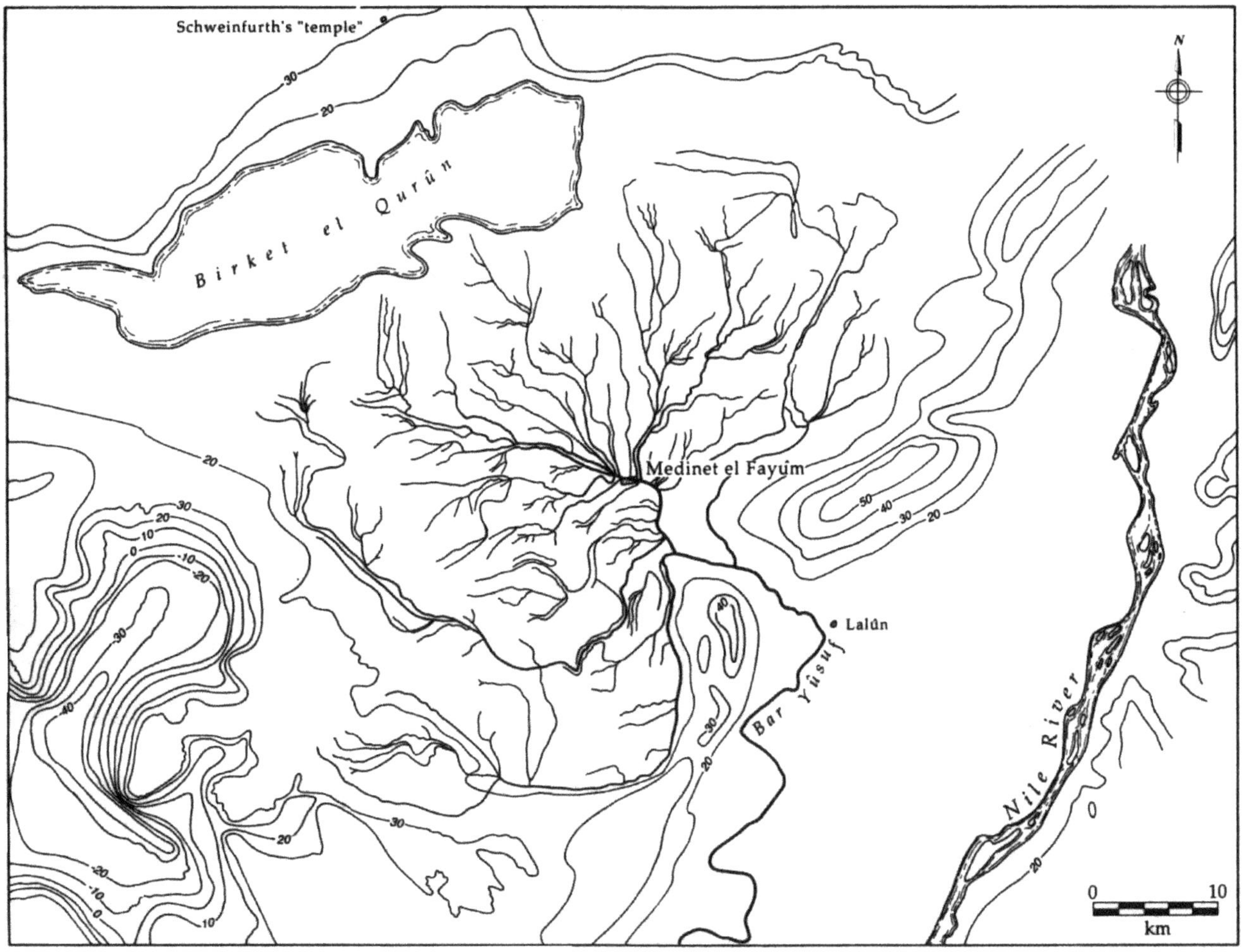


Figure 3.3. Detail Map of the Fayum Depression.

thin or incomplete, rendering it difficult to correlate them with those of the Valley and Delta (Said 1990:487).

The desert to the east of the Nile Valley is composed of high, rugged mountains parallel to the Red Sea. The igneous parent material is carved into valleys and ravines, though the eastern drainage pattern of these mountains differs from that of the west. As the run-off flows eastward toward the Red Sea, numerous small independent channels form. Between the highlands and the shoreline is a gently sloping coastal plain of calcareous silt; the width varies from essentially nil at the Gulf of Suez to approximately 8–25 km in Sudan. Predictably, the plain nearer the hills (i.e., further inland) is covered with coarse boulders while toward the Gulf the composition becomes much finer (Hume 1925). The shoreline and coastal plain is broken into a number of bays and lagoons dominated by *Avicennia marina* grass (Kassas and Zhran 1967, cited in Goodall 1986). Reeds such as *Phragmites* and *Typha* dominate in saline swamps or deep estuaries respectively (Ayyad and Ghabbhour 1986).

Rain on the eastern side of the watershed is characterized as "less than 30 mm per year…occasional and unpredictable" (Ayyad and Ghabbhour 1986:149). It condenses and falls as moisture-laden winds cool with rising elevation, forming a typical rainshadow with little moisture to fall on the western slope. Where the surface deposits are mixed gravel and sand, and receive little runoff, *Indigefer sinosa* dominates, while species of *Acacia* (especially *Acacia seyal*, camel thorn) predominate in areas of better water availability (Ayyad and Ghabbhour 1986). These plants are suitable for goats, but not sheep or cattle, although succulents occur at wide intervals throughout the desert. Bomann and Young (1994:27) noted that these plants tend to "be concentrated in a series of lines and groups, centrin [sic] over underground…streams," and would likely have been useful locators of sources of water for humans and their herds. The lower elevations of the north and northeast slopes are occupied by *Moringa*, while at higher altitudes "ferns, mosses and liverworts abound" (Ayyad and Ghabbhour 1986:162),

In the western drainage of the Red Sea Hills, the small streambeds coalesce into a few great wadis, whose mouths are in direct contact with the Nile (Hoffman 1991:241–251 [citing Winkler 1938]). The primary routes crossing the eastern Delta, north Sinai and the Eastern Egyptian Desert are well known (see Figure 3.4; Bomann and Young 1994). These include Tell Abu Sefa to el-

Ariash (the 'Way of Horus'), the Wadi Tumilat, the Wadi Gasus to Safaga, the Wadi Hammamat to Quseir, and the Wadi Abbad to Berenice. Wilkinson concludes that the main route in the 'Middle Egypt' region during the New Kingdom (and perhaps earlier) was the Wadi Araba, whose estuary opens into the Gulf of Suez at Zarafana (1823:29–33).

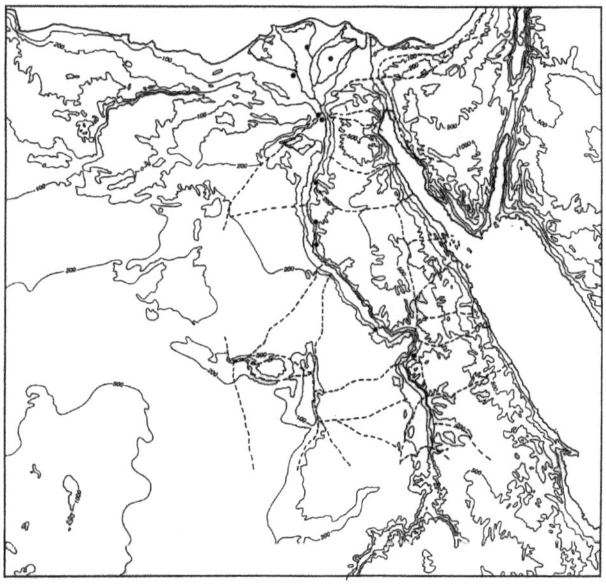

Figure 3.4. Primary Desert Wadis and Routes of Travel (after Bates 1970: inside back cover).

On the southern and southwestern slopes of the Red Sea Hills, similar species of plants are confined to the channels of the western drainage system due to the reduced precipitation in the rainshadow. Here, there are "no major routes" crossing the Nile Valley to the Gulf of Suez and the Red Sea, but connections "can be made through somewhat more circuitous routes" (Bomann and Young 1994: 28–9). Indeed, Hoffman contended that the Eastern Desert could have supported a more dense, if still highly mobile, population than the Western Desert at least during the Predynastic and early Dynastic times (1991:247). Interaction of Eastern Desert populations with immigrants or caravans from southwest Asia would have facilitated transmission of cultural ideas in addition to the numerous trade goods found in Delta and Valley sites. The Wadi Abu Had lies in a strategic position between a number of copper and gold mines utilized at least by the Old Kingdom and again during Roman and Byzantine times. To the east are galena mines adjacent to the natural harbor at Zeit Bay. These were probably mined before the Middle Kingdom until they were eventually exhausted during the New Kingdom. These various routes provided easy access by valley dwellers to seasonal highland pastures as evidenced by the rock art (chapter seven).

Beyond the Fayum Depression to the west of the Nile Valley is the Libyan or Western Desert. It is essentially the easternmost extent of the Sahara. It is a flat plateau with numerous closed-in depressions, except for the uplifted area of Gebel 'Uweinat on the extreme west Sudano-Egyptian border (see Figure 3.1). The Gebel 'Uweinat lies at 1907 m above sea level, in stark contrast to the great Qattara Depression, which lies at nearly 40 m below seal level. Northeast of the Gebel 'Uweinat is broad high ground extending some 200 km, gradually sloping to the north to the Dakhla and Kharga Oases (with elevations of 400 m and 200 m above sea level respectively). The northern boundary of these oases is a high escarpment formed by the southern edge of Eocene limestone, which lies at 500 m above sea level (see Said 1990:10). Surrounding these and a few smaller, ephemeral oases is the Great Sand Sea. In this barren region, the very hot, dust-laden *khamsin* winds occasionally blow during spring, contributing substantially to deflation and erosion of archaeological materials. Attia noted that plants often die from root exposure as a result of soil loss, as well as from scouring damage to stems and leaves (1954). In addition, grit carried in these winds can spread diseases and suffocate animals (Hume 1925).

Stratigraphic and paleoenvironmental studies are relatively new phenomena in Sarahan North Africa. Concisely presented by Banks in her investigation of early Sarahan pastoralism (1984:19),

> [m]ost of these studies have been in lowland regions, such as Kharga Oasis (Caton-Thompson 1952; Wendorf and Schild 1980), Dungul and Kurkur Oases (Hester and Hobler 1969), Siwa Oasis and its environs (Hassan 1986, 1978), Gebel 'Uweinat and the Gilf Kebir (Wendorf et al. 1976, 1977; Wendorf and Schild 1980; Williams and Hall 1965; Maxwell 1980; de Heinzelin Haesaerts, and Van Noten 1969), [and…] Nabta Playa and Bir Kiseiba (Wendorf et al. 1976, 1977; Wendorf and Schild 1980; Wendorf, Schild and Close 1984).

These studies vary in detail and quality, and large gaps remain in the database. It appears that from Mauritania to the Sudan, early Holocene (9000–7500 B.C.) groundwaters were high and there is mounting evidence of numerous lakes at the base of mountains, and between Lake Pleistocene dunes (Faure et al. 1963; Williams 1971, 1984).

The crucial factors influencing lake levels are rainfall and temperature; temperature of course affecting the evaporation of shallow lakes, etc. (see Butzer et al. 1972). Considering the geomorphological, floral, faunal data and the modern environment, it seems likely that rainfall rarely exceeded 200 m per year even during the most mesic periods of the Holocene (Hassan 1988:146). Analysis of charred wood remains from Gilf Kebir suggest that between 6050 and 3050 B.C., water was seasonally available and would have supported small, mobile human populations even if rainfall did not exceed 100 mm annually (Neumann 1987). Today, the Western Desert receives approximately 1.0 mm rainfall annually, usually in a few concentrated storm bursts during December and January (Ayyad and Ghabbhour

1986:149). Monsoonal rains are posited to have extended to the southern reaches of the Tibesti and Aÿr Mountains (Servant and Servant 1970, 1972). During and immediately following these rains, water would have pooled briefly in carbonate-floored depressions between the giant sand ripples (Wendorf et al. 1985:136; Gabriel 1977:22–24).

McHugh et al. (1989) recognized that storm water may have drained long distances along sand-filled channels to feed playa lakes and perhaps supported vegetation that produced pollen and other indicators of higher rainfall than actually occurred. The southern region of the Western Desert seems to have been covered by an open Mediterranean-type vegetation, in contrast to the much drier northern and eastern portions of the rest of the Sahara (van Zinderen Bakker 1976). Pachur and Roper (1984) noted that there was enough water to support at least discontinuous patches of vegetation, allowing fauna—and human populations following them—to migrate through areas which are now totally desert, including the Great Sand Sea northeast of Gilf Kebir, the Western Desert, and further south, the plains around Wadi Howar.

Rock art depicting elephant, hippopotamus, giraffe and rhinoceros, historical records of their presence along the fringe of the desert, and the identification of some of these species among the fauna from archaeological sites attest to a fairly high biomass in some areas of the Sahara during the Holocene Wet Phases (Mauny 1957; McHugh 1974; Signey 1965; Dekeyser 1955). These data provide some idea of the carrying capacity, although a discrepancy exists between the rock art and recovered faunal remains, suggesting that the faunal remains are more indicative of human exploitative preferences than habitat structure. Osteological evidence of many of the larger herbivores depicted in the rock art is rare; the majority of remains consist of smaller herbivores, particularly *Gazella* (Banks 1984).

Beyond Egypt's western border, faunal data from the Eastern Sahara are fairly detailed because of the quality of preservation and the numerous assemblages that have been recovered and studied (Banks 1984: Table III:1). There is a general lack of diversity among the assemblages, a high frequency of carnivores of generally small size (implying stiff competition for resources), and a generally low biomass and thus carrying capacity, in which faunal communities congregated around the playas. Mid-Holocene assemblages suggest a semi-arid to steppe environment with a carrying capacity lower than areas further west.

## The Annual Ecological Cycle and Resource Scheduling

Several researchers have proposed that Egyptian foragers adopted (southwest Asian) domesticates as only one more set of resources to exploit, as they continued to hunt and gather (Brewer 1986, 1989; Hassan 1986a, b, 1987; Wenke 1991; Wenke et al 1983; Wetterstrom 1993). The attraction of these new food sources seems to have been their predictability, for although Egyptians of the Epipaleolithic had a seemingly successful and stable subsistence pattern, they remained at the mercy of annual Nile floods. With domesticated animals, foragers had predictable and mobile resources that could effectively compensate for the unpredictability of such floods. Above, the different habitats in the three regions of Egypt suggest that resources in some areas were more abundant or predictable than in others. Throughout much of the Holocene, the southern Delta and the Valley floodplains would have provided the most abundant, diverse and predictable plant and animal resources. Some researchers have suggested, however, that while the Upper Egyptian floodplain is not a truly circumscribed habitat, the geology restricted plant and animal (including human) populations to a comparatively narrow band along the Nile, and caused the food supply to be relatively less predictable than in the north.

Nile ecology created special categories of land: for example, the high riverbank levee, the low riverbank itself, swampland, etc.. Eyre (1994:70) noted that the Egyptians themselves were aware of different qualities of land, usually attributed to the likelihood of being naturally flooded (Table 3.1). The low gradient of the floodplain resulted in vast differences in inundated land, even with only minor fluctuations in flood height (Butzer 1976; Hassan 1993). This led to the development of irrigation mechanisms during the late Predynastic and perhaps slightly earlier in the Amration (see Van Lepp 1995). Efforts were made to raise the overall water table and thereby distribute water across a wider area, increasing the amount of high quality land. Excess water was also retained and distributed to outlying areas after the floodwaters themselves had already retreated; irrigating fields during the growing season increases the strength and productivity of plants which might not otherwise survive in such areas, further expanding the amount of usable land.

The deposition of silts annually renewed soil quality and different basins held water for longer or shorter periods before draining; the amount and quality of products to be raised on a given plot would also vary. A mosaic of smaller habitats based on this variability is more plausible than the overly simplistic impression of a distinctive habitat for each of the three major regions. Nonetheless, resources in the Delta were more predictable or more abundant *on average* than in the Valley. This mosaic pattern likely factored into the quality and amount of land an individual could own, beginning in the late Predynastic, as social stratification became clearly evident (see chapter six).

Thus, the wide range of available resources encouraged locating settlements close to floodplains, and a subsistence strategy maximizing the seasonal nature of those resources would have been ideal. Hassan (1984:60–

Table 3.1. A Variety of Terms Relating to Land (Brewer et al. 1994; Eyre 1994).

| | | |
|---|---|---|
|  | *iww mꜣwt* or *ꜥmꜥt* | **mud flats** |
|  | *ḫrw* | **lowland** |
|  | *qꜣyt* | **high ground (requiring irrigation?)** |
| 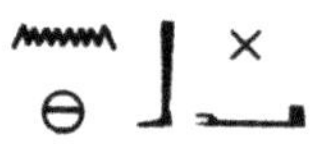 | *nhbw* | **virgin plowland** |

62) has described a scenario for economic scheduling in ancient Egypt, reflecting the influence of Nile floods on human activities (see Figure 3.5). The association between annual inundation and natural cycles of plant and animal production was clearly understood by the Egyptians themselves, as indicated by their names of seasons: *Akhet, Peret* and *Shemu* (Kadish 1988).

*Akhet* denotes the beginning of a new year, and is marked by the beginning of the inundation—although one should bear in mind that this occurred a few weeks later in the north. Rising water level has been shown by Brunton (1979) to trigger spawning in the Nile catfish (Family: Clariidae). Brewer (1987) has demonstrated that catfish were commonly collected during the late spring/early summer and the summer/fall, corresponding to the flood minimum and maximum. Similarly, Brewer (1991a) suggested that another common archaeological taxa, the Nile perch (*Lates*), was collected primarily during the period of rising and receding floodwaters, or during *Akhet* and *Peret*. Fish became abundant and easy to catch from lagoons, streams and basins as these areas drained. Corvée labor projects across Egypt during the Dynastic Period are likely to have been concentrated during *Akhet* because many localized activities (agricultural pursuits in particular) were postponed until the floods began to recede.

*Peret* means "coming forth," as the earth was reborn out of the floodwaters and represented perhaps the most important season (roughly November through February in the south). This was the season of growth and harvest of plants for both human and animal consumption. As will become evident in the next chapter, this was also the period in which the highest potential for milk production and weight gain occurs among animals—especially by the young (see also Bar-Yosef and Khazanov 1992:70). Hassan proposes that this season was also marked by ceremonial gatherings and feasts (1984:61).

The third season, *Shemu,* is translated variously as "lacking water" or "warmth" (Kadish 1988:187). Although the exact translation is unknown, the link remains clear that it denotes a season of minimal influence by the Nile, and suggests a time of difficulty as pastures and ponds are exhausted. Exploitation of wooded gallery near the river would have intensified as local resources were depleted, and some segments of the population may have moved their herds to remaining pastures some distance from settlements. The increased mobility may have encouraged exchange between regions, particularly if the flood and consequent harvest in one area had been insufficient. There is an indication from the Middle Kingdom that some activities were suspended during the annual drought. The example is of mining in the Sinai (Gardiner et al. 1955), but conceivably other corvée labor projects would also have been limited because of the heat and reduced resources.

## Conclusions

Through this examination of geological, palynological, and zooarchaeological data, the resource potential of the regional habitats have been defined, and seasonal and long-term climatic shifts for each have been reconstructed. Random organization of Nile distributaries in the delta rendered intercommunity communication or cooperation more difficult, but the high wild resource potential and higher water table resulted in greater food availability and predictability. In contrast, vegetation in the deserts would have been minimal, a "discontinuous grass cover and a few scattered acacia trees" highly dependent upon winter rains (Hassan 1980:440; see also Brewer et al. 1994:7–8). The Fayum depression and other oases scattered in the Western Desert were highly susceptible to climatic fluctuations, and their vegetation and animal communities similarly sparse. The Valley appears to have been intermediate between these two extremes, with much higher resource predictability and yield than in the desert regions but restricted to smaller expanses than in the vast deltaic plain.

Geologic and climatological research and evidence from growth rings in fish (*Clariidae* and *Lates*) indicate that Egypt's Predynastic climate (ca. 3500–3100 B.C.) was becoming progressively more arid, with increasing variability in winter temperatures and possibly winter rainfall (Brewer 1991a, b, 1992; Brewer and Yokell 1996). This was accompanied by a decrease in the volume of Nile floods (Bell 1970; Hassan 1980). The combination of these variables would have reduced resource productivity and predictability for the human inhabitants of this area (Brewer 1991b:299). With this decrease, many desert sites were apparently abandoned. A corresponding increase in archaeological sites along the Nile (e.g., Hassan 1980) suggests that portions of the desert populations were moving closer to the main Nile channel, bringing their domesticated animals and cultural beliefs with them. With decreasing environmental stability, increases in population density and, potentially, the need for more complex social structures within the population (e.g., Brewer 1991a, b; Brewer and Wenke 1992), the inception of the domestic animal complex and the rise of the first dynastic cycle are perhaps not unexpected.

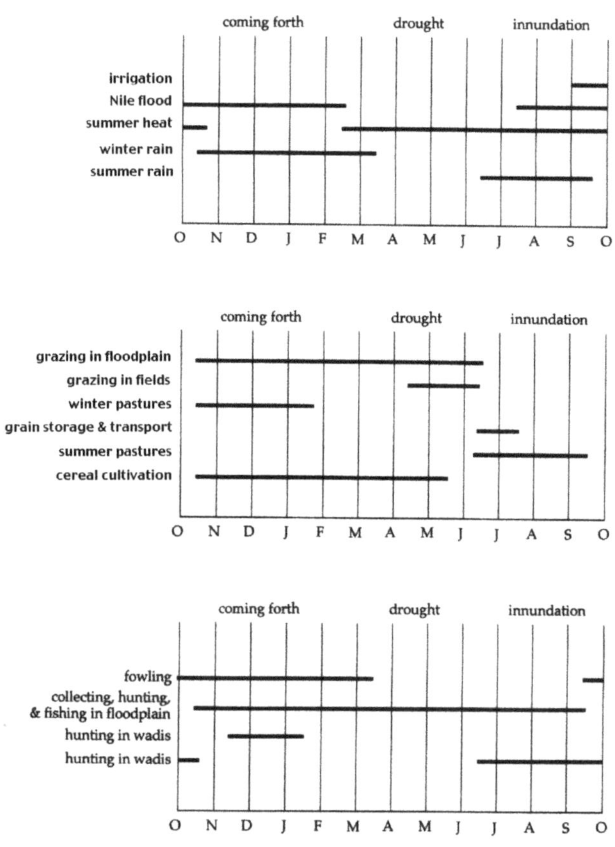


Figure 3.5. Proposed Seasonal Resource Scheduling in Ancient Egypt (after Hassan 1984:60–62).

The cultures of Upper and Lower Egypt and its Deserts were noticeably different during the Predynastic (see chapter six), and the co-evolution of human societies and domestic taxa should have followed different trajectories in each region. In the next chapter, a detailed description of the biological and physiological adaptations of the four domestic species to certain environmental conditions is presented in order to suggest which taxon (or complex of taxa) might have been particularly attractive economically to the ancient Egyptians of a given area.

# 4. COMPARATIVE ECOLOGY OF FOUR DOMESTICATED SPECIES

## Introduction

Modern faunal distributions do not accurately reflect the biogeographic landscape in which domestication took place, because significant environmental changes have occurred throughout and since the Holocene (beginning ca. 10,000 B.C.). In general, the colder periods (ca. 6000–4500, 2500–500 B.C.) were characterized by greater dryness in tropical regions, and greater humidity in the northern margin of the Sahara. In tropical areas, the appreciable decrease in rainfall was counterbalanced by decreased evaporation; this aridity controlled the central Sahara as far south as the Tanzanian plateaus. During the warmer phases (ca. 8000–6000, 4500–2500 B.C.), this extensive region received much more precipitation from the equatorial rain system. The vegetation zones expanded and migrated further north, east, and south into the surrounding deserts.

Regardless of the cause(s) of environmental change, resultant changes in the location and extent of forest/grassland (i.e., forage) have had an important impact on the distributions of various species, and thus the human populations dependent upon them. With an understanding of the major climatic oscillations (documented primarily for North and East Africa) which affected the distributions of grassland habitat available as forage, it becomes possible to reconstruct areas of resource abundance or scarcity, and the degree of resource predictability or seasonality. Without *determining* the nature of occupation, the specific environment and climate of an area do *limit* the population density and subsistence alternatives available to its inhabitants (plant, animal, or human). The ecological and physiological requirements of the species comprising the Egyptian domesticate complex are now presented in order to determine when, where, and to some degree how, human populations could have relied on pastoral modes of subsistence.

## Comparative Attributes

### *Thermal Stability*

A mammal produces metabolic heat when transforming food into work; it also absorbs heat from direct or indirect solar radiation. This cumulative 'heat load' must be balanced by the animal's heat loss in order to maintain thermal stability. In tropical and subtropical areas a mammal has five defenses against excessive heat: behavioral avoidance, temporary storage of heat, evaporative cooling, the reflective and insulative characters of the coat, and lowering of its metabolic rate (which reduces metabolic heat production).

Cattle dissipate excess body heat primarily by sweating and panting, the former allows greater volume of fluid to be evaporated and results in more efficient cooling (Macfarlane 1968b:171–172). *Bos indicus*, the Zebu or Brahman cattle, secrete approximately six times more sweat than they evaporate by panting, whereas the European cattle (*Bos taurus*) secrete only three to four times more sweat. Additionally, the heat-tolerant Zebu also has a shorter, smoother, and more highly reflective coat than *Bos taurus* (Macfarlane 1968a:172; 1968b:266; Schmidt-Nielsen 1979:78). Macfarlane (1968a:168) cites Turner and Schleger's (1960) study that demonstrated a high correlation between a short, smooth coat and the rate of tissue growth, the production of meat rather than fat, the fertility and food conversion efficiency of cattle. While the Zebu is a more recent breed and was not present in Egypt before the Middle Kingdom (Epstein 1971; Marshall 1990), it demonstrates important adaptive strategies.

In contrast to cattle, thermal stability is maintained in sheep and goats primarily by panting (Macfarlane 1968a:171–172; Redding 1981:194–199; Schmidt-Nielsen 1979:98–100). Body temperature in Middle Eastern goats rises more than sheep, suggesting that goats are better able to tolerate heat (Redding 1981:194). Sheep rely so heavily on water in the circulatory system for evaporative cooling that Ghosh and Khan declare it to be "decidedly less desert-worthy than the goat" (1980:26). Tropical and desert sheep typically have hairier fleece than other (e.g., more northern) breeds, permitting convective cooling and reflection of incoming radiation without trapping water or heat (Macfarlane 1968a:168, 1968b:266). Woolly and hair-wool fleeces do provide considerable insulation from temperature extremes, but also *trap* heated air in the interstices of the wool to which the sun penetrates; this may cause them to overheat in direct sun (Russell 1988:56).

Pigs lack the ability to sweat, and body temperature is maintained through behavioral avoidance (if shade is provided or available), by wallowing, or panting, rendering its environmental requirements more stringent than those of other large food animals. Newborn pigs dissipate relatively more heat than adults because young pigs lack insulating layers of fat (Mount 1968), and because smaller bodies have a greater surface area to volume ratio. As with other species, pigs lower their food consumption under heat stress, thereby producing less heat and reducing problems of heat dissipation. Of course, the less they eat, the less they grow. Spaulding and Spaulding (1989) reported that pigs generally seek moisture in which to wallow when air temperatures rise above about 30°C, the subsequent evaporation providing the needed cooling effect. This has been used as an argument for the idea that pigs are maladapted to survival in hot, arid environments (e.g., Harris 1974, 1985). However, much of the literature Harris used is derived from studies of modern, European breeds kept in the tropics—an area in which they did not evolve. In contrast, Redding (1981) noted in his study of Middle Eastern herding strategies that temperature was *not* a major limiting factor of pigs, having encountered sounders of active wild pigs where temperatures exceeded 47°C. Thus, of the four domestic species, goats are best able to maintain thermal stability in water-restricted areas, followed by sheep, cattle, and lastly, pigs.

## Water Balance

From the discussion of heat dissipation, it is apparent that water loss is a limiting factor. In addition to evaporation, fluids are lost through urination and defecation. Obviously, all water loss must eventually be replaced by an equal intake; generally by drinking, but also from water contained in food (or the oxidation of hydrogen in food [Hafez 1968b:13]).

Cattle, particularly calves, are generally unable to meet their water requirements merely through consumption of fresh plants, and Schmidt-Nielsen (1979:78–80) noted that their water consumption is high relative to sheep and goats. Banks noted that cattle should graze and water at least every other day, although they can survive up to three days without water (1984:216). Often, movements will alternate daily between water and pasture, especially during dry seasons when the spatial distance between water and pasture is at a maximum (Deshler 1964). Under heat stress, water intake increases more than is required to cover increased evaporation (Russell 1988:57). Heat-stressed cattle drink to reduce body temperature directly rather than merely to offset dehydration.

Both sheep and goats are able to meet much of their fluid requirements from plants during periods of lush grazing and browsing, and generally require less frequent watering than cattle during dry seasons (Dyson-Hudson and McCabe 1985; Dahl and Hjort 1976; Redding 1981; Russell 1988). Overall, sheep use approximately half the amount of water as cattle, and goats use less than sheep (Macfarlane 1968a:176, 1968b:270–271). Goats are able to dramatically reduce their water loss via excretion of concentrated urine (i.e., by using water from cells and gut), and having an excretory system that is twice as effective as that of most breeds of sheep (Macfarlane 1968a:175–176; Redding 1981:200). Given these water requirements, Russell concludes that while cattle can survive only three to five days under water deprivation, sheep and goats can survive for approximately six to ten days (1988:58, citing Sato 1980:11).

Complete water deprivation in all three species leads to a 20–30% loss in body weight (Ghosh and Abichandani 1981:13). Restricted water intake, however, actually led to an *increase* in overall body weight in the same three species. This is attributed to a slower rate of passage of feed through the gut (Purohit 1972), and an increase in the digestibility of crude fibers (Purohit et al. 1976). Further, the recovery of lost body weight is almost fully achieved on the first day of rehydration (Ghosh and Abichandani 1981:24–25). Nearly 84% of lost weight among cattle and 70% among sheep and goats was achieved the first day (Mcfarlane 1968a). Schmidt-Nielsen (1964) hypothesized that the ability to rapidly replace lost water results from an animal's need to drink quickly at a water hole and escape before being brought down by a predator. While remaining untested, it seems probable that domestic species have maintained this pattern of behavior from their wild ancestors.

Data were unavailable on the ability of pigs to survive for extended periods without water, but van Loon noted that pigs fed wet garbage or slop diets may not need additional water (1978:95). It is recommended that water allowances for pigs raised on hot, dry conditions not drop below between 1 and 5 kg per day (Devendra and Fuller 1979:Table 6.4), depending of course on pig size. This may be mediated to some degree by access to wallows. Redding (1991:23) suggested that the Egyptian Delta "may have been ideal for maintaining pigs, since even if the local breeds experienced heat stress the high water table and seasonal floods must have created abundant wallows." Pigs require more frequent access to water than other domestic species, and thus would be a less preferred species in hot, *arid* environments, but well-suited to hot, *moist* environments such as the Delta or portions of the Valley. Thus, the order of domestic species does not change when ranked according to minimum water requirements and efficiency of water usage.

## Feeding Ecology

The feeding patterns of cattle, sheep, goats, and pigs are highly significant for determining the relative productive potential of these herd species in specific locales. Broad taxonomic variation exists between nutritional values regardless of the time of year, and individual parts of a plant vary in nutritional value throughout the year. Gordon and Sampson (1939) found that as plants pass through leaf, bloom and drying phases, the crude protein content of all plant types decreases. Phosphorous and potassium content also decrease, while fiber content increases in grasses and herbs. Berton et al. (1964), Tomlin et al. (1965), and Redding (1981) noted that lignin content increases substantially with maturation; digestibility is negatively correlated with the amount of lignin. Thus, deciduous shrubs and trees always maintain a higher protein level than grasses, broad-leaf shrubs and non-deciduous shrubs. Legumes have a lignin content equal to or greater than that of grasses, are less digestible and pass through the digestive system more quickly (Tomlin et al.1965; Redding 1981).

Cattle are basically grazing animals, but will browse occasionally on available bushes. Their multiple stomach chambers enable them to graze during the cool morning periods, and chew cud with only a minimum of effort during the midday and afternoon heat. As Smith noted, this feeding schedule requires that cattle be put to pasture at first light so that they have sufficient time to fill their stomachs before noon, and has encouraged herders to keep calves close to camp so that cows will return in the evening on their own to feed them (1992b). This has the added bonus of preventing the calves from suckling at will, which obviously would reduce the amount of milk available for human consumption. At most, cattle move between 22 and 25 km per day to fresh pastures even with adequate watering (Stenning 1959; Gulliver and Gulliver 1953; Deshler 1964), and are typically restricted to within a 4 to 13 km radius of water sources during the dry seasons (Dahl and Hjort 1976; Torry 1973; Breman and de Wit 1983). They are capable of adjusting slowly to the harsh conditions of the dry season, and may lost up to one-half of their normal weight in the process (Smith 1992b:106). At the lower weight, daily energy requirements are also lower, decreasing nutritional needs by roughly one-half as well (Topps 1977:102).

Huston (1978) postulated that sheep rely on collecting and storing nutrients when graze is available, for use when forage is scarce or of poor quality. Williamson and Payne (1977:454) maintained that sheep are selective grazers, preferring short grasses, legumes and herbs, and noted that sheep are reluctant to try new forages. Sheep prefer grasses more than trees and shrubs.

Goats tend to prefer browse over grasses (except when kept in paddocks). Goats utilize or ignore different plant species according to the stage of maturity (French 1970:166–168); green new growth is more nutritious. Goats are also selective in the utilization of parts of plants (Cory 1927:17; Thalen 1979:221–223). Goats graze when plant species present are higher in nutritional value than browse, shifting to premarily browse as the dry season approaches. Despite their preference for certain types or parts of plants, goats are inquisitive feeders and will try virtually anything (grass, greens, weeds, leaves, bark, young shoots, seed pods, paper, clothing, etc.). This low selectivity allows goats to utilize habitats that would not meet minimum nutritive needs of sheep. Thus, goats are better adapted for success/survival in more harsh areas than sheep, and should be more abundant archaeologically in such areas. Goats spend less time at one feeding locality and search more frequently for food. The average daily distance traveled by goats is 1.6 times greater than sheep: 10 km versus 6.3 km (Cory 1927:14).

Although not primarily grazers *or* browsers, pigs generally prefer tubers, grains or even plants such as clover (Barker 1985)—and therefore compete to a small degree with other domesticated animals. Citing Dardaillon's (1987) study—conducted in an area of coastal France reminiscent of the modern-day Egyptian delta—Redding noted that the list of non-domestic food plants consumed by pigs "matches very closely the plant list for the Old Kingdom deposits of Kom el-Hisn," also in the Western delta (1991:22). This potential for competition with other domesticated animals can be reduced by fattening hogs on gleanings from cattle manure, as 25% of whole grains may pass through the bovine digestive system unscathed (Devendra and Fuller 1979:127).

However, a more important consideration is that pigs root in uncultivated forests or fallow garden plots, and owing to their digestive anatomy, can eat many of the same foods as humans. This has been interpreted by some as competition for food between humans and pigs, and has consistently been presented in the literature as a justification for *not* raising pigs in regions with limited or unpredictable resources (e.g., Harris 1974, 1985; Kemp 1984; Redding 1991). Dogs also eat many of the same foods as humans, yet are not considered competitors or inappropriate in limited habitats.

Pigs are beneficial in that they will eat cast-off food remains and even human waste. This not only eliminates them from direct competition for resources with humans (or most other domesticated food animals), it may also provide the added benefit of reducing available matter for disease-carrying decomposers such as flies or rats. Among the *zabbalin* refuse collectors of Cairo today, pigs are being used in an urban waste management project reminiscent of rural Greece (Miller 1990:126, fn 7). In areas of extremely dense low-income (and presumably Christian) population in Cairo, the *Wahiya* garbage brokers bid for or inherit the right to rent collection routes throughout which pigs are allowed free range to feed on domestic waste, which otherwise would simply continue to accumulate[1] (Haynes and el-Hakim 1979). Perhaps restricting what type of waste was given to each species could account for the continued acceptance of both 'competitors'. For example, while similarities in diets exist between pigs and dogs, Devendra and Fuller (1979:105–107) and Redding (1991:29, fn 3) note that the most valuable food sources for managing pigs are proteins and oils in fish meal, made generally from fish processing wastes. Youatt also commented that "refuse wash and grains and other residue of breweries and distilleries may also be given to swine with advantage, and seem to induce a tendency to lay on flesh..." (1847:137). There is no evidence suggesting dogs were fed these types of food, rather that they consumed primarily scraps from large herbivores, and more rarely smaller taxa such as rodents (Brewer et al. 1994).

Fish processing offal as well as bread-/beer-making residue are two food sources readily available in ancient Egypt, further reducing the importance of the traditional notion of pigs competing with either humans or other domesticates. Devendra and Fuller (1979:17) noted that an integrated system of pig production combines fish farming, vegetable production and/or duck keeping. This would have been an ideal means for widespread pig production in Egypt because "major sources of animal protein for rich and poor appear to have been fish and wildfowl" throughout ancient Egyptian history (Miller and Wetterstrom 1996).

[1] Here, streets are not wide enough for garbage trucks, which in any case are too few in number to handle the vast quantities of domestic refuse produced by the ever-increasing population of Cairo.

### *Aspects of Productivity*

There is little argument that the products available from various taxa affect their relative merit to human populations. For example, pigs yield considerably fewer products than other domesticated taxa because of their comparatively small size, soft bones, and their inability to produce milk for human consumption. However, physiological adaptability to environmental stresses also affects productivity, in terms of meat, fat, milk, growth rates, reproduction, etc. While debate continues over the validity of various measures of meat or fat yield, for example, from archaeological taxa (Blumenschine 1986; Blumenshine and Caro 1986; Brooks et al. 1977; Daly 1969; Guilday et al. 1962; Lyman 1979; B. Smith 1985; Stewart and Stahl 1977; Weiner 1973), the seasonal variation in such yields has been poorly studied or documented even among modern herds. For example, in 53 African countries in which tax increases are closely tied to herd number and yield, carcass weights of cattle did not vary from an optimum carcass weight (projected by various governments) between 1969 and 1978 (FAO 1978). Having established the relative physiological adaptivity of each of the four domestic species to environmental stressors, the products of these taxa are also usefully compared in the same fashion. Their relative productivity affects how human populations attempt to maximize herd growth, stability, and off-take; these issues are addressed through examination of ethnographic accounts of modern pastoral societies (chapter five).

- **Fat**

Fat is the main food reserve allowing all these species to survive on restricted or low-nutrient resources during dry periods of the year (or in the case of northern distribution, during winter). According to Noddle (1989:27), ruminants may even withdraw fat from their bone marrow during exceptionally long drought seasons; unfortunately, few controlled experiments with marrow fat of domesticated animals have been carried out (but see Brooks et al. 1977 for details on several African ungulate species). Intramuscular, peri-renal and tail concentrations have received more study.

Cattle are relatively efficient converters of feed into energy; converting approximately 43% in a hot environment (Yousef et al. 1968). In dairy cattle, surplus nutrients are converted to milk, while in beef cattle, surpluses are deposited as flesh and fat. Thus, each has different functional level require-ments of hormones and enzymes, and led Butterworth (1985) to conclude that beef cattle are more susceptible to humidity stress than dairy cattle. Gross anatomical differences may also contribute to this difference: modern dairy cattle are typically thin, angular, with a deep paunch and capacious udder, while beef cattle are more rounded due to thick layers of subcutaneous fat. The greater body surface area exposed by dairy cattle, then, effects greater heat dissipation (Yousef et al. 1968). It may never be possible to determine when these breeds became sufficiently

Figure 4.1. An Example of the Egyptian Fat-tailed Sheep (from Description de l'Egypte 1994[1809]:762, plate 7).

differentiated that the environment produced a discernible effect, or if these differences influenced the herders' decisions.

Dahl and Hjort (1976:204–205) noted that goats generally do not build up concentrations of fat, while sheep deposit it intramuscularly, particularly in the tail or rump. The "fat-tailed sheep" of Egypt is a common example (see Figure 4.1). The lumps of fat deposited at the base of the tail may weigh up to "4 to 5 kilos; the rest of the animal may weigh only 25 kilos" (Brewer et al. 1994:91); whereas a mature goat with a total weight of 40 kg will typically only provide 1.7 kg of fat (Redding 1981:77). Quoting from early descriptions of Cape sheep, Youatt noted that the fat was a semi-fluid like thick oil, and was frequently used for oil and butter (1837). A comparison of tail and body fats among Iranian fat-tailed sheep similar to those in Egypt indicated that tail fat is indeed quite soft, contains more iodine, more unsaturated fats, and was reported as more palatable (Parvaneh 1972).

Pigs also deposit fat in layers between bands of muscle. Van Loon noted that many fats are absorbed and deposited unchanged; it is easy to change the flavor of pig fat merely by modifying the diet even a few weeks before slaughter (1978:90). Fish meal with high oil content or even garbage diets lead to "soft" pork, containing a large amount of soft unsaturated fats, but switching to crop residues a few weeks before slaughter returns the fat and meat to normal consistency and taste (Devendra and Fuller 1979). At least since the Medieval Period and continuing among non-Muslim populations in the Sudan, pigs have been raised primarily as a source of meat, but also to supply fat "used as a dressing for the hair and skin" (Chessman 1936:371, cited in Spaulding and Spaulding 1989:8).

Terrill noted that while sheep decrease food consumption during heat stress, temperature does not affect the efficiency of feed conversion (1968). Further, the metabolic rate of sheep is lower than that of cattle—thus fat stores last longer than the metabolically active cattle when food supplies fail (1968). Comparative rates of efficiency of feed conversion or fat utilization under stress were unavailable for pigs.

### • Meat

Just as the different taxa vary in their physiological needs, they differ in their ability to convert forage into meat. Meat provides a wider range of amino acids than plants, contains the essential vitamin $B_{12}$, and more iron, although the quantity—and to a lesser extent the nutrient content—of meat depends on animal breed, nutritional state, age, sex, and season at death. Spotty coverage in the literature "renders it impossible at present to estimate age- or sex-related variability in nutrient yield" (Redding 1981:137–138), nor do available data permit estimation of seasonally specific values for quantities or content of meats.

Determination of which species will be used in an area is not as simple as calculating the amount of meat or calories. Especially in harsh or unpredictable habitats, humans must consider the relative efficiency of each species. Obviously one adult cow, bull or steer provides more meat than a single sheep, goat or pig, but it may be advantageous to raise the latter if they are more efficient at converting their food (plants or waste) into human foods (meat or fat). On average, pigs convert one-fifth of consumed food into meat (Strickon 1965:233), although Pimentel and Pimentel (1979:59, cited in Redding 1991:29, fn 2) give a yield of only one-tenth. Even with this variability, pigs are more efficient than cattle. A modern beef steer, which presumably has been bred for high meat yield, converts less than one-twentieth of consumed food into meat (Strickon 1965:233).

The documented reduction in the overall sizes of various species following domestication and the lack of comparable osteological studies on modern species from which slaughter yields are derived makes an "accurate evaluation of the applicability of [these] data to the prehistoric past extremely difficult" (Russell 1988:24). The reductions are on the order of 20% for cattle (A. Smith 1980:494–496), 20–22% for goats, and "similar reductions" for sheep (Clutton-Brock 1979:153, Table 6). Data were unavailable for pigs.

Analyses of meat yields from unimproved[2] Near Eastern breeds of sheep and goat demonstrate that sheep of either sex consistently yield more meat than goats (see Table 4.1). Such detailed information was unavailable for breeds of cattle or pigs from the Near East. Sudanese cattle in poor condition have dressing percentages (proportion of the animal's life weight remaining after slaughter and evisceration) of 47%, and 50% for well-fed animals, yielding between 90–108 kg per individual (Dahl and Hjort 1976:165). Meat weights from tropical pigs were calculated by Devendra and Fuller (1979) as approximately 10% of the total live weight, and African pigs attain up to 250 kg total weight[3]. Thus, pigs provide roughly the same amount of meat as adult male sheep or goats, and while they yield about one-fourth the meat of cattle, pigs also require only about one-half as much food. The amount of food provided would of course be less if the pigs were allowed to feed on domestic garbage. Haynes and el-Hakim (1979:104) noted, however, that modern pigs fed on urban waste in Cairo attain slaughter weight (of about 40 kg) after eight months, while the

[2] While recognizing that selective breeding since the beginnings of domestication has undoubtedly led to improvements in habitat tolerances, product yields, etc., I refer to "unimproved" breeds raised by modern indigenous African pastoral societies to distinguish these animals from recently introduced breeds with exceptionally high tolerances and yields, such as the Fulani and Boran cattle in tropical habitats of Africa.

[3] Adult weights of African pigs vary considerably, but little is known concerning their heritage or origin. The 'Ashanti dwarf,' averaging only 80 kg, may not be indigenous (Devendra and Fuller 1979:22-23). The 250 kg variety mentioned approximates the size of pigs depicted in Egyptian art, and occurr in the Middle East, from where they may have originated.

Table 4.1. Weights for Three Age Classes of Unimproved Sheep and Goats by Sex (from Redding 1981:146, 152, Tables V-2 and V-4).

| Sex | Age Class | Live Weight (kg) | Carcass Weight (kg) | Meat Weight (kg) |
|---|---|---|---|---|
| Female sheep | birth | 4.0 | 2.0 | 1.4 |
| Male sheep | birth | 4.3 | 2.2 | 1.5 |
| Female goat | birth | 1.9 | 0.9 | 0.6 |
| Male goat | birth | 2.1 | 1.0 | 0.6 |
| Female sheep | yearling | 30.0 | 15.6 | 11.8 |
| Male sheep | yearling | 41.0 | 21.3 | 16.2 |
| Female goat | yearling | 26.0 | 13.0 | 8.9 |
| Male goat | yearling | 41.0 | 20.5 | 14.1 |
| Female sheep | adult | 40.0 | 20.8 | 15.8 |
| Male sheep | adult | 68.0 | 35.4 | 26.9 |
| Female goat | adult | 35.0 | 17.5 | 12.6 |
| Male goat | adult | 65.0 | 32.5 | 23.4 |

same weight can be achieved in intensive feeding programs in 14–18 weeks.

### • Milk

Milk differs from meat or fat in that it is a renewable resource, with each lactating female providing a new supply each day, whereas the other products require the loss of the animal. Milk and dried milk products are not made from the milk of pigs because this species (and, in fact, most mammals) store milk in an alveolar system rather than the large cistern-type systems of cattle, sheep, goat and camels (see Russell 1998:28). Three aspects of milk yield are important for comparisons of productivity between species: quantity per lactation[4], length of lactation, and nutritional composition (Redding 1981:166). Length of lactation, and to some degree, even the quantity of milk, can be increased through human milking activities (Russell 1988:25). Altering herd structures for greater numbers of females and staggering breeding are means for human populations to increase the amount of milk or lengthen the period of its availability.

With adequate forage near the end of the rainy season, unimproved breeds of cattle in Uganda may produce up to 2.5 liters of milk daily for human consumption (Dyson-Hudson and Dyson-Hudson 1970:113). In contrast, Deshler reported for the same population and season that only one liter of milk may be produced beyond that needed to feed their calves (1965). Goats, however, produce up to 1.7 liters surplus per day with adequate food (Mackenzie 1971). Sheep produce between 0.9 to 1.7 liters of milk a day, and a ewe raising twins will produce about 50% more milk than one with a single lamb (Ryder 1983). That lactation can be increased beyond the normal production level without human control of breeding implies that more milk might have been available for humans than previously thought.

The length of lactation for sheep averages 135 days, and 210 days for goats (Redding 1981:169, 171). Data for cattle demonstrate the extreme plasticity of milk yield in response to environment (and also breed, which were rarely specified). Lactation generally varies from 210–250 days in marginal drylands, but may be much shorter in highly seasonal environments (Dahl and Hjort 1976:143). Presumably, then, lactation would have been longer for herds kept along wadis and desert margins, but shorter in the Valley and Delta.

Sheep milk contains more fat and protein than other species, containing 7.5% fat and 5% casein, while cow's milk contains 4% fat and 2.5% casein (Ryder 1983:721). Goat milk contains slightly more fat (4.5%) than cattle, but the same amount of casein (Mackenzie 1993:247). Although pig milk (4.5% fat, 7.5% casein and other proteins [Mackenzie 1993:247] ranks above cow or goat milk, the suid alveolar storage system renders milk unavailable for human use. Combined with lower heat tolerance, pigs are poorly suited for exploitation by humans relying on milk for subsistence.

The milk yield of all mammalian species undergoes seasonal variations, primarily a reduction in output in high humidity and temperatures above 27°C (Hafez 1968b:74). While Karimojong cattle in Uganda may still provide one-fifth to one liter of surplus milk during the dry season (Deshler 1965; Dyson-Hudson and Dyson-Hudson 1970), sheep and goat produce virtually no surplus milk (A. Smith 1980:469).

Perhaps more important for human consumption is the composition of milk under extremes of temperature. While the percentage of fats decreases between 21° to 27°C, and then begins to increase, non-fatty solids exhibit the reverse pattern (Hafez 1968b:76). Kamal et al. (1961) noted that high temperatures caused a decrease in potassium, citric acid and calcium, while sodium was unaffected. These temperature-related changes represent an important consideration during the dry season: although *overall* yield may be lower, *nutritional* yield may not be significantly lower, as fats, solids, and important nutrients become more concentrated.

Seasonality of breeding has important implications for milk storage and availability of alternative food sources. Survival on fresh cattle milk in areas of mono-seasonal

[4] Data for sheep and goat expressed in kilograms were converted to liters by dividing the specific gravity of milk for each species. Redding (1981:168) cites 1.0366 for sheep and 1.10316 for goat milk.

breeding would be virtually impossible, and milk storage and alternative foods are of major importance. In areas in which cattle breed year-round, the proportion of lactating cows remains constant, and the need to store milk for later consumption is considerably less. However, the combination of livestock species has implications for the seasonal composition of the human diet not yet discussed. The shorter gestation period of goats, for example, means that they give birth and begin to lactate during the dry season. That goats tend to give milk in seasons when bovine milk is scarce may mitigate the seasonality of milk availability.

- **Wool**

Little information was found regarding the impact of habitat on the amount of wool available from sheep or goats. Ghosh and Abichandani (1981:11) report that water restriction "had no effect on wool production and lambing performance." That goats appear to be much better adapted to arid environments suggests that periodic water restriction—unless very severe—would likewise have minimal impact on hair production or kidding. Data on relative amounts of wool or hair from sheep and goats was limited. Under extensive husbandry, Middle Eastern breeds of sheep yield an average of 1.75 kg of wool per year, while goat breeds under similar conditions yield only 0.5 kg of hair annually (Watson 1979:107). Clearly, herders would prefer sheep over goats if the goal is wool production.

## Natural Herd Growth Factors

The environment and its resources plainly affect the productivity of *individuals* of each species to the degree that species-level differences in suitability to particular habitats can be determined. The availability of resources also serves as a limit on the growth potential of the *herd* itself—lack of adequate water or food may stress the animals sufficiently to decrease successful reproduction, to increase the mortality rate, and thereby to put the whole herd at risk. Ideally, such information as the number of young, age at first pregnancy, total lifespan, etc., is based on the biological capacity of each species, but the scarcity of these data for unimproved breeds necessitates reliance on ethnographic data.

### *Comparative Reproduction*

Seasonal variations in forage quality and abundance affect more than the weight of an animal. While even modern stock retain the capacity to maintain a fœtus at the expense of their own body tissues, severe seasonal malnutrition may result in resorption or rejection of below-average birth weight individuals by their mothers (Noddle (1989). As has already been shown, milk yields vary seasonally with adequate food supplies, and thus seasonal food supplies encourage seasonal breeding. Areas with only one rainy season exhibit a tendency for cattle reproduction to be mono-seasonal. Where there are two rainy seasons, calf births are more evenly distributed throughout the year (Dahl and Hjort 1976:265).

The nine-month gestation period of bovines generally requires a spring œstrus, whereas sheep are autumn breeders (Noddle 1989). Cattle normally begin to breed as early as their second year, producing a single calf every two to three years (Russell 1988:Appendix A), although herders may delay this by several years under harsh conditions. In contrast, sheep and goats are typically allowed to bear offspring as soon as they are biologically able, beginning between one and two years of age, gestating for three to six months, and producing one—or occasionally two—young (Redding 1981:126). Areas of particularly good pasture enable successful breeding of sheep twice a year, up to three times every two years (Dahl and Hjort 1976:92).

While pigs may not necessarily compete with other domesticates or humans for resources, they *do* represent an alternative and could displace other taxa in an economy under certain conditions. Perhaps the pig's saving grace for human economic and subsistence issues is the ability of this species to increase in number and size rapidly. They reach sexual maturity at about eight months, have a short gestation period of about four months, and also have considerably more young than do domesticated ungulates; tropical pigs typically have been 4 and 12 young per litter (Devendra and Fuller 1979:46–47), for 8 years (Grigson 1982). Ppigs return into œstrus only a few days after weaning, and have been documented as non-seasonal breeders since Roman times (Forster and Hefner 1968). It is unknown at present if ancient Egyptian pigs were able or permitted to breed seasonally or not. The strong seasonality of natural resources suggests that foraging pigs would have been seasonal breeders, but fish- or bread-processing residues as pig food would certainly have permitted non-seasonal breeding. The average piglet weighs slightly less than 1.5 kilos at birth, doubles its weight during the first week, and reaches nearly 100 kilos within six months (van Loon 1978). Although these figures are based on ideal conditions, they do indicate the ability of the species to rebound more quickly from environmentally or human-induced losses than the other domestic species.

### *Comparative Mortality*

The death rate of a pastoral herd results from both natural mortality and human cropping strategies. In Dahl and Hjort's model of "normal" cattle herd growth (1976:45–48, 64–65), cattle have a maximum lifespan of 13 years, with 36% of all newly born calves dying before their fifth year, and the total adult population having a mortality rate of 5% a year. In Redding's models of sheep and goat herding strategies, both species have a maximum lifespan of nine years, with 32% of all lambs and 42% of all kids dying during their first year, and both adult ewes and does subject to a mortality rate of 18% per year (1981:80–136). He further postulated that a herder who lost most or all of his flock could achieve a subsistence level again more quickly by herding goats rather than sheep or cattle (1981:121–136). The theoretical minimum for a herd to double is 6.5 years for cattle and 3 for sheep or goats (Dahl and Hjort 1976). Clearly small stock offer a quicker recovery, and provide a sense of security.

Denvendra and Fuller report a 25% mortality rate prior to weaning (between six and eight weeks of age) as typical for pigs (1979:119), but the larger litter easily offsets this higher loss rate. Data were unavailable for adult natural mortality, and age at slaughter varies considerably as it is dependent upon the length of time needed to reach a desired weight.

Pigs have the greatest potential for herd growth or rebound after losses because of their early breeding age, short gestation period, large litter sizes, and the capacity for non-seasonal breeding. The tendency of goats to produce twins and the general tolerance of habitat conditions allows them to recover quickly as well. Sheep are slightly below goats in their ability to rebound. The higher mortality, slower maturation, and delay in first breeding of cattle renders these herds the slowest of the four species to recuperate.

## Summary of Comparative Attributes and Conclusions

Variations in the physiological tolerances may be characteristic of different populations of the same modern breed, but "even if the data were available, it is unlikely that meaningful values for Middle Eastern *breeds* of sheep and goats for the ability to withstand temperature- and water-related stress could be established" (Redding 1981:191, emphasis in original). However, it is clear that variations in evolved characteristics of cattle, sheep, goats, and pigs render each better adapted to specific ecological conditions, affecting their relative desirability as herd animals.

Goats generally have the greatest ability to withstand heat, water restriction, and low quality forage, and produce surpluses of milk for most of the year. Sheep are intermediate in their degree of tolerance, and cattle somewhat lower in their tolerance of adverse conditions and ability to convert forage into products. Further, as rainfall decreases, the ability of sheep and cattle to successfully forage declines, as the percentage of the year with good forage drops with dwindling rainfall. Such low rainfall areas, if they maintain some vegetation year-round, should support goats in some numbers. Thus, goats are perhaps best adapted to hot, arid environments such as the desert regions of Egypt, with sheep, cattle and pigs successful in hot environments when provided sufficient access to water. Sheep might be expected to outnumber cattle given the higher quality of milk produced by the former under similar conditions. Thus, if the herder's goal is a nutritional reliance on milk or milk products, sheep should be more abundant than cattle in either the Valley or Delta. However, if the goal is meat production or a mixed product strategy, cattle should predominate because of their absolute higher yields, and bearing in mind that cattle represent an extended investment. Pigs fall toward the bottom of such rankings: highly susceptible to heat stress—without daily access to moisture—yet quite tolerant of a variety of foods. These characteristics, combined with the probability that pigs may have been fed fish processing or bread-/beer-making residues, suggest that pigs would have been favored sources of meat and hides of the working classes in areas of the Valley or Delta near the Nile or its distributaries.

Clearly, an environment limits, but does not itself specify, the manner or intensity of its exploitation by plants or animals. Competition between and within species results in the survival (and reproductive success) of those that are biologically or physiologically best adapted to the habitat conditions. Unfortunately, the human ability to alter (rather than merely adapt to) their environment complicates understanding the impact of environment on humans. Ultimately, though, humans are still animals, and must operate within the bounds of nature. The question then becomes: How might the human-constructed environment differ from the natural one? That is, by what means did humans modify the natural adaptations of the four domesticated species to their own purposes? In the following chapter, human modifications of herd structures are presented, followed by generalized strategies compiled from ethnographic literature in regions similar to ancient Egypt's.

# 5. Contributions of Domesticated Animals to Economic and Social Production

## Introduction

The complexity of relationships between humans and land or animals underscores the importance of an ecological approach to studying prehistory. The physical environment is only one aspect of the entire model, and the efficiency of adaptation to specific habitats is dependent upon the costs incurred in maintaining the livelihood of the social group (Russell 1988). Different strategies are used to procure food, and in many cases seasonal variation in resource availability requires scheduling of activities, for harvesting an assortment of foods, and collecting other raw materials. Thus, a dynamic model of resource exploitation must encompass a yearly cycle within a framework of long-term fluctuations in rainfall or other environmental pressures affecting those resources (Smith 1992b:2; Larson et al. 1996:218). Ethnographic studies document the variety of responses to these fluctuations by detailed description of the relationships between humans, animals, land, and one another.

Before describing the diverse forms of these relationships, it is necessary to replace vague or misapplied concepts and terminology with more precise, theoretically rigorous ones. First, an important distinction often blurred or ignored in the literature is that between 'subsistence' and 'economy'. *Subsistence* is what people live on—the plants and/or animals in their diet. The *economy* of a population consists of the mechanisms for the management and mobilization of its resources (Barker and Gamble 1985). The use of the term 'subsistence economy,' therefore, is an attempt at precision, to distinguish food procurement and production from other aspects of the economy such as craft production, wage labor, etc. Second, *production* can be defined either ecologically or economically. Ecological production refers to the thermodynamic process whereby energy from the sun fuels the creation of organic matter *in* nature, whereas economic production refers to the expenditure of human (and I argue, animal) energy in order to procure resources *from* nature for consumption (after Ingold 198083, 219–221). These two types of production are distinct but complementary.

Values assigned to labor and its products must "be *socially* rather than *physically* defined..." (Ingold 1980:221, emphasis added). The natural increase of herds is a process of ecological production brought about through animals' labor (movement and grazing). The artificial increase through human labor) is not economically productive, however. Although herds are *socially* appropriated and reproduced as the property of particular social units, they remain *organically* as much a part of the natural environment as their wild counterparts (E. Marx 1964:89–90). The essence of economic production lies not in tendence but in slaughter, in husbandry rather than herding (Ingold 1980:222).

Earlier, I provided an introduction to the complex interactions between the natural environment (chapter 3) and the means by which animals survive in particular habitats (chapter 4), to give some measure of ancient Egypt's ecological productivity. The physiological adaptations of the four domesticated species clearly influence their relative fitness—and productivity—in a variety of habitats similar to those of ancient Egypt. These adaptations permit production, in the biological sense, of the extraction and consumption of energy (food) for maintenance of the individual animal. To some degree, these adaptations influence maintenance of the species; one component of the environment is an individual's conspecifics, affecting herd growth and reproduction. That certain species are relatively better adapted to this organic production in differing habitats than other species suggests that when human populations became dependent upon those taxa, different processes were necessary for production, in the social/economic sense, of human-derived measures of optimal herd size or productivity.

Inquiry into such processes need not be based on guesswork, because there are numerous studies of societies (relatively) unmodified through contact with Western societies. Ethno-graphic and -historic sources are particularly valuable because they offer dynamic and current information to help interpret the static remains preserved archaeologically. In the following sections, several models of subsistence and economic production are presented. While all share some components—domesticated animals and/or plants—they exhibit remarkable variety in the degree of control over those domesticates, and over land.

Referring to nomadism, Ingold (19880:123) stated that "[f]ew terms have been used less consistently...Strictly speaking, it refers to no particular system of productive relations, but to a pattern of movement." Such a narrowly defined meaning is of little use in the present investigation of social consequences of the interactions of several economic production systems. Some scholars have defined nomads as all those leading a mobile way of life, independent of the economic base (see Lee and DeVore 1968:11–12). Other scholars have described nomads as extensive herders and mobile groups who either have nothing to do with farming, or only limited involvement with it as a secondary or supplementary activity. Khazanov (1978, 1984) and Ingold (1980, 1988b) reject mobile hunter-gatherers as nomads because such groups have too little in common with other mobile economies (such as some forms of pastoralism). The bases of their economy—food extracting versus food-producing—are different in principle and thus "their reasons for being mobile are different and the character of the mobility is different" (Khazanov 1984:15). Further, Spooner maintains there is

> a tendency to treat nomadism as a type of culture or a category of society. This approach is misleading, since there are no features of culture or of social organization that are common to all nomads or even that are found exclusively among nomads (1973).

Therefore, I advocate (with Bennett 1984:290–291) that the term be avoided, or used only as a modifier (e.g., nomadic pastoralist). With this restriction of the application of the term in scientific literature, the movement of human populations is readily perceived as part of the subsistence strategy, without masking the significant distinctions between the economies of quite dissimilar mobile groups.

However, similar problems of definition and consistency have been found with other terms important to the present study. For example, even in a volume in which the editors "drew [to] the attention of the participants…the necessity of developing and elaborating a commonly accepted terminology just to be able to understand each other" (Bar-Yosef and Khazanov 1992:2), the terms 'nomadic pastoralist,' 'pastoral nomadist,' and 'developed pastoralist' were in one article equated and in another set in opposition. Likewise, Chang and Koster noted that even today 'pastoralism' "remains theoretically unsatisfying and amorphous…[resulting in] the unfortunate and intellectually sterile debates that normally ensue when academics are faced with the needs of 'splitting' or 'lumping' behavioral categories (1986:98–99). Their frustrations are understandable. It is impossible to develop and test a model if its components are not carefully operationalized. Thus, while my definitions may not be accepted by all, it is imperative that I explicitly state what I consider to be relevant characteristics of various economic systems to have any hope of investigating social change resulting from interactions between those systems. I hope that the suggested precision in defining the relevant processes under consideration might allow significant cross-cultural or -regional generalizations to be made regarding similarities or contrasts between specialized animal-based economies. Also, following Ingold, I wish to demonstrate

> the possibility of achieving a working synthesis between economic and ecological approaches in anthropology, which neither reduces the economy to economic relations of production nor, as in so much economic anthropology, ignores production altogether in favor of an exclusive focus on forms of exchange and distribution (Polanyi 1957, Vayda 1967, see Cook 1973). [Ingold 1980:10]

Clearly, a wider perspective is required to demonstrate the interrelationships of several variables in order to view an essentially static model of animal-based economies not only as a series of strategies along a continuum, but also as a dynamic system resulting from changes in the environment and/or the societies. The characteristics comprising each stage along the continuum must be presented before attempting to reconcile the modern examples with archaeologically testable measures.

## Pastoralism

As a means of subsistence, pastoralism is perhaps easier to define in a broad sense: human populations raising livestock. Pastoralism, too, has been subjected to intense debate in attempts to distinguish its forms, relying variously on geographic distribution, herd composition, distance, direction or periodization of migrations, degree of sedentism, relative reliance on domesticated plants, etc. (e.g., Bar-Yosef and Khazanov 1992; Barth 1962; Clutton-Brock 1989; Ingold 1980; Khazanov 1978, 1984; Smith 1992b; Uerpmann 1979). Similar to the distinctions made by Khazanov (1984:18–24), I attach greater importance to the ratio of animal versus crop production in an economic system than the degree or direction of mobility, although the degree of reliance on crops is generally inversely correlated with mobility.

While Khazanov (1984) and other anthropologists insist that pastoralism can only develop from a society that practices farming, many others argue that this may not apply in some areas of Africa, perhaps because of the variety and/or localized abundance of wild plant foods for both animals and people (Clutton-Brock 1989; Robertshaw 1989; Klein 1986; Russell 1988). Pastoral economies are adaptive responses to habitats frequently characterized by a marginal, non-contiguous, and/or unpredictable distribution of resources (Dyson-Hudson and Dyson-Hudson 1980; Spooner 1971). They can be subdivided into five major classes on the basis of ecological-economic criteria (e.g., herd species used, the nature of movements, and dietary factors [following Clutton-Brock 1989; Khazanov 1984; Ingold 1980]):

a. *Nomadic pastoralism* or *'pure' pastoralism.* Practiced by members of those groups which rely fully on animals and characterized by the absence of a regular reliance on plant crops (Khazanov 1984; McGreevy 1989).

b. *Semi-nomadic pastoralism.* The emphasis is on herds, and the periodic changing of pastures throughout the bulk of the year, but members also grow crops in a secondary and supplementary capacity. The degree of mobility of course varies considerably and is largely dependent upon ecological conditions.

c. *Semi-sedentary pastoralism, Transhumance*[1], or *'distant pastures husbandry'.* Also referred to as

[1] Khazanov argued the original Spanish term denotes *vertical* movement of herds to highland pastures by an agriculture-based lowland population, and should not describe other migrations (1984:22–24). However, it has been used for more than 50 years to describe transfer

'sedentary cultivators with auxiliary herding' (Forde 1963:404) and more commonly as 'mixed farming' (Barth 1976:75). These forms are extremely difficult to separate among published ethnographic accounts. The majority of the population is sedentary and occupied with agriculture, which varies from being an equal to slightly dominant component of subsistence. Herding plays a comparatively smaller role, and livestock are maintained all year on pastures located quite far from settlements. Generally, animals are kept in enclosures or pens, and require laying-in of fodder; economic competition may develop between land devoted to animal fodder and to crops for human consumption. The seasonal migrations may be of separate pastoral sub-groups or merely families within the society.

d. *Agro-pastoralism* or *Sedentary animal husbandry*. In this form, animals generally do not form the basis of an economy, but rather supplement an agriculturally oriented one. This type of pastoralism is characterized by the stockpiling of fodder for maintaining livestock confined in stables or enclosures within or adjacent to the settlement. Khazanov identifies this as "*household-stable animal husbandry*" (1984:24), and it has also been referred to as the 'penned farming' of animals. Again the provision of fodder is a potential problem, particularly when land is at a premium.

e. *Ranching*. This form was defined most succinctly by Ingold as "the *predatory* exploitation of animals which nevertheless constitute objects of property, for sale in a money market" (1980:4, emphasis added). This emphasizes a fundamental distinction from the above pastoral strategies, in which the relationship between humans and their herds is viewed as essentially symbiotic. An additional important criterion is the divided access to land, whereas in other forms of pastoralism land is typically held in common. For these reasons, ranching is sometimes separated from other forms of pastoralism. The degree of interaction between modern pastoral and agricultural groups indicates that nearly all participate in a market economy, if even on a very limited basis.

## *The Ethnographic Sample*

Studies examined were primarily restricted to the Nile Valley and other North or East African populations utilizing cattle, sheep, and goat to various degrees (see Figure 5.1). No detailed studies were found of populations in these regions that included pigs or ranching. Additional examples identified through the *Ethnographic Atlas* (Murdock 1967) and the Human Relations Area Files (HRAF) were also included from other regions which demonstrated significant parallels to (or divergences from) the near-tropical—yet often marginal—habitats which formed much of the ancient Egyptian landscape. Although each major group exhibits significant differences, it can be extremely difficult to differentiate between them archaeologically. The data to distinguish groups using archaeological remains may not yet be available in some instances—e.g., between small, semi-nomadic pastoral populations and the mobile segment of an otherwise sedentary society. Understanding this limitation in the present study is crucial for correctly interpreting ambiguous assemblages, and will be overcome most easily by other evidence, such as documents or artistic depictions.

The primary objective of the ethnographic examples is to explore the diversity of domesticated animal uses under a variety of deliberately limited environmental conditions in order to be consistent with archaeological data. In this way, the ethnographic cases are not used in a purely descriptive sense, but rather to determine the degree to which a common pattern is in evidence. As a result, the argument is essentially one of enumeration. Weaker than a true causal argument, the combined body of evidence nonetheless makes a strong case for the various contributions of domesticated animals and their importance to different economies. This type of argument has considerable explanatory power in its own right, and can also be used as a starting point to develop a causal argument with future research (Raish 1992:3).

## Nomadic Pastoralists

With the definition sufficiently restricted to avoid confusion, members of this category are almost exclusively found in grassland habitats, including steppe and tundra regions of the Far North (Ingold 1980; Khazanov 1984). Ethnographies of Ma'aza (Hobbs 1989; Murray 1935), Tuareg (Keenan 1977; Nicholaisen 1963) and Samburu (Spencer 1965, 1973; Pavitt 1991) provide much of the information needed to identify a "nomadic pastoralist" strategy.

The Ma'aza Bedouin occupy the northern half of Egypt's Eastern Desert (Figures 5.1 and 5.2), and provide the closest information concerning the ancient Egyptian economic and social patterns in this rocky, arid landscape. Although there is no unequivocal evidence why and when they came to Egypt from the Arabian peninsula, oral histories suggest that an extended period of migration began during the eighteenth century (Hobbs 1989:12–17). Because the Ma'aza came so recently from the region of probable origin of domesticated sheep and goat, it seems reasonable to postulate that the roles of animals in this society may most closely reflect those established or adopted when the ancient Egyptians incorporated these same species.

of herds between two areas of differing climate (Carrier 1932, cited in Ryder 1983:654). By this connotation, 'transhumance' is a viable option in Egypt—or other places—with significant habitats separated by latitude rather than altitude.

Figure 5.1. Map of Africa Showing Distributions of Selected Pastoral Populations.

The Tuareg are Berber-speakers who live throughout the central portions of the western Sahara and northern portions of western Sudan (Nicholaisen 1963; see Figure 5.3). They live in comparatively fertile savanna in the south to barren desert in the north; the plains between various mountain massifs allow some predictability of seasonal resources (1963:28). The main livestock are goats; sheep are bred only on a limited scale, and cattle can be raised only in the Sahel region. The Tuareg may allow insight into aspects of the lives of the ancient Egyptian desert-dwellers and their herds. The Samburu are Maa-speakers and live in northern Kenya south of Lake Turkana in an area of arid savanna grasslands and semi-deserts where climate precludes farming (see Figure

5.4). Instead, the Samburu manage large herds of cattle and smaller herds of sheep and goat.

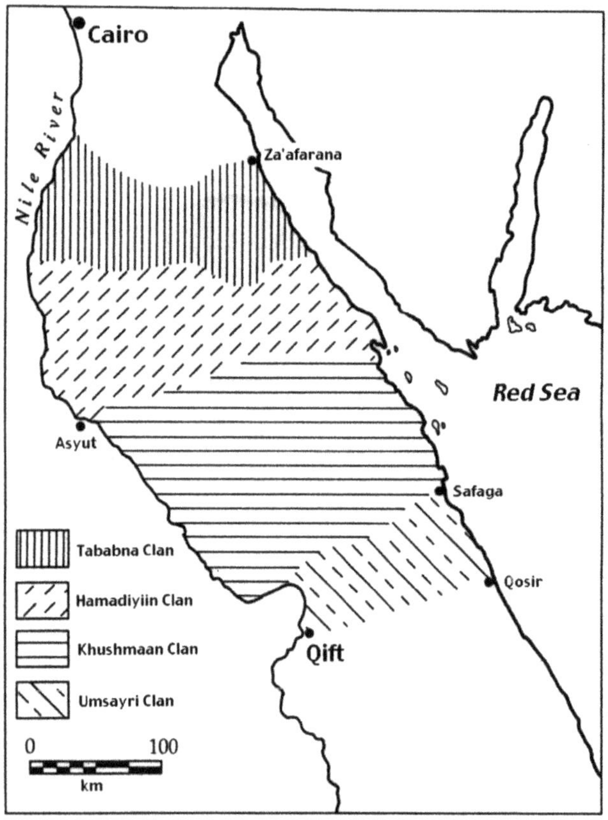


Figure 5.2. Ma'aza Geographic Distribution (after Hobbs 1989:map3).

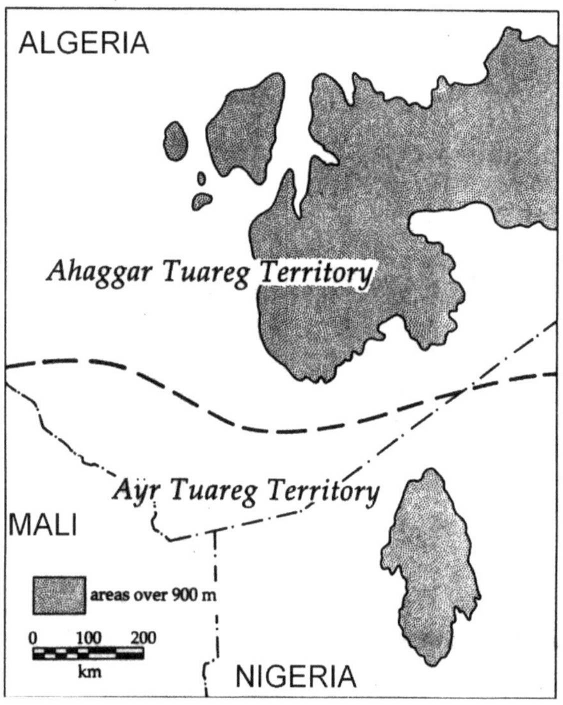


Figure 5.3. Geographic Distributions of the Northern and Southern Tuareg (from Nicholaisen 1963:figure 1).

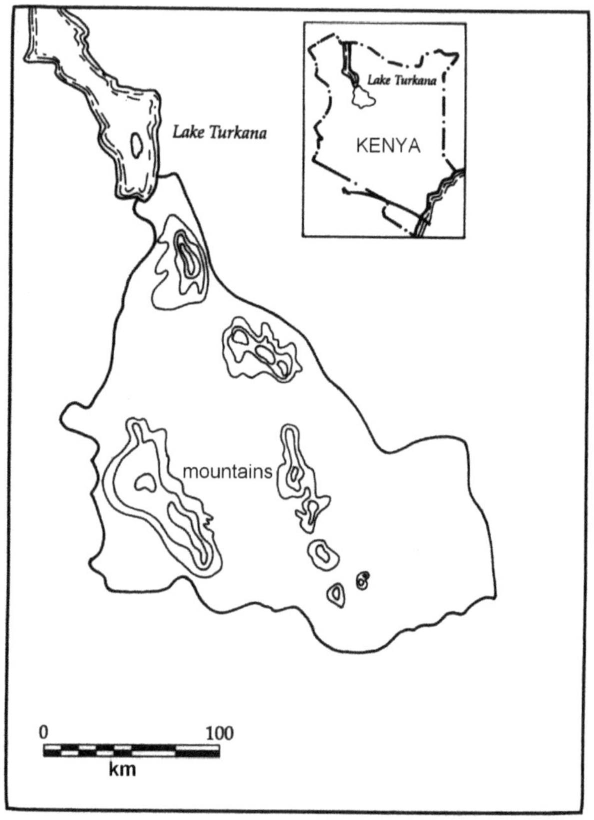


Figure 5.4. Geographic Distributions of the Samburu (after Pavitt 1991: frontispiece).

## Semi-nomadic Pastoralists

By definition, semi-nomadic pastoralists are more sedentary than groups in the previous category. This is due, at least in part, to the relatively better ecological conditions which permit higher quality or broader distributions of forage. Animals do not need to move as often; in some regions agriculture can be practiced on a small scale. Much of the information needed for identifying a 'semi-nomadic pastoral strategy' was gathered from ethnographies of the Jie (Gulliver 1955), Karimojong[2] (Gulliver and Gulliver 1953; Dyson-Hudson 1966; Dyson-Hudson and Dyson-Hudson 1969, 1970), Dodoth[3] (Deshler 1964, 1965), Turkana (Gulliver 1951, 1955; Smith 1992a, b), and Dasanetch (Carr 1977). Each group occupies a roughly similar habitat (or range of habitats), and the similarities between these groups are remarkable. Even limited involvement with agriculture exerts a considerable influence on many aspects of the lives of pastoralists: the species composition of herds, the routes and seasonal prevalence of migrations, division of labor, etc. (see Khazanov 1984:19–20, and references cited there).

[2] Variously spelled Karamojong or Karimajong.
[3] Also spelled Dodos, although this is a more antiquated spelling.

The Karimojong are a group of some 60,000 people occupying a plateau in northeast Uganda (see Figures 5.5 and 5.6). The habitat is savanna grassland, and while the rainfall is adequate for agriculture, it is too unpredictable for the Karimojong to depend upon it as a sole means of subsistence (Dyson-Hudson and Dyson-Hudson 1970:96). This is consistent with reconstructed habitats of the Nile Valley margins. Three ecological regions inhabited by the Karimojong and Jie are exploited in different ways (the fourth region is mountain forest and is not discussed here). The Dodoth are considered a northern Karimojong tribe, and provide additional details. The Jie inhabit a semi-arid plain in northern Uganda (see Figure 5.5) with an annual rainfall of approximately 635 mm, adequate for agriculture. During the dry season, the Jie concentrate around a series of wells in the western territory (Gulliver 1955) in much the same way that ancient Egyptians may have clustered around oases or ponds established by large wadis during the flood season.

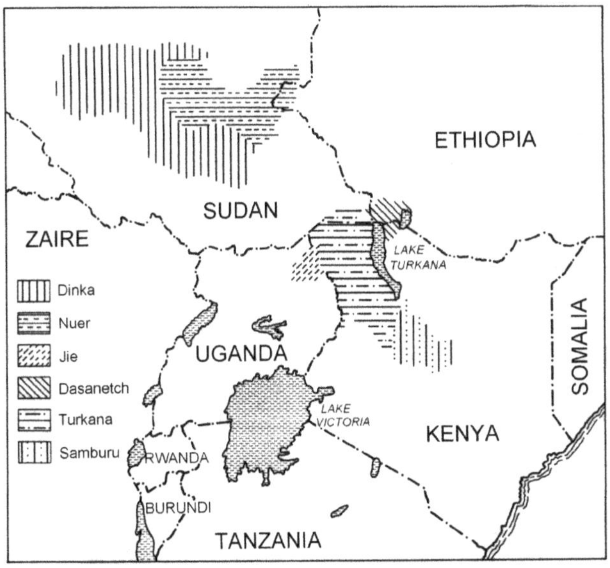


Figure 5.5. East African Regional Map Indicating Several Modern Pastoral Populations.

The Turkana are a Nilotic pastoral people with camels, cattle, and small stock living on a hot and semi-arid plain primarily to the west of Lake Turkana (see Figure 5.5), and claim a common origin with the Jie (Gulliver 1955). The average rainfall is considerably less than the areas occupied by the Jie, typically between 300 and 400 mm fall on the plains and less than half that in the more arid regions. Because the environment is more arid and resources are more sparsely distributed, the Turkana exploit a larger territory than the Jie, are more mobile, maintain more small stock, and with the addition of camels, rely on a greater variety of livestock (Barfield 1993:33). The habitat corresponds to the reconstructions of marginal regions of the ancient Egyptian Nile Valley margins and the deserts.

The Dasanetch live along the Omo River in southwestern Ethiopia in an area of divergent grazing potential ranging from bare to minimal shrub steppe vegetation through tree/grassland areas into uninhabitable tsetse-infested areas (see Figures 5.5 and 5.7; Carr 1977:Figure 2.20). They were originally a fully pastoral society, but continued loss of territory to other governments since the 1800s has necessitated that nearly all members practice some agriculture; the increasing reliance on crops corresponds to a more sedentary lifestyle and a corresponding decrease in social status (Carr 1977:187). This group is included here to illuminate some of the pressures and possible effects encountered by prehistoric Egyptians practicing similar strategies during and following the political unification.

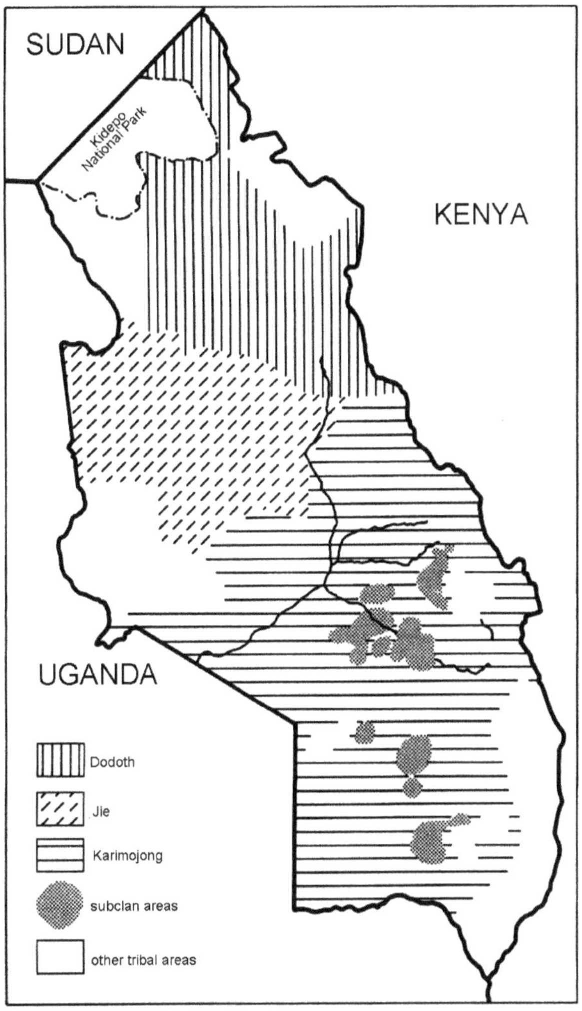


Figure 5.6. Distributions of the Karimojong, Jie and Dodoth.

## Sedentary or Transhumant Pastoralists

Territories utilized by human populations practicing a combination of transhumance and cultivation often overlap with those of semi-nomadic pastoralists (at one extreme), andagro-pastoral groups (at the other).

Similarities in their seasonal diets and their economies render them difficult to distinguish. The majority of semi-sedentary pastoralists occupy habitats of even greater resource abundance and predictability than their more mobile counterparts and live at least part of the year in areas which consistently support agriculture in sufficient quantity that herding becomes secondary to plant crops in subsistence and the economy. Here, groups such as the Nuer (Evans-Pritchard 1940) and the Dinka (Bontkes 1991; Deng 1972; Schwabe 1978) will be examined.

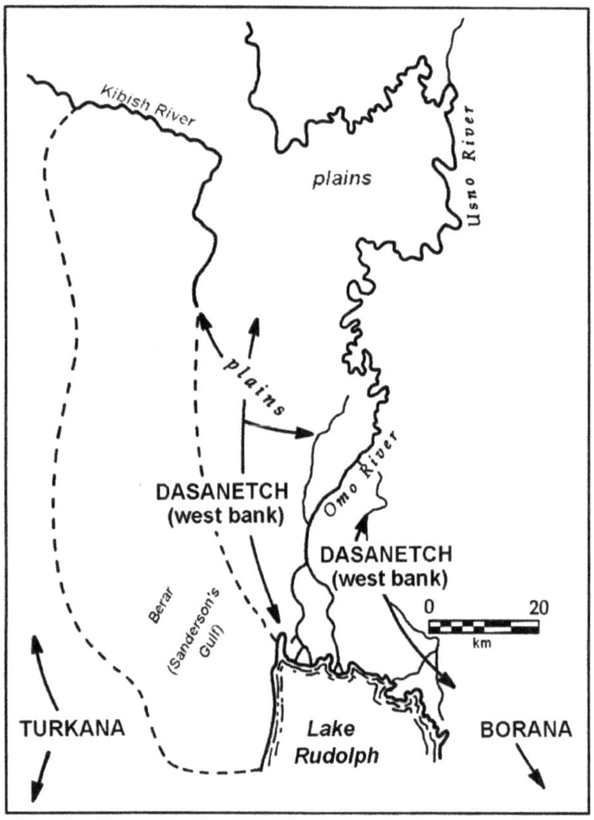


Figure 5.7. Geographic Distribution of the Dasanetch (after Carr 1977:Figure 2.20).

The Nuer live in the Upper Nile province and between the Sobat and While Nile Rivers, occupying an area of extensive grasslands (see Figure 5.5). The seasonal inundation of the low-lying floodplains causes the Nuer to retreat to higher elevations, where they have established communities. The Dinka live on the eastern bank of the White Nile in southern Sudan, in an area with a single rainy season and considerable grassland, portions of which flood seasonally (see Figure 5.5; Bontkes 1991:13–15). The rivers allow these Nilotic pastoral peoples to fish following the rainy season, as faunal analyses and tomb decorations document that the ancient Egyptians did (e.g., Brewer and Friedman 1989). The more stable and predictable habitats of the Nuer and Dinka allow permanent settlements near rivers or permanent sources of clean water, such as would have been prevalent along the length of the Nile Valley, perhaps in the Fayum, and in the Delta.

## Agro-Pastoralists

In many of the above categories, agriculture was undependable or not possible as a primary resource due to poor soil conditions, insufficient or extremely unpredictable rainfall. The increased reliance on crops and the ability to keep sedentary herds indicate better habitat conditions among the semi-sedentary pastoralists. Agriculture has long been viewed as requiring more intensive—but seasonal—labor than herding pursuits, and the devotion of one-half or more of the production to plant resources resulted in many changes over more mobile strategies.

Considerably fewer quality ethnographies of agro-pastoralists were located, and the Tswana are the only modern group presented here. Linguistically and culturally a part of the southern Sotho people, the Tswana live in areas of the Northern Cape and eastern Botswana with good rains and fertile soils (see Figure 5.1; Breutz 1991). They practice mixed agricultural and traditionally have large herds of cattle. They are gradually overtaking lands of the hunting-gathering Basarwa; the Tswana believe that setting up stock posts around new waterholes provides rights of usufruct over surrounding grazing lands (see Hitchcock 1978:176). The comparatively rich Tswana owners even hire Basarwa to manage their herds at stock posts. This is essentially a form of indentured labor and costs the herd-owner virtually nothing (Smith 1991b:185, 248–250). It is expected that the Tswana and their interactions with the Basarwa may clarify interactions between some Valley or Delta populations with the desert dwellers who moved to more fertile regions during times of climatic deterioration or environmental crisis.

### *Uses of Domesticated Animals*

The major uses of domesticated animals from the ethnographic sources are: *(a)* dietary importance of meat and animal by-products, *(b)* use of dung as a fertilizer, *(c)* reliance on animals as a means of amassing wealth and as a form of live storage, *(d)* use of animal traction for transport and plowing (Raish 1992:45). Animals as 'live storage' is practiced variously as a fundamental basis for survival or as protection again lean periods. Additionally, *(e)* the use of dung as fuel, *(f)* religious or other non-economic significance attached to animals, *(g)* population movements motivated by animals' needs, and *(h)* settlement organization, were identified during this research. In general, the ethnographic sources demonstrate that domesticated animals are used both as a primary food resource in the more mobile populations and as a supplemental resource among sedentary groups. In both gross categories, animals serve as a means to diversify the subsistence base. In addition, they renew the fertility of certain types of agricultural fields and lead to further intensification with use of the plow or in threshing.

## Components of the Diet

### *Plant Resources*

The categorization of nomadic pastoral societies as dependent solely upon animals is somewhat misleading, in that all include fruits, grains, and vegetables in their diet. The distinction made here is the means by which those foods are obtained: nomadic pastoralists harvest wild plants or trade with other groups, while all other forms grow plants themselves, albeit to differing degrees. Vegetable consumption among all pastoralists has also been correlated with sex: women consume more vegetable foods than do men (Dyson-Hudson and Dyson-Hudson 1970:100). In general, North and East African pastoralists apparently consume fewer vegetables than similar pastoralists in the Near and Middle East (Khazanov 1984). The reason for the lower plant consumption among African populations is unclear, but may reflect a significant—if unquantified—difference in available resources between the two regions.

Despite a heavy reliance on animals and plant products, the Ma'aza "do not despise agriculture, only agriculturalists," and grow a variety of crops on small plots (Hobbs 1989:45). The topography and unpredictability of rainfall prevent agriculture from having a strong, consistent place in the economy. Similar, the Tuareg have been slowly migrating toward better grazing conditions in the southern reaches of their territory for centuries, and today there "are no Tuareg who subsist without agricultural products: obtained largely through trade (Nicholaisen 1963:216–217). Grains and dates are utilized principally during the dry season. The Samburu do not even maintain household garden plots, instead obtaining needed vegetables and fruits exclusively through the gathering of wild plants (Spencer 1965).

The better soil and water access among semi-nomadic pastoralists allow crops to be cultivated in fields adjacent to settlements and stored in granaries within stockaded homesteads. Karimojong have a strong sexual division of labor, and crops are primarily the work of women. They grow numerous varieties of tall sorghum for use in porridge, beer or storage, and the cucurbits (melons, etc.)—a distant second but still important food crop—are planted between the rows of sorghum (Dyson-Hudson and Dyson-Hudson 1970:114). Finger millet is planted in swamps as a specialty crop, but it needs so much water that it is never a significant contribution to the diet. The Karimojong claim they cannot subsist by agriculture alone and believe cattle to be more reliable than agriculture (Deshler 1965, 1965; Gulliver and Gulliver 1953). Karimojong women subsist mainly on these grain foods, with milk from goats and a few cows to supplement their diet after feeding their children.

Similarly for the Dodoth, grains such as sorghum, small millets, and corn provide the major portion of the diet, with total yields adequate to meet household needs for 4–7 months a year (Deshler 1965:166). The main sources of food provide only about 25% of the total diet in terms of calories; the remainder is obtained from gathered foods such as termites, wild onions, spinach, fruits, or grasses (Deshler 1965:167). When crop yields are inadequate, additional grain is redistributed through ceremonies, trading and begging from relatives living in areas with surpluses. This is an effective means of establishing reciprocal ties of obligation by using resources which would otherwise go to waste (sorghum, for example, cannot be kept more than one year). When these supplies fail, the Dodoth will grudgingly trade cattle to other tribes for grain. Although the Dodoth exhibit a much stronger reliance on plant crops than their Karimojong neighbors, Dodoth social activities are more clearly marked by exchange or sacrifice of animals.

Among the Dasanetch, horticulture has traditionally been a seasonal supplement to the products of animal-based subsistence. Because yields vary considerably from year to year, horticulture is not considered a stable alternative to herding, and carries a stigma of poverty for those who rely upon it as their primary means of survival. Nonetheless, members of all but the wealthiest tribal segments practice horticulture to some degree. Millet and maize are the dominant crops, although tobacco, two types of beans and several gourd varieties are also grown (Carr 1977:190). Within the past two decades, the number of Dasanetch who rely heavily on crop plants has increased dramatically and horticulture no longer plays the supplemental or stop-gap function that it once did. Instead, it has become the basic means of subsistence for the majority of the population. For those who can afford to do so, grain surpluses are used for consumption at ceremonies or, more commonly, for barter to obtain other products or to increase small stock herds.

Both the Nuer and Dinka rely heavily on plant crops, but also raise cattle, sheep and goat (in decreasing order of importance). Despite the regular reliance on agricultural staples of sorghum and maize, Evans-Pritchard noted that the structure of the Nuer production cycle clearly gave precedence to pastoralism (1940:81; see also Barfield 1993:28). Evans-Pritchard postulated that even if it were possible for the Nuer to be fully reliant on agriculture, their pastoral belief systems would first have to change (1940).

Little information was available on African agro-pastoralists, and unfortunately, the few studies available for Middle Eastern agriculturalists who maintain a few head of livestock are quite old, and focus on groups heavily involved in market subsistence (Demarchi et al.

1962; Kligler et al. 1931). However, these studies do provide a baseline for examining potential deficiencies in an agriculturalist's diet. As in the various nomadic pastoralists' diets, the agriculturalist relies heavily on grain and grain products for the majority of the calories ingested, up to 65% to 70% (Redding 1981:229). Among the Tswana, for example, the chief crops grown are maize and several varieties of sorghum, but in areas with particularly good rainfall, beans, groundnuts, melons, may be grown. Before governmental provision in the late 1950s of European vegetables for cropping, wild vegetables were also collected (Breutz 1991:20). Together, these products yield more calcium and iron per portion than meat, and more iron than milk (Pellett and Shadarevian 1970, cited in Redding 1981). Thus, although agro-pastoral groups have a more diversified food production strategy than mobile pastoralists in terms of the variety of products consumed, the bulk of the diet in *all* pastoral groups is high in plant foods.

## *Animal-Derived Resources*

The seasonality of breeding, overall reproductive and mortality rates are important natural factors in the structure and size of any herd, but equally important for the continued existence of a *domesticated* herd are the management and productive strategies practiced by the humans controlling these animals. Cultural factors such as belief systems and the practical ability to maintain a healthy herd become particularly important in this regard. All herders studied routinely interfere with the natural reproduction and survival of their animals to suit their own purposes, for example, choosing to delay the age of first breeding under less than ideal pasture conditions, maintaining an artificially greater number of females, castrating certain males, etc. (e.g., Devendra and Fuller 1979; Ingold 1980; Khazanov 1984; Mackenzie 1993; Noddle 1989; Redding 1981; Russell 1988). Unfortunately, not all of these factors leave recognizable or measurable evidence archaeologically.
Among the nomadic and semi-nomadic pastoral populations in Africa, "the conversion rate between plants and humans can be as low as 1:5000" calories (Ryder 1983:650). This loss is mitigated by customs of ingesting milk and blood, as well as meat, of their animals. Because of variation in productivity by sex, age, and season between the four species presented in the previous chapter, the subsistence uses of these animals will be discussed separately below. Dahl and Hjort (1976:23) list the basic animal products of pastoral subsistence in order of decreasing importance: milk and milk products, meat, and then blood. However, this belies the highly seasonal nature of the diet, particularly among nomadic/semi-nomadic populations. In general, proportions of milk and blood decrease as pasture diminishes and more grains are harvested (see Figures 5.8 and 5.9; S. Smith 1980:471). The simple ranking of resources by Dahl and Hjort also blurs the relative contributions of different species to human subsistence, which dramatically alters the structure of herds, the degree of human mobility, and other factors discussed below.

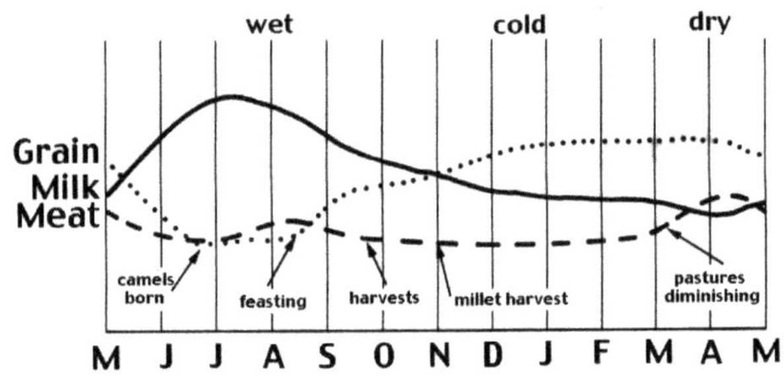


Figure 5.8. Generalized Sahelian Nomadic Pastoralist Seasonal Diet (modified from A. Smith 1992:figure 1.4).

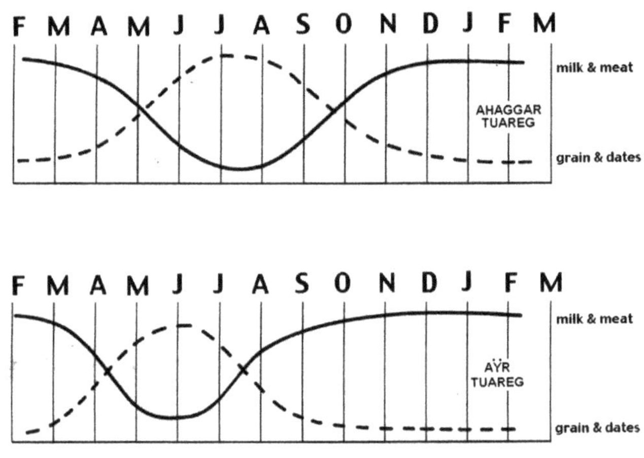


Figure 5.9. Detailed Tuareg Seasonal Diet (after Nicholaisen 1963:figures 3.1, 3.2).

- Milk

Whereas meat represents about $^{1}/_{10}$ the protein eaten by animals and because only about 40% of a carcass is eaten by humans, milk protein is equivalent to about ¼ the protein consumed in producing it (Ryder 1983:650). A blood and milk diet is not only an effective herd management technique—animals need not be killed for their products—but because the water content of the animal itself reduces human water requirements. This also indirectly increases the sources of available water since animals are able to drink more saline water than humans. While Brewer et al. (1994) are correct in noting that only a small percentage of cows may be lactating at any given time, this number can be regulated according to the demands of the human population for the different kinds of animal products, activities (e.g., transport), and various other cultural reasons (see Spooner 1973:12; Dahl and Hjort 1976:28, fn 32; Khazanov 1984:28).

For the Samburu, milk from cattle and goats is the primary component of the rainy season diet, and milking is considered the task of females. In the low country and during the dry season, the small stock thrive and a heavier reliance on their milk is suggested—although not explicitly stated— by Spencer (1965). The habitat of the Tuareg is not conducive to cattle survival, and goats play a much stronger role in meeting basic human subsistence needs. Milk and meat consumption are highly seasonal (see Figure 5.9), and the Tuareg sometimes complain of fatigue and stomach pain when they are forced to eat nothing but milk (or milk products) for weeks or even months at a time (Nicholaisen 1963:209; Monod 1975:102). Nicholaisen (1963:221) noted that the method of milk preparation varies by region: in the north it is generally consumed fresh, while in more southern populations it is regularly soured and conserved in skin bags. In both areas, butter and cheese are consumed daily. No specific data were available for the amount of milk produced or consumed by Ma'aza Bedouin, although Hobbs reported that it was an important component of the diet (1989:45).

Data for milk production and consumption among the Karimojong, unfortunately, were reported only for cattle despite statements that goats are kept near the permanent settlements to supply milk to women and children. Less than half the total number in a given herd are potentially milk cows, and with a lactation of generally less than eight months, only about 25% of total cattle holdings actually give milk at any one time. However, these cows produce an average of five pints per day at the end of the rainy season, and slightly more than two pints daily even at the end of the dry season (Dyson-Hudson and Dyson-Hudson 1970:13). Some *ghee* (boiled butter) is stored, but by the end of the rainy season, only a few quarts remain.

Among Dinka herds, total milk production per lactation is 750 kg, and an average of 525 kg is allotted to a (female) calf. This is an effective way of maintaining a herd structure dominated by females, whose productivity is responsible not only for herd survival and growth, but also that of the human population as well. Other important food sources are meat, other cultivated plants, fish, bush meat, and wild fruits and vegetables (Figure 5.10), all of which are obtained and consumed by the local populations as there is little trade.

Among the Tswana, a strong sexual division of labor is evident, and this division is carried over into their diets. Herders live adjacent to the grazing grounds and subsist primarily on soured milk, in contrast to the farmers' diet of a maize-porridge. Milking, then, is a male task. In contrast, women are so intimately associated with agricultural pursuits that the threshing floor is reserved as their traditional burial site (Breutz 1991:22).

- Blood

Although the caloric content of blood is considerably less than that of milk, it becomes an important source of nutrients—particularly iron—in the dry season when supplies of milk are insufficient (Deshler 1965; Dahl and Hjort 1976; Spencer 1965). Nicholaisen mentioned that the Tuareg will only bleed camels, and apparently not other species, when they lack water during desert journeys and the blood "never constitutes a proper dish" (1963:235). Its near absence is unexpected because all other mobile pastoralists practice blood-letting regularly. This may be due to the Tuareg's adoption of Islamic law, which prohibits the consumption of animals or products under certain conditions.

Every evening, Karimojong boys living in temporary herding camps collect approximately one to two pints of blood from the jugular vein of an adult bovid, or one-half pint from a cut above the eye of sheep and goats, sharing it between the herdsmen (Deshler 1965:162; Dyson-Hudson and Dyson-Hudson 1970:100).

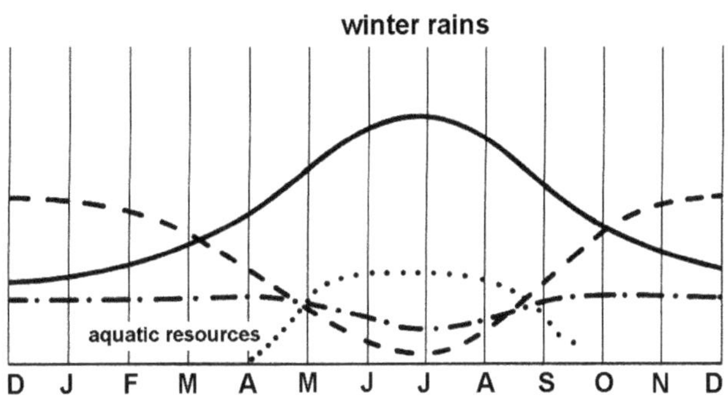


Figure 5.10. Seasonal Diet Among the Nuer and Dink (after A. Smith 1992:figure 1.4).

However, an individual animal is bled only about once a month during the wet season and less often during the dry season. Young men who work with the herds consume the majority of this important nutrient source. While staying at the stock camps, the diet is almost exclusively blood and milk, supplemented by grain foods—usually in the form of beer—which the women may bring with them on their occasional visits from the permanent settlements. A large number of wild plants and fruits are eaten, especially during the dry season, and although the men will not go out of their way to hunt, they will kill game if it is easy to get (Dyson-Hudson and Dyson-Hudson 1970:100).

- Meat

Ingold noted that "men avoid having to convert their domestic animals to food for the mundane, pragmatic reason that these animals fulfill the purposes assigned to them only whilst they are alive" (1980:100). Killing them contradicts the very purpose of their domestication.

The meat component of the nomadic pastoralist's diet is primarily obtained from small stock, although some nomadic pastoralists depend on hunting for the majority of the meat they consume. Cattle (and other large stock, when kept) are generally much more highly valued than small stock, and are usually eaten following the animal's natural death, slaughtered or sold under extreme conditions, and used as a cash crop to pay taxes, purchase grain or other supplies. The mixing of species within herds maximizes resource utilization because of the different grazing and browsing patterns (see chapter four), but also helps the herdsmen to survive epizootic infestations, and to more quickly recuperate from catastrophic losses in one species.

Meat is not a regular component of the Tuareg diet, but is consumed more often among the southern populations. The majority of meat comes from sheep, with only a lesser proportion from goats (A. Smith 1992:125), although goats outnumber sheep nearly 10:1 (Cranstone 1969:250). The preference of sheep for sacrifice and/or consumption, and of goats for milk, certainly affects herd size and structure of the two species. Among both Samburu and Tuareg populations, cattle are consumed only when they die of natural causes or at ceremonies. The value placed on large stock as foci of social relationships "altogether underrates the economic importance of sheep and goats [which among the Samburu]...are an important source of food in the dry season" (Ingold 1973:79–80; see also Spencer 1965:2–6). Among the Dodoth semi-nomadic pastoralists, cattle meat is generally limited to about 30–40 pounds per year per individual (Deshler 1965:165). Sheep and goats no doubt contribute to the diet, but "no quantitative information existed...at the time of field study" (Deshler 1964:166). The traditional centrality of cattle among the Dasanetch is clearly evidenced by their complex terminology for the species, the adoption of herding terms to denote human relationships, and their common use as themes in songs, dances, and rituals (Carr 1977:99–100). A stock owner who can successfully subsist with only sporadic horticulture commonly has 40 to 50 cattle, but the economic role of sheep and goats is "highly significant" and will have fewer cattle than either sheep or goats (Carr 1977:177).

The Dinka seem to rely slightly more on plant crops than the Nuer, but also attach considerable cultural significance to herding. The Dinka concentrate on cattle herding, although they also raise small numbers of goats, sheep and poultry. Bontkes (1991) calculated that small ruminant herds account for only 3.4% of domestic stock, when expressed in 'animal units'[4]. Normally cattle are not killed for consumption, but almost every animal that dies is consumed. Cattle may also be killed for ceremonial purposes and, reluctantly, in times of famine. The Dinka are disinclined to sell cattle and will do so only when they require money to pay for necessities and when sorghum is insufficient (Bontkes 1991). They sell males first, then dry cows, and finally calves and heifers. Cattle are instrumental in maintaining their system of reciprocal obligations.

[4] The number of smaller animals needed to equal the slaughter yield from a hypothetical animal of standard size and weight, in this instance, cattle.

The Tswana raise goats primarily for meat, and to a lesser degree, for milk. However, goat meat is not obtained through slaughter but rather from animals which die of natural causes (Breutz 1991:15–20. Assuming a minimum of ritually slaughtered animals, the distributions of age classes in an archaeological sample should approximate a natural curve. The Tswana also breed long-horn cattle and use them as sacrificial animals as well as the larger portion of bride-wealth. Their meat is reportedly never consumed as a meal, and only on festive occasions following a ritual sacrifice (Breutz 1991:15). Clearly, as in previous categories, cattle and goat age distributions would be markedly different archaeologically.

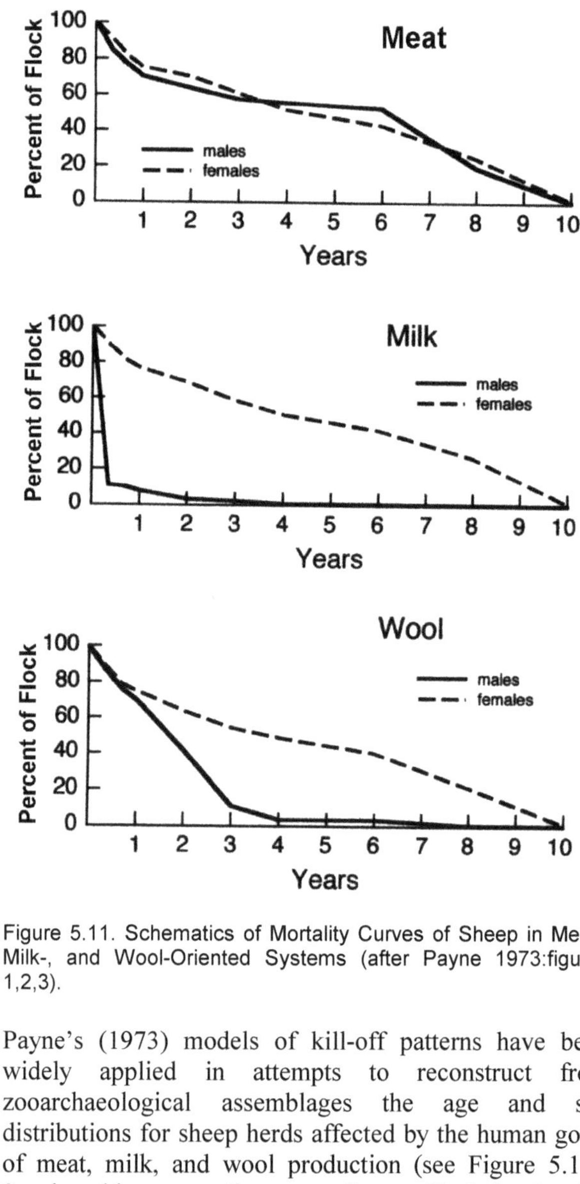


Figure 5.11. Schematics of Mortality Curves of Sheep in Meat-, Milk-, and Wool-Oriented Systems (after Payne 1973:figures 1,2,3).

Payne's (1973) models of kill-off patterns have been widely applied in attempts to reconstruct from zooarchaeological assemblages the age and sex distributions for sheep herds affected by the human goals of meat, milk, and wool production (see Figure 5.11). Survivorship curves (i.e., mortality profiles) for females are identical in meat-, milk-, and wool-oriented systems: few are killed off until well into maturity when production declines. Milk kill-off patterns should be characterized by a high percentage of males less than six months of age, and in the 'meat model', male mortality peaks at around three years of age. High numbers of males in addition to the brood flock are retained to maximize wool production, exhibiting essentially the opposite pattern of a milk herd.

These models can be adapted for other taxa as well by adjusting the Payne's original scale to reflect relative growth, maturation rates and ages of productivity for the other species (given in chapter four). The overall patterns are the same (see Figure 5.12). However, since pigs do not provide renewable resources such as milk or wool, the relevant data can only be applied to the meat-based strategy.

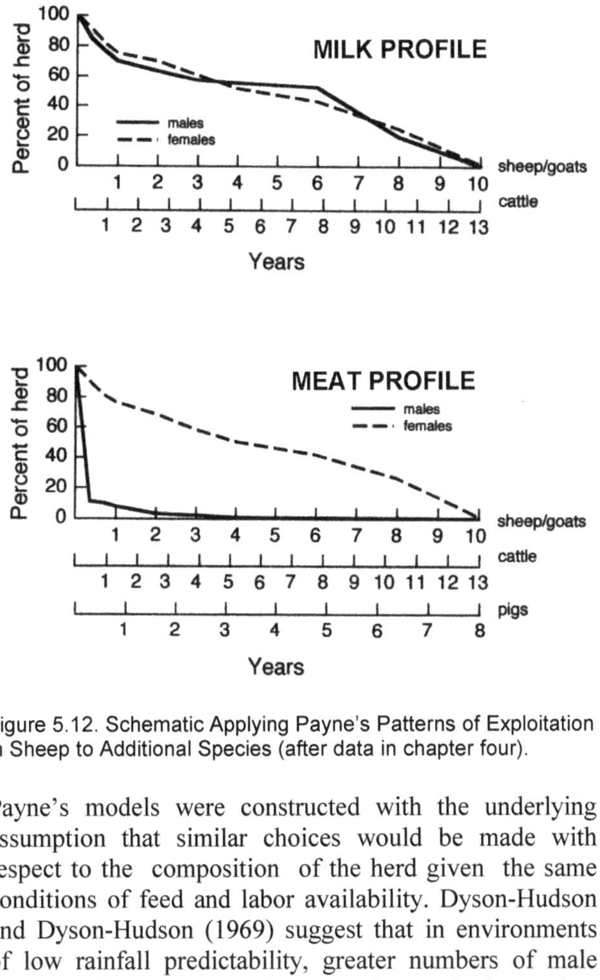


Figure 5.12. Schematic Applying Payne's Patterns of Exploitation in Sheep to Additional Species (after data in chapter four).

Payne's models were constructed with the underlying assumption that similar choices would be made with respect to the composition of the herd given the same conditions of feed and labor availability. Dyson-Hudson and Dyson-Hudson (1969) suggest that in environments of low rainfall predictability, greater numbers of male stock are likely to be kept into maturity as a hedge against adversity. Thus, throughout the desert regions and the marginal areas of the Valley in Egypt, archaeological remains should be indicative of the models developed by Dyson-Hudson and Dyson-Hudson, including a higher proportion of males than predicted by Payne's models. Clearly, in those regions it would be difficult to distinguish the wool-producing herds from a milk-based strategy in which greater than predicted males were kept as 'insurance'.

# Economic Production

## *Herd Structure*

The unpredictability of resource abundance, quality, and location have led some scholars to conclude that long-term increases in production (i.e., increased herd size) are incompatible with nomadic pastoralism (see for example, Dahl and Hjort 1976:271; Khazanov 1984:76–78). To the contrary, other scholars believe that all pastoralists attempt to maximize herd size in good years in order to offset the low rate at which the animals reproduce and to counterbalance the loss of herds during bad years (e.g., Spooner 1973; Deshler 1965; Spencer 1965, 1973). Still others argue that social factors and values must be considered, such as the desire to prolong the lactation period through an increase in the number of young animals (Stenning 1965). Perhaps the most influential factor affecting the slow increase in herd size is the dramatic increase in meat consumption through animal sacrifice during periods of drought (Schneider 1957:278–300). Khazanov argues that "the sacrifice of livestock...is linked to institutions of reciprocation necessary to the society"(1984:77).

While most nomadic pastoralists of North and East Africa consider themselves cattle pastoralists, in reality this species rarely monopolizes the herds. As indication of the (mundane) importance of a species can be gained from the number of specialized terms relating to it. The Tuareg, for example, have twelve terms to indicate the age and sex of goats, and seventeen for the color, but fewer than ten for cattle (Cranstone 1969:251). They explain this by the fact that cattle were unimportant to their subsistence in the past (Nicholaisen 1963:53). In contrast, the Nuer have six main terms for cattle horn shapes, ten for colors, twelve more for shades or combinations of white and gray, and still others denoting age and sex (none were reported for other taxa, but this almost certainly an oversight by Evans-Pritchard).

There is a consistency among groups for the ratio of large to small stock which is apparently related to the reliance (or lack thereof) on agricultural produce (Smith 1992b). For example, Tuareg, who do not grow plant foods, have a 3–4:1 ratio of small to large stock, while the Jie and Karimojong, who do have gardens, have a ratio as low as 1:1 (Gulliver 1955:38; Dyson-Hudson and Dyson-Hudson 1970:107). The Ma'aza herd sheep and goat, and maintain a few camels as beasts of burden. Camels are not well adapted to the steep inclines and loose rocks of the stony Eastern Desert, and must be left below when the Ma'aza travel into the mountains (Hobbs 1989:37).

Due to the low quality forage in Dodoth territories, depressed growth rate, and high mortality among cattle, nearly 25% of the herd is under one year of age, and there are extremely few mature animals (Deshler 1965:161). This rather unusual age distribution might be misinterpreted in an archaeological sample as a deliberate alteration of the herd structure, when in fact it is related to environmental factors.

## *Herd Size*

Herding success depends on the number of pastoralists (usually male) available to herd and water the animals, although herd size can be manipulated in order to maximize effective care with only a minimum of human involvement. Dahl and Hjort noted that cattle are usually pastured separately from small stock, while sheep and goats are often pastured together (1976:250). This is not unexpected given differences in feeding ecology (chapter 4). However, the adaptive capacities of these species are not necessarily related to economic effectiveness or appropriateness of herding them together. For example, in the southern Aÿr region, the Tuareg herd more sheep than goats, and do so because sheep wool is of higher quality. Goats are included in the herds primarily to act as flock leaders. Because goats feed faster, they lead sheep to new pastures more quickly than they would have progressed on their own. In the northern Tassili region where wool is of less importance, the physiological adaptiveness—rather than economic benefits—of the species is the deciding factor in herd composition; here, goats predominate among small stock (Nicholaisen 1963:45–46).

What was sometimes overlooked in several ethnographies, however, is that a number of families closely connected (whether by reciprocal relations, kinship, etc.) herd their animals together (Ingold 1980; Nicholaisen 1963; Gulliver 1955:156). In his study of the Dodoth, for example, Deshler stated that men can only be independent by having large herds and many sons, and a man with many cattle but few sons must herd his animals together with a man with many sons but few cattle (1965). Combining herds reduces the number of herdsmen to watch over them, reinforces the idea of communal access to land and resources, and also fosters shared obligations between families (ostensibly so debts can be repaid in the future). The significance of different levels of decision-making is addressed further under the heading "*Social Organization: Authority and Decision-making*".

The size of the female herd must allow sufficient milk for calves *and* the pastoralists, and also include enough pregnant or immature animals to be productive by the time the other cows run dry. The Tuareg deliberately stagger the pregnancies of goats across the available breeding season to increase the number of lactating individuals (Nicholaisen 1963). Breeding is sometimes delayed or staggered throughout the herd to ensure that the majority of females will give birth during the wet season, when there is sufficient high-quality pasture for the greater nutritional demands of the pregnant animals and for several weeks after birth to strengthen the young. The semi-nomadic Karimojong pastoralists do not allow cows to breed until they are nearly four years old, and use several methods of animal contraception to separate repeated calving by approximately 14 months (Dyson-Hudson and Dyson-Hudson 1970). This is accomplished most simply by herding the males separately from the females (Nicholaisen 1963:43). Other methods include tying the penis or hobbling the males to prevent them from mounting receptive females (Cranstone 1969:256). Efforts are made to preserve females, and high calf mortality (17%) necessitates postponing castration until males reach one year of age.

Herding success is also affected by breeding programs to limit the numbers of males in the herd while maximizing the numbers of females since milk is more important in caloric/nutritional terms than meat (see Russell 1988:73–102 for an extended discussion). Among those herders whose diets are particularly dependent upon milk and milk products, there is strong incentive to maintain breeding stock until they are beyond reproductive age, when they are then sold or slaughtered for local consumption. Only one or two males need to be kept in the herd for breeding; the remainder is castrated. This is the most typical method of controlling breeding, and all pastoralists studied believe it has the added effects of rendering the animals easier to control and causing them to accumulate fat (e.g., Cranstone 1969:255; Gulliver 1955:27). Scientific documentation corroborates such beliefs. Metabolic and somatic effects typically include delayed ossification of the long bones (resulting in thinning and attenuation), elongated and fine-boned cranial structure, relatively weak muscle development, suppression in the nervous system of aggressiveness and excitability, and a more delicately textured and flavored meat lacking the strong odor and taste characteristic of bulls (Baîburtcjan 1963:2). Lowered oxidation and improved carbohydrate assimilation tend to favor fat deposition over muscle, and typically steers exhibit greater loin development than bulls, which are usually larger in the forequarters (Turton 1962:447). Thus, although castration results in slower development, the multiple benefits (easier handling, higher carcass yield, better taste, and possibly higher nutritive content) would seem to argue for castration as a management option (particularly in beef production strategies).

The most commonly used method of castration is to open the scrotum with a knife or spear tip to remove the testes. A second group of methods involves damaging the testicles without removing them, by tying the scrotum of a young animal with cord so that the testicles atrophy, or by crushing them between two stones (Cranstone 1969:255). Indentations along the length of the horn core were thought to be archaeologically recognizable evidence of castration (Noddle 1983), although this is now known to be incorrect. Cross-sectional analyses indicate these indentations are actually showing periods of nutritional stress, and occur more often in breeding females (Siegel 1976). Unfortunately, there is currently no reliable means for identifying castrates in an archaeological population (see the heading "*Physical Criteria*" in Appendix A).

The importance of the females to herd (and thus human) survival is most evident in the ethnographies of the Tuareg nomadic pastoralists and the Tswana agro-pastoralists. Male calves are restricted from suckling to ensure that female calves and human children receive enough milk (e.g., Nicholaisen 1963; Breutz 1991). To accelerate weaning, a male may be totally separated from its mother, or its access may be restricted. There are two main types of devices associated with weaning: those which make suckling difficult or impossible for the offspring, and those which cause pain for the mother (Cranstone 1969:257–260; Nicholaisen 1963:Figs 6, 19, 31, 41). In the former, cords or sticks are tied across the mouths of the young like a bit, preventing them from sucking but not grazing. Also, cuts may be made on their noses, making it painful for them to suck. In the latter type of devices, a ring of thorns or forked sticks are tied to the calf's nose, making its attempts to suckle painful for the mother. Also, sticks or roots may be passed through the calf's nasal septum, admitting air when it tries to suck, again painfully poking the mother. When the need for extra milk is temporary, the Tuareg tie a goat's hair net bag over the udder of a lactating female (Nicholaisen 1963:61, figure 41). Restricted feeding contributes to the higher mortality rate for males. As much as 40% of male calves are killed before reaching one year, compared with the natural 5% mortality rate among female calves (Dyson-Hudson 1985:173).

Redding proposed that the size of herds kept by families practicing primarily agricultural activities (i.e., agro-pastoralists) must be less than half that of groups *not* involved with agriculture because labor resources must be divided between agricultural and pastoral activities (1981:230). This initially seems logical, until one considers that family size—and overall settlement population—is generally *higher* among agriculturalists than pastoralists. Khazanov (1984:129) and Hassan (1973:536) noted that the sedentarization[5] of pastoral groups typically corresponded to an increase both in family size and the number of generations within a family (a decrease in length between generations). Those result partly from the increased birth and survival rates, but also reflect the economic basis of needing a larger workforce for meeting agricultural labor requirements. The subsistence base is broader, more productive, and presumably more stable with the addition of a variety of crop plants, thereby reducing the overall importance of animals to basic survival. Herd sizes might be further reduced as social exchanges (such as bride wealth and overall prosperity) come to be based to some degree on these other resources.

Family size is generally larger among agriculturalists, increasing the number of people available for either herding or agricultural activities. This would further offset the increase in duties resulting from the splitting of efforts between pastoral and agricultural activities. I agree that herds tend to be smaller in agricultural villages, but Redding's figure of half the size of pastoral groups seems arbitrary and severely reduced. Further, I do not accept that the splitting of efforts between pastoral and agricultural activities is the reason for the smaller herds. It is difficult and inefficient to control small herds below a certain size (depending on the species). Coalescing them into larger, more manageable herd units allows a greater absolute number of animals without increasing the number of human herders or labor input, provided there is sufficient access to pasture or fodder to sustain these herds. Further, herd animals grazed on the higher quality forage or fodder available in areas in which agriculture is a viable economic alternative consistently produce stronger young and more milk and meat (chapter 4). Agro-pastoralists need not keep excessively large herds as a means to rebound from catastrophe. Herd size, then, should fall naturally with an increase in reliance on agricultural pursuits. Finally, the higher quality and productivity of plants—and therefore also of animals—permits the production of surpluses, thereby offsetting the absolute increase in amounts of food needed (for both animals and humans), perhaps without any additional labor.

## *Fodder and Dung*

Modern nomadic or semi-nomadic pastoralists allow their herds nearly free access to plant resources, moving them to new areas or better pasture as needed, since land is essentially held in common. Ryder stresses that with transhumant populations, serious conflict may arise concerning the passage of herds through cultivated land (1983:654). In the regions and groups discussed above, however, the herds are generally moved away from land under cultivation to natural pastures in the wet season, and brought to the better agricultural lands only during the dry season (i.e., after the harvest). Thus farmers probably welcomed the animals in order to obtain their manure. Conflicts may have arisen more rarely during periods of drought, when there was insufficient water for crops or when desperate herders emigrated from even drier areas. This general pattern is also more likely to have occurred in Egypt, given the similarities in habitat and seasonality of resources.

Dung is a very important product as well, particularly for nomadic pastoralists wishing access to the stubble of harvested fields belonging to more settled peoples. While in some areas the pastoralists must pay for the food their animals consume, in others the farmers pay (usually in grain) for the fertilization of their fields (Allchin 1963; Ryder 1983:735). Folding—restricting animals within temporary pens—in arable fields is likely to have been an early expression of this practice, and continues today in deltaic Egypt (personal observation). Unfortunately, little

[5] That is, the process of becoming sedentary, often written 'sedentization.'

documentation could be found about the amount of manure for each species, and nothing on the relative improvements in plant production.[6] Noddle (1989:40) incompletely cites several studies which indicate that manure derived from modern animals fed protein-rich feed contains "more plant nutrients than that of earlier stock" but which still only provides 50% of the needs of most modern plants.

Dung is often allowed to dry, collected and burned as fuel, especially in desert habitats where there is little else to burn (Hobbs 1989; Voigt and Plug 1985, cited in Noddle 1989:41), including the deserts and southern villages in Egypt (Brewer personal communication). Preparing cakes of cattle dung mixed with straw and chaff is typically the task of women and children (Miller 1984:76). Sheep and goat dung are considered the hottest burning, although cattle dung readily burns with no smoke (Ryder 1983). It is often used in smudge fires to ward off mosquitoes (Lincoln 1981; Nicholaisen 1963). Cattle dung is often used as 'plaster' in construction among many East African populations (Lincoln 1981:14). No information was found concerning pig dung, but since pigs are shown treading in seed on Egyptian fields (Hartmann 1923), it seems likely that their dung was 'applied' directly to the fields. Dung used for fertilizer is known in Arabic as *jillah*, and that used for fuel (primarily from stabled animals) is known as *bakh biladi* (Ayrout 1963:44-45). Ancient Egyptians identified dung as *ḥyr* but apparently no distinctions were made between dung used for fertilizer and that used for fuel.

With larger numbers of animals, or those kept by sedentary populations, plant resources become much more limited—especially among agricultural groups whose goal is to grow crops for human rather than animal consumption. A means of reducing this competition between human and animal needs is through fodder conservation. Penned animals require less space, and also require less food by saving energy previously expended in traveling to pasture and water. Pens can sometimes be identified by analysis of phosphate concentrations from animal urine remaining in the soil (Bradley 1978; Fleming 1978).

Anywhere grain has been harvested there will be an abundance of plant stalks that can be dried and stored. This food source is likely to have been more nutritious than modern straw because of the higher weed content (Noddle 1989). Silage (fresh, green plants provided to animals) is likely to have been widely used in Egypt, and remains of vetches or clovers are documented in Egypt at least by the Neolithic period (Wetterstrom 1993:214). It is unclear, however, if such plants were wild or cultivated in plots (Brewer et al. 1994). Chowdhury and Buth (1970) identified cotton seeds among sheep dung from an archaeological village in the Nubian desert (ca. 2500 B.C.), and suggested that cotton was used as fodder since there was no evidence of cotton manufacture. Tree foliage is also a possible fodder, and would have been fairly ubiquitous along the drier, higher hillocks, or the outer floodplain–desert margins. The thorns of the acacia render it less desirable, but the leaves and seed pods would probably have been consumed by herd species, as they are today.

However, in any region supporting sedentary human populations, especially in which animals are kept with limited mobility, local forage may be overgrazed. Habitat degradation resulting from overgrazing has been repeatedly documented worldwide, and can be postulated for the past by analysis of plant remains from stratified archaeological sites, as Wetterstrom did for the late Predynastic in Egypt (1994). With the depleted food supply, three subsequent shifts by herders are expected. First, higher proportions of goats to sheep allow utilization of the less desirable but dominant plant species (Redding 1981:278, 1984b:163). Second, fodder could be provided (a defining characteristic of the agro-pastoral societies defined here). Third, in extreme cases, "the environs of a human settlement eventually become so severely degraded that it can no longer support large animals. [And] the prospects for survival of wildlife, humans and livestock are threatened, so scavenging species might be expected to increase to fill the continuing need for meat source" (Miller 1990:137). In other words, scavengers mirror and expand the increase in ecosystem productivity begun with the shift to goats, and speed nutrient flow to greater numbers of smaller organisms which can thereby be supported in orchards, garden plots or near residences. Thus, longer-term survival may have been assisted by recycling waste from meat production through scavengers such as pigs. The subsequent shift to hardier or more tolerant taxa is testable archaeologically through examination of recovered faunal samples from stratified sites.

## Social Production: Redistribution & Sacrifice

Among all ethnographic cases, meat is usually eaten fresh, and the distribution of this resource is tightly controlled by social customs. While the specific customs of any one society would not be directly applicable to the archaeological record in Egypt, an overall pattern is apparent which should allow the discrimination between faunal assemblages accumulated by different types of pastoral economies.

For example, meat distribution and consumption of small stock by nomadic pastoralists occurs at the household[7]

[6] Van Loon (1978:5) noted that a modern feeder pig produces 12 kg of nitrogen, 10.5 kg phosphorous, and 8 kg potassium, but he does not report the type or nutritional content of the feed, or the water content of the dung.

[7] A fundamental social unit, the household can serve as a basic analytical unit. However, it is "a unit of economic and social production that does not necessarily live under a single roof" (Wilk

level. Under conditions of ideal preservation, this would result in an archaeological distribution of whole animals within one or a few closely associated structure(s). The social preference for slaughter and consumption of small stock on a regular basis suggests further that the age range of remains would be fairly narrow, with a majority attributed to males for those remains which could be reliably sexed. These patterns are markedly different from those of cattle. The restriction of cattle consumption to those animals that die of natural causes or that have lived beyond productivity should result in either a normal mortality curve or one dominated by older females. Additionally, meat from this large taxon is redistributed at the settlement level in order to reinforce social relationships and obligations. Archaeological remains should reflect this pattern through the recovery of meat-bearing elements across the site, and cattle remains should be comparatively rarer since fewer are raised or killed.

Ryder noted that social customs among some African and Middle Eastern semi-nomadic pastoralists dictate "3/4 of any available meat" must be shared among friends (1983:69). Thus, although tribal practice allows for the sun-drying and long-term storage of (surplus) meat, the societal requirement of sharing means that only a few kilos are available as reserve dry season food (Deshler 1965:118). Only castrated males and barren cows killed during religious ceremonies (usually during a period of poor rainfall) constitute a culling of stock. Unfortunately the specific social mechanisms for distribution of small stock were not clearly reported, although their importance economically has been noted.

Both sheep and goats are regularly slaughtered for food among nomadic and semi-nomadic pastoralists, but cows are kept for milk, and steers are surrounded by a system of beliefs restricting their consumption to ritual occasions. Interestingly, transhumant Khoikhoi herders of southern Africa use *sheep*—not cattle—in ceremonies, leading Wilson (1969:56) to conclude that the Khoikhoi were sheep-herders before they were cattle-herders. Reconstructions of develop-mental chronology based on zooarchaeological data suggest that this is indeed the case (Klein and Cruz-Uribe 1989; Sealy and Yates 1994). This preference for the earliest domesticate in sacred activities may be useful in determining the origins of some ritual practices of the ancient Egyptians, or why some use certain taxa in rituals and others do not.

Barfield noted that "non-ritualistic consumption of animals that die, particularly cows, is pervasive," and that the "ritual slaughter of steers occurs frequently enough to provide a regular supply of beef (1993:26). Schneider noted that the most common ritual occasion is a feast "given by a member of the neighborhood who requests prayers and goodwill of his neighbors"—often at the request of those same neighbors (1957:290). A large number of people are invited, not only to ensure that no meat is allowed to spoil, but because those who attend must reciprocate. While not formally linked with a need for food, the regular spacing of these events nonetheless creates a situation in which ritual feasts play an important—if unacknowledged—role in meeting key subsistence needs. Ryder further suggests that "[o]ne might speculate whether the religious sacrifices—those designed to produce rain for instance—originated as a necessary culling, which was only later invested with magical properties" (1983:70). Unfortunately, this may never be known for either extant or archaeological populations.

Meat is of greatest importance in all groups when milk is scarce; this is also true of blood. In a purely practical sense, cattle are of unique importance in most traditional East African societies. Although fish and agricultural products are consumed, milk and meat remain the primary elements of the diet and the majority of objects of material culture are derived from cattle (Evans-Pritchard 1940:28–30; Deng 1972:3; Crazzolara 1934:301–303). Thus, cattle are highly prized and are a clear measure of a man's wealth and prestige; the animals are used in all social transactions. Underlying this economic and social value is the religious use of the species. Ultimately, all oxen are intended for sacrifice, and returned to the creator god who provided cattle originally (Evans-Pritchard 1951, 1953). Cows are typically offered only at funerary ceremonies (Crazzolara 1934). But animals other than cattle are often sacrificed, and the absolute numbers of sheep and goats may exceed cattle (Evans-Pritchard 1951, 1953). Among the Dodoth, for example, most cattle are slaughtered at public ceremonies, and men eat most of the meat (Dyson-Hudson and Dyson-Hudson 1970:103, unnumbered plate). Accumulated wealth (in large herds) allows for slaughter during periods of shortage, and the donor gains support from his neighbors.

Since slaughter permanently eliminates a potential source of milk or blood, it is "loaded with symbolic and emotional connotations, involving restrictions on when and how an animal can be slaughtered, how the meat is to be redistributed..." (Dahl and Hjort 1976:265). Ritual slaughter nearly always involves communal sharing, and should be viewed as an institutional means of ensuring that all members have at least some meat at all times throughout the year. Sharing then, is an alternative to each household absorbing the cost of losing a renewable resource, and avoids the necessity of storing sufficient meat for personal consumption. Ethnographic analysis cannot describe the human–land relationships that existed in each archaeological case, but it can suggest a range of alternatives which may provide clues to further archaeological investigation.

---

and Rathje 1982:620–621); a house structure should not be equated with a single household.

## Relative Mobility and Settlement Patterns

Patterns of mobility among modern groups of course cannot be directly applied archaeologically. However, an understanding of the mechanisms driving the population movements and the decision-making process for when or where to move will be invaluable for developing an archaeologically testable model.

Samburu nomadic pastoralists typically maintain a seasonally mobile stock camp and a comparatively more permanent settlement known as a homestead. Distances between the two camps will usually not be more than a half-day's walk. The homesteads are occupied by the less active members of a family (the very young and old), and consequently these settlements are habitually located in areas of better grazing so that fewer relocations are needed. The majority of small stock remains nearby, as does a 'subsistence herd' of milk cattle. In contrast, the stock camp includes the remainder of the cattle which are driven by the more active members of Samburu society. The location of the stock camp is dependent upon three variables: pasture, water and salt. Since all three rarely occur together, the strategy for maintaining optimal resource exploitation must balance the distance between resources with the quality of the resource and the condition of the animals. During the dry season, pasture in areas where salt is also found is used up rapidly, thus these pastures tend to be left for the wet season. Cattle may be taken to salt licks one day per week, four days per month, or for one month in six depending on the distance between the salt and other needs (Spencer 1973:23). Only rarely is salt taken to the herds.

Unlike the Samburu, neither the Tuareg nor Ma'aza maintain separate homesteads and stock camps; rather, the animals are pastured in the immediate environs of the tents themselves. Camps are always located around wells, pools, or other sources of water, but never closer than one kilometer because "there is little pasture, many foreigners and consequently little peace" close to a water supply (Nicholaisen 1963:164). Saliferous plants are common in northern Tuareg territory, and in the Aÿr region, the Tuareg feed their animals salty earth (Nicholaisen 1963:129–131) to meet the animals' dietary needs. Reed huts with rags or animal skins thrown over the top are constructed in the wet season in areas where greater sedentism is likely (Smith 1992b:165). Herds of different households are prevented from intermingling (and interbreeding) by setting up tents a few hundred meters from one's neighbors on the same pasture (Nicholaisen 1963:146–149). Smith noted spatial distance reflects kinship distance (see 1992b:165–167). This has important implications for interpreting archaeological campsites.

Nomadic pastoralists tend not to have substantial, permanent dwellings or storage structures, and the majority of their technology is made from perishable organic materials. On the whole, they leave few archaeological remains. Woven hair or coarse wool tents are now used in the Middle East and North Africa, but it is unknown when these materials replaced animal skins. Ryder (1983:649) postulated that the change from wild animal skins to domestic hair and wool as tent materials probably resulted from a desire or need to minimize the number of animals killed. The shift may just as likely have resulted from hair and wool becoming more readily available or efficient to process into tent material and to transport than skins, the restriction of skins for use in clothing or other purposes, or the greater longevity of felt tents. Precise figures of skin tent durability were unavailable in any of the ethnographies examined, but tanned and oiled waterskins of the Egyptian Ma'aza Bedouin harden, crack and require patching or replacement after only two to three years (Hobbs 1989:50). Replacement of a skin tent would necessitate the loss of several animals—depending on the size of the tent and the species used. Drying attributed to exposure to dung fires (although the sun is no doubt also a factor) requires replacement of felt tents after five or six years (Ryder 1983:264). Felt tents can be replaced without affecting herd numbers or structure.

Some scholars in the Levant have turned to ethno-archaeological methods to clarify the type and nature of archaeologically significant remains likely to have been generated among pastoralists (e.g., Banning and Köhler-Rollefson 1986, 1989; Simms 1988). Goat-herding Bedouins of Petra (Jordan) and in Syria consistently use space regardless of whether the camps are traditional goat-hair tents or cinder-block structures provided as part of government development programs (Simms 1988). Goats are tethered at night, and their dung is routinely collected for fuel. Typically, hearths are merely shallow impressions and are rarely lined with stones; unburned kitchen debris was tossed into abandoned hearth basins. These features and other activity areas produce only light concentrations of refuse, and were routinely altered significantly or destroyed by dogs (Banning and Köhler-Rollefson 1986:12). Wind deflation of sites also contributes to scattering of refuse.

Stone platforms used in the processing of milk into soured products (*laban*) remained at many abandoned camps and have been noted in sites throughout the Petra region (Banning and Köhler-Rollefson 1983; Banning 1986; Russell and Simms n.d., cited in Simms 1988). These perhaps represent the only archaeologically visible evidence of milk processing. The composition of a particular site would depend on the length of occupation, the number of people and activities, and the subsequent disturbance following abandonment. Thus, not all sites would exhibit the identical pattern, but suggest that such mobile populations would be nearly invisible archaeologically.

The semi-nomadic Turkana herders follow either of two patterns of mobility. In the first, two homesteads—one with cattle and the other with small stock and camels—move in concert, allowing contact and cooperation between the two camps. In the second, the homesteads move in opposing directions. Cattle are moved from wet season pastures on the plains to dry season pastures on the hills, and the goats and camels continue across the plains. Most of the year, the two parts of the family do not see each other, and this strategy is reserved for lean or drought years. The tendency to go to the same area every year is highly dependent upon the quality of pasture. Rights to water are maintained on the basis of the work a man and his family put into digging and maintaining wells. However, since watering takes place every second day, two families have alternate use of the same water hole (Gulliver 1951:64). A Turkana wife usually owns and cultivates a garden around the wet-season oasis.

The average Karimojong herd owner has 100–150 cattle, 100 sheep/goats, and needs six herd "boys" (6–25 years old) to manage the herd during the year (Dyson-Hudson and Dyson-Hudson 1970:109). When possible, they are driven to water once a day. During the dry season in the western plains and eastern highland areas of Uganda there "is neither sufficient time nor water for cattle to drink all they want…[temporary] stock camps are built between the water source and grazing" (Dyson-Hudson and Dyson-Hudson 1970:107). Herds are driven to pasture one day and to water the next.

Permanent homesteads are built and occupied by women and children. Goats and sheep are penned near the permanent settlements year-round, eating the leaves of the scrub vegetation, and providing a little milk for the children. A few milk cows are allocated to the settlement by husbands to their wives for additional milk during the difficult dry season. These cattle graze freely during the day and are corralled at night, but are fed neither grain nor hay. Men have an area in the homestead near the stock corral that is theirs, but a man may enter the yard of a woman (even his own wife) only with her permission. A similar pattern was noted among the Dasanetch as the ideal, but permanent settlements are becoming increasingly common—and more crowded (see Carr 1977:206–208).

Despite individual variation among the strategies utilized by the mobile segment of the semi-nomadic population, there is a consistent opposition of the central settled portion—associated with women, their hearths and agriculture—to the periphery, associated with men, the cattle camps and pastoralism. Thornton (1974:5) noted that the "critical factor in defining [Jie] social and physical space is the location of the permanent settlement at the center." Both the Dodoth (Thomas 1965:figure 11) and Jie (Gulliver 1955:75) tend to have fenced animal compounds (*kraals*) next to their houses, while those of the Karimojong are clustered together on one side of the settlement apart from the houses (Dyson-Hudson 1966:106). Such compounds are prevalent in areas with a frequent threat from predation, such as in East Africa, but they are less common or absent in areas where the threat is minimal, such as in the western Sudan or other parts of northern Africa (Barfield 1993). Around these homesteads are the fields owned by individual women, and each settlement has a rainy season watering point and ritual grave. While it cannot be assumed that all semi-nomadic pastoral groups would conform to these particular patterns, the idea of a central point is expected to "underlie all concepts of spatial use by pastoral peoples" (Smith 1992b:27), resulting in a common outward-looking world view.

Migrations of semi-sedentary (transhumant) pastoralists tend to be "shorter in both duration and distance than the migrations of semi-nomadic pastoralists *in the same kind of environment*" (Khazanov 1984:22, emphasis added). This characteristic is particularly interesting because it suggests that ecological constraints influence movements less than economic considerations. This may have important implications for distinguishing between semi-nomadic and semi-sedentary populations using archaeological materials.

Among the transhumant Nuer, the entire population moves to the dry season camps. In the rainy season, the low-lying areas flood and families retreat with their herds to higher ground where horticultural activities take place. Generally, the older people return first to wet season villages, followed a few weeks later by younger members, who also move out again first to begin fishing at the start of the next dry season. Thus, the diet of the Nuer is highly seasonal (see Figure 5.10), but the addition of nutrients from fish reduces the overall reliance on milk. The beginning of the wet season is the most challenging because they cannot yet fish the flooded river nor are grain crops ready for harvest. This is the period during which milk plays its most important role. Conversely, the season when food is plentiful is also when Nuer are more likely to go on raiding parties against the neighboring Dinka (Evans-Pritchard 1940:97).

Dinka cattle are divided into two groups: a smaller one remains close to the house or owner (for household milk), the other is herded together with others' animals in large herds, managed outside the village by young unmarried males. These cattle graze in the savanna during the rainy season. Toward the end of this period, grass quality decreases, and animal growth slows. By November, large herds are brought to the lower-quality grassland zone, resulting in further reductions in growth (or beginning losses of body weight and mass). In January, cattle are moved to the toic zone, where grass is of minimal quality and insufficient quantity. Here, cattle lose further weight, up to an additional 15 kg).

Among transhumant populations such as these or in ancient Egypt, permanent occupation of village sites for part of every year could be expected to yield clear archaeological evidence in the form of extensive middens, the remains of substantial structures, and specialized tool kits. The same is true of camping sites occupied by smaller populations year after year. Also, the larger scale of agriculture suggests that threshing floors would be a part of the archaeologically recognizable remains of a village site, particularly when animals were used for traction.

Agro-pastoral settlements are much larger than previous strategies could support, with between 5000 and 10,000 people, and are organized according to a typical layout. The Tswana household includes a married woman and her children. The living area includes a single sleeping hut, and a combined storage/kitchen hut, and often a front yard with a garden plot. A reed, thornbush or cactus 'wall' surrounds each household's yard to keep out cattle (Breutz 1991:68).

The physical arrangement of different households within the village reflects first the importance of cattle to the society, and second the rank system of the clan members. The sun must rise first over the cattle *kraal*, and distance from the single opening of the *kraal* is inversely correlated with social position. Stock owners tend to their gardens as any other village inhabitant, and the day-to-day management of the herds falls to young boys and single adult males.

Block plots are larger expanses of arable land controlled by different clans; married men must apply to the headman for a subdivision of it (Breutz 1991). Typically located 3–15 km away from the settlement, a large portion of the village will move to temporary shelters in the fields following the first rains (Breutz 1991:22). These plots are not generally fenced because they are used as communal pastures (within a clan) after the harvest, and it is the responsibility of the stock owner to keep his herds from damaging crops grown on block plots. Most clans have block plots in different areas as protection against localized disease or damage.

The only mobile segment of Tswana society is comprised of the young boys or unmarried herdsmen who keep cattle and goats on grazing grounds located considerably further from the settlement (as much as 60 km). Keeping the stock at some distance from the block plots reduces the likelihood of damage to crops by wandering cattle, and allows better use of some of the marginal lands inadequate for crops. Unfortunately, it also means that the fields are not manured, and some crop rotation is necessary to maintain productivity. Although a single field may remain under cultivation for as long as ten years, the majority continue to produce a surplus.

Breutz (1991:24) noted with some disdain that it has become increasingly common for Tswana farmers to sell "too much" of their crop in order to obtain credit. They must then buy back this grain during the lean period preceding the next harvest; they are becoming economically dependent upon traders. This is apparently a relatively recent problem, however, and represents an important change. Previously, surplus grains were used solely to increase an individual's cattle herds, and now the goal is to maximize profits, as in ranching endeavors (see the heading "*Ranching*" below for social implications).

## Social Organization— Authority & Decision-making

The myriad ways in which pastoralists share ecological zones with agriculturalists have been most comprehensively studied by Barth (1956, 1959–1960, 1964a, b). I agree with Khazanov, however, that Barth views the two groups as "different species of animals which utilize natural resources in different ways" and that Barth minimizes the dynamic and expansive nature of both general groups when he defines the character of their interactions as symbiotic (1984:35). While both groups benefit from the social and economic interaction or interdependence, much more often the balance of the relationship tips towards the agricultural groups. The dietary distinctions given in the above categorizations of pastoralism assume—because pastoralists are necessarily very involved with the domestic stock that underlie their economy—that this structures their social organization as well. The major differences, then, are not in how 'pure' they are in terms of the above categories, but as Smith (1992b:19) suggests, in the "rigid hierarchies and political centralization of some groups, as opposed to others that are acephalous and egalitarian." In the former, labor is strictly controlled from the top and surplus is accrued to strengthen power relationships; in the latter, decision-making is in the hands of the relatively autonomous collective group.

While the autonomous component of the pastoral communal system—the household—is the most noticeable, the larger community organization should not be forgotten. A community comprises a group of independent households (rarely more than 20–25 people) who move together year-round, jointly pasture livestock, and are linked by other ties of mutual responsibility and aid (Khazanov 1984:132). A Turkana community typically includes two to five households (Gulliver 1955:11–12), while the Samburu live with six to seven households (Spencer 1965:18–19). In favorable seasons, these communities may coalesce into much larger aggregates for celebrations, marriages, etc. The number of families may vary from 10–20 among the Tuareg (Nicholaisen 1963:146) and Turkana (Gulliver 1955:12) to more than 70 among the Samburu (Spencer 1973:22).

The question of how consensus is reached concerning when or where to move has for many years been the subject of studies of camp polity (see N. Dyson-Hudson 1966; Gulliver 1955; Evans-Pritchard 1940; Irons 1979). More recently, a cross-cultural study of 19 pastoral populations demonstrated that among mobile pastoral societies in which the household or tent leader is the basic organizational unit, camp size seldom rises above 14 units, and the optimal size is six units (Johnson 1983). For consensus to be reached in larger groups, other organizational factors must exist. Absolute camp population numbers are less important than how the camps are organized politically (see Johnson 1983). This is fortunate given that difficulties in establishing true contemporaneity of various structures at any archaeological site render determinations of absolute camp population numbers problematic or uncertain.

Heads of households must constantly make economic and political decisions with regard to where the herds are grazed, how many are slaughtered (or given away) as symbols of status or power, etc. "The implied egalitarianism of the nomadic pastoral situation is restricted by rank and prestige" (Ryder 1983:653). Strikingly, almost all nomadic pastoralists are exclusively patrilineal in kinship organization (Barfield 1992); descent, residence and inheritance rules are through the male line. The Tuareg are an exception, however, because they have adopted Islamic laws of kinship (Nicholaisen 1963). Among the typical nomadic pastoralist kinship patterns, marriages invariably require the payment of bridewealth, transferring goods from the groom's family to that of the bride's. However, the status of women in most mobile pastoral societies is generally higher than their sedentary counterparts (Barfield 1993:15).

There is considerable division of labor between the sexes within semi-nomadic pastoral society, as members of all these groups consider farming primarily the work of women. Care of animals is more evenly distributed between the sexes, although ownership and decisions are made primarily by men. Ownership of the herd is vested in the eldest brother and passes on to the next-eldest brother after the death of the eldest, and so on. When the last of the brothers in this generation dies, the herd is broken up according to the number of sons of the older generation; each son inherits through his mother's allotment and the offspring of that allotment (Gulliver 1955:86). For both the Karimojong and Dodoth, authority is in the hands of the age-grade elders, but wealthy men—with large herds—increase their power base beyond this system and have wide influence over their peers (Deshler 1965). Authority is vested by public acclaim and influence as needed; there are no formal or permanent chiefs.

Issues of group size and settlement patterns are variable even within the same geographic region; the patterns seem determined less by environmental factors than those of social organization. Figure 5.13 graphically depicts some of these patterns for the pastoral strategies so far discussed. One characteristic common to all is that the 'family' most often coincides with a separate physical household. Ownership and economic production are usually carried out at the family level among the mobile pastoralists (Khazanov 1984). As indicated above, however, multiple families of mobile pastoralists often herd their animals together on communal pastures. Thus the production unit—the household or family—bears virtually no resemblance to the social or political unit—the community. However, among the sedentary Tswana agro-pastoralists, the production unit itself is comprised of two independent parts: herding and agricultural production. Herding plays such a secondary role in the society that its production is maintained by only a small segment or subset of the household. In contrast, agricultural production is carried out by several households for the clan that owns the land.

## *Ranching*

While ranching has not received the intense investigation as some of the above forms of pastoralism, defining has proven less difficult. A useful and commonly accepted definition is provided by Strickon (1965:230):

> That pattern of land use which is based upon the grazing of livestock, chiefly ruminants, for sale in a money market. This pattern of land use is characterized by control over large units of land, extensive use of that land, and extensive use of labour on the land.

Ranching has typically been considered an arid lands adaptation, following the assumption that primarily land useless or of marginal use for crops will become ranch land (e.g., Webb 1931). However, South American ranching is carried out on lands that are "perfectly good for commercial agriculture" (Strickon 1965:231). Before human population expansion in North America, cattle ranching in particular thrived in a variety of New World habitats, from "tropical savannas to subtropical pine barrens and midlatitude prairies, from fertile lowland plains to rugged mountain ranges, from rainy districts or semi-deserts" (Jordan 1993:9). The system which operated in the southeast and midwest United States during the 1700s and 1800s is expected to shed light on ancient Egyptian ranching in similar habitats. Components of 'Carolinian' ranching evolved as enterprises moved westward, eventually producing a much-altered—and better-known—system referred to as the 'Anglo-Texan.'

Numerous non-industrialized cattle-ranching enterprises worldwide, including those of the coastal and riverine habitats of South Carolina during the late 1700s, also raised herds of swine (Jordan 1993). Interestingly, such operations typically occurred in outlying areas such as marshes. Available food, salt and water were sufficient for near year-round exploitation of these areas by cattle, and pig sounders thrived unattended on the roots and shoots of the adjacent gallery forests. Jordan (1993) reported that tidal marshes were particularly heavily utilized during the winter months. Not only were troublesome insects scarce during the winter, but plants in these areas were tender and nutritious, and eliminated a need for winter fodder. The remainder of the year cattle depended upon the resources of the local 'wet-savanna' or sedge bog habitat. Hogs were permitted to root in the understory of forests and along streambank woods. Resources—including land—were sufficiently abundant that herds were permitted to roam freely. This is known as open-range or free-range ranching.

Obviously, the expansion of ranch territory is not without limits, however, and the rancher must either maintain his herd within pasture capacity, or improve profits through increased *quality* of product. This can be achieved through purchase of higher quality stock or improvements in forage crops and disease control, but more likely by selective breeding. By enclosing tracts of land, the breeder could prevent mixing of his stock with that of his neighbors (Ingold 1980:247; Osgood 1929:139). However, fencing has the disadvantage of limiting the mobility of animals, thus increasing the likelihood of losses as a result of environmental unpredictability. Whereas practitioners of all other forms of pastoralism derive security from a combination of maximizing herd size and mobility, ranchers do so from a combination of herd size limitation and territoriality (Ingold 1980:247–248).

## Economic Production

### *Herd Structure*

While other pastoral strategies may incorporate commercial sale into their economies to a limited degree, livestock are not produced as commodities *per se*, but as objects of multiple use and personal ties (Galaty 1989:216). Thus market calculation is only one, and an imperfectly developed, means of determining livestock value. Typically the goal of such strategies is to maximize herd size for the sufficient amounts of products obtained from living animals, long-term stability, and for social exchange and status reasons. In ranching, however, the goal is maximize profits from the sale of animals; the object is the greatest offtake which leaves a reproductively stable herd. With only seasonal access to markets, most ranchers sell according to immediate cash needs, devote little or none of the profits towards improving the quality of the animals, and only a small portion of the off-take is actually consumed by ranch households (Rivière 1972:18–20; Ingold 1980:241).

Archaeologically, these goals may be visible only through negative (and possibly textual) evidence. That is, maximizing the number of animals sold to consumers elsewhere effectively *removes* the bulk of the herd population from the ranch site and consequently from the archaeological sample (Fig 5.13). Thus, the animals consumed locally will be the few which die of natural causes or which were deemed unsuitable for sale, belying the importance of certain age classes or sex. The number of these animals are typically insufficient to meet the dietary (or perceived) needs of the ranchers, and small numbers of swine (in marshy areas) or sheep (in the prairies) are also commonly raised. Otherwise, a portion of the profits would have to be allocated for the purchase of meats, milk products, and/or wool/leather goods.

Another important distinction between ranching and other forms of pastoralism, in terms of recognizing the former archaeologically, is the singular focus of the large-scale production in ranching. That is, herd structure is geared toward maximizing production of meat, milk, or wool of a single species, but not often in combination. While hides or fat may be sold as supplemental profit on a "meat-ranch" (regardless of the animal species), milking would not likely be practiced on a sufficiently large a scale as to affect herd structure. Similarly, milking is not practiced in specialized production systems emphasizing wool because castrated males are preferred for their particularly fluffy fiber (Payne 1973:284). No evidence was found of "milk ranches" in non-industrial societies. This may, be due to the difficulties in processing large quantities of milk into storable (and distributable) products. Regardless of the product intended, ranches focus on one species raised for a single product.

### *Herd Size*

While mobile and agro-pastoralists require regular access to their herds for subsistence, the rancher needs only to round up his stock twice a year—once for branding and once for selecting animals for slaughter (Ingold 1980; Jordon 1993; Webb 1931). Because the relationship between humans and animals is not continuous through time in free-range ranching, herd sizes can be considerably larger. The ideal herd size among various forms of subsistence pastoralism is around 150 cattle and 400–500 sheep/goats (Dyson-Hudson 1966:49; Gunnison 1966:68–69; see also Redding 1981). In contrast, ideal herd size among ranchers is 1000 cattle or 2500 sheep/goats (Strickon 1965:245). This relatively low labor intensity not only reduces labor costs, but also enables ranchers to make best use of available pastures by allowing animals to free-forage within ranch territory. It also reduces the development of personalized ties between humans and animals (Galaty 1989; Ingold 1980). Ultimately, in open-range marsh ranching, the lack of control over breeding results in animals returning to a near-feral state (Jordan 1993:23–24). Such ranching might have occurred in Egypt's desert oases, since animals were essentially restricted to the area by available food and water. Similarly, discrete Delta basins may have been ideal for ranching, as animals would have been unable to traverse swampy areas. In either case, animals would not have required daily attention.

The reduced interaction between herders and animals within a ranching strategy also results in a reduced ability of humans to protect their investment from predators or mixing of stock between ranches. Fencing-in a territory dramatically reduces these problems, but raises another. Territorial ranches are subject to the same fundamental problems as mobile pastoralists: maintaining the herd at the optimal size given the quality and abundance of forage. However, the flexibility of mobile pastoralists to move frequently to new areas with fresh forage is unavailable to the rancher. Thus, the total number of animals a region can support under ranching may be considerably lower than that under other forms of pastoralism, unless there is a reliable mechanism for obtaining fodder from other areas. Obviously,

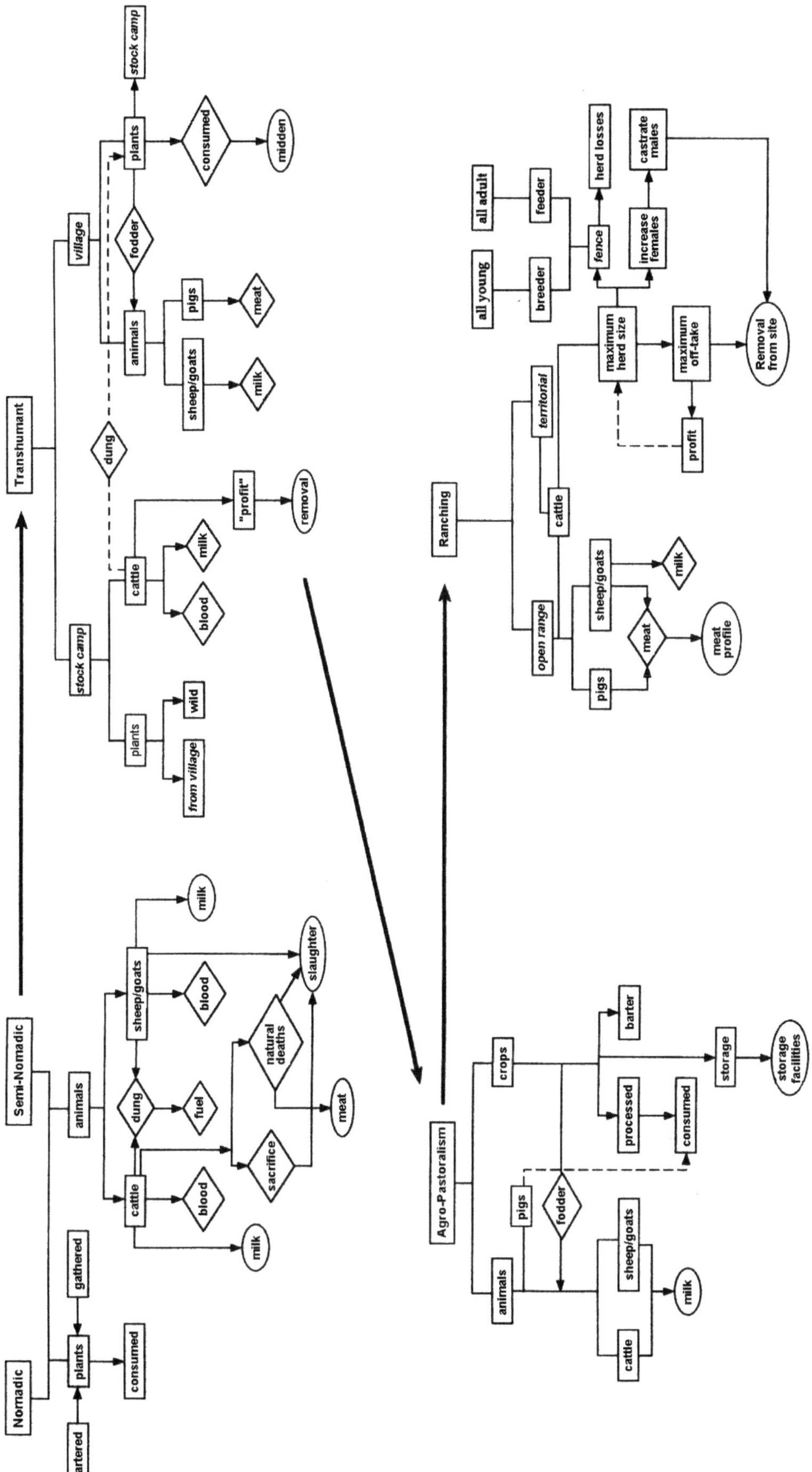


Figure 5.13. Model of the Animal Exploitative Continuum.

provisioning herds of over 1000 animals is costly, and cheaper alternatives are constantly sought. But the energy expenditure and dangers of the large-scale relocation of ranched herds to fresh pastures limits the practicality of this means of reducing feeding costs. In North American ranching enterprises, the 'normal pattern' of open-range cattle raised for meat evolved into a reliance on separate 'breeder' and 'feeder' districts linked by a network of established trails over which cattle were driven (Jordan 1993).

## Social Production

Ecologically, ranching more closely approximates hunting in that the relationship between "[h]uman and herds is one of predation;" socially, ranching resembles mobile types of pastoralism in that "ranching contains a principle of divided access to live animal property" between ranch owner and employees (Ingold 1980:235). This combination of relation-ships has encouraged the development of several changes from the various forms of pastoralism described above.

"Livestock marketing, enhanced by a growing commoditiz-ation of stock and the creation of new political institutions among pastoral people, has brought about changes in social relationships and had an effect on land use and herd management" (Smith 1992b:228). Transference of the perception of animals from the realm of subsistence to a commodity or means for profit reduces the reliance on animals for status. This can now be measured in terms of money or status-items (including the amount/quality of land owned), and animals no longer play significant roles in the religious arena. In addition, a "general decline in adherence to traditional practices as vesting authority with government, not owners" is also noted (Smith 1992b:228). Both of these important changes should be visible archaeologically, particularly during periods with written documents.

Rigby (1985:160) cautions, however, that where governmental systems lack the personnel and/or facilities to effectively manage all the marketing needs of its population, herders quickly discover ways to take advantage of such short comings, for example, selling their animals directly to local buyers in areas where meat is scarce due to delays in distribution of governmental provisions. Thus, documents may underrepresent the amount of meat and products actually consumed by a population, and more important, may undervalue the profits obtainable by herders. There is considerable potential for such actions to have occurred in ancient Egypt. It is commonly accepted that local practices at variance with national religion or politics were tolerated, so long as government taxes and tributes were paid.

Ingold (1980:240–243) noted an important distinction between Strickon's (1965) 'Euro-American ranching complex' and the 'subsistence ranching' or 'proto-ranching' documented in the New World prior to penetration of the capitalist market and in regions of unrestricted land (e.g., Rivière 1972; Osgood 1929). The relationship between owners and workers in industrialized (i.e., territorial) ranching is one of employer/employee, in which the employee has little possibility of economic independence. In contrast, the relationship between owners and subsistence ranch-hands is one of "economic kinship" (Rivière 1972:86). Ranch hands are considered family members, are raised by the owner, and at the end of a season are paid bonuses in animals for the purpose of building up a herd of one's own (see also Leeds 1965). The possibility of recognizing this type of ranching archaeologically is clearly related to an understanding of the availability of land.

In territorial ranching, land has been privatized or is perceived to be scarce. Thus it is in the financial interests of the owner to limit competition by preventing his employees from accumulating enough wealth to purchase their own lands or herds. Among subsistence ranchers, however, land is freely and readily available, and allowing ranch hands to build their own herds is not viewed as competition. Rather, the close relationship between ranch owner and workers encourages bonds of obligation; if the ranch owner loses a portion of his stock to natural catastrophe, he can reasonably demand or expect to be given animals from his employees' herds. This system is highly reminiscent of pastoralism described earlier in which sharing and reciprocal obligations were essential to survival. Indeed, it may be difficult to distinguish small-scale ranching from large-scale agro-pastoralism solely from archaeological remains.

Within a market economy, the decision of devoting land to plants or animals is, dependent upon the relative profit perceived from either resource (see especially Barker and Gamble 1985: Clutton-Brock 1989), echoing the spatial land-rent model proposed by Heinrich von Thünen. In his idealized model (1966), concentric zones of land use are arranged around a centralized market (see Figure 5.14). In reality, the shape and size of different zones are distorted by habitat variability, population density and proximity to other markets[8] (e.g., Christaller 1966; Lösch 1954), and fluctuates with perceived need (i.e., demand). Generally, however, the most intensive forms of production—such as agriculture—tend to be located closest to the market, with the most extensive forms relegated to the outermost regions and requiring the greatest outlays for transporting goods to market. Increase in demand for a particular resource causes that zone to expand in size, forcing subsequent zones to relocate outward (Figure 5.15). The limited participation in those markets by the majority of mobile pastoralists helps explain how groups such as the Tswana were marginalized.

[8] In "Central Place Theory," circular zones of land use surrounding markets overlap with those of nearby settlements; overlapping segments are bisected. This forms hexagons with no land unaccounted for, a major limitation of von Thünen's circular model. It is the size and shape of the hexagons which are further distorted by natural and cultural factors.

First, most pastoralists consider land to be a communal resource, while agriculturalists and ranchers view it as a commodity to be bought and sold. Second, while competition for land between herders and agriculturalists grew in demand (and subsequently, in price), the subsistence-oriented (rather than profit-motivated) strategy of the mobile pastoralists did not allow them sufficient surpluses to purchase land, and certainly not the most expensive lands close to markets.

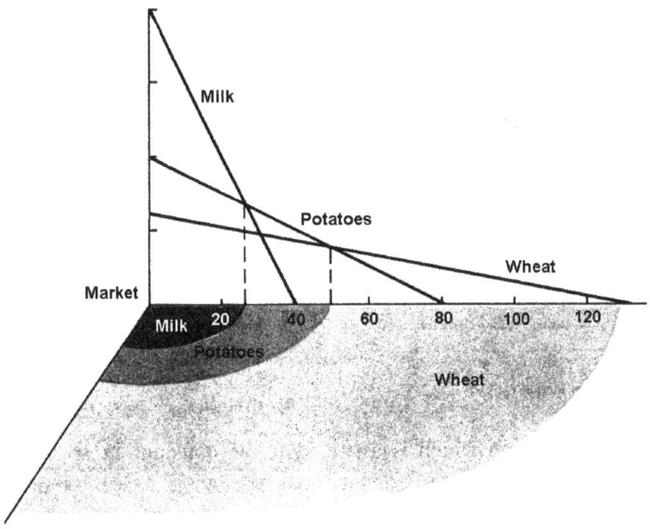


Figure 5.14. The von Thünen Model of Land Rent (after Lloyd and Dicken 1977:figure2.16).

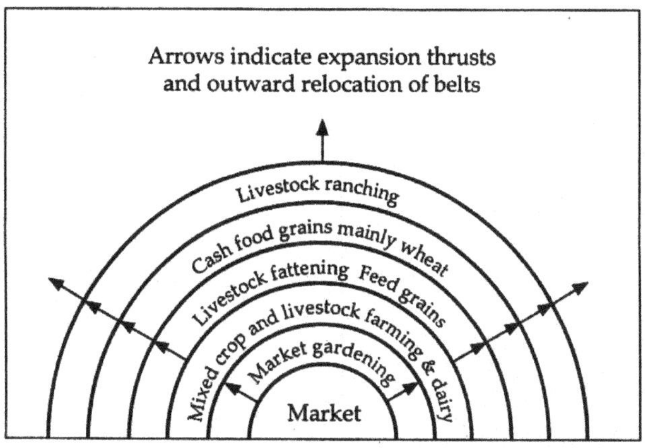


Figure 5.15. Hypothetical Expansion and Relation of Various Land-use Zones, Demonstrating the Shunting of Ranching into More Remote Regions (after Jordan 1993:figure 1).

From a more ecological perspective, ranching enterprises themselves contributed to outward expansion of these zones (Jordan 1993:11–13). Maintaining unnaturally high numbers of females, depriving ranchland of fertilization by removing animals before death, specialized overgrazing, trampling and soil compaction resulted in an overall decrease in range carrying capacity. This ultimately resulted in a decrease in herd fecundity and health. Repeated relocation to new, undamaged habitats became an adaptive strategy, and cattle ranching took on a mobile character as it moved toward the North American prairies. In such outlying areas, land was comparatively inexpensive, but drives over these large distances to market resulted in lower quality animals and consequently lower prices/profits. The solution: 'breeder' and 'feeder' districts. Animals were raised in outlying areas until they approached slaughter age and were then driven to 'feeder' areas of lush grass near markets to fatten before being sold or slaughtered (Jordan 1993).

Hilliard (1972) noted that a combined cattle and hog focus was typical of ranching in southern North America (i.e., from the Carolinas to Louisiana), shifting away from pigs only as ranching moved into the nearly treeless prairies of Texas and the Midwest. The major changes included increased size of cattle herds, the replacement of sounders of pigs with flocks of sheep, and the production of winter fodder. The centrality of pigs to ranching enterprises in North America has been minimized despite decades of study; the importance of pigs in similar habitats in ancient Egypt—such as desert oases and the Delta—has surely been overlooked as well. The relative unavailability of large tracts of land in the Nile Valley might have led to an early appearance of this 'industrialized' ranching, while subsistence ranching may have occurred in the Delta, even throughout the Old Kingdom. Population and other expansion would have put a premium on land soon after the unification, thus encouraging a shift to 'industrialized' ranching throughout available territory.

As fundamental to the emergence and expansion of the modern ranching complex as the existence of large urban populations of consumers of its product is a massive complex of processing and transportation which linked producer to consumer. The ecological necessity of diffusing livestock over a grazing area makes it impossible for even the largest ranching operation to be the sole supplier for a modern, heavily capitalized, packing house operating year-round. Processing plants are built peripheral to both supply and the centers of demand (Strickon 1965:236–237). The idea of center / periphery is crucial to understanding the location of land devoted to livestock versus processing facilities in Egyptian ranching. The Nile was heavily utilized for redistribution of a myriad of goods (Wente 1990). The river played the same role as the modern railroad in overcoming transportation distances and costs, particularly with regard to the feasibility of 'breeder' and 'feeder' districts. Previously, archaeologists have assumed that ranching, processing and distribution centers were part of the same location, and it will be interesting to test this alternative.

## Discussion and Conclusions

Much of the early anthropological research into African pastoralism stems from Herskovits' (1926) idea of a 'cattle complex' in which ritual relations between a herder and his cattle were viewed as structural elements in the social system. This concept was based on anthropological attempts to reconstruct indigenous pastoral lifeways prior to significant Westernization, and proponents viewed those reconstructions as the 'ethnographic present.' Unfortunately, vital elements of the system were ignored. In particular, the "familiarity [of indigenous herders with the concept of] markets and the commercial value of their animals and their skill with trading and symbiotic relations with cultivators and townsmen" (Bennett 1993:303) was denied.

Subsequent anthropological work has redefined pastoralism as a complex system involving many economic activities, including involvement in markets and commercial relationships. Particularly with regard to research associated with internationally funded development programs, interest has arisen in the importance of herding economies in almost all African countries, and the wide range of cultural responses that revolve around domesticated animals (see Rigby 1985 and references cited there). Recent investigations have correlated ecological context with degree of mobility (Ambrose 1984; Ambrose and Lorenz 1987) and social complexity (Clark and Brandt 1984; A. Smith 1980; S. Smith 1980). These studies document correlations—*not* causes—between certain ecological conditions and human adaptive responses, which are manifested in quite different forms of subsistence, mobility and economic strategies. The studies developed in part in response to anthropological debate that pastoralism is a branch off the mainstream of social evolution (Barth 1969; Cohen 1974; Isaac 1971). The inference that pastoral societies are 'residuals' from earlier evolutionary stages or somehow less viable than agricultural ones fails to consider that herding is often the most effective means of resource exploitation and land use in grassland habitats. That ecological context contributes to the degree of reliance on herding in an area is true, but the variety of socioeconomic responses to habitat documented among modern groups has not yet been widely applied to pastoralist societies known only through the archaeological record.

Patterns of prehistoric subsistence based on hunting, herding, transhumance, and pastoralism (here including ranching) all depended to various degrees on the exploitation of herd animals, as is the case in many African societies to the present day. These modes of subsistence can no longer be viewed as points along a 'cultural evolutionary continuum'—rather, as adaptive responses to cultural *and* environmental influences. That different responses to the introduction of domesticated animals were possible—indeed, required by the indigenous hunting and gathering populations—is evidenced by the subsequent changes in human social structure and economy. For many, the shift to food production marks a threshold beyond which societal changes are explained primarily through political or religious means.

The models of domesticate-based subsistence presented above and summarized in Figure 5.13 are based on ecological and evolutionary assumptions, but are neither unidirectional nor deterministic. They do not address *why* some societies shifted from primary dependence on wild foods to domesticated ones. Rather, they seek only to specify a series of animal-exploitative activities and associated ecological effects arranged along a continuum (see Harris 1989:18) of control over animals, and also to some degree the availability of land. The benefits and ramifications of a reliance on domesticated animals for meeting subsistence needs are numerous. It increases the stability of the resource base over the unpredictability of hunting, allows more complete use of environment (domesticates eat food humans cannot digest), increases the number of people supportable in an area, and improves nutrition and health. When human food waste is given to animals, it *reduces* competition by animals for humans' food. This is an important point, in that it opposes the argument used to justify the taboo against pigs in marginal habitats (e.g., Harris 1977), and it may improve overall human health by reducing trash dumps (populated with disease-carrying creatures). Domesticates may improve agricultural output with fertilizer, reduce the human workload by providing traction (threshing, plowing, trampling seed), and also transport. In economies in which secondary products are used, sexual division of labor (men herd but women milk, or social rank provides meat and others provide clothes, etc.) may be encouraged. The continuum is also conceived as a gradient of increasing input of human energy per unit of exploited land (Boserup 1965; Christenson 1980), but this correlation cannot at present be demonstrated quantitatively and must remain hypothetical (Earle and Preucel 1987, *contra* Russell 1988).

No real attempt is made to determine whether this trend of increasing energy input (or output) per unit area of exploited land was a function of increased population density, sedentarization, social stratification, or other demographic factors in varying combinations. The present aim is to introduce a descriptive—not explanatory—model. This can then be applied to archaeological data to better understand the patterns appearing during the crucial formative period and culminating in the first unified Egyptian state.

Ingold (1980) has argued that the change from hunting to pastoralism was not simply a shift in ecological relations from herd pursuit to herd management, but involved a major transformation in the social relations of production and the ideology of prestige. Regular hunting among many pastoral peoples seems a rare phenomenon (e.g., Carr 1977; Huntingford 1953), and is often viewed with contempt (Evans-Pritchard 1940; Gulliver 1963; Dahl 1979). However, Robertshaw (198:211) cautioned that the rarity of hunting may be due, at least in part, to the underreporting of hunting by ethnographers who misinterpreted the negative connotations of hunting as a lack of exploitation of wild game. The shift in *ecological* production is indeed considerable; the pastoralist must delay immediate satisfaction of hunger for the long-term goals of herd maintenance, although Ingold has perhaps overstated the case with regard to changes in *social* production. The products of a kill in both hunting and nomadic pastoralist societies are shared; ensuring that members receive at least some meat throughout the year. Most sedentary pastoralists, however, rarely share beyond the family or household; the exception is the distribution of ritually slaughtered animals. Archaeological faunal assemblages indicating a combination of pastoralism and hunting, then, should not be unexpected.

The physiological tolerances of various species render each uniquely able to cope with different environmental stressors (chapter three). Studies in the Near East and North Africa determined that mixed-taxa herds offer a more stable response for human populations against losses due to insufficient forage or water, or catastrophic losses due to species specific epizootic infections (Redding 1981; Smith 1992a, b). Mixed herds would be particularly useful responses in less stable or predictable habitats in Egypt, such as the deserts or margins of the Nile Valley.

While pastoralists have the (theoretical) potential to see their herds grow exponentially, a farmer increases output only additively, by enlarging lands under production, or increasing the labor devoted to the same acreage. This labor may take the form of fertilizing, weeding, irrigation, or plows. However, a farmer has the added security of being able to store (or sell off) surpluses for future use while the herder's surplus animals are continually at risk. These high risks of constantly caring for surplus animals can be offset by their use "to bind marriages, create friendships,[9] and buy political support" (Barfield 1993:15). Such investment in social relations is particularly widespread among nomadic pastoral populations living in areas where sedentarization is not a viable alternative, and where networks of friends and relatives provide an economic safety net in times of disaster.

Part of the difficulty in reaching a consensus of definitions and trait lists is because the human/animal relationships described occur in a unique setting—the particulars of the environment and its habitats vary through time and space. This is not to imply that no significant similarities exist; otherwise there would be no point in attempting regional or cross-cultural analyses. Marx (1978:45) noted: "Differences must be studied in their wider context, and meaningful comparisons can be made only where there are broad underlying similarities between societies...[An] anthro-pologist compares several descriptions or case studies of similar social phenomena in roughly comparable social contexts." In this chapter, I have tried to do the same, by defining an economy and summarizing ethnographic research of several groups utilizing it. In the following chapters, those expectations will be applied to Egypt's archaeological and historical records in an attempt to define prehistoric economies there, and then to account for and explain the localized factors causing a lack of fit among the Egyptian data.

[9] I would argue it is more accurate to refer to these relationships as based on reciprocal obligation rather than friendship.

# 6. Development of the Egyptian Domesticated Animal Complex

*"To understand a phenomenon we have not only to know what it is, but also how it came into being."*

Franz Boas (1940:305)

## Introduction

Meadow (1992:267) noted that "researchers [of Levantine pastoralism] tend to assume, based on analogy with the modern situation and usually with no firm archaeological evidence, that pastoralism...in the past was based chiefly on caprines." Bar-Yosef and Khazanov investigated this in their long-awaited synthesis of archaeological, anthropological and historical approaches to the study of pastoral and agrarian-urban societies in the region (1992). Somewhat similarly, I attempt to correlate those same lines of evidence in Egyptian proto- and historic sites. However, my goal is not to determine the loci or dates for the *origins* of pastoralism in Egypt, but to investigated social change within the pastoral and agrarian societies *during* and *following* their coalescence into the formally united society characterized by the Dynastic periods.

Maintaining the life of a herd animal is of considerable interest to owners or keepers. It is therefore relevant to investigate livestock husbandry in prehistoric Egypt not only by drawing analogies from the performance and husbandry of non-industrial and often poorly maintained livestock of the present day, but also by using the available literary and archaeological evidence. Caution must be used when relying on the written documentation from Egypt, however. The majority that have been preserved and studied relate to upper classes and priesthood rather than to lower classes, who would have been involved in the daily activities of farming and animal husbandry. Still, these sources provide certain clues to the relative importance of various animal species for different purposes, in different regions, and time periods (see the heading "*Nature of the Data*" in chapter two).

From modern groups (chapters four and five), insight was gained into natural and cultural aspects of herd maintenance not easily accessible archaeologically. Through appeals to uniformitarianism, physiological and ecological requirements of modern breeds are assumed to reflect the natural tolerances of the major food-producing domesticates in ancient Egypt. The *expected* distribution of domesticated taxa across Egypt (from chapter four) can then be tested against the available archaeological record. In doing so, the first group of questions (chapter one) can be addressed:

> What is the distribution of domesticated taxa across Egypt? How does that distribution change through time? Are there areas where certain taxa predominate?

However, the distributions or abundances of taxa are not expected to exactly mirror the purely zoological/natural distributions, because of influences by humans. Generalized models of human-constructed environments to which these taxa had to adapt, and within which they continued to evolve, are important for interpreting such a complex history. These models from the last chapter indicate that a diversified strategy—a reliance on multiple species—is more stable or dependable than a highly specialized one, particularly in areas of limited or unpredictable resources. Thus, while the local habitat influenced which species could have survived or thrived in an area (over the long-term), the ancient Egyptians themselves modified that environment (in the short-term) by creating a subsistence strategy based on a domesticated animal *complex*, in which animals were valued for the ability to complement other taxa within the complex. It is therefore more important to the present research to investigate how the different species were utilized in a cohesive system. The current state of knowledge on the origin and spread of the four domestic species so important to Egyptian society is complicated, as are the networks of social interactions between the inhabitants of each region. The appearance of each domesticated taxon will be summarized, subsequently allowing the development of the complex itself to be traced geographically. Sites mentioned appear on Figure 3.1.

### *Early Remains of Cattle in Egypt*

There is now general agreement among zooarchaeologists that the progenitor of all domestic cattle was the extinct aurochs (plural: aurochsen), *Bos primigenius*, which was common across northern Africa and parts of the Near East since the late Pleistocene (Brewer et al. 1994; Gautier 1984; McHugh 1974). Gaps in our knowledge about the relationship between various specimens led to the description of a separate wild 'species' thought to represent the predecessor of the modern domesticates for each region (e.g., Grigson 1969, 1976, 1978, 1980). Two wild species were recognized in North Africa: *B. primigenius* and the smaller *B. ibericus* or *B. africanus*. Greater precision in archaeological dating and further investigation of the bones has shown that these 'species' are instances of a morphological geographic cline in diagnostic features (such as horn size or shape) and sexual dimorphism. The small forms were females of *Bos primigenius*; more recent specimens are probably the remains of small domestic cattle (see Banks 1984; Gautier 1980, 1988). The problem of distinguishing wild from domestic cattle is complicated in North Africa by the presence of buffalo (genus: *Syncerus*) since the Pleistocene, and the loss of many osteological collections, preventing restudy.

Wild *Bos primigenius* was native to southern Europe, North Africa and the Near East. It continues to be impossible to refute independent domestication in each region. A complex of playa lakes and swamps 500–600 km east of the Gebel 'Uweinat in the southwest Egyptian Western Desert provides evidence of hunter-gatherer groups in the area, and the well-known rock art demonstrates that cattle were not uncommon at least by the early Holocene (Brandt and Cardner 1987; Brueil 1934; Clark 1954). Evidence suggests that these populations and their domesticated cattle[1] occupied the area during the drier seasons of the year by circa 7000 B.C. (Gautier 1976c, 1980, 1984). Reported dates become more recent with increasing distance from this desert region. *Many* early sites are probably buried under deep layers of alluvium or subsequent occupation, but it seems contrived to postulate domestication, spread, and continued use within the Valley (e.g., Wendorf and Schild 1994) when the earliest known domesticated cattle remains there (at el-Shaheinab[2], ca. 6000 B.C. [el-Mahi 1988]) clearly post-date the Saharan remains. A more parsimonious explanation is domestication occurred outside the Nile Valley. However, this does not necessarily preclude an Egyptian or African locus of domestication.

The bovid bones recovered from the eastern Sahara are slightly younger than morphologically domesticated cattle in Greece (see Berger and Protsch 1973; Protsch and Berger 1973), supporting a model of stimulus diffusion from there into Africa (Jarman 1969). Also, these sites potentially predate those in Tell Mureybit, Syria (7000–9000 b.c.), previously the earliest recognized domestic cattle remains in the Near East. This casts doubt on the popularly held belief that they spread from the Near East, through Egypt and into other regions of Africa (see Shaw 1977:107). A third possibility has only recently come to light: domesticated cattle spread from the southern reaches of the Arabian peninsula, across to Eritrea/Horn of Africa and into the Sahara, reaching the Nile Valley somewhat later (Marshall 1990; F. Marshall personal communication).

Recent and on-going DNA testing may eventually resolve the complicated issue of the (general) geographic origins of domesticated cattle (Bradley et al. 1996; Loftus et al. 1994). These tests strongly suggest a "predomestic separation for the ancestors of African and European bovines" (Bradley et al. 1996:5131) and the simplest—but not yet definitive—explanation for that divergence is independent domestication on each continent. Depending on the eventual chronology, however, it may also result from stimulus diffusion of the idea of domesticates from one area into others. While DNA research cannot reliably determine if Egyptian or other North African herders were 'the first' to domesticate cattle, it is nonetheless apparent that they were already experimenting with potential domesticates contemporaneously with herders outside of Africa. Consequently, even if domesticated cattle were brought into Egypt, the osteological effects of adoption would expectedly be minimal and difficult to separate archaeologically from independent domestication.

## Early Remains of Goats and Sheep in Egypt

The origins of domesticated goat and sheep seem to have been the focus of most of the research on domestication in the Near East. Although even today it is difficult to distinguish between the two species osteologically, numerous methods for determining wild–versus–domestic status have been employed (e.g., Boessneck 1983; Bökönyi 1974; Chaplin 1969; Ducos 1969). This problem is compounded by mixed species herds (see Redding 1981). There is a general consensus, however, that both domesticated goat and sheep were introduced into Egypt. All domesticated goats are descended from *Capra aegagrus*, the scimitar-horned goat of western Asia (Clutton-Brock 1993:68). This particular wild goat species has never inhabited any part of Africa, and thus domesticated goats in Africa must have been introduced. Similarly, domestic sheep in Africa (*Ovis aries*) are descended from the Asiatic mouflon (*Ovis orientalis*). The indigenous mountain sheep of northern Africa, the wild Babary sheep (or *aoudad, Ammotragus levvia*), is not directly related to domestic sheep (Ryder 1983).

Caprine (goat/sheep) remains found in the Eastern Shara have been dated to 7300 B.C., as well as in Egypt's Fayum region by 5800 B.C. (Gautier 1984). El-Mahi's (1988) metrical reanalysis of remains from the Sudanese sites of Kadero and el-Shaheinab—dated to ca. 4800 and 3300 B.C. respectively—contradicts earlier interpretations (e.g., Bates 1953) that the smaller remains were of domesticates. Although the metrical analysis was not definitive with regard to their wild/domesticated status, el-Mahi concluded that the 'dwarf' specimens are more likely the *young* of a wild goat population. While sheep and goat were perhaps spreading slowly east toward the Nile from the Western Desert, they also spread northward, appearing by 5000 B.C. at Haua Fteah cave on the Cyrenaican coast (Bate 1955). The direction and mechanism for their introduction into Egypt remains uncertain.

[1] Gautier (1984) identified cattle remains as domestic because the severe environmental conditions precluded them from occurring there naturally. Based purely on osteology, they are inconclusive, falling within the range of small wild or large domestic specimens. However, integrating cultural and environmental factors increases the likelihood that he is correct.

[2] Occasionally reported as es-Shaheinab (e.g., Arkell 1937). This error apparently stems from a lack of familiarity with rules of Arabic pronunciation. The prefix 'el' is replaced with the first letter of words beginning with the 'sun' letters (including those producing 's' or 'sh' sounds), in this particular instance producing the 'esh' sound.

### *Early Remains of Pigs in Egypt*

The wild boar—the progenitor of domesticated pigs—was common throughout Europe, Asia and North Africa following the Pleistocene, and thus determining the origin of domesticated pigs in Egypt is subject to many of the same problems as the origin of domesticated cattle. Unfortunately, pigs have not received the scientific attention as other domesticates, particularly in Egypt. Their lack of secondary products and the erroneous perception that pigs compete with humans for food has led to the popular (if incorrect) belief that pigs were never important economically. As previously demonstrated, the pig's omnivorous diet effectively removes the species from competition with humans, and their rapid and prolific reproduction increases the likelihood that they would be used as a dietary or economic supplement.

Epstein believes that domesticated pigs were introduced from southwest Asia along with sheep and goats (1971:349). However, arguments abound that pigs must have been domesticated locally because they are not easily herded over distance, and also most commonly brought under control after other domesticates are known (e.g., Brewer et al. 1994:65–96; Newberry 1928:215; Zeder 1991:30–32; Zeuner 1963:260–262). The absence of pig remains throughout Wendorf and Schild's surveys of Egypt's Western Desert was interpreted by Gautier (1976a, b, c, 1980, 1984, 1988) to indicate that they were not native to Egypt. Thus, pigs *may* represent an example of the domestication of a local species through application of the idea or technology introduced from another area (perhaps in the form of an introduced domesticated taxon). However, the lack of pigs in Fayum or desert assemblages is not unexpected on biological principles and likely reflects the ethnographically based probability that pigs would be utilized by partially or full settled agricultural groups, which would not have been found in the deserts.

At least by the Epipaleolithic, wild pigs were consumed throughout the Valley (Sandford 1934:86; Gaillard 1934:66–72; Brunton and Caton-Thompson 1928:77), Delta (Hayes 1964:71), and Fayum (Caton-Thompson and Gardner 1934). Domestic pigs are known first in the north at the western delta site of Merimde Beni-salâme[3] (ca. 5000–3500 B.C.; Boessneck and von den Driesch 1985; Yokell in prep A) and the eastern delta sites of Ma'adi and el-Omari (Boessneck et al. 1989; Brewer 1989b; Menghin and Amer 1932; Hecker 1982; Debono 1948). Pigs had been considered as imports from outside of Egypt because of the low representation in archaeological remains relative to other domesticated species (e.g., Kees 1961; Darby et al. 1977:173–175), but Brewer et al. (1994:96–96) proposed an ecological explanation. Only with further work in deltaic Egypt can either hypothesis be viewed with greater certainty (see chapter seven).

## Development of the Domesticated Animal Complex

As is clear from even such a brief survey, most of the domestication research in Egypt has focused on identifying wild versus domestic status of animals at various sites, in order to locate 'the earliest' occurrences. This has led to numerous attempts to discriminate between independent invention and diffusionist approaches to acquisition. The prospect of simultaneous—but independent—domestication of cattle in southwest Asia, southern Europe, and North Africa cannot yet be eliminated. The local inhabitants had clearly been experimenting with the idea of domestication, and readily adopted domesticate-based strategies regardless of the mode of introduction. The current state of research is incomplete, but suggests that sheep and goats were adopted from southwestern Asia somewhat later (see Brewer et al. 1994; Ducos and Helmer 1980). Sufficient data are presently lacking, but indigenous domestication of pigs by fairly settled Egyptian populations may have occurred soon after the introduction of sheep and goats. Recognizing the *direction* of spread is more important than the specific location of initial domestication, because of the probability that cultural practices were transmitted to the Egyptians during the period of adoption of a single species and in particular in the development of the core complex.

## The Complex in the Deserts

Available archaeological evidence suggests, then, that cattle were the first domesticated taxon incorporated into the economy of the highly mobile human populations utilizing Egypt's Eastern and Western deserts. Faunal remains are somewhat limited, however, and it is not possible to reconstruct age profiles or utilization strategies as defined in the previous chapter. Nonetheless, those models provide patterns with which to more completely interpret these data.

Throughout the Western Desert, remains have been discovered which date first to the period of initial cattle domestication and second to the introduction of domesticated sheep and goats (Close 1990; Wendorf and Schild 1980, 1994). Similar to sites scattered throughout the Saharan desert plain, these *Steinplatze* (literally, 'stone places') contain small concentrations of potsherds, flint blades and bones of animals (Gabriel 1977). These sites are viewed "as the traces of groups of herders—perhaps young men and boys—driving domestic animals to graze across grasslands that would have sprung up on the sand sheets after the summer rains" (Close 1990:94). The light density of artifacts indicates that these sites were occupied only briefly, perhaps water and/or grazing

[3] In the literature, the Arabic prefix 'el' has been dropped, and the name is commonly simplified further to just Merimde. The final 'e' in both words of the name are sometimes replaced with 'a'.

were not available in sufficient quantity or quality to permit extended occupations. Analysis of lithic raw materials and refitting of artifacts and flakes from successive occupational levels and nearby sites demonstrates that routes were traveled repeatedly, suggesting established patterns of movement (see Close 1990).

The minimal archaeological debris is consistent with the signatures of nomadic pastoralists presented in the previous chapter. Considerably more work is needed before reliable patterns can be identified concerning the nature of the exploitation, however. If expectations defined by the model are met, cattle would not have been a primary source of meat, which would have been obtained from hunting of wild species also found at these sites. Rather, cattle would have been utilized primarily as a renewable resource; i.e., for the milk and blood. As indicated from the previous chapter, blood would have been especially important during the dry season when other resources were restricted.

Work conducted in the Fayum area indicates that during the later period of Saharan occupation—after sheep and goat had been incorporated into the economy—populations were still highly mobile, and segments of that population were involved to some degree with agriculture (Brewer 1989a; Caton-Thompson and Gardner 1934; Kozlowski and Ginter 1989; Wendorf and Schild 1976; Wenke and Brewer 1992; Wetterstrom 1993). Extensive research suggests that "some of the plants and animals...were beginning to show signs of domestication" (Wenke and Brewer 1992:177).

Table 6.1. Relative Abundances of Identified Taxa Recovered from Selected Fayum Sites, Calculated from NISP Values. (Data from Brewer 1987; Gautier 1976c).

| | Brewer (Sites 1,3,4,5) | Gautier (Kom W, E29G3) |
|---|---|---|
| *Bos* | 6.8% | 12.4% |
| cf. *Bos* | 58.3 | - |
| *Ovis* | - | - |
| *Capra* | - | - |
| *Ovis/Capra* | 23.1 | 78.6 |
| *Gazella* spp. | 6.4 | 3.5 |
| *Sus scrofa* | - | 2.5 |
| Other mammals | 5.4 | 3.0 |

In both Brewer's (1986, 1989a) and von den Driesch's (1986a) analyses at specialized hunting/fishing camps along the shoreline, the most abundant mammalian resources were dominated by cattle, while other, smaller taxa—including wild species—contributed to the diet in nearly equal proportions (see Table 6.1). Nearby Kom W exhibited a much different pattern dominated by sheep/goats; Gautier (1976c) cautioned that sample sizes were extremely small.

Proportions of mammalian remains at Kom W were nearly identical to those from nearby Kom K (Gautier 1976c); few details on faunal remains were included in the site report for this latter site (Caton-Thompson and Gardner 1934). Gautier reported that the occupation at Kom W was similar to but on a larger scale than at Kom K. Fish remains were not systematically collected from either site. It is unknown how uch piscine resources actually contributed to the subsistence economies, although fish remains were clearly a major component of the diet at other Fayum sites (Brewer 1987). For none of these samples could age or sex profiles be determined, so it is not possible to reconstruct herd structures or whether domesticates were utilized for meat, milk, blood, or some combination thereof. Considering the continued reliance on hunted species and the abundance of fish in light of the ethnographic data in the previous chapter, it is unlikely that any of these mammals would have been exploited regularly for meat. Milk—probably from goats—would have been used seasonally, with blood from either sheep or goats being used as an occasional supplement.

The importance of plant resources is most evident at Kom K, with basketry-lined communal silos containing seeds and other grains (Caton-Thompson and Gardner 1934:37–41). In spite of repeated seasonal use and storage, remains of structures or permanent occupations were not found, indicating that despite the involvement with cultivation (or domestication[4]) of plant crops, the populations should be characterized as semi-nomadic. The north–south arc of oases (*wꜣḥ·t,*) throughout Egypt's Western Desert (Figure 3.5; also Banks 1984; Trigger et al. 1983:119–121) could have linked these desert populations both the Delta and Valley inhabitants on at least a seasonal basis. For example, the immigration and settlement of desert populations has been postulated in Upper Egyptian and Nubian sites. The incised and combed ceramics and microlithic tools are not typical of other sites in the Nile Valley, and they are termed 'Saharan' or 'Pan-grave' as a result of their similarity to artifacts found in the Sahara. Unfortunately, aside from preliminary analyses, the bulk of these artifacts remain unpublished (see Bagnold et al. 1939; Mond and Meyers 1937). Although the comparatively lush habitat of the oases would have almost certainly encouraged seasonal congregation and logically produced a richer archaeological assemblage than shorter-use desert sites, there has as yet been little excavation there.

Zooarchaeological data for the Eastern Desert are lacking for this period of initial adoption or domestication. This is extremely unfortunate considering that at least sheep and goat came from the Near East, perhaps across Sinai and either into the Delta or south into the Eastern Desert. Based on the relative ages of sites with domesticates, it appears that in the Western Desert and Fayum regions at least, the full complex appears to have been developed

[4] While Wetterstrom (1993:210) does not explicitly state that cereals from Fayum sites were domesticated, she remarks that "domesticates appear to be an addition to a forager food base" and repeatedly sets cereal grains in opposition to sedges and various grasses which are clearly designated as wild foods.

somewhat earlier than in the Delta or Valley. If cattle were indeed domesticated locally west of the Nile Valley, this might have permitted other taxa (namely sheep and goat) to be incorporated more easily upon their introduction to the area (see the heading: "*The Secondary Spread of Domesticates*" in chapter two). During this period of domestication or adoption, the habitat was more hospitable than today and supported an essentially grassland/steppe biotic community (see chapter three). The low resource availability could support only fairly small mobile populations for whom domesticated animals provided meat storage, milk, and other renewable products, and eventually some transportation (i.e., as beasts of burden) by the larger taxa. Wild animals were plentiful, at least until the Predynastic, but less predictable than the 'walking larder' provided by domesticates (Clutton-Brock 1989), and a more immediate cultural and economic response resulted than elsewhere in Egypt. The need to move to fresh water and pasture probably encouraged the establishment of trade contacts along established routes. Further, rock art in the Eastern and Western deserts provides graphic evidence of an early cattle 'cult' (Winkler 1938, 1939; McHugh 1974; Muzzolini 1983, 1986, 1992, 1993).

Wetterstrom (1993:208) concluded: "there is little to differentiate animal exploitation patterns from the Qarunian [i.e., Epipaleolithic] and neolithic times except for the addition of some sheep/goat and small quantities of cattle." In other words, food production was *added* to a diversified or generalized extractive strategy but did not replace it. Although the faunal data from the Predynastic are ambiguous with regard to sharing meat or blood from hunted animals (or domesticates lost through natural causes), the communal grain storage facilities are suggestive of the distribution of animal products as well. Sharing of available resources is an important component of nomadic and semi-nomadic pastoral economies. The repeated seasonal use of sites—while leaving only minimal archaeological and structural debris—is another typical trait of mobile pastoral populations. Again, the data are limited, but what little is known about inhabitants of this region conform to the expectations defined in the model for nomadic and semi-nomadic pastoralists.

## The Delta Data

Domesticated pigs appear in the Egyptian archaeological record at sites in the Delta or along the Valley flood plain. These sites—discussed below—were apparently occupied for extended periods, as is expected from the ethnographic cases in the previous chapter. Whether the decrease in population mobility is a cause or result of involvement with more intensive use of crop plants is unknown. Reconstructions of habitat and seasonality of resources for both the northern (Delta) and southern (Valley) regions (see chapter three) strongly suggests that none of the four taxa would have needed to be driven to water during the wet season. Rather, they would have obtained sufficient water from a variety of locally available plants. For example, the Valley would have been characterized by a mosaic pattern of interrelated microhabitats such as the *Cyperus–Panicum* meadows along the flood plain, limited marshes surrounding oxbow lakes, a narrow savanna woodland on natural hillocks and levées, and with acacia and tamarisk trees giving way to various grasses in the wadis and desert margins. In contrast, marsh- and salt-tolerant plants would have been highly abundant following the inundation in the Delta, with the few available shrubs and trees restricted to the better-drained soils such as dunefields at the delta's outer margins. The continued absence of pigs from nearby Fayum sites—particularly in light of evidence of interaction between inhabitants of these two areas—raises the probability that the Fayum and desert inhabitants were aware of the species but resisted adopting it because it was not suited to their highly mobile existence.

Archaeological investigations document the appearance of Predynastic sites in the Nile Delta and Valley between ca. 5000 and 4400 B.C. Early development of Predynastic sites along the Nile correspond with a period of aridity in the Sahara and declining Nile floods. A period of severe droughts has been suggested as the primary cause of immigration of farming communities into the Nile region (Stanley and Warne 1993a, b; Hassan 1980, 1988; Wenke 1991). The fundamental differences between Upper and Lower Egyptian archaeological remains and the similarity of Delta remains with sites outside Egypt's borders led Hoffman to conclude that all of the domesticates were "new to Egypt in the early 6$^{th}$ millennium B.C. and had been brought into the Delta either by migrants or by the diffusion of ideas from the rest of the Middle Eastern and circum- Mediterranean worlds" (1991:176–177). Faunal remains from the Predynastic sites of Ma'adi, el-Omari, and Merimde Beni-salâme are given in Table 6.2.

Ma'adi is a well-known site located on a low desert ridge at the mouth of a major wadi. Hundreds of graves—containing differing amounts of quality pottery, stone vessels, stone and shell jewelry—as well as the segregation of the poorest graves at the western end of the cemetery are clearly indicative of some social differentiation (see Hoffman 1991, Wenke 1991 and references cited therein). The site also exhibited specialization in activity areas, with craft production zones and buried storage silos around the periphery of the settlement, the core of which was composed of dozens of semi-subterranean pit houses. Stone tools, pottery and other artifacts demonstrate that the inhabitants were involved in exchange throughout Egypt and perhaps as far east as Palestine. Bökönyi (1985) argued that remains of donkeys are evidence that these animals may have made such interactions over distance feasible, particularly in light of the relative ease of access to the east through the wadi. This location is nearly ideal as part of a redistributive network, and Hayes has suggested that desire by Upper Egyptians to control access to this trade route led to the burning and destruction of the site

Table 6.2. Relative Abundances of Taxa Recovered from Selected Predynastic Delta Sites.

| | Ma'adi[5] | el-Omari[6] | Merimde Beni-salâme[7] | | |
|---|---|---|---|---|---|
| | | | Batrawi | Early | Late |
| *Bos* | 32.7% | 13.5% | 14.0% | 18.4% | 14.3% |
| *Ovis* | 6.2 | - | - | 6.4 | 2.6 |
| *Capra* | 6.2 | - | - | 0.2 | 0.2 |
| *Ovis/Capra* | 22.7 | 9.8 | 9.2 | 41.4 | 16.4 |
| *Sus* | 17.5 | 7.3 | 8.4 | 29.0 | 27.9 |
| Other lg mammals | 3.3 | - | 5.2 | 1.6 | 2.2 |
| *Clarias* | 0.08 | 15.0 | 12.2 | 1.1 | 17.7 |
| *Lates* | 3.4 | 12.4 | 9.4 | 0.4 | 2.5 |
| *Synodontis* | 7.7 | 11.4 | 31.3 | 0.5 | 8.5 |
| *Tilapia* spp. | 0.1 | - | 4.0 | 0.3 | 4.8 |
| Other fishes | 0.2 | 30.6 | 6.3 | 0.6 | 2.9 |

[5] Boessneck et al. (1989)
[6] Brewer (n.d.)
[7] Batrawi (Yokell in prep A); Early and Late (Boessneck and von den Driesch 1985)

(1965:123). Despite numerous reiterations of such statements in support of the hypothesis of conquest of the Delta by Upper Egyptians, the authors of a reanalysis of the original field notes and artifacts were quite explicit that the evidence of burning "is not widespread" and "a violent conflagration cannot be proven and is not very likely" (Rizkana and Seeher 1989:83).

The identified faunal sample from Ma'adi is large and diverse, and exhibits a pattern of mammalian exploitation grossly similar to that in the Fayum (Brewer 1989; von den Driesch 1986a; Gautier 1976c). Wild animal resources contributed to the assemblage, but domesticates dominated, while fish provided only limited protein (Boessneck et al. 1989). An interesting difference from the Fayum and desert assemblages is the heavy reliance on cattle *and* pigs at Ma'adi, each of which is considerably more abundant than either sheep or goat. Boessneck et al.'s (1989:tables 7, 8) detailed analysis determined that cattle herds were dominated by cows, and that the majority of this species were killed well before their third year. Both of these traits are typical for milk-based strategies. In contrast, proportions of males to females of identified remains for both sheep and goats were nearly equal (Boessneck et al. 1989: tables 11, 12), suggesting that they were utilized for purposes other than milk. The limited age distributions indicate that individual sheep and goats were killed during their prime (Boessneck et al. 1989: table 10). This is at least suggestive of meat-based strategies. Unfortunately, it was not possible to reconstruct any discernible butchering or redistributive pattern from the anatomical parts represented.

The data from nearby el-Omari are extremely limited, but appear to show some parallels with the Ma'adi samples. Dozens of semi-subterreanean circular structures and clay- or basketry-lined granaries were also noted, suggesting similar patterns of permanence of occupation and access to goods as at Ma'adi. With regard to faunal remains, Debono did not provide actual counts, but did list pig first in his account of species recovered, while species at the end of the list were represented only by single elements (1949:567; see also Hayes 1965:119). Subsequent analysis of the remains could not conclusively separate sheep from goats, and bovids were again the most abundant mammalian taxon (Brewer n.d.). Despite these limitations, remains of adults dominate the age distributions, but because they were inconclusive with regard to domestic or wild status, the interpretability of this assemblage is limited.

Few Neolithic sites in Egypt have received as much attention as that of Merimde Beni-salâme, located in the western delta. It is one of the few which exhibit a well-stratified sequence of (archaeologically accessible) occupations, and Hassan has estimated the temporal span to be nearly a millennium (ca. 5000—4100 B.C.; Hassan 1988:151). Only a portion of the faunal remains have been published (Boessneck and von den Driesch 1985; Hawass et al. 1988) despite 12 seasons of excavations by two research teams (Junker 1928, 1929, 1930, 1932, 1933, 1934, 1940; Eiwanger 1978, 1979, 1980, 1982, 1984, 1988). In 1993, the faunal remains excavated by Junker were analyzed, and a publication will be forthcoming (Yokell in prep A). The present discussion is based on the combined faunal analyses, and illuminates the earliest occurrences of the traditional distinctions between Upper and Lower Egypt.

The earliest remnants of a community at Merimde are reflected in the lowest levels of the site by a few scattered hearths and 15 burials. Traces of postholes suggest round or oval structures 1.6 to 3 meters in diameter, possibly covered with matting, hides or other organic materials (Eiwanger 1979:26). The lithic assemblage from this occupation more closely resembles the Epipaleolithic took kit with its emphasis on blades rather than the bifacial tools that are typical of the later levels at Merimde and other neolithic sites. The earliest ceramics and burial practices differ from later occurrences as well (Eiwanger 1979, 1980, 1984, 1988; see Hoffman 1991:179). Comparison of these traits (i.e., lithics, ceramics, structures, and burial practices) with sites such as those in the Fayum (Caton-Thompson and Gardner 1934; Brewer 1986, 1989a) indicates that the first inhabitants of Merimde (or at least a portion of that early population) were likely seasonally mobile.

The earliest phase was separated from succeeding ones by a significant hiatus of unknown duration. Two new types of structures appear during the final phase of occupation, identified by Eiwanger as 'Phase V' (1978, 1982). While the postholes of oval house structures were found throughout the settlement and in all levels, larger, semi-subterranean mud structures measuring 1.5 to 4.0 meters in diameter appear only in a portion of the site, in the uppermost levels (Eiwanger 1982:68). 'Foundations' or walls of up to one meter high were built above ground out of blocks of Nile mud (Eiwanger 1982; Junker 1932). While these were purported by Junker to represent the standard house type of the later occupation, the larger size and spatial concentration suggest a special function (Wetterstrom 1993:214). The other innovation at this time was the basket silo, located in front of house structures (Eiwanger 1978:37), and differs from the communal silos in the Fayum. Wheat and barley were the predominant cultivars, and although *Vica sativa* might have been grown for fodder, its association with cereal grains may indicate that it was merely a weed (Hawass et al. 1988:36).

The Merimdens utilized a wide variety of fauna (Table 6.3); eight piscine and seven mammalian genera in addition to the domesticate complex. The site may, in fact, represent the earliest occurrence of the full complex in this area. However, fishing contributed substantially to the economy as indicated by the abundance of net weights, harpoons and fish-hooks (Eiwanger 1982:82) as well as the faunal remains themselves. The wild fauna included hippo, crocodile, turtles and an unidentified species of antelope. The smaller quantity and limited variety of wild taxa suggest that they contributed less to human subsistence here than in the Fayum. Mammalian remains identified in samples from Merimde Beni-salâme and the Fayum provide intriguing evidence not only of an increasing reliance on domesticated plant and animal taxa, but also hinting at environmental changes.

Table 6.3. Number of Identified Specimens per Taxon from Merimde Beni-salâme.

| Taxon | Junker[8] | Eiwanger[9] Phase I | II | III | IV | V | Totals |
|---|---|---|---|---|---|---|---|
| **Pisces** | **476** | **144** | **2235** | **33** | **4022** | **2226** | **9136** |
| *Mormyrus* spp. | 1 | 2 | 58 | - | 90 | 58 | 209 |
| *Clarias* spp. | 98 | 65 | 1275 | 7 | 2016 | 1013 | 4474 |
| *Schilbe* cf. *mystus* | 1 | - | 1 | - | 4 | - | 6 |
| *Synodontis* spp. | 252 | 28 | 305 | 13 | 895 | 563 | 2056 |
| *Bagrus* spp. | 11 | 5 | 79 | 1 | 177 | 93 | 366 |
| *Lates niloticus* | 76 | 26 | 193 | 5 | 316 | 121 | 737 |
| *Tilapia* spp. | 32 | 16 | 307 | 6 | 474 | 344 | 1179 |
| *Tetraodon fahaka* | 5 | 2 | 17 | 1 | 50 | 34 | 109 |
| **Mammalia** | **321** | **1482** | **4957** | **234** | **9182** | **4145** | **20321** |
| *Sus scrofa* | 68 | 241 | 1474 | 76 | 3397 | 1380 | 6636 |
| *Bos* spp. (domestic) | 113 | 250 | 838 | 36 | 1725 | 724 | 3686 |
| (wild) | 2 | - | 6 | - | 5 | 2 | 15 |
| *Beisa Oryx*? | 7 | - | - | - | - | - | 7 |
| *Ovis/Capra* | 74 | 695 | 1752 | 26 | 2018 | 794 | 5359 |
| *Ovis* - | 138 | 242 | 8 | 322 | 130 | 840 | |
| *Capra* - | 2 | 8 | 1 | 26 | 1 | 38 | |
| *Alcelaphus buselaphus* | 5 | 2 | 48 | 14 | 52 | 9 | 130 |
| *Gazella* spp. | 7 | 7 | 22 | 3 | 71 | 28 | 138 |
| *Hippopotamus amphibius* | 18 | 5 | 11 | - | 146 | 73 | 253 |
| *Canis* spp. | 11 | 20 | 167 | 8 | 224 | 89 | 519 |
| *Vulpes* spp. | - | - | 7 | - | 14 | 5 | 26 |
| *Peocilictis libyca* | 8 | - | - | - | 72 | 14 | 94 |
| *Lepus capensis* | 3 | - | - | - | - | 1 | 4 |
| *Crocidura flavescens deltae* | - | 1 | 7 | 1 | 10 | 14 | 33 |
| *Arvicanthris niloticus* | - | 61 | 321 | 25 | 488 | 349 | 1244 |
| *Meriones* spp. | - | 38 | 10 | 32 | 537 | 427 | 1044 |
| *Gerbillus* spp. | - | 14 | 10 | - | 29 | 27 | 80 |
| *Mus musculus* | - | 8 | 24 | 4 | 45 | 54 | 135 |
| *Jaculus jaculus* | - | - | 10[10] | - | 1 | 24 | 35 |
| cf. *Eliomys* spp. | 5 | - | - | - | - | - | 5 |
| **Totals** | **797** | **1,626** | **7,192** | **267** | **13,204** | **6,371** | **29,457** |

[8] From the Derry Batrawi collection (Yokell in prep).
[9] Boessneck and von den Driesch 1989.
[10] This value excludes 10 elements belonging to a single skeleton.

In the faunal assemblage from later excavations at Merimde, domesticated sheep were considerably less abundant than goats (n=38 and n=840 respectively; von den Driesch and Boessneck 1985:6). Less than 15% (878 of 6063) of all caprine remains from Eiwanger's work at Merimde could be assigned to these genera, but they reveal the same pattern. Redding (1981:79) noted that while sheep typically dominate in areas with a high density of grazing forage, they are less successful than goats in similar areas with lower rainfall (i.e., as at Merimde). In both samples, quantities of cattle and pig were nearly equal (von den Driesch and Boessneck 1985; von den Driesch 1986a: Gautier 1987:175, Yokell in prep A). While the fragmentary nature of the remains limited the number which could be measured, six of the *Bos* remains in the Batrawi collection were well within the 'domesticated'limits proposed by von den Driesch and Boessneck (1985:11–13). Three were considerably larger and more consistent with the 'wild' parameters (see Appendix D, Table D.1; Yokell in prep A). Domestication reduces sexual dimorphism while decreasing overall size, and metrical analyses cannot always conclusively distinguish wild from domesticated specimens (see Appendix A). However, the abundance of remains from Merimde which fall below the size range for wild taxa argues for control by humans.

The location of Merimde adjacent to the desert and near a Nile channel was ideal; inhabitants could—and did—exploit both habitats. This yielded a wider and much more stable resource base, enabling the inhabitants to survive insufficient floods by relying more heavily on wild resources, or to support larger numbers of inhabitants than the desert habitat could support. Using elements from both habitats would have allowed the Merimdens to store excess foods; that this was done is evident from the storage structures found. The increasingly elaborate storage facilities also suggest that they were shifting to a greater focus on farming. Further, Hawass et al. (1988:36) propose that the abundance of *Rumex* seeds "may indicate that the fields were not efficiently weeded, and that salinization problems might have been encountered in this early phase of agriculture." The potential for habitat degradation resulting from the shift toward heavier reliance on domesticates is discussed briefly at the end of the chapter.

Based on the faunal and other data from these three sites, the lifestyle of the prehistoric delta dwellers was based on large, essentially self-sufficient agricultural villages, in which resources were held in common. There is also growing evidence from various delta sites that nomadic pastoralists of the deserts exchanged foreign trade items such as Red Sea shells (Kantor 1952; Hoffman 1991). From the ethnographic models, the seasonal influx of desert peoples would have occurred after the delta crops were harvested, and perhaps trade items were exchanged for seasonal pasturage in the stubble of agricultural plots (providing manure). This interaction may have encouraged the mercantile-based economy typical of the later Predynastic in this area.

# The Valley Complex

Roughly coeval with these delta sites were fully agricultural communities along the Nile Valley; two of the largest were Naqada and Hierakonpolis. Nine sites (ca. 3850–3650 B.C.) were tested in the Naqada region, located in a marginal desert zone adjacent to the western floodplain. Similarly, a regional survey around the well-known site of Hierakonpolis located several dozen sites; only two with adequate faunal samples are discussed here. Both Naqada and Hierakonpolis exhibit the complete domesticate complex, although the data from Hierakonpolis are more detailed (see Table 6.4).

Meager evidence of settlements recovered near Naqada include "traces of hearths, pits, animal pens and possibly huts, as well as...dense scatters of organic refuse and artefacts, a small dump of ash and charcoal, traces of a carbonated-cemented floor, ...[and] a circular storage pit... " (Wetterstrom 1993:232). Hassan noted that the sites appear to have been repeatedly abandoned and reoccupied (1988:155). Plant remains at Naqada show heavy emphasis on cultivars such as emmer wheat, six-row barley and flax, but also abundant and diverse wild plant remains (Wetterstrom 1993:223). The economic importance of cultivars is by no means definitive, but it is strongly suggested by the ubiquity of cereals from virtually every level in every square meter excavated, as well as the presence of field weeds (inadvertently cut off with the cereal stalks and removed from the crop plants through subsequent processing). The abundance of seeds of the field weed clover (*Trifolium*) is suggestive of the provision of fodder plants for the domesticated animals. In the previous chapter, this characteristic appears only in agro-pastoral or fully agricultural societies. Surprisingly, however, the above-ground storage facilities and substantial dwellings of such societies were noted but not well documented by the researchers at Naqada.

Table 6.4. Relative Abundances of Identified Remains of Taxa Recovered from the Predynastic Upper Egyptian Site of Hierakonpolis. (See Appendix D, Table D.4 for NISP values.)

| | Totals | Locality 29 | Locality 11 |
|---|---|---|---|
| *Bos* | 52.6% | 22.6% | 41.5% |
| *Ovis* | 2.5 | 4.2 | 3.1 |
| *Capra* | 6.5 | 5.4 | 6.1 |
| *Ovis/Capra* | 27.6 | 62.8 | 40.7 |
| *Sus* | 9.2 | 4.2 | 7.3 |
| *Canis* | 0.9 | 0.6 | 0.8 |
| other mammals | 0.7 | 0.3 | 0.5 |

Hoffman (1982:123-124) noted that the Predynastic settlement pattern at Hierakonpolis exhibited a hierarchical structure of large 'core' sites surrounded by smaller 'outliers' of varying size and function, revealing early the "industrial, residential and perhaps even military and administrative aspects" by which the site (and Egypt in general) has been characterized during the Dynastic period. Locality 29—the 'Predynastic Town' in subsequent literature—was identified as a large 'core' site which had well-preserved faunal remains. Locality 11 was a smaller satellite site surrounding another major 'core' site. Architecture at Locality 29 consisted of "semi-subterranean houses with wattle/daub superstructures, small outbuildings of light construction, extensive yards enclosed by reed? fences, and a large simple pottery kiln" (Hoffman 1982:14). In contrast, excavations at Locality 11 revealed a multi-component site characterized by a number of trash middens, habitation zones, and a cemetery. One area of the site was determined to be a specialized zone for the threshing and milling of grain (Hoffman 1982:18). A series of wooden fence posts associated with several circular basins (thought to have held large water jars) and two shallow troughs are interpreted as evidence of a livestock compound. Despite these features and the abundance of pottery fragments surrounding a kiln, habitation structures and hearths were scarce. Hoffman (1982:25) concluded that pottery production and livestock maintenance were the primary activities carried out at the site.

The level of preservation at Hierakonpolis was excellent, often "including dried muscle, ligaments, tendons and articular cartilage...any patterns present...result from cultural activity rather than the vagaries of poor preservation" (McArdle 1982:116). Although McArdle's data were preliminary and sample sizes were small, the age distributions for each domesticated taxon are suggestive of different strategies for utilization (see Figure 6.1 and discussion below). Although fish and birds were consumed, they "were not a major aspect" of the diet (McArdle 1982:121). Raw data were not published.

At Localities 11 and 29, pigs were regularly slaughtered at about the time they reached maximum body size; they were probably used for meat. The majority of cattle were not slaughtered until they were well into adulthood, probably when females had stopped producing milk and both sexes had long since achieved maximum body size. This suggests, at least tentatively, that bovids were not a regular supply of meat for the inhabitants of either locality. Rather, they were maintained for other purposes (milk, traction, etc.) and only eventually eaten. This pattern mirrors that found in most of the pastoral strategies defined in the previous chapter.

The ovi-caprid remains, however, show a different mortality pattern at each locality at Hierakonpolis (again, see Figure 6.1). The full range of ages were discovered at Locality 11, while 80% of the ovi-caprid remains at Locality 29 are of near-adult or fully mature animals.

McArdle (1982:118) offers three alternative explanations:

1) Locality 11 inhabitants emphasized caprine husbandry
2) Locality 11 was only seasonally used during and/or following the birthing season
3) Locality 29 inhabitants kept only mature sheep/goats

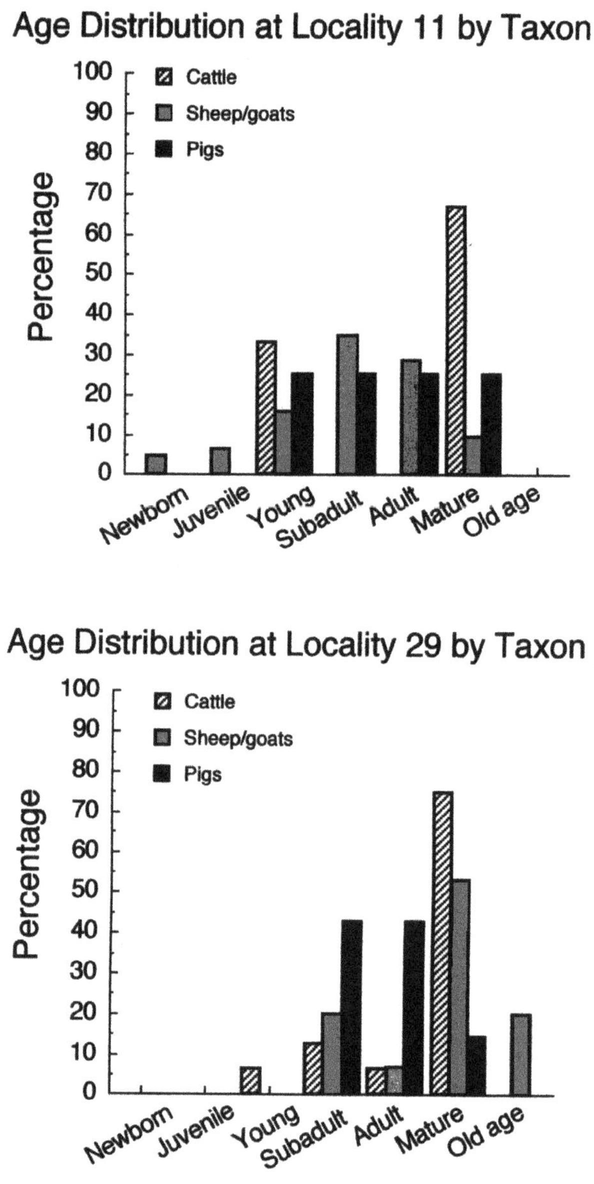


Figure 6.1. Age Distributions by Locality and Taxon from Predynastic Components of Hierakonpolis, in Upper Egypt (from data in McArdle 1982).

In the first instance, year-round inhabitants of Locality 11 utilized pigs for meat and maintained flocks of sheep and goat for other purposes, probably milk and wool but conceivably also for blood. In the second, McArdle postulates that the locality was used only until newborns and young individuals were sufficiently physically mature to be herded to the main village. However, peak mortality occurs in subadults, or approximately when the animals have reached mature body size. In a meat-based strategy, there is little further to be gained by maintaining the animals beyond this point. In this third potential explanation, McArdle contends that the inhabitants of Locality 29 maintained flocks with artificially high numbers of mature sheep and goats (i.e., as breeding stock). In light of the preference for slaughtering adult cattle at this same locality, it seems more likely that the sheep and goats were maintained until productivity began to decline with advancing age. It is even possible that the inhabitants did not raise the animals at Locality 29, rather 'importing' them from other satellite sites specifically for slaughter. The variability between faunal assemblages at Localities 11 and 29 may merely be the result of seasonal availability of pasturage, but may also represent alternative strategies of food production practiced by social groups within the same community.

Gautier (1987:175) noted a pattern similar to Locality 29 in successive occupations at Naqada: while sheep and goats dominated in earlier levels, a gradual shift toward pigs and cattle occurred (1987:175). He concluded that subsistence de-emphasized desert resources over time. An equally plausible explanation in light of ranching techniques presented in the previous chapter is that the shift toward a combined cattle/hog focus may indicate 'proto-ranching' to serve the growing populaces at Naqada and Hierakonpolis.

From five human coprolites from Amration levels at Hierakonpolis (Locality 14), Hoffman concluded that the diet "consisted primarily of starchy and vegetable foodstuffs—another sign that the herds were already being treated as "capital" wealth and that meat was not commonly consumed..." (1991:159). While the possibility for this early appearance of "capital" wealth is intriguing, his conclusion that meat was not commonly consumed is incorrect—in light of the faunal evidence indicating that primarily young animals were consistently utilized by the inhabitants of nearby Locality 11. The diets of hunter–gatherers are dominated by plant resources, although such populations were long thought to subsist primarily on meat obtained through hunting, and who exhibit little or no evidence of concepts of "capital" wealth (e.g., Lee 1968, 1969). Plant foods also predominate among all groups with domesticated herd animals, presumably an effort to maintain the herds by reducing slaughter for human consumption. Populations in marginal environments are an important exception. There, animal blood and milk comprise the majority of the diet as a means to obtain needed protein and calories. Concepts of wealth and animal worship are most prevalent among these populations (see chapter five). Thus, if Hoffman's conclusion of capital wealth is restricted to bovids, he may be correct.

Archaeological research in this region also yields occasional evidence of contact with the desert nomadic pastoralists, predominantly in the form of 'Saharan' ceramic styles, decoration and fabrics (e.g., Mond and Meyers 1937; Hoffman 1991:227–233). The similarities between Western Desert rock art and the decoration on a terracotta model curated by the Royal Ontario Museum are striking, and further suggest sustained or repeated contact between Desert and Valley (McHugh 1990). Originally identified as a house model, McHugh convincingly argues against this possibility; in fact, the model (stable?) has no close Nilotic counterparts "either in form, architectural features, or decoration" (1990:278). Further, the scene on the model features kids suckling their mothers—nearly identical to scenes in the rock art of Gebel 'Uweinat in southwestern Egypt (see Van Noten 1978; McHugh 1974; Muzzolini 1983, 1986, 1993). In contrast, depictions of domesticated animals are rare in early Predynastic art of the Delta or Valley despite their abundance in faunal assemblages.

## Discussion and Conclusions

The generalized models in chapter five described a range of variation in subsistence strategies and other aspects of the human control of animals in relation to the environment roughly corresponding to the reconstructed ecological conditions in each of the three regions of ancient Egypt. The introduction and adoption of domesticated taxa there occurred comparatively later than in areas to the east beyond Egypt's borders. Butzer has suggested that "broad spectrum hunting/gathering subsistence on the Nile floodplain" was sufficiently successful that "exotic cultigens and domesticated animals were resisted" (1976:107).

Although somewhat brief and lacking data in some areas, the information presented in this chapter answers the first part of the first research goal: To determine the distribution of the domesticated animal complex across Egypt. The available archaeological evidence suggests that each of the four domesticated species was adopted in areas in which it was well adapted and viable as an economic pursuit. Wetterstrom suggests that "initially, lifeways were not dramatically changed with the introduction of domesticates...[t]he first farming settlements are not significantly different from earlier hunter-gatherer camps (1993:167). There is continuity in both animal and plant taxonomic composition, use of storage facilities, etc., between sites throughout much of North Africa during a still poorly understood period of initial spread, but vast discrepancies in the centuries which followed. Various taxa appear to have been incorporated with a minimum of disruption or modification to Egyptian economy, forming a core complex *complementing* wild resources and domesticated plants rather than rapidly *replacing* those resources. It is interesting to note that in all these sites the frequency of wild game is minimal (except aquatic resources and occasionally birds, which seem to be understudied archaeologically), supporting the premise that domesticates served as an extension of an established diversified strategy.

The proportions of the four species differ significantly between each region (see Figure 6.2 below), most probably motivated by a human desire or need to overcome highly seasonal yet still unpredictable (and worsening) local environmental conditions. Data are plotted as percentages of the total faunal sample from a given site. In a hypothetical example, a site in which the three species contribute exactly equal amounts to the identified sample, data would be plotted by a single data point in the center of the triangle. Increasing distance from a corner denotes a decreasing contribution of the labeled species. Relying purely on differences in habitat preferences or tolerances (as described in chapter four), the general similarities in plant communities postulated for the Delta and Valley habitats were expected to result in taxonomically diverse assemblages. In contrast, the less predictable and limited resources in the Deserts were expected to exclude pigs, and emphasize the drought- and heat-tolerant sheep/goats. Discrepancies between faunal assemblages from various sites were not attributed solely to ecological factors, however. The tentative beginnings of regional preferences can be discerned by the late Predynastic, perhaps influenced by exposure to other possibilities through trade and contact with or immigration of nomadic pastoralist populations from the desert regions.

Broadly, desert sites were characterized by a reported (but often unquantified) abundance of fish and hunted species, a consistent dominance of sheep or sheep/goat among mammalian remains, with fewer bones of cattle, and a paucity of pigs. Data from Gautier's (1976c) analysis of Kom W followed this pattern closely (see Figure 6.2). Sheep/goat dominated the assemblage, and pigs were very rare. Data from Brewer's (1989) work at nearby sites demonstrated a higher reliance on cattle (indicated on the same figure by the symbol's proximity to the '*Bos*' corner) and the total absence of pigs. The reason for the emphasis on cattle is not clear, and may result from cultural or ecological factors (or a combination of both).

Other data related to these sites are inadequate for more definitive statements, but what patterns are present are consistent with expectations defined for nomadic pastoralists in the previous chapter. Structural remains of settlements were rare and of insubstantial construction, suggesting that more durable materials were unavailable or unnecessary. Similarly, storage facilities along the Fayum lake margin were uncommon, and when recovered, indicated communal access to stored goods. Again, this mimics patterns among modern nomadic pastoralists, in which food sharing is essential for survival by creating reciprocal obligations.

Predynastic sites in the southern delta were typically more generalized, with cattle contributing heavily to subsistence at all three Delta sites examined. The clumping of two Delta sites (Ma'adi and el-Omari) together slightly to the left of the center of Figure 6.2 indicates the nearly equal contributions of cattle and sheep/goats with the lower emphasis on pigs. In contrast, cattle and pigs contribute nearly equally at Merimde Beni-salâme, and the near absence of sheep/goats is indicated in the figure by the placement of the data point almost on the axis opposing the 'sheep/goat' corner.

Age and sex distributions for cattle remains reflect similar patterns for milk-based strategies: cows dominated herds, and the majority of this species were killed well before their third year. In contrast, sheep and goats at Ma'adi and el-Omari appear to have been utilized for meat rather than milk: proportions of males to females were nearly equal, and the limited age distributions suggest that they were killed during their prime. The reliance on sheep/goats rather than pigs is most likely an adaptive response to the drier and perhaps more unpredictable habitat conditions near Ma'adi and el-Omari in comparison with Merimde Beni-salâme.

More data are expected to strengthen contentions made here, but the available evidence seems to reflect patterns similar to those for modern agro-pastoral strategies. The pairing of cattle and hogs in semi-sedentary, agro-pastoral and 'open-range subsistence ranching' strategies identified in the previous chapter may perhaps partially explain the dominance of pigs at Merimde. While there is insufficient evidence to argue that Merimdens were participating in a true market economy (necessary to meet the definition of ranching), habitat conditions surrounding the site were ideal for permanent (i.e., year round) occupation and would readily have supported agriculture. With abundant high-quality forage, cattle herds would have thrived, and pig sounders could have rooted largely unattended in the nearby desert margin shrubland or in gallery forests along channels.

Remains of (and within) fairly substantial semi-subterranean structures and clay- or basketry-lined granaries indicate both the greater permanence of occupation and involvement with agriculture at Delta sites.. Additionally, social stratification in burials as well as specialized activity areas (and sites) is further evidence of more complex society in the Delta during the Predynastic. Unfortunately, it was not possible to reconstruct any discernible butchery or redistribution pattern from the anatomical parts represented at any of these sites, which might have furthered our understanding of early distribution networks in the Delta. Despite the social ranking evident in specialized craft production zones (and sites) as well as differential access to burial goods—including long-distance trade or luxury items—it appears that villages remained largely self-sufficient with regard to subsistence.

Data for Upper Egyptian or Valley sites were restricted to faunal assemblages from a single major site. The data are less clear, and cannot be considered truly representative of the entire region. Instead, they reinforce the range of alternatives available to the inhabitants (see Figure 6.2). The placement of the data points for Localities 11 and 29 near the axis opposite the '*Sus*' corner indicates that this species contributed only minimally to subsistence at

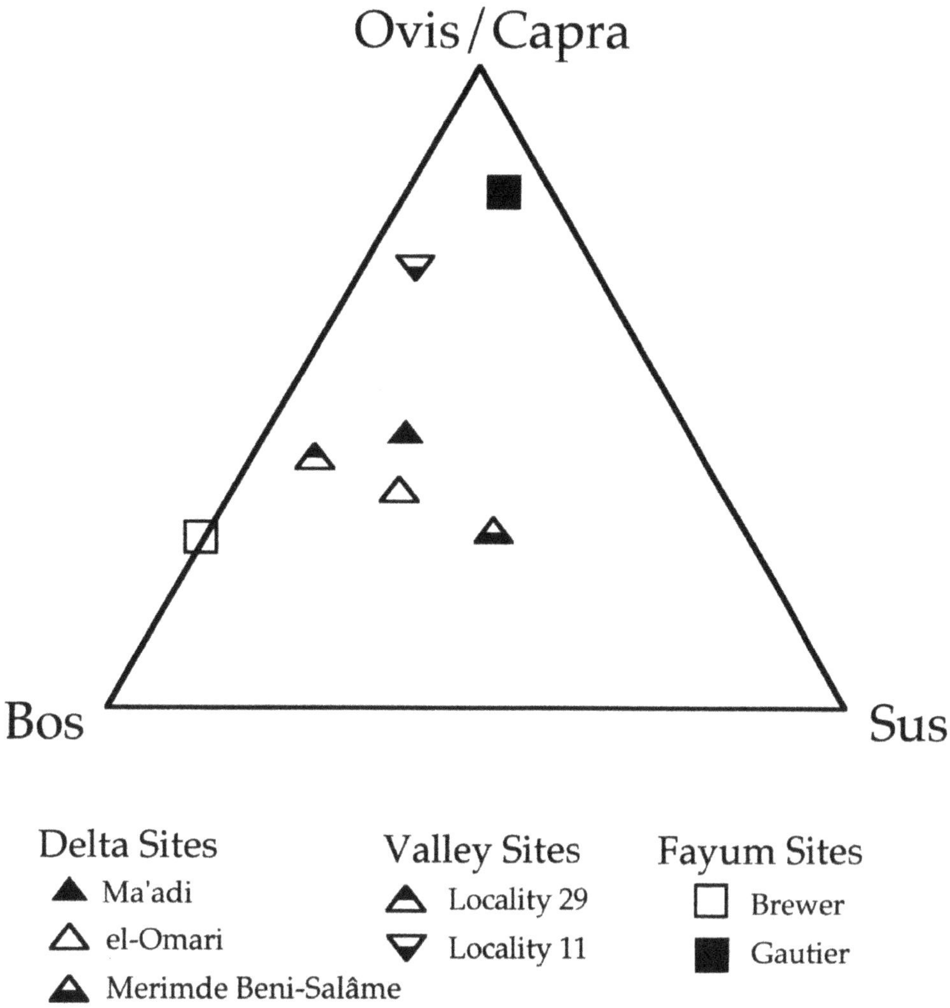


Figure 6.2. Scatterplot of Faunal Data from Various Predynastic Egyptian Sites.

either site. The greater reliance on sheep/goats at Locality 11 may in part reflect available habitat (the site was located farther from sources of seasonal water), and inhabitants *may* have preferred the more adaptable species. However, in the detailed discussion of these sites, it was also suggested that Locality 11 was a seasonal pasture camp, and ethnographic data indicate that sheep/goat are often pastured away from large stock. Interestingly, the data point for Locality 29 is plotted close to those for Ma'adi and el-Omari, reinforcing statements in the detailed discussion that Locality 29 was a more permanent settlement, albeit on the desert margin.

Mortality patterns for pigs suggest that they were a consistent source of meat at Locality 11, perhaps replacing the hunted resources utilized in other areas and in earlier time periods. Ovi-caprid and bovine herds were perhaps utilized for milk, although different age distributions at the two localities suggest that at least some segment of the population was still seasonally mobile. Over time, the ancient Egyptians in all three regions combined and modified these indigenous and/or introduced domesticated animals to serve their own unique purposes, albeit within the limits of the animals' natural ecological tolerances.

In summary, economics of late Predynastic Delta settlements were dramatically different from that in Upper Egyptian villages. Although the core domesticate complex and the acquisition or distribution of luxury/foreign goods[11] were major components of both economies, such activities apparently held little religious or social significance for the inhabitants of the Delta. In the Valley, however, pastoral development entailed a continuing elaboration of material culture, socio-political structures and economic practices (Gautier 1987; Krzyzaniak 1978; Krzyzaniak and Kobusiewicz 1984). The inhabitants of Upper Egypt participated in a display- and status-oriented society at least by the Gerzean period

[11] The adoption of the donkey during the Predynastic resulted in the elimination of size and weight limits on foreign goods by 3500 B.C. (Hoffman 1991). Ripinsky claims that camels were similarly used (1985:141). On foot anatomy, camels would be suited to the Western Desert and donkeys to the Eastern. While intriguing, it falls outside the present scope (see chapter eight: *Directions for Future Research*).

(ca. 3600–3100 B.C.), and many political and religious traits characteristic of the Dynastic period appear to have developed here. For example, the association of the political leader with an animal is first documented in art at Hierakonpolis,[12] which is also postulated to have been the first capital of Upper Egypt. Although military conquest of the north by the south has been a popular explanation for the eventual unification, to date there is still no unequivocal evidence. Rather, it appears that trade contacts outside Egypt shifted the developmental focus from south to north as early as mid-4th millennium B.C. Clearly, a regional—rather than site-based—approach is a useful framework for any realistic inquiry into prehistoric social and economic production strategies, integrating a variety of subsistence and non-subsistence data in consideration of long-term trends in resource exploitation, and of the models available to explain them.

The continuing shift in emphasis from hunting to herding and agricultural strategies since the beginning of the Holocene is postulated to have led to environmental deterioration in several areas of the world (e.g., Baker 1974; Bohrer 1975; Clason and Clutton-Brock 1982; A. Smith 1992a,b; Wetterstrom 1993). In the valleys of southeastern Europe this deterioration is attributed to overgrazing by non-local grazers such as goats adapted to the flora on the mountain slopes of Iran/Iraq (Clason and Clutton-Brock 1982). Similar habitat impact is thought to be a contributing factor to the abandonment of many Levantine neolithic sites (Köhler-Rollefson 1988). Additionally, cutting of trees and brush for fences and food is also postulated to have contributed greatly to habitat shifts toward grassland, particularly in East Africa following the introduction of iron (A. Smith 1992b:81–82). While interesting, this avenue has not been widely accepted in North Africa—but is applicable to the fragile balance of humans and habitat in Egypt.

The annual renewal of soil, nutrients and water through the floods might be expected to minimize the effects of soil nutrient loss from crop harvesting in the Valley and Delta. Paleobotanical analyses of several sites in these areas from the late Predynastic and early Dynastic yield "tantalizing, suggestive data but no unequivocal evidence for environmental degradation" during the Predynastic (Wetterstrom 1994:7). For example, the limited stands of *Acacia* and tamarisk would have been quickly exhausted from cutting for use either in construction or as fuel (directly burned or processed into charcoal). Components of Delta samples shift from ubiquitous evidence of wood and charcoal to increases in fodder plants, and cattle dung as the predominant fuel source (Wetterstrom 1994:9). The combined impact of clearing and grazing would have resulted in a gradual loss of annuals with a concomitant proliferation in less palatable perennials.

Marshes would have been subjected to seasonal grazing and plant collecting, and meadows would have been profoundly impacted by a shift or loss in plant cover due to intense grazing and cultivation. Over time, such degradation may have been reflected in competition between land for agriculture versus fodder or a shift among utilized faunal species for animals with greater tolerances for lower quality resources and/or those which are able to more quickly rebound (see chapter four). The most severe pressure would most likely have occurred during the spring and summer (drought) periods, and over time the degradation may have encouraged relocation of entire communities to areas whose resources had not been depleted (Wetterstrom 1994:6), as has been demonstrated repeatedly among ethnographic studies of modern herders (see chapter five).

Without oversimplifying an immensely complex problem, these data are highly suggestive of environmental degradation contributing to (*not* causing) the viability or eventual need for intensification and redistribution networks by which dynastic Egypt is characterized. Climatic worsening (i.e., an increase in aridity, decreased precipitation and perhaps lower or more unpredictable floods [e.g., Brewer 1991c; Hassan 1981, 1988]) is also noted for the end of the Predynastic and would have exacerbated the ecological imbalance resulting from settled agricultural villages and animal husbandry practices. The general climatic worsening has been suggested by some to have encouraged desert populations to move toward the Valley and Delta. A dramatic increase in the number and size of sites in these areas of greater stability and resource abundance is evident at this time (Hassan 1984b). In the Delta, at least, there would have been abundant land and resources to support the increased population, and the general adaptiveness of the domesticated species to such habitats suggests that the immigrants could easily have maintained their traditional lifestyle, or adopted a more settled pattern. Although there is at present no clear evidence for population pressure within the narrower Nile Valley, quality land for agriculture or grazing was comparatively more limited than in the Delta (see chapter two), and immigrants might not have been as readily absorbed by the existing population. According to the ethnographic models, mobile immigrants who attempt to maintain their traditional lifestyle under such conditions are likely to be marginalized, socially as well as geographically.

Additionally, as both populations and settlements increased, available land eventually had to be divided between agriculture and grazing (and fodder?). Van Lepp (1995) has proposed that examples of irrigation techniques (weirs, dikes, basins, and canals) are preserved in the decorations of some ceramic vessels dating between 4100 and 3600 B.C.. He postulates that the size of these irrigated fields were small, averaging approximately 3.30 hectares (8.15 acres; Van Lepp 1995:208). While these are interpreted as single-family plots, some representations indicated much larger

[12] In the lowest register on the reverse of the Narmer Palette, a bull is depicted destroying the brick walls of a settlement. This has been interpreted as the king conquering an enemy (Hoffman 1991:130).

holdings (e.g., 22.40 hectares or 55.33 acres; Van Lepp 1995:209).

Irrigation would have provided a variety of options for expanding the usable territory, and methods for flood control of the natural catchment basins have been postulated as strong stimuli for cooperative labor (Butzer 1976). With food production freeing members of society for other tasks, the structural arrangement of irrigated fields and the labor-intensive process of construction and maintenance indicate cooperation at the village level (and beyond?). The planning and organization necessary to execute such tasks is indicative of the developing society, and it is conceivable that peoples newly arrived from the desert regions might have been conscripted more easily since they lacked their own land.

The various qualities of land dictates that better quality land (i.e., naturally inundated but well-drained, see Table 3.1) would be the most highly prized, and therefore the most expensive (according to von Thünen and Central Place models, see chapter five). Brewer et al. (1994:15–16) contend that *access to* water was the crucial factor determining the quality—and thus value—of land. In contrast, Eyre (1994) argues that it was the *drainage of* water from land that determined its value. For example, whereas the term oAyt is interpreted by Brewer et al. to indicate land which requires irrigation, Eyre interprets it to denote land reached by an average inundation but which was high enough to drain satisfactorily. A similar discrepancy is seen with xrw which Brewer et al. suggest did not need irrigation. Eyre views this as land which could not be counted on to drain satisfactorily for grain crops. Brewer et al.'s interpretation may underrepresent the amount of land requiring irrigation and Eyre's may overestimate it. The difference between the two interpretations could be significant, when one considers labor input. It is not known at present whether irrigation/agricultural tasks were carried out by hand—as a large proportion of similar activities still are today in Egypt—or if domesticated animals were used. The nature of the data do not permit this question to be answered, but the ethnographic uses of animals certainly suggests that cattle would have been preferred for digging canals, and plowing, while small stock aided in threshing.

Less desirable lands would be cheaper, but also produce lower yields, require more investment such as irrigation, and/or be utilized for purposes better suited to the available drainage rather than products which obtain the highest prices. For example, areas free from full inundation, such as desert margins or an extended expanse of land higher than the surrounding floodplain within the Valley itself, might have been chosen as the site for an orchard or plantation, on which were raised luxury products such as olives and wine (Eyre 1994:59). These same lands are also best suited to grazing, and once again the possibility of conflict arises between animal husbandry and agricultural activities. The habitat preferences and requirements of the various taxa dictate that decreasing quality of land would be suited for raising cattle, pigs, sheep, and goats, respectively (chapter four). The comparatively slower growth, higher absolute food intake, etc., for larger species similarly denote higher costs of feeding and raising these animals, and the greater yields obtainable from them would also increase their price (or barter value). This idea is reflected in the few surviving prices for the various taxa (see Table 6.5).

Thus, although I repeatedly refer to a generalized "Valley" habitat, a complex mosaic of plots would actually have existed (chapter three), with each devoted to one or a few of the crops or animals for which the land was best suited. While the wealthiest Egyptians probably owned a variety of types of land producing a wide array of items, in a general sense this mosaic should also be reflected in the relative wealth or social status of the landowners. As a result, the bulk of the population, the peasantry *yʿḥty* or *yḥwty* would not have owned land, instead renting and working land owned by another for a share of the yield (Wente 1990:58–60, see leases discussed by Eyre 1994:60).

Table 6.5. Prices for Domesticated Animals During the 19th and 20th Dynasties (from Cerny 1954:907).

| Price Each | Source |
|---|---|
| YOUNG CATTLE: | |
| 30 deben | Ostrakon Breasted |
| CATTLE: | |
| 120 deben (copper) | Turin Papyrus No. 9754, Ostrakon BM 5649, Ostrakon Del el-Medina 113, Ostrakon Turin 9753 |
| 130 deben | Papyrus Chester Beatty |
| Ox Hide: | |
| 12 deben | Ostrakon Gardiner 36 |
| 15 deben | Ostrakon Berline 1268, Ostrakon Turin 9753, Ostrakon Cairo Cat. 258000, Ostrakon Edgerton 9, Ostrakon Deir el-Medina 113 |
| up to 20 deben | Ostrakon Petrie 48 |
| SMALL CATTLE: | |
| 40 deben[13] | Ostrakon Del el-Medina 113 |
| up to 1 deben | Ostrakon BM 5643 |
| up to 3 deben | Ostrakon Petrie 4, Ostrakon Aberdeen 1317, Ostrakon Der el-Medina 73 |
| Goat Hide: | |
| 2 deben | Ostrakon Petrie 48 |
| PIGS: | |
| 5 deben | Ostrakon Del el-Medina 113 |
| 7 deben | Ostrakon Berlin 12405 |

Leases were typically for one year, and the rate was not finalized until the prospects for the inundation (and thus eventual yield and profit) of the individual plot became clear (Eyre 1994:60, and references cited there). A Demotic land lease from Darb el Gerza (Philadelphia,

[13] This is the only recorded price not specifically for goats and is clearly more appropriate for young cattle. It is perhaps either an error in recording or in translation.

P.Bm 10560), however, is clearly marked as an eleven-month duration (Martin 1986:163). This lease is more important for the description of the tasks falling to the lessee for compliance with the agreement: the crops to be farmed were declared by the lessor, but the equipment (and obviously labor) was to be provided by the lessee. There is also tantalizing evidence from the New Kingdom and later that workmen loaned or rented their draft animals to others as a source of additional income (McDowell 1992) reinforcing that they were expensive and unaffordable by segments of the population. Information from other documentary sources concerning differences between social classes will be presented in more detail later.

Throughout Egypt during the Predynastic, increasing economic specialization, social differentiation and the elaboration of status markers has been documented. The available faunal data are somewhat limited, but similarly suggest a shift from the sharing of land and resources to private ownership, and to a much stronger reliance on domesticated food sources. Although this evidence is tentative, it further suggests that raising or eating cattle would have become prohibitively expensive to the average Egyptian. Alternative sources of milk and meat (and conceivably also hides and traction) would be required. These alternative sources might expectedly be found in heavier reliance on smaller, less social desirable taxa (including aquatic resources and pigs) by these lower social classes (see the heading: "*Dietary or Economic Differences Between Social Classes*" in the next chapter).

Considerably more work is necessary, however, particularly with regard to the distribution of meat. Whereas acephalous and/or egalitarian pastoral strategies were shown in the previous chapter to utilize meat only seasonally, and to share beyond the household level, pastoral strategies among ranked societies generally relied on aquatic sources for protein (stabilizing protein intake), and sharing of domesticated animal meat was restricted to households or performed within sacrificial/sacred contexts. Although the ethnographic data were not clear, it also seems likely that individuals of higher status would also claim preferential right to certain anatomical elements (the meat-bearing joints in particular). It is not possible from the currently accessible Egyptian evidence from these early periods to answer questions of differential access to domesticated animal resources by social classes.

# 7. FROM ARCHAEOLOGICAL DATA TO INTERPRETATION

## Introduction

Many researchers see the environment as a constraint on the development of complex polities dependent upon population growth. In this view, emerging elites act as brokers in a wider system designed to produce a surplus in one area to offset shortfalls in another; i.e., acting as redistributive agents to stabilize an inherently unstable resource base, while the conversion of surplus into tokens of social status stimulates further entrenchment of the elite roles within the society as a whole (Barker and Gamble 1985; Renfrew 1973, 1977; Renfrew and Shennan 1982:100, 106). Within such a system, the majority of the human population is dependent upon the aid of that society's beneficent leaders. An alternative view characterizes elites as exploiters of production to suit their own ends, "controlling a subject population by destabilizing local subsistence systems that are inherently self-sufficient" (Gamble 1981; Barker and Gamble 1985:17). Both views have been applied to Egypt and its cultural development, but what is of interest here are not elites' underlying intentions, but the visible effects of their decisions.

A multi-tiered economy is suggested by monumental architecture of the early Dynastic period and complex social stratification in the urban sector is abundantly evident from written records of the Old Kingdom (Baer 1960). According to Butzer, irrigation provided the economic resource base necessary for complex society of Old Kingdom, but the actual shift is one of scale (Butzer 1976:107). In other words, there was a shift to intensive exploitation and surpluses, but the base itself did not change.

An extended discussion of the complexities of either the religion or the redistributive economy characteristic of the Dynastic Periods is beyond the scope of the present research, but each is a visible mechanism of social control. For example, at least by the Archaic, a new leader justified his authority through association with the mythical figures in his home village (Trigger et al. 1983). The interrelationship between rulership and religion dictates that government control of resources reflected to some degree the deities emphasized or popularized by the reigning pharaoh. In theory at least, the accession of a new king might have required the establishment of new cults, and new temples at which to glorify those gods. In reality, however, succession usually passed peacefully within a family bloodline and little change in cult worship (although exceptions certainly occurred). Even when a break in succession resulted in changes in the *official* deities, the cults of previous rulers were not always discarded, and a new ruler often emphasized similarities to the previous pharaoh in order to justify his right to rule. The curation of more popular theologies served to entrench the prominence of the associated cult animals as well. However, with the exception of the Amarna Period, little effort was apparently made to prevent or abolish existing local traditions; inhabitants of each village continued to worship local gods but incorporated pieces of national religion as necessary. The proliferation of temples and estates—which enjoyed a tax-exempt status—placed an increasing burden on the redistributive economy for increasing volumes of goods and land for their maintenance.

Nome[1] capitals were most probably primarily rural in character, as they are still today, with fields, shops and mansions. Nome capitals were seats of political and religious power and as such served as centers for economic activity including manufacture, services and the distribution of goods (Hassan 1993:552). These capitals were the major centers for collecting annual taxes on cereals, cattle and other products (Helck 1974). They also controlled the rural labor force and mobilized them for local agricultural projects (e.g., building dikes) as well as military operations (O'Connor 1972b). Connected to the nation's capital via the Nile, regional capitals paid taxes (typically collected in kind [see Cerny 1954) by boat, and various goods were brought on the return.

Fundamental to understanding the redistributive economy, or the roles of domesticated animals within that system, is recognizing that ancient Egyptian transactions were "named according to the ultimate destination of the products" described as either *inw* or *b3kwt* in various preserved records (Bleiberg 1988:157). The term *inw* refers to products destined for the king's private use, and in all cases indicates the exchange of goods between two individuals. In contrast, *b3kwt* indicates exchange between groups of people (e.g., members of a particular profession or social class) and a geographical destination such as a temple. *B3kwt* was apparently used to furnish and repair temples, in divine offerings, or as rations/rewards for service (either military or corvée labor, but see Lorton [1974] for an alternative interpretation). This corresponds well to Janssen's (1979) interpretation of the redistributive economy: goods collected by temples were then transferred back to the populace for consumption. Payment of *b3kwt* by temples for services rendered would almost certainly have reinforced the beneficence of the associated gods.

If Bleiberg is correct in concluding that the Egyptian redistributive system "require[d] an Egyptian temple to administer it [*b3kwt*] for *local* distribution" (1988:165, emphasis added), interpreting zooarchaeological remains at sites across Egypt would require more emphasis on economics than ecology. That is, faunal remains would not necessarily reflect culling of local herds, as suggested

[1] "Nome" is a Greek term for the ancient Egyptian provinces. These administrative units changed throughout the Dynastic period. During New Kingdom times when they are perhaps best documented, there were approximately 18 nomes in Lower Egypt and 22 in Upper Egypt.

by four of the five pastoral strategies defined in chapter five. Rather, the presence of a species (or parts thereof) might be the result of redistribution of goods donated to a local temple from other areas. Redistribution of processed goods would typically be recognizable archaeologically in the ages, sexes or anatomical portions of the animal brought into the site (in the case of meat, probably emphasizing adult males, or skeletal elements which provide the greatest yield). Additionally, the range of species utilized might be narrower, because of regional or religious proscriptions against the consumption of certain taxa; a temple obviously could not distribute goods it did not receive. However, because *bꜣkwt* is apparently not profit-motivated, sites heavily subsidized through this mechanism may not fit the ranching model, which was expected to clarify economic and social relationships between regions during the Dynastic period.

Janssen (1982) demonstrated that even on an individual level, redistribution was a fundamental aspect of social interaction; the fact that the quality, quantity and origin of gifts were carefully recorded implies a reciprocal obligation. This trait is still common among many of the indigenous African populations from which the pastoral model was developed. Village-level redistribution of meat from highly-prized (but privately owned) large stock is socially mandated among several nomadic (e.g., Hobbs 1989; Nicholaisen 1963) and semi-nomadic pastoral groups (e.g., Dyson-Hudson and Dyson-Hudson 1969, 1970; Gulliver 1951). Members depend on such reciprocal obligations in order to survive lean years. Regrettably, Egyptian settlement data are rarely adequately detailed to reconstruct redistribution at the individual level, but this may be possible in the future. The present analysis necessarily stressed site-level and inter-regional economies.

## Development of Breeds

Although the subsistence bases of Upper and Lower Egypt were highly similar during the Predynastic, the cultures were noticeably different. Consequently, the co-evolution of human societies and domestic taxa should have followed divergent trajectories in each region. The first distinction is in differences of utilization of each species and the evolution of specialized breeds. Investigation of differences comprised the second set of research questions (see chapter one). Zooarchaeological techniques are somewhat ambiguous with regard to separating domesticated from wild animal remains (see Appendix A for more discussion). Reliable determination of subspecific variation (i.e., breeds) from osteological material is extremely rare, perhaps because the majority of traits selected for by humans (e.g., coat color or increased milk production) do not produce measurable skeletal effects or occur so gradually that they cannot be distinguished from variation within a population. For these reasons, the evidence for the evolution of breeds must be sought in other sources, primarily artistic depictions, but also written sources.

### • Cattle

Brewer et al. (1994:82–85) and Darby et al. (1977:85–169) provide thorough discussions of the types, names and dates of appearance of four morphological types of cattle in ancient Egypt. Both authors indicate the specialized uses of each, and only a brief summary is warranted here. See Table 7.1 for common terms relating to cattle. I contend that there may be three—rather than four—breeds, and that one is actually a discrete (sub?)species introduced later from outside Africa.

Table 7.1. A Variety of Terms Relating to Cattle (after Darby et al. 1977:table 2).

| Transliteration | Meaning |
|---|---|
| *mnmnt* | Cattle |
| *nfrt* | |
| *ḫtmw* | |
| *iht* | Cow |
| *idt* | |
| *ḥmt* | |
| *sꜣbt* | Dappled Cow |
| *bḥs* | |
| *ms* | |
| rny | |
| *tꜣy* | |
| *wšb* | Bull |
| *kꜣ* | |
| *iḥ* | |
| *id* | |
| *pry* | Ferocious Bull |
| *ngꜣw* | Long-horned Bull |
| *smꜣ* | Wild Bull |
| *mry* | Fighting Bull |
| *tpiw* | Ox |
| *iwꜣ* | |
| *skꜣ* | Plough Ox |
| *nḥbw* | Yoke Oxen |
| *tntt* | Sacred Cattle |
| *iryt* | |
| *mhit* | |
| *mnʿt* | |

The first morphological type of cattle is *ngꜣw*, described as "tall, lean, standing high on muscular haunches, with wide everted horns" (Darby et al. 1977:93). It may be a descendent of the (native African?) wild bovid, *Bos primigenius*. Bulls of this type are depicted fighting, jumping or struggling against lassos (but significantly, never in stalls). These same animals also exhibit more tame behavior such as plowing (see Figure 7.1). Cows are depicted calving or milking (see Figure 7.2). Dieties such as Hathor and Apis are attributed to this variety.

The second morphological type recognized by Darby et al. (1977) is the *iwꜣ*, but it is not likely a separate breed. Bulls of this type were specially fattened for sacrifice. They stood "exceedingly low on their haunches, with pendulous bellies and wide everted horns that were often artificially twisted asymmetrically or removed during their youth" (Darby et al. 1977:98). These animals are typically restricted standing in stalls and being hand-fed (see Figure 7.3). As Brewer et al. (1994:84–85) noted, the excessive weight and extremely inactive lifestyle would have rendered these stall-fed animals "muscularly weak," and their hooves to be "overgrown and turned upward." Because females were not depicted, some have contended that the animals were imported from the south. However, it seems unnecessarily complicated to import animals from great distances when locally-or regionally-available cattle could acquire the same traits with quality fodder and inactivity. A more parsimonious explanation is that particularly fine specimens of Egyptian cattle were selected for sacrifice during annual tax censuses.

A three-dimensional model from a Middle Kingdom Theban tomb has four obese cattle in fattening stalls (Gilbert 1988). Two animals are force-fed by attendants; Winlock identified the fodder not unexpectedly as grain and straw (1955:22). Papyrus Harris only mentions bulls in fattening stalls (see Breasted 1906[IV]:145, 164), and that such bulls had been "purified from every evil in their fields" (Breasted 1906[IV]:149), indicating that hand-feeding was a change from an earlier diet. Altering diet a few weeks before slaughter improves the taste and texture of meat from free-range animals (chapter four). All four animals in the model lack genitalia, suggesting they had been castrated.[2]

In addition, Gilbert (1988) draws the conclusion that the additional expense of a soft wooden door sill was worth preventing sore-footedness in these special animals, because such pain frequently seriously affects eating and/or mating behaviors. A large-scale ranching operation of such animals (e.g., at Kom el-Hisn) is unlikely given the astronomical amounts of human labor required to hand-feed and maintain them for the approximately three years needed to obtain their mature stature. Rather, it is much more likely that the most promising specimens from ranching or private herds were selected, perhaps by priests (as Herodotus described, see also Brewer et al. 1994:84), then moved within proximity

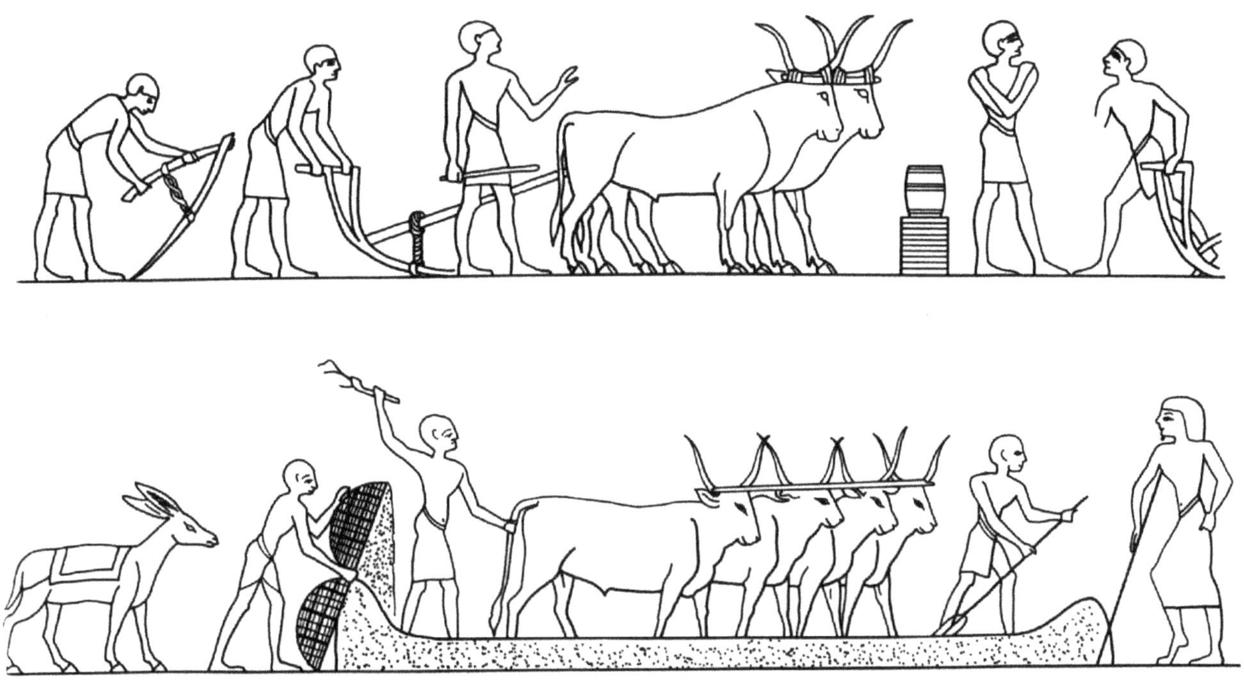

Figure 7.1 Examples of the *ngꜣw* Cattle in the Service of Humans.

[2] Castration is usually accomplished by damaging—not removing—the testes (see chapter five).

Figure 7.2 An Example of the Care Given to *ngꜣw* Cattle.

Figure 7.3. The Second Morphological Type of Egyptian Cattle and Their Stalls.

of their eventual slaughter, and fattened in smaller groups. This hypothesis accounts for the lack of *iwꜣ* cows, and more closely approximates strategies from modern pastoral groups.

The next type of cattle is a short-horned variety known as *wnḏw* which replaces the short-horned variety as most commonly represented during and following the New Kingdom (see Figure 7.4). Smith (1969) offered literary evidence that *wnḏw* were imported from Syria (1977:98), and based on similar morphological changes among central and eastern European bovids, (1994:84) noted that the shortening of horns may be "the evolutionary product of human control and the accompanying move from desert steppe to the Nile Valley and Delta." Thus, the *wnḏw* may be a true breed, or merely represent the long-term effects of the shift orchestrated by humans from the southwest Asian steppe to cooler and wetter Egyptian habitats. These cattle appear in similar situations as the *ngꜣw* bulls and cows, so even if *wnḏw* were deliberately developed by the ancient Egyptians, it does not appear to have been for a new purpose, but rather a modification of the existing form (perhaps merely to reduce the size of the dangerous horns).

Figure 7.4. An Example of the Short-horned *wnḏw* Cattle.

Figure 7.5. A Depiction of the Hornless *hredᶜebᶜ* Cattle.

The fourth variety recognized by Darby et al. (1977) and the third by Brewer et al. (1994) is the hornless type (*hredᶜebᶜ*), which appeared at least by the Old Kingdom. Described as 'fancy' cattle, these animals were never utilized for traction, and were sometimes depicted with bells or necklaces by peasants (see Figure 7.5). Ruffer (1919) suggested that these specimens were merely polled and do not represent a legitimate breed. This seems more likely than a special breed of an expensive animal merely for peasants' amusement. Rather, I would suggest that these animals represent prizes awarded to peasants during various festivals and/or contests (see Wilkinson 1988[1854]) which could then be sold or added to an existing herd. At some point in the future, zooarchaeological investigation of crania[3] may perhaps explain the absence of horns.

The final variety, the Zebu, represents a distinct species rather than merely a breed (see Figure 7.6). Appearing during the New Kingdom, *Bos indicus* was introduced from the Near East, perhaps across the Horn of Africa. Morphologically, it can be distinguished in artistic scenes by the large 'hump' on the back of the neck. This is visible archaeologically in a different skull shape and in the bifurcation of the neural spine of (several) thoracic vertebrae (Clutton-Brock 1993:67). This variety would have been attractive economically because its much higher tolerance for heat means it requires less watering, and it is also largely immune to diseases borne by the tsetse fly, perhaps allowing expansion into new areas previously unsuitable for cattle husbandry.

Figure 7.6. Zebu Cattle.

How far back can the cattle cult be traced? *Perhaps* as far back as the Narmer Palette, by which time the bull is already closely associated with kingship (Vandier 1952:592–599). Bullfights are described in Pyramid and Coffin Texts, and tomb scenes (see Figure 7.7) were common during the Greco-Roman period. They have been attributed to scenes of daily life because they are found in proximity to review scenes, herdsmen are often present, and in some scenes the victorious bull is permitted to mate. Galán interprets them as a means of describing the struggle to maintain social position in the Netherworld (1994:92–93). Perhaps more reliable evidence is in the similarity between certain anatomical elements and Egyptian hieroglyphs. Bovine thoracic vertebrae resemble the ankh sign (☥). The last three lumbar vertebrae together with the sacrum exhibit remarkable similarity to the *djed* sign ( 𓊽 ). These two symbols form part of the representation for the royal staff or scepter (*wꜣs*) in use by the First Dynasty. These similarities, in connection with an *Egyptian* understanding of the male reproductive

[3] When the horn sheath and underlying bony core are removed from beef cattle between two and five months old, very little scar tissue forms and hair quickly covers the wound (Beattie 1980). Horns removed from older animals, or if the bud is improperly removed, produce a distinctive scar and are much more likely to become infected. Animals which are hornless from birth lack the horn bud altogether.

system,[4] seem to have led to the association between the staff and a bull's penis (Schwabe 1978; Gordon and Schwabe 1995; Schwabe et al. 1982).

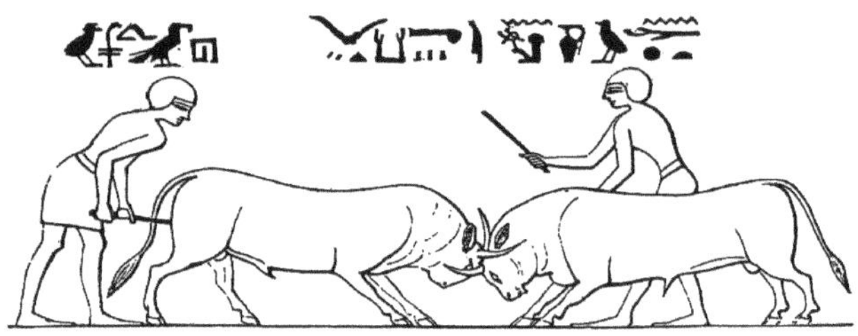

Figure 7.7. An Example of a Bullfight.

The association between the bull's spine, its penis and reproduction may have been based on an erroneous conclusion, but without dissecting the human reproductive system, Egyptians would have been unaware of their error. Thus, the parallel between the penis as a conduit for semen and the scepter as a conduit for royal power makes logical sense. These data are intriguing but hardly incontrovertible, so extending cattle cults farther into the past is hazardous. Darby et al. (1977) hypothesized that the wide fertile plain of the Delta would have been the ideal location for cattle to have become objects of worship, but both the use of the horns to mark graves at Halfan sites and the abundant images of cattle in desert rock art to the importance of the species in marginal areas much earlier. Granted, such uses do not necessarily indicate formal worship, but do indicate that the species was accorded special value.

### ♦ Sheep and Goats

Despite the long and detailed history of cattle husbandry in Egypt, comparatively less is known about breeds of sheep and goats. In contrast to the early appearance of special purposes for cattle in the deserts, and possibly the Delta, the habitat tolerances of sheep and goats would have rendered them preferred species in the Valley. Surprisingly, there are few words for either species (see Table 7.2), nor apparently as many depictions as there are of cattle. If the modern pastoral populations are any indication, however, the preeminence of cattle in social production belies the importance of the greater numbers of smaller taxa; the same is likely true for ancient Egypt as well. Since the majority of surviving documents and artistic depictions are attributed to members of the upper social ranks, the paucity of information concerning sheep and goats may indicate these species were utilized primarily by middle or lower social classes.

Table 7.2. A Variety of Terms Relating to Small Cattle[5] (after Darby et al. 1977:211) and Pigs (from Dawson 1928:600).

| | | |
|---|---|---|
|  | *iwt* | Small Cattle |
|  | *rri* | Pig |
|  | *šꜣi* | |

Two breeds of sheep are currently recognized, although from the available evidence it appears that during the Middle Kingdom the woolly breed rapidly replaced the earlier hairy type. A single breed of goats was utilized (see Figure 7.8), although it evolved over time from having scimitar-shaped to 'corkscrew'-shaped horns (Brewer et al. 1994:93).

Figure 7.8. Typical Activities of Egyptian Goats.

7.9. A Statue Indicating the Characteristics of Egyptian Sheep.

Slate palettes in the shape of sheep are known from the Gerzean II period (ca 3300–3100 B.C.), depicting smooth 'hair' coats, short erect ears, long tails, and either 'normal" or corkscrew horns (Ryder 1983:105). During

[4] In bulls, the penis is attached to the vertebral column by two retractor muscles. To Egyptians, the spinal cord was considered a bone, and since bones were the source of semen, semen created the white parts of a fetus including its bones. The symbols are interpreted by Gordon and Schwabe (1995:fn25) as an orthographic representation of the bull's generative system as the source of his power of life, stability and dominion. A dried bull's penis may be used as a staff of power, in the same way that carved wooden staffs are utilized among modern Nilotic pastoralists.

[5] The abundance of pig remains and the occasional use of the hieroglyphic sign for pig as a determinative after 'small cattle' suggests it may also refer to pigs. Several modern populations include pigs in the term (e.g., Spanish ranchers [Jordan 1993:29]). The assumption that pigs were unimportant in Egypt may have led to this erroneous exclusion.

the whole of the Early Dynastic period (3100–2613 B.C.), however, the only sheep depicted were of the corkscrew-horned type (see Figure 7.9), although with lop ears (Zeuner 1963). Coat color ranged from white to black, and included pie-balds. Until the Middle Kingdom, sheep were of a hairy, thin-tailed breed, and despite excellent preservation conditions, woolen textiles are scarce. This led Ryder to suggest that neither sheep nor goats were utilized primarily for that purpose (1964, 1969). Similarly, Brewer et al. (1994: 93) noted that Egyptian tomb illustrations depict only short-haired goat varieties that could not have supplied much wool, and proposed that they were kept primarily for meat or hides. Wilkinson noted that a district in Thebes was exclusively appropriated to leather cutters and indicated that the skins were predominantly of smaller taxa (1988[1854]:II:102). Hides were also used for parchment before the widespread use of papyrus; the taxon involved has not yet been determined. Wilkinson concluded that hides may have been imported as tribute payments (1988[1854]:II:104–105), but these were largely exotic taxa such as leopard, used for fancy costumes.

Even by the late third millennium B.C., sheep were woollier and exhibited year-round growth rather than a spring moult (Ryder 1964, 1969). By the Middle Kingdom (1991–1633 B.C.), fat-tailed sheep appear in artistic depictions (Lortet and Gaillard 1907; Ryder 1983; Zeuner 1963). Scented fats had become a luxury burial item at least by the Predynastic, and there are numerous depictions during the Dynastic period of Egyptians wearing cakes on their heads at various functions (Figure 7.10). With the explosion in class distinctions between the Predynastic and Dynastic periods, the perceived need for scented fats as a marker of that status would have required a similar increase in the source of the fat. While the fat base has not been determined, the common use of ox-grease in medicinal compounds would suggest that the fat used in scents was from another species—perhaps the fat-tailed sheep. The changes toward woolier and fatter-tailed sheep suggest selective breeding.

Figure 7.10. Party Participants Wearing Cakes of Scented Animal Fat (after Wilkinson 1988[1854]:I:143).

According to H. Smith (1969), sheep and goats were kept as cult objects in addition to subsistence purposes, but were not specially fattened for sacrifice. Detailed descriptions of the fattening and slaughter of cattle for meat and/or sacrifice are known, but at least two authors state that there is as yet no documentary evidence of eating meat from goats, sheep, or pigs (Montet 1958; Gilbert 1988). Despite this, the ram was worshipped at several sites; not surprisingly most are in Upper Egypt. The goat was apparently not the object of formal worship, unless it was confused or deliberately chosen to replace the ram at some sites (e.g., Mendes) during the Greco-Roman period (see Darby et al. 1977:222–223). Large numbers of "small cattle" recorded as tax or tribute (e.g., Harris Papyrus [see Breasted 1906(IV)]) attest to the economic (i.e., non-ritual) values of sheep and goats. These discrepancies suggest that accepted beliefs about the roles played by sheep and goat need to be reexamined.

### • Pigs

Despite the archaeological evidence of domesticated pigs by the Predynastic in areas of natural resource abundance, pigs (*rerr*) are rare in depictions and documents. They are absent from Dynastic hunting scenes, but wild[6] suids appear in Middle Kingdom marsh scenes at Beni Hassan. (Newberry 1928). No depictions are even suggestive of multiple breeds. The relative paucity of pig depictions may be due, in part, to misidentifications. For example, Old Kingdom depictions of Seth resemble semi-feral/feral swine worldwide: the upright, rigid tail is typical of modern pigs when angered and all young suids show the longitudinal stripes of light/dark color along the body of the Egyptian cult animal. Seth is identified as a hippopotamus at the temple of Edfu (237–257 B.C., see Newberry 1928; Darby et al. 1977:179–180). The association of Seth with evil has encouraged interpretations that pigs held low value or was even abhorred (see the heading: "*Dietary or Economic Differences Between Social Classes*" below).

Ruffer (1919:21) states that pig-shaped cosmetic palettes are proof that swine were not *universally* abhorred (emphasis added). Further, pig parts are used in medicinal compounds, suggesting that the animals could be obtained when necessary (see Darby et al. 1977:189–190). Although strict adherence to Horian and Osirian beliefs would not have allowed such uses of pigs, followers of Seth would have readily accepted them. One must keep in mind that a "basic feature of Egyptian thought was the acceptance of local deities not... worshipped elsewhere in the land" (Darby et al. 1977:195). This concept of local or regional customs contrary to the state religion is essential for interpreting the often seemingly conflicting archaeological and Egyptological data. First it is necessary to examine the available faunal evidence for regional strategies during the Dynastic Period.

[6] Wild pigs were hunted in the Fayum during Roman times and survived in the Delta and Fayum until the late 1800s (Brewer et al 1994:94).

## Continuing Nomadic Strategies in the Deserts and Oases: Insufficient Evidence

Population densities in desert areas were expected to be low based on the model defined in chapter five. These populations, characterized by highly mobile herders of drought- and heat-tolerant animals, left behind a minimum of archaeological remains. Even with only a few published analyses to consider, this was the pattern at least throughout the late Predynastic. Statements that climatic worsening at the end of the Predynastic encouraged (or even forced) nomadic pastoralists to concentrate in the Valley and Delta has contributed to the general perception that the deserts and oases were virtually unoccupied throughout the Dynastic period. But were the desert regions abandoned following the unification? The presence of considerable numbers of Bedouin in these areas today under comparable climatic conditions as well as a few scattered surviving documentary mentions by the ancient Egyptians themselves shows this perception is incorrect.

The view of desert populations as 'foreigners' or simply unworthy of consideration as part of 'civilized' society (Redford 1986; Posener 1956; Kees 1961) certainly implies the area was not completely devoid of inhabitants but that they occupied only a marginal position in Dynastic Egyptian society. For this reason and in interests of maintaining clarity between bedouin populations and governmentally sponsored activities in the deserts, "Egyptian" in the discussion below is used in an artificially restricted sense and excludes bedouin.

Desert dwellers—or *Medja*—from the Red Sea Hills were sufficiently identifiable to warrant invitation by the Middle Kingdom court at Thebes, although the same sources[7] also indicate that *Medja* were subjected to surveillance and aggression (see Trigger et al. 1983:121–122). There is also some indication that nomarchs of Middle Egypt, bearing the title "Administrator for the Eastern Desert" employed *Medja* as a form of regional police (Kees 1961), indicating not only the importance of the area to the Egyptians but also of a perceived threat to travel through or activities in the area.

Hieroglyphic inscriptions found throughout the Eastern Desert demonstrate that both Egyptian and indigenous desert laborers were employed by expeditions at least by the Old Kingdom (Rothe et al. 1996). While many inscriptions bear the titles and names of those in charge of work gangs and expeditions, two document improvements to wells or the digging of new ones (Rothe et al. 1996:91, 97–98).

In the Western Desert at the metropolis of Wadi el-Natrûn, the capture by King Amenophis III of 96 wild bulls from a herd of 170 was recorded on a series of scarabs (Ritner 1986). Even accepting the odds of exaggeration, the original herd must have been considerably larger to include so many bulls. If conditions were sufficient for wild cattle, it is also likely that herds of domesticated cattle (and presumably other taxa) were raised in the environs. In fact, these 'wild bulls' may have been part of a domesticated open-range herd which had returned to a feral state through lack of control over breeding. To the south, Farafra Oasis was known as "Cattle Country" at least by the Middle Kingdom, although "small cattle" and pigs were also raised there (Lichtheim 1973:170, 182; Kees 1961:131). As during the Predynastic, these herders appear to have been bedouin rather than transplanted Egyptians. Small groups of nomadic pastoralists are recorded in both the Western and Eastern Deserts throughout the Dynastic Period, but the Valley and Delta Egyptians considered them relatively unimportant or backward marauding tribes. To date, little archaeological work has been conducted in the deserts for the Dynastic Period and the nature of the exploitation of these areas by indigenous inhabitants remains essentially unknown at present.

Unfortunately, the extremely limited investigations into Dynastic Period desert occupations have concentrated primarily on mining and quarrying of raw materials for monuments and funerary equipment. Considerable effort has been expended among Egyptologists to determine the locations of various mines and quarries from remaining papyri or other sources. Shaw's recent work concerning the size and degree of governmental control at settlements associated with expeditions from Old Kingdom through the Greco-Roman Periods (1994:108) highlights important factors regarding uses of domesticates in such contexts.

A key consideration raised by Shaw is that the vast majority of quarrying expeditions would have been sponsored by particular temples or the government itself,[8] and so cannot be expected to conform to the model for the desert habitat. Nonetheless, such sites are critical for understanding the mechanisms underlying animal management during the Dynastic Period. The permanence of a quarrying settlement reflects the perceived value of mining a specific substance at that location, and the duration of exploitation should affect the faunal component. A short-term occupation resulting from a preliminary mining survey would allow reliance on storable provisions such as dried or cured meats, in much the same way that staging posts were provisioned in southern Canaan (see Redford 1986:142). The faunal assemblage at such sites would be dominated by anatomical elements from high meat–yield animals not necessarily well adapted to local conditions. Thus remains recovered from provisioned sites should indicate governmentally controlled (or at least socially accepted) species. In contrast, long-term expeditions would also be

[7] For example, the Papyrus Bulaq 18 and the Execration Texts.

[8] Several excursions and requests for desert goods are recorded in private letters (e.g., Wente 1990:38). These most likely refer to travel through the region to obtain particular items. Private mining expeditions are unlikely.

provisioned, but contact with Bedouin raises the probability of trade/exchange for local species well adapted to the area. Additionally, a small contingent may develop that locally raises such animals; these may or may not be governmentally sanctioned. Despite documentary evidence for long-term and intensive use of mines and quarries throughout the Dynastic Period, associated settlements have been subjected to little archaeological attention over the last century and illustrate a sizable gap in the accumulated data.

## Where Ranching Prevailed: The Delta

Whereas the delta region had previously been considered by scholars as an uninhabitable swamp and thus unimportant to Egyptian cultural development (Baumgartel 1947; Arkell and Ucko 1965:162–165), new studies suggest that the region was densely populated and highly productive economically at least by the Old Kingdom (Butzer 1976; Brewer et al. 1994; van den Brink 1988; Kroeper 1989; Wenke and Brewer 1996; Wenke 1991). Murnane suggests that even when fully developed, the delta "remained a land of gardens and vineyards, with cattle-grazing a main occupation in several areas," that during the Old Kingdom only two-thirds of the region was occupied, and that "judging by the number of estates from land devoted to mortuary cults of high officials, virgin territory was freely available" (1983:19). Wenke and Brewer (in press) have also suggested that the Delta may have functioned as an economic reserve due to its greater environmental stability compared to the Valley proper. Any one of the four core domesticated species would prosper in the fertile Delta, and the relative abundances are expected to fluctuate based on human social needs rather than merely perceptions of the most effective or stable economic strategy, as was apparently the case in the deserts.

"Only a few comparatively well preserved but functionally rather specialized settlements have so far been excavated, although there is still considerable scope for settlement archaeology in Egypt in spite of the difficulties" (O'Connor 1972b:79). The tendency to situate villages in close proximity to the inundation often resulted in their "obliteration by violent floods…[and] the siltation of the floodplain since the Old Kingdom is likely to have covered many older settlements with a thick layer of mud" (Hassan 1993:559; similarly Brewer and Wenke 1992:191). And, lateral shifts in the position of the channel of the Nile had an impact on the preservation of many settlements (Butzer 1976). Located a few kilometers south of modern Cairo, the site of Memphis is perhaps the best documented example (Michael Jones, 1995 personal communication).

### *The Sites and Faunal Data*

There are still few sites with large identified and published faunal samples with which to fully test the model. Material from three sites from two different time periods were chosen for the present analysis in order to alleviate concerns of the representativeness or appropriateness of generalizing from a single assemblage. Faunal data from Tell Ibrahim Awad, Mendes and Kom el-Hisn are summarized in Table 7.3.

Tell Ibrahim Awad and Mendes are both of Archaic date, and Kom el-Hisn dates somewhat later, during the Old Kingdom. Tell Ibrahim Awad is useful for illuminating the roles of animals in rural delta settlements. Mendes was a provincial capital and located in closer proximity to a major Nile distributary, allowing greater access to and/or influence by other areas than perhaps occurred at Tell Ibrahim Awad.

Kom el-Hisn provides important insight into governmental control and the intensive exploitation of both the geographic potential of the Delta and the taxa best suited to survival there. Future work with new datasets will only help to more fully test or to refine the model proposed here.

#### • Tell Ibrahim Awad

Faunal remains were recovered from both settlement and burial contexts, although the published data were combined. Boessneck and von den Driesch (1988:117–118) noted, however, that cattle bones were predominantly found amidst human remains, while pigs were nearly absent from this context. They may represent the remains of feasting or provision of food to the dead. That bovid remains are the preferred taxon *may* indicate a cultural preference for the species in this context, but it is premature to make a definitive statement based on the available evidence.

Table 7.3. Relative Abundances of Various Taxa Recovered from Selected Dynastic Delta Sites.

| | Tell Ibrahim[9] | Mendes[10] | Kom el-Hisn[11] |
|---|---|---|---|
| Mammals: | | | |
| *Bos* | 24.3% | 12.2% | 1.3% |
| *Ovis* | 4.2 | - | - |
| *Capra* | 0.3 | - | - |
| *Ovis/Capra* | 2.2 | 10.8 | 27.9 |
| *Sus* | 35.9 | 35.5 | 35.6 |
| *Alcelaphus bucalephus* | 1.3 | - | 1.4 |
| Hippopotamus | 4.5 | 0.3 | - |
| Donkey | 3.2 | - | 3.7 |
| other | 0.3 | 1.0 | 1.1 |
| Fishes: | | | |
| Catfishes[12] | 16.0 | 24.7 | 0.5 |
| *Synodontis* | 1.0 | 10.8 | 7.4 |
| *Lates* | 3.2 | 0.3 | - |
| other | 3.8 | 4.2 | 21.1 |

[9] Boessneck and von den Driesch 1986:Tables 1,2.

[10] Combined from data in Brewer and Wenke 1991:Table 1, Yokell n.d.a.

[11] Wenke et al. 1988:Table 2.

[12] The genera *Clarias* and *Heterobranchus*, which can be difficult to distinguish osteologically.

Although raw data were not published, the authors noted that the majority of pigs were slaughtered at about one year of age and a few females lived well into adulthood; cattle remains were of young or subadult animals (Boessneck and von den Driesch 1988:119). These distributions are consistent with meat-based husbandry practices. The few measurements possible on the highly fragmented remains suggest that the cattle were a large, long-horned variety, perhaps representing incipient domestication. On the basis of horn shape and strength, the few sheep remains were attributed to adult female specimens of the 'hairy' breed (see heading: "*Development of Breeds*"), suggesting an interpretation of a milk-based strategy, although samples sizes were insufficient to reconstruct age or sex profiles for sheep or goats.

Remains of fish, hartebeest (*Alcelaphus bucelaphus*), hippopotamus, and a few migratory birds indicate a minimal reliance on locally available resources. Boessneck and von den Driesch (1976, 1988) cite similar patterns of taxonomic abundance for nearby Tell el Dab'a and the west delta site of Buto (Tell el-Fara'on). Thus, zooarchaeological analysis of remains from these sites confirm that the shift begun during the Predynastic—away from wild resources and toward domesticated ones—was continuing.

### ♦ Mendes

For much of its long history, this eastern delta site served as a district capital and from epigraphic evidence was associated with the ram god, "Great Spirit, Master of Ḏdt" (*B3 ng ḏdt*). Excavations were designed to shed light on the nature of provincial life during the crucial developmental period leading into the first Dynastic cycle (Wenke and Brewer 1991:4), principally through analyses of ceramic styles and fabrics. Evidence of trade or contact with southwestern Asia was revealed, but the extent is not presently known.

The initial faunal sample was inadequate for reliable statistical analysis and subsequent excavations revealed a slightly different pattern (see Table 7.3; Brewer and Wenke 1992; Yokell n.d.a). The assemblage is dominated by fishes, which is not surprising considering the proximity of the site to a major Nile distributary. While pigs dominate among the mammalian remains in both samples, the margin is considerably narrower in the larger sample size. The greater abundance of pigs reiterates a sedentary component as described for earlier Delta settlements. However, hunted wild mammal species were not identified at Mendes, indicating a shift to a much narrower subsistence base. From the combined sample, only eight specimens were from subadult mammals and it is not possible to reconstruct age profiles for any of these species. However, the paucity of immature specimens indicates that all taxa were utilized most heavily after achieving maximum body size. Excepting the abundance of fish remains, the overall pattern is highly similar to that from Tell Ibrahim Awad and suggests that the species were being utilized primarily for meat.

### ♦ Kom el-Hisn

This large rural west Delta community has been postulated to have served as a cattle breeding center during the Old Kingdom (Redding 1992; Wenke et al. 1988; Moens and Wetterstrom 1988). The excavated structures and artifacts indicate that the site was occupied primarily between ca. 2500–2100 B.C. (corresponding to the 5th and 6th dynasties, see Table 1.1). The flora and fauna from three seasons of excavation in residential areas have been intensely studied. The pattern of the faunal remains is initially misleading in comparison with the previous two samples; extremely few bovid bones were recovered and sheep/goat and pigs were found in nearly equal numbers (see Table 7.3; Redding 1992:101). The rarity of cattle remains suggests that the species was unimportant economically. However, the floral and epigraphic evidence allow quite convincing recreations of the site not only as a pastoral area emphasizing cattle-raising, but one involving transport of animals off-site for consumption elsewhere. For example, Kom el-Hisn was the provincial capital of the Third Nome of Lower Egypt, a district that included the "Estate of the Cattle" (Helck 1974). The principal deity of worship was the cow goddess Hathor, and a derivitive form of Hathor known as Sekhat-Hor, the protectress of cattle, was also worshipped here (Redding 1992). Additionally, the bulk of floral remains recovered were typical of the burning of duncakes in domestic cooking, and many other floral remains are of plants commonly used as fodder (Moens and Wetterstrom 1988; Wenke et al. 19988:19). Evidence of sheep/goat dung (*ḥyr*) was rare, and because such pellets are commonly preserved, their absence supports the inference that cattle dung was the primarily fuel (Moens and Wetterstrom 1988). While not inconclusive, these titles and floral evidence certainly suggest that cattle played an important role at the site.

I agree with Redding (1984b, 1992) that sheep/goat remains are evidence of small supplemental herds for milk products. The sex and age distributions of these species are typical of milking strategies: predominantly female, with the majority of males culled between one and two years of age (see chapter four). Nor is the frequency of pigs unexpected when one considers that they can be raised on grains which have passed through the bovid digestive tract. This is especially important at sites such as Kom el-Hisn where abundant cattle did not contribute much meat to the local inhabitants' diet; pigs were needed as a protein source. These patterns are typical of expectations for ranching systems outlined in chapter five. In light of the ethnographic evidence for nomadic pastoralists exchanging dung and other goods for use of pastureland, and documentary evidence of contact between such groups and delta inhabitants throughout Egypt's long history, these remains *may* be either seasonal camps by desert populations or of payment in the form of animals for access to post-harvest stubble. The pig to ovicaprid ratio suggests permanent herds were more likely.

I disagree with Moens and Wetterstrom (1988), however, that bovids at Kom el-Hisn were ritual *iwꜣ* cattle, kept in pens and fattened on high quality fodder before being transported elsewhere for sacrifice. Recovery of bones of cattle less than two years of age argues against the use of Kom el-Hisn as a "feeder" ranch—which would include only adults (and mostly males). It is much more likely that the majority of cattle at Kom el-Hisn were beef cattle, raised for slaughter and redistribution/ consumption, not sacrifice (see the heading below: "Development of Breeds").

## Where Farming Strategies Prevailed: The Valley

The comparatively circumscribed habitat in the Nile Valley would have resulted in more intense competition between land for agriculture and for fodder/grazing than in the Delta, and thus greater effects of social production on species abundance are expected. This southern area would have been better suited to the husbandry of the smaller taxa, which (as indicated by the habitat preferences and relative productivity of the various species in chapter four), require less room, less water, lower quality forage, rebound more quickly from unpredictable environmental stress, and still provide humans with meat and secondary products. And contrary to popular belief, Upper Egypt was nearly ideally suited to raising pigs.

### *The Sites and Faunal Data*

Considerably more excavations have been undertaken in this southern region and sites of earlier periods are more readily accessible than in the Delta. However, the majority of effort focused at temples and tombs while only limited work has been directed toward settlements, and still fewer have published fauna. Thus it is necessary to distinguish sacred contexts from settlement data in the following presentation.

Perhaps the best known faunal assemblage from a Dynastic Period settlement in Upper Egypt is Tell el-Amarna. Supplemental information is included from a similar context at Giza. These assemblages are in marked contrast to faunal remains from offering temples and tomb scenes such as those from Memphis and Elephantine. The data are summarized by site in Table 7.4. As with the desert and Delta discussions, further research will only improve the strength of the interpretations offered here.

#### Tell el-Amarna

The "workmen's village" at Tell el-Amarna has received considerable attention in terms of excavations by archaeologists, analyses by faunal specialists, and Egyptologists' examination of related documents (Hecker 1982, 1984; Kemp 1984–1987; McDowell 1992). It is one of the few Upper Egyptian settlement sites and faunal assemblages with sufficient data for the present investigation (see Table 7.4).

Animal pens were identified throughout all phases of occupation. Analysis of goat coprolites indicates that they subsisted only on grasses, perhaps suggesting that they were provided with silage or fodder (see chapter four), and human waste[13] identified within the animal pens has been used to support the idea that pigs were raised in some numbers. The excavator contends that pig-raising was illogical given their ecological requirements and low prices (Kemp 1984). However, as demonstated previously, pigs were well adapted to habitats available in the Nile Valley. As individual households and groups of households raised pigs which recycled organic waste, they were rewarded with resources (dung[14] and meat) that could be exchanged for commodities available to others with greater access to fields, markets and river banks where other commodities would be in greater supply than those of the tomb workers. Deir el Medina records to which Kemp refers indicate that pigs were sold cheaply, but it should be noted that they obtained a higher price than sheep or goats (see Table 6.1). At least two of the five prices involving pigs concern their exchange for coffins or for coffin decorations (Janssen 1975; Valbelle 1985). Because coffins and related items would have been needed at short notice, pigs represented a low investment source of income which could be liquidated quickly (Miller 1990:132). Thus, the faunal complement of the workmen's village at Tell el-Amarna apparently represents both an adaptive response to the regional environment by humans and a mechanism for overcoming the limitations of governmental provisioning.

#### Giza

Mark Lehner's recent work at a workmen's village near Giza provides further insight into site provisioning, as suggested by both Tell el-Amarna and Kom el-Hisn. The worker's area is adjacent to a large complex apparently of the 4th dynasty royal institutions, including storage buildings, campsites and bakeries (AERA 1996:5,8). While bread- and beer-making activities have been excavated in close proximity and appear in Old Kingdom tomb scenes as closely connected endeavors, "the recovery of fish fins, gills and cranial fragments were unexpected in this context" (AERA 1996:5). Neither

[13] Eggs resembling parasitic *Taenia* spp. worms were found in human fæces deposited in the pens (Donald 1984:56–7). The eggs are produced by the adult worm living in humans, while the immature larvae inhabit pigs.

[14] Cruz-Uribe infers from Papyrus Louvre that the desired price of dung is "so low that it would not warrant a legal suit to get payment" (1985:130). That unknown amount may have been substantial to the lower social classes. A 19th Dynasty letter describes the exchange of four ass-loads of dung (Wente 1990:161). While these examples are rare, they reinforce the contention made here that dung was an important economic resource.

quantities nor taxonomic identifications have yet been published. However, laborers were often paid in allottments of fish (Janssen 1975) as well as bread (see Wetterstrom and Moens 1993), and large-scale processing centers would have been necessary considering the large corvée workforce. Fish are precisely the type of remains which should be expected in close proximity to a large bakery.

Presented only in summary form, the mammalian faunal data further support the idea of governmental provisioning at Giza. The assemblage is dominated by remains of cattle less than two years old followed by young adult sheep, a few goats and only rarely, pigs (Redding 1992). Redding interprets the abundance of bovid remains as evidence of governmental provisioning, but does not provide details of the elements recovered. Had he done so, it might have been possible to compare them to 'cuts' of meat represented in a model slaughterhouse found in Meketre's tomb, also discussed by Gilbert (1988) and shown in Figure 7.11. Because the three-dimensional models were included in a tomb, they represent nourishment of the soul in the afterlife, but they also reflect to some degree aspects of actual beef cattle husbandry as were conducted on the estate of tomb owner during his lifetime (Gilbert 1988).

Figure 7.11. Tomb Scene of Slaughter and Subsequent Processing of Cattle into Standardized Portions (after Wilkinson 1988[1854]:I:171,175).

Table 7.4. Relative Abundances of Various Taxa Identified from Selected Upper Egyptian Sites.

| | Tell el-Amarna[15] | Giza[16] | Memphis[17] New Kingdom | Memphis[17] Greco-Roman | Elephantine[18] |
|---|---|---|---|---|---|
| Mammals: | | | | | |
| *Bos* | 16.5% | 44.6% | 42.0% | 13.9% | 6.8 |
| *Ovis* | - | 6.9 | 6.3 | 0.6 | - |
| *Capra* | 26.9 | 3.0 | 0.7 | 0.3 | 62.0 |
| *Ovis/Capra* | - | 42.5 | 17.5 | 6.2 | 6.9 |
| *Sus* | 41.3 | 1.0 | 23.8 | 2.8 | - |
| other | 1.5 | 1.9 | - | 2.5 | 0.9 |
| Fishes: | 13.6 | - 9.8 | 72.6 | 23.7 | |

[15] From Hecker 1982:table 11.1, excluding faunal remains outside the walled village and animal pens. The 'other' mammal category here only includes carnivores and not miscellaneous unidentified mammals. Fish had not been systematically examined.
[16] Data from Kokabi 1980.
[17] New Kingdom data from Jeffreys et al. 1986, Greco-Roman data from Yokell n.d.b.
[18] Combined from Boessneck and von den Driesch 1993:tables 1,2.

Although the scale is not consistent, the models are in general agreement with the plans of three actual slaughterhouses discovered elsewhere in Upper Egypt thought to have been in use during the Old Kingdom (Verner 1986:181–90). The models and archaeological remains of slaughterhouses included three 'stations' where individual animals were killed; with an estimated 12 animals slaughtered per day, the amount of meat, viscera and bones produced annually must have been staggering. Gilbert (1988:80) concludes that cattle were trussed, pushed onto their sides to expose the throat, which was then cut using long straight-backed knives with convex blades. Blood was a captured in bowls and transferred to larger bowls in two earthenware braziers in the corner. Vandier (1969:173–174) describes tomb scenes in which blood is collected and carried away, and Fischer (1976) notes that blood was used as food by the Egyptians.

The high ceiling with large openings at the top of the front wall of the model are attributed by Gilbert as a design to aid cooling and drying of meat hanging from two ropes strung across a rear balcony (1988). Indeed, the Old Kingdom hieroglyphic rendering for slaughterhouse combines 'chopping block' with 'cool' (Geolet, in Gilbert 1988:79, fn 35). Unfortunately, direct comparison of the model with faunal remains from real-life meals of the tomb owner or of the actual slaughterhouses and their contents is impossible. Analysis of more than 13,000 osteological fragments from excavations at East Karnak is as yet incomplete (Yokell in prep B), but may soon shed light on the process of disarticulation as well as the systematic distribution of large taxa between villages, priests, and temples.

At Tell el-Amarna, it appears this deficiency was overcome by a reliance on smaller taxa, and the abundance of ovicaprid remains at Giza may reflect similar efforts. Redding attributes the relative paucity of pigs to their utility in "rural, mixed farming/herding communities" (1992:106). However, Zeder noted in Mesopotamian sites that pigs become less commonly utilized when there is evidence of greater centralized control (1991:31). The residential area at Giza would have been highly visible by visitors to other temples and tombs on the plateau, and if pigs were not a sanctioned resource, their use "may have been discouraged" by those controlling the provisioning (Zeder 1991:32). Sheep and goat would have provided meat and renewable resources for those workers who could afford them. However, if workers were paid in grains as Cerny (1954) suggests and the average Egyptian obtained protein largely from fish (Moens and Wetterstrom 1993), then the proximity of a fish processing center to a large governmental bakery/brewery is not unexpected.

## *Redistribution for Religious or Political Purposes*

A small offering assemblage from the offering temple associated with a 1st or 2nd Dynasty pyramid at Giza provide insight into uses of animals beyond maintaining the nutrition of the vast Egyptian workforce. Only domesticated animals and a few birds were recovered (Table 7.3; Kokabi 1980). Cattle or sheep/goat dominated depending on whether the remains were tabulated using NISP or MNI (see Appendix B for a discussion of these terms and how they are derived), but pigs were comparatively rare by either measure. The sample sizes are too small for reliable statistical analysis, but the assemblage is particularly important because it demonstrates that all four species of the core complex *were* suitable as offerings. All of these animals were adults and would have long since achieved maximum body size, probably indicating their use as offerings of meat. The presence of 'less desirable' species—pigs—is perhaps related to an obligation by the tomb owner to provide for his servants.

The involvement of the royal estate itself in pig raising during the New Kingdom might be suggested by the gift of 1000 breeding pairs of pigs to the Ptah Temple at Memphis by Amenophis III (L. Bell in Hecker 1984:157–8). The continuing importance of pig raising in domestic (artisan?) contexts at Memphis is attested by the frequency of pig bones there, second only to cattle (Jeffreys et al. 1986). The dominance of cattle is not unexpected considering the Apis (bull) Temple was located there. Analysis of faunal remains from Greco-Roman occupations at Memphis[19] suggests that by this late period, however, pigs were far less abundant than other members of the core complex (see Table 7.4).

On a much larger scale, literary evidence supports redistribution for political and religious purposes. Breasted (1906[IV]:87–206) recounts the "invaluable treasure of facts and statistics" from the Papyrus Harris (EA. 9999). Ramses IV compiled the list of benefactions carried during his father's 31-year reign (1184–1153 B.C.). The property of several temples is listed, totaling 421,362 large and small cattle for the Temple of Amon at Thebes, 45,544 for the Re Temple at Heliopolis, 10,047 for the Ptah Temple at Memphis, and 13,433 for several smaller temples. In an average year, then, more than 13,500 animals were property of the Amon Temple, 1460 at Heliopolis, 325 at Memphis, and more than 425 at the smaller temples. Although these temples possessed nearly 750,000 acres of land (Breasted 1906[IV]:96–7), this would have been distributed between the temple grounds, pastures, agricultural land, as well as habitation zones for priests and workmen. Along the narrow floodplain of Upper Egypt where these temples were located, there simply would have been insufficient pastureland among

[19] The data from Greco-Roman levels at Memphis were collected while I was employed by the American Research Center in Egypt (ARCE) Field School as an Archaeological Site Supervisor and faunal analyst. The ARCE Field School subgrant project is financed by the Egyptian Antiquities Project of ARCE, Inc. under its grant from the United States Agency for International Development (USAID), "Restoration and Preservation of Egyptian Antiquities" (USAID Grant No. 263-0000-G-3089-00). I am grateful for their permission to include these data here.

the temple property to raise such large numbers of animals. Indeed, there are indications that several of the estates were located in the delta (Wente 1990:118–119), one of which was clearly located on a canal in the *western* Delta (Breasted 1906[IV]:125, fn c), where habitat conditions were particularly suited to pasturage (see chapter three). One fragmentary document from a royal scribe of the 19th Dynasty limits herd sizes to 500 for deltaic estates belonging to Amon as 500 cattle; unfortunately, the corresponding number of herders has been lost (Wente 1990:119).

Additional sections of the Harris Papyrus document animals donated to the temples for use in traditional annual feasts; that is, not part of the actual herds raised on estates, but only the animals *culled* from other, larger herds for sacrifice and redistribution. These numbers are considerably smaller: the total donations for all the temples combined were only 30 or so head of cattle per year. These animals would have been transported from across Egypt, perhaps as part of annual taxes paid to the king. These are perhaps the *inw* cattle which were transferred to the temple estates for fattening and eventual sacrifice. Similar to the Harris Papyrus, a late 20th Dynasty papyrus recovered from Thebes discusses the requisitions for goods from the Upper Egyptian temples of Elephantine, Kom Ombo, Edfu, Hierakonpolis, el-Kab and Esna (Janssen 1991). The destination is unclear, but the description suggests that they were probably delivered to the Amun temple, perhaps as a tax for the installation of a priest (a practice known during the Ptolemaic period) rather than formal tax paid to the pharaoh and his court. Interestingly, cattle are provided only by northern sanctuaries (beginning at Edfu), not from Elephantine or Kom Ombo (see Figure 3.1 for locations). Given the Nile as means of transportation, the increased distance is not likely the reason. However, southern sanctuaries do provide items unique to those areas or even imported from more distant regions, perhaps replacing cattle, which could then be reserved for local use. A brief report from the 25th and 26th dynasty Chnum temple at Elephantine indicates that cattle *were* utilized locally for offerings, although in much fewer numbers than goats (see Table 7.2; Boessneck and von den Driesch 1993). The significance is not yet understood, but may eventually be related to the specific ceremony or occasion for which offerings were made.

The Harris Papyrus is typically cited as an example of the loss of royal power to the temples; such immense quantities of land were donated (and thus removed from the tax base) that much of the country was in the hands of the priests. While this is almost certainly true, the large numbers of herders and workers of the temple estates were also considered property of the estate, and their subsistence needs were apparently partially or completely provisioned (see Bleiberg 1988; Breasted 1908[IV]: 123–126). Thus, the loss of governmental income resulting from the transference of property to tax-exempt religious estates probably had less impact on the lives of average Egyptians (such as temple employees) than on the funding and provisioning of national (corvée labor) projects which were fundamental to reinforcing the power/authority of government.

## Discussion: Beyond Regional Strategies of Intensification

Clearly, additional settlement studies and faunal analyses are needed in all three geographic regions, but the preliminary patterns presented here for Upper and Lower Egypt appear to closely approximate those patterns expected by the models defined in chapter five. An apparent lack of exploration of Dynastic occupations in the deserts rendered it impossible to evaluate continuity or change. Three Delta sites were examined; two from the Archaic Period and one from the Old Kingdom. Several assemblages were studied from Valley sites: one recovered from the habitation zone of the laboring class, two from a similar zone adjacent to a major temple, and two from offering or tomb contexts. These data are graphically depicted in Figure 7.12. Predynastic data are included on the graph to facilitate recognition of continuity or change between time periods within a geographic region.

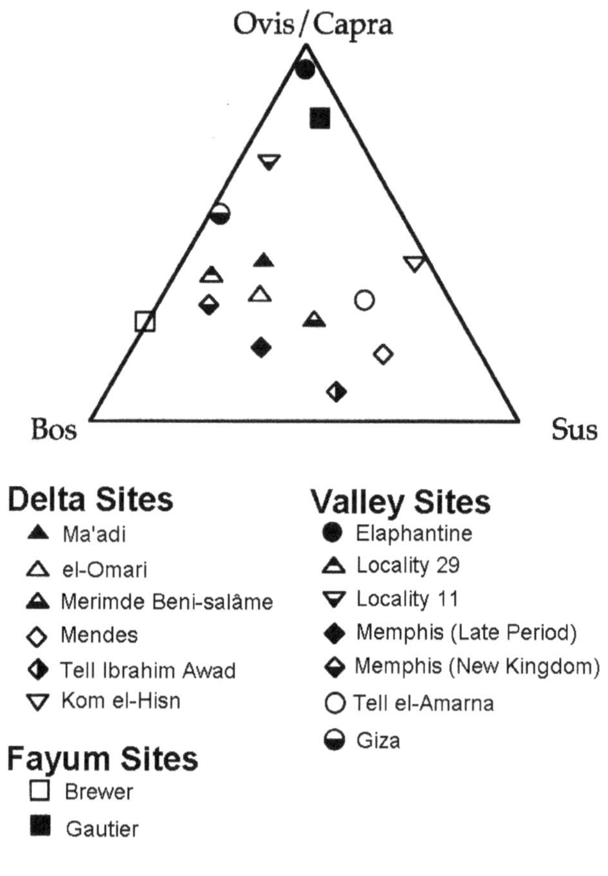


Figure 7.12. Scatterplot of Faunal Data from Predynastic and Dynastic Sites in the Three Geographic Regions.

The faunal remains from the three Delta sites exhibited marked differences which were clearly not the result of differences in available habitat. Mendes and Tell Ibrahim Awad—the Archaic Period sites—were quite similar in species utilization. Hunted animals were extremely rare, indicating that the shift begun during the Predynastic toward a full reliance on domesticated animal resources was nearly complete. Both assemblages were dominated by pigs, with cattle also contributing significantly to subsistence; sheep and goat were rare at either site. This pattern represents a shift towards pigs following the Predynastic. Because pigs were only associated with agro-pastoral or ranching strategies among the ethnographic cases, this shift is interpreted as highly suggestive of the permanent occupation of agricultural villages. Age and sex distributions could not be constructed for the Mendes faunal remains. The restriction of cattle remains to burial contexts at Tell Ibrahim Awad may hint at the growing importance of this species for marking social status. Unfortunately, detailed settlement data such as the size and location of storage or processing facilities were not readily available, and patterns of faunal data are insufficient for definitive statements on social or economic production.

The faunal remains from the Old Kingdom site of Kom el-Hisn were intriguing. As Figure 7.12 indicates, the assemblage was comprised of nearly equal proportions of sheep/goats and pigs; cattle bones were conspicuously rare. Characteristics of open- or free-range ranching in the New World were helpful in interpreting this site as a beef cattle ranch, with the prime specimens exported away from the site. The ovi-caprids and pigs served as supplemental sources of nutrition. Age and sex distributions were typical of milk-based exploitation of ovi-caprids, and meat-based exploitation of suids. The reliance on pigs for meat, in particular, was typical of modern non-territorial ranching strategies. In combination with Egyptological evidence that the region and site were well-known during Dynastic times as producing abundant and high quality cattle, recognition of the non-territorial system eliminated the possibility that the cattle herds were privately owned and had been transported to the Delta for access to seasonal pasture. Clearly, the information recovered from Kom el-Hisn indicates that the occupants of at least this one site specialized in raising cattle for trade with other areas (the third original research question).

Surprisingly, a reliance on blood, milk and related products from cattle was predicted for inhabitants of Upper Egypt and the Delta, but little evidence was recovered for the Dynastic Period. Artistic and written sources document that cow milk was fed to human infants, and was also the subject of a chapter of *The Book of the Dead,* in which a dead prince drinks from Hathor's udder and is restored to new life (Darby et al. 1977:58). Milk was depicted stored in ovoid pots (*nms't*) stoppered with grass, keeping out insects but not air. Ryder (1983:113) notes that several Egyptian words exist for milk products, although their exact translation (e.g., fresh milk, butter, cheese) is unknown. Several texts mention milk from or for young cattle (Breasted 1906:IV), certainly suggesting that the milk in jars is from this species and not sheep or goats. Letters from the Middle and New Kingdoms by regional officials and servants alike include requests that "freshly jugged milk" be provided (Wente 1990:69;93, 159). Cattle milk (as well as numerous organs) was often incorporated into medicinal compounds (see Darby et al. 1977:159–161). Before the importance of milk and its products can be fully understood, larger sample sizes more complete age/sex distributions of bovid osteological remains from a variety of sites throughout Egypt are necessary.

Assemblages from Valley sites also exhibited interesting and enlightening patterns. Settlement data were again rare, but contrasted strongly with assemblages from offering and tomb contexts. The remains from the workmen's village at Tell el-Amarna emphasized the local raising of pigs. This was a departure from Predynastic assemblages at Hierakonpolis, which contained few suid bones. Much of the difference is due to Predynastic inhabitants being only partially involved with agricultural pursuits, relying on a diversified strategy of animal utilization as protection against unexpected losses, while Tell el-Amarna inhabitants had a level of security 'built-in' by governmental provisioning of subsistence.

Previously viewed as an unexpected occurrence given habitat constraints, the presence of pigs at Tell el-Amarna was predicted both by the re-evaluation of species tolerances (in chapter four) and the agro-pastoral model defined in chapter five. The redistributive network—particularly the *b3kwt* rations—was apparently insufficient for the needs of the workers, and pigs were raised as supplemental sources of protein and income. Preliminary data from a similar site at Giza was suggestive of the same pattern, but raw data were not available. Giza was important, however, for the addition of information concerning the labor involved in provisioning such large workforces; it appears that large-scale fish processing was closely tied to bread- and beer-making.

The limited data from offering contexts documents neither adaptive strategies to local habitat conditions nor economic importance of various species. Rather, assemblages from Elephantine and (a different site at) Giza indicated that all four species in the domesticate complex were suitable as religious offerings. These data were somewhat surprising, considering the long-held beliefs that pigs were undesirable or prohibited animals. Not surprisingly, however, there was general concordance between the deities worshipped and the proportions of different species prepared as offerings. For example, the assemblage recovered from the Chnum Temple at Elephantine—dedicated to a god identified as a ram—was almost exclusively sheep/goat, as indicated on Figure 7.12 by the data point plotted at the apex of the triangle. These two sites demonstrate quite clearly that domesticated animals were incorporated into religious practices, and that the case for the taboos/proscriptions against certain taxa has been overstated (answering the fourth original research question; see also the heading: "*This Little Piggy…*").

The distribution of domesticated taxa across Egypt could be determined in only isolated instances because of limited faunal and settlement data. A corollary to this research question was the change through time. This has been documented in each region through examination of sites of varying age, but it is unknown at present how representative any one of those sites may be of other sites in that region. In light of the bias in available settlement data in combination with the knowledge that the religious and political goals of the government permeated Dynastic Egyptian society, the regional approach employed thus far will temporarily be set aside. In its place will be an examination of the accumulated evidence regarding the research questions relating directly to the economic and religious aspects of the core complex.

Although based on a barter system, profit was certainly a concept well understood by the ancient Egyptians, and the mosaic of quality land has already been suggested as a source of competition. Ranching, for example, would have been limited to "gentlemen farmers" who could afford to purchase large numbers of expensive cattle as well as to support sufficient numbers of herders to care for the animals (including transport and access to seasonal pasturage in the Delta). Systematic annual taxation necessitated inspection of the herds (see Figure 7.13); painted and three-dimensional model "reviews scenes" have been discovered in tombs at least by the 12th Dynasty (e.g.,Wild 1966:pl 168; Newberry 1893–4:pls 18–19; Posener 1962:157).

The largest and most detailed of these is a three-dimensional model of cattle review showing a Middle Kingdom Theban noble seated beneath a tented pavilion upon a dais and surrounded by four scribes, various servants and stewards while cattle are paraded before him a yard (Gilbert 1988:71). While Winlock identifies the animals as beef cattle because of their size relative to their handlers (Winlock 1955), Gilbert (1988:72) is correct to caution that size relationships between cattle and the human figures may not be precise or accurate, and the small size of the animals may merely represent a cohort of weanlings. *Both* Winlock's and Gilbert's contentions are supported by the careful representation of all the animals as males, the majority of which would be removed from the herd as young adults in a meat-based ranching strategy (see chapter five).

Winlock (1955:19–20) attributes the scene to the official head count for tax purposes, and it is thus a demonstration of Meketre's wealth and prestige. These occasions would also have provided an ideal opportunity to select animals for culling. The best animals were likely selected to become *inȝ* bulls, others used to pay taxes, and others donated to temples favored by the herd owner in attempts not only to contribute to the quality of his afterlife, but also to curry favor with current political leaders. However, the recovery of such models and artistic scenes in the tombs of Upper Egyptian officials should not be construed as evidence that the herds were maintained on Upper Egyptian pastures. In fact, the large size of some of the herds (Fischer 1959) argues that they would have been kept on pastureland in the Delta. Many of the wealthiest officials owned land in the Delta, for use as vineyards, pastureland or a variety of other profit-based ventures (Wilkinson 1988). Herds owned by such wealthy families could have been maintained on those Delta properties year-round, and may have taken on characteristics similar to the probable ranching strategy at Kom el-Hisn, albeit on a smaller scale. Other 'gentlemen farmers' in the Valley may have rented Delta pasturage on a seasonal basis. Most likely, herds would have been driven down the Valley or transported by boat following the *Delta* harvest. The more limited pasturage in the Valley would have decreased in quality or been completely exhausted at about the time that crops were reaching full maturity in the Delta (because flood and recession occurred later in the north; see the heading "Seasonal Resource Scheduling" in chapter three).

Tomb scenes depict herds crossing bodies of water, with herders or owners in boats protecting the animals from dangerous aquatic species (see figure 7.14). Young animals are pulled into the boats, perhaps to save them from drowning or to entice the cows into the water. Although the scenes are recorded in Upper Egyptian tombs, the Nile would have been too wide and deep for herds to swim across, and thus these scenes must reflect the movement of herds across canals or distributary channels in the Delta. Private letters and surviving poetry are from the sons and employees of wealthy Valley farmers, sent to the Delta to care for herds for extended periods. Many lament the time away from home, and eloquently describe Valley-dwellers' unwillingness to leave the familiar Upper Egyptian landscape—sharply bounded by high limestone cliffs—to live in the unnervingly flat, open spaces of the delta (Fischer 1959; Helck 1974).

The seasonal movement of herds to better pastures falls within several of the subsistence strategies outlined in chapter five. However, there are indicators among the Egyptian sources that it was either agro-pastoralism or ranching being practiced. It is the opinion of this author that ranching is better supported by the limited evidence.

Agro-pastoralism, as defined here, requires animal husbandry to be a secondary or supplemental economic component. Animals are typically maintained with fodder in stables or enclosures within or adjacent to settlements. Production is comprised of two essentially independent parts: agricultural and herding pursuits are carried out independent of one another. Egyptian sources do not indicate that 'gentlemen farmers' utilized fodder or kept herds in enclosures, and while their involvement with agriculture can be inferred from other tomb scenes, the relative contribution of animals versus plants cannot be

Figure 7.13. A Cattle Census (after Wilkinson 1988[1854]:II:177).

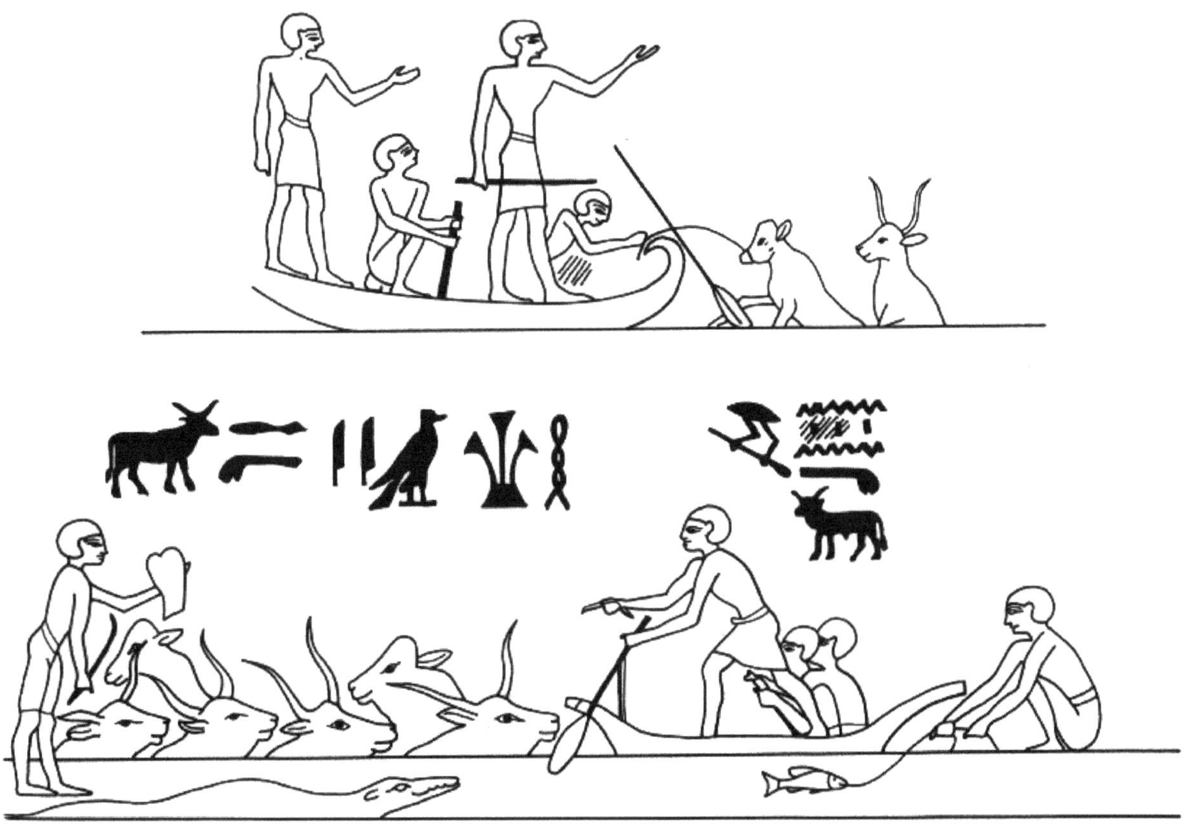

Figure 7.14. Cattle Herds Being Driven Across a Nile Channel.

reliably determined. These factors seriously challenge the likelihood that these individuals were practicing semi-sedentary pastoralism. In contrast, evidence from other tomb scenes and legal documents indicates that similar officials were heavily motivated by profit and off-take from herds; this is a fundamental aspect of ranching (Wilkinson 1988[1854]. Seasonal movement of herds is an effective means of maintaining quality and amount of yield equivalent to the 'breeder' and 'feeder' districts described for territorial ranching.

## Dietary or Economic Differences Between Social Classes

Having addressed the research question concerning the development of breeds, some effort must now be devoted to answering its correlate: what the social or economic functions of the various breeds were. The development of the different breeds is closely tied to the increasingly complex redistributive economy, and again the bias in scholarly efforts necessitates restriction of the following discussion primarily to cattle.

Although few records survive of actual wages or salary of the three principal social classes of the New Kingdom (field laborer, priest and government official), the basis of workmen's food and wages alike was evidently emmer wheat and smaller portions of barley (Cerny 1954:916–917). These payments were made monthly and although they varied considerably between individuals, there is little variation in wages over the 200 years documented. Cerny justifiably concludes that the economy remained stable; irrigation, taxation and redistribution systems operated efficiently, and no shortage of food occurred to create a decrease in wages (1954:920). Fragments of New Kingdom papyrus include the range of products to be delivered to workmen at the Deir el-Medina necropolis: "vegetables, fish, firewood, pottery, small cattle, and milk" (Wente 1990:134). The inclusion of small cattle—and the absence of large cattle—hints that protein for this social class did not include beef.

While grains were clearly an important dietary (and economic) component for most Egyptians, I agree with Moens and Wetterstrom (1988) that fish would have provided the bulk of protein for the middle and lower social classes. The Nuer and Dinka agro-pastoralists heavily utilize fish on a seasonal basis, and the importance of fish to Egyptian subsistence has been documented at least by the Upper Paleolithic (e.g., Brewer 1989a, 1991a; Brewer and Friendman 1989; Brewer and Yokell 1996; von den Driesch 1986b). The reported abundance of fish remains at all Dynastic archaeological sites along the main Nile or its delta distributaries argues for piscine resources to have maintained their dominant position in the diet. Indeed, it seems highly likely that as domesticated animals and the land on which to graze them became more expensive, the "average" Egyptian would have turned increasingly to aquatic resources and to pigs, which remained comparatively inexpensive.

Fish were often depicted in market scenes being purchased by barter (Eyre 1987), and are also typically more abundant than other taxa in lists of provisions/rations for corvée laborers (e..g, Wente 1990; Breasted 1906). Tomb scenes indicate that fish were prepared in a variety of ways: sun-dried, smoked, pickled, or salted (Montet 1925); all of which would permit the fish to be transported over distance and/or consumed over a period of time. In order to process such large amounts of fish into provisions for workers, massive processing centers would have been required; the first indications of such were recently discovered near Giza.

In light of the vast redistributive network, only prohibitive cost would prevent a heavy reliance on fish protein by 'average' Egyptians living far from the Nile. That is, costs associated with the labor required to process fish for long distance redistribution may have outweighed the value of the fish itself, particularly if inexpensive, locally available sources of meat/protein could be obtained in place of fish. Long touted as unsuitable for raising in Egypt, it now appears that pigs were ideal to fill this economic 'niche.'

Similarly, the association of pig remains with a low species diversity consisting primarily of small meat-yielding animals was interpreted by Hecker (1982) as utilization by lower class individuals in site areas with large percentages of high meat-yield animals and that exhibited a greater range of species. Evidence that pigs were indeed consumed by lower classes is found in a 25$^{th}$ Dynasty laboring class mummy, which had *Trichinella* cysts in his body tissue (Millet et al. 1980). Identification of disease in lower social ranks should not be construed as proof that pig meat was restricted to these classes (see below). The "workmen's village" at Tell el-Amarna seems a similar case, in which inhabitants were supplementing governmental provisions.

### *This Little Piggy Stayed Home: The Case of the Missing Taboo*

Classical authors and recent scholars have suggested that raising or consuming pigs was unfavorable or even prohibited, or at least an inappropriate food for the afterlife. Cultural biases have been revealed among the classical writers (e.g., Darby et al. 1977:176–180; Dawson 1928). Similarly, an investigation of published reports concerning the uses or prohibitions of pigs from the Egyptian economy and pantheon has revealed that significant and incorrect assumptions or biases persist among modern scholars (Yokell 1997). As demonstrated in chapter four, water rather than temperature appears to be the limiting factor for the distribution of pigs. Thus, suids are well adapted to ecological conditions typical of much of the Nile Valley and Delta regions. The ability of pigs to consume the same foods as humans does <u>not</u> place them in competition with their keepers but rather renders them uniquely adapted to village contexts, whereas competition may develop between land devoted to agricultural pursuits and land (and labor) devoted to fodder or grazing plants for the other taxa. The rapid and prolific breeding of pigs increases their desirability as a regular source of meat, allowing some degree of specialization on the part of herders (who can therefore reduce their dependence on (off-take from) other species and build up these herds for security or profit).

If the frequency that certain taxa are represented in tomb scenes has been linked to their relative desirability, as Vandier (1969) has concluded for Old Kingdom piscine representations, this *might* suggest that pigs were in fact a less desirable resource. From the above summary of breeds, however, it is clear that the paucity of pigs is due at least in part to the failure of scholars to recognize suid depictions. Still, 'less desirable' need not denote a prohibition, merely that if the average person had a choice, he/she would choose another animal. And because the vast majority of scenes studied are from upper social ranks, the importance of pigs to a particular tomb owner may have been minimized in favor of more highly prized animals. Therefore, the near absence of pigs may reflect both an Egyptian preference for other species and biases in tomb art studied by modern scholars.

The Harris Papyrus provides an extensive list of acceptable and desirable Old Kingdom religious offerings, and pigs are conspicuously absent (Breasted 1906[IV]:87–206). Again, this document concerns activities of upper social ranks, and if pigs were 'less desirable,' they would not be included among items used to demonstrate generosity and piety. The Harris Papyrus also documents the oft-cited rivalry for food between humans and pigs, describing a year of famine in which "food is robbed from the mouth of the swine, without it being said, as before, 'this is better for thee than for me,' for men are so hungry" (Harris 1985:84). This statement should perhaps be considered more indicative of the importance of pigs than of their inappropriateness. Only under conditions of extreme human need is food taken from pigs, suggesting that normally they were consistently fed. If the species was undesirable during normal conditions, it is unlikely that the owner would have apologized for taking food away from such an animal in more dire circumstances. And, additionally, unless the animal was valuable (or its meat prohibited), one might expect the animal to be slaughtered to satisfy its owner's hunger.

Even by the Middle Kingdom, there is no evidence for an implied or mandated taboo. The earliest literary mention is in the 3rd Dynasty biography of Methen, a Lower Egyptian official, who inherited "small cattle" with the hieroglyphic determinative for pig (Sethe 1906–1909, cited in Newberry 1928:211). That pigs could be raised and inherited without stigma by a member of upper classes certainly suggests that pigs were not abhorred, nor were they restricted to particular social classes. Only during and following the New Kingdom does pork avoidance seem to be an actual phenomenon for certain classes of Egyptian society: the divine king and the royal officials and priests who served him or other gods (e.g., Darby et al. 1977; Dawson 1928:599; Kees 1961; Newberry 1928). In contrast to this, however, recall that pigs were among the more abundant species at Memphis. Again, this may be due to a relationship between cattle- and pig-raising not explicitly defined by the model, but certainly explainable within it (e.g., as at Kom el-Hisn).

However, Zeder (1991:31) noted in Mesopotamian sites that pigs appear to play a more important role during times of weaker political integration, and become less commonly utilized when there is evidence of greater centralized control. She attributes this to the species' lack of secondary products and relatively greater human labor input per yield over other species. Similar to their treatment in ancient Egypt, pigs are rarely depicted, mentioned in documents, or included in temple offerings in Mesopotamia; nonetheless, pigs are ubiquitous at most urban sites there (Zeder 1991).

## Summary and Conclusions

The variety of cattle in depictions and records appears to reflect a social emphasis placed on the species; association of particular breeds with certain—especially ritual—activities further emphasizes the point. However, one must remember that the vast majority of scenes in which cattle appear are from upper classes, and from previous descriptions of land and animal prices it is clear that the average Egyptian was unable to afford land or the more desirable species.

The "intricate problem of acceptance versus avoidance consists [of] sorting out contradictory statements and evidence, in clarifying ambivalent attitudes" and trying to fit them into a valid framework (Darby et al. 1977:72, 380). The bias in available artistic or literary data has created an illusion of a more homogeneous society than actually existed, and because these data are primarily from upper social ranks, reconstructed economic and social uses of each species are distorted. Dietary differences were due to social status rather than governmental or religious prohibitions. It appears that true taboos involved only a few meats, which varied between districts regardless of changes in formal edicts during various historical periods. Generally, avoidance was restricted to certain ceremonies, particular holy periods (especially the five epagonemal days), or to restricted (i.e., higher) classes.

Without question, more data is needed to fully evaluate the models, but minimally the predictive model for the ranching strategy appears successful based on available data from the western Delta. The workmen's village at Tell el-Amarna is the best indication of a localized subsistence economy, in the form of a sedentary agricultural community. The success of this strategy in marginal areas of the Valley was not unexpected once long-held biases and assumptions— particularly the roles of pigs—were reexamined and tested against modern ethnographic examples.

The other strategies are difficult to test at present, for several reasons. The pervasive redistributive network during the Dynastic Period complicates the interpretability of faunal assemblages, necessitating a reliance on multiple sites and other lines of evidence. Unfortunately, Egyptian settlement studies are a comparatively new avenue of research, and few sizable assemblages from domestic contexts were available for testing expectations in the Nile Valley. Nonetheless, comparisons of settlement data with faunal assemblages from ritual/offering contexts provided some needed insight into cultural preferences of different ranks of Egyptian society. Continuing excavations will no doubt improve the interpretability of the data presented here by augmenting sample sizes with material from additional sites and contexts in each of the three geographic regions.

It is readily apparent that the Nile was of fundamental importance to survival, affecting not only the seasonality of labor and subsistence activities, but also permeating Egyptian mytho-theology. The concentration of scholarly efforts on the roles of domesticated animals perhaps has underrated the importance of aquatic resources in the diet of the bulk of the population. Many sites mentioned here reported remains of fish and waterfowl as abundant but, unfortunately, those remains have not yet been fully identified or quantified. As indicated by chapters three and five, riverine resources certainly played a major seasonal role in basic subsistence in Dynastic Egypt—especially by human populations in rural areas at or beyond the limits of the redistributive economy. A few works document the importance of fish/fishing (Brewer and Friedman 1989; Brewer and Yokell 1996; Darby et al. 1977; Gamer-Wallert 1970) and birds (Houlihan 1986), but few provide quantifiable data documenting the relative importance to subsistence.[20] While the task would be massive, a combined analysis of domesticates and aquatic resources would be invaluable for understanding the totality of Egyptian uses of animals.

At least by proto– and early–Dynastic periods, the beginnings of animal cults and uses of animals for traction and secondary products are evident. The cattle cult has received the most attention, and is suggested by at least the 1st Dynasty, when the bull had already been associated with kingship and power. Even by the late Archaic, the majority of depictions of field preparations using hand-held hoes were replaced with plows drawn by oxen and donkeys (Hartmann 1923). For lower social classes, however, tomb art continued to include hoes, suggesting that these ranks did not have access to (i.e., could not afford) technological innovations associated with the larger species. Recent and on-going investigations provide corroborative evidence for the appearance of many of these traits much earlier, and document the antiquity of the complex relationship between social control and subsistence production in Egypt. Currently, there is insufficient evidence to determine the underlying *causes* of intensification strategies. It was first necessary to determine *what sorts* of mechanisms were devised to incorporate such dissimilar societies into a single unified one, and philosophical reasons for *why* this was done can be investigated in the future.

[20] The few reports that include numerical data rely on NISP, which is highly biased in favor of taxa with exceptionally diagnostic traits. For example, because catfishes' cranial fragment only a few millimeters long can be assigned to genus, NISP severely over-represents their true abundance.

# 8. THE VALUE OF ZOOARCHAEOLOGY IN MODELING SOCIO-ECONOMIC EVOLUTION AND CONTINUITY: RETROSPECT AND PROSPECT

## Introduction

The basic thesis in this study was that significant advances in the understanding of the development of complex societies are unlikely unless human–(plant)–animal relationships are investigated within the context of general theories which address the underlying principles affecting both subsistence and social behaviors. The aim at present was to present a descriptive—not an explanatory—model based on numerous ethnographies of modern pastoral populations in a variety of habitats. This model was then applied to archaeological data; specifically, to better understand the patterns appearing during the crucial formative period and culminating in the first unified Egyptian state.

Archaeological investigations in Egypt had concentrated until recently on sites yielding information about the higher social classes during the Dynastic Period. Comparatively little work had been conducted at settlement sites, and not a lot has been known about the daily lives of the majority of the population. Without such data, it had proven impossible to fully comprehend the mechanisms by which disparate regional societies were subsumed into the unified Egyptian 'state.' Osteological remains of domesticated animals had been previously considered to contribute little to scientific knowledge of a society, and to be of marginal utility in understanding the process of integration in Egypt. Their primary functions had been as paleo-environmental indicators or to determine the geographical origin of food production in North Africa. Recent analyses of faunal assemblages had attempted more cultural interpretations for the proportions and distributions of various domesticated species at some archaeological sites. Regional and status differences in taxonomic utilization began to appear among the data, but previous analyses either did not test these patterns of did so on only a limited basis.

I have sought here to examine such differences from a wide range of faunal assemblages from different geographic regions and through several thousand years. The overall design of the research presented here was similar to that proposed by Bar-Yosef and Khazanov for the Levant (1992:1-2). Evolutionary ecology, and to a lesser extent economic, theories were applied to ethnographic and archaeological data in an attempt to further our current understanding of the development, adoption and perpetuation of alternative food production strategies in ancient Egypt, and how those strategies also influenced other aspects of Egyptian society (chapter 2). Thus the focus of this research was not to fully examine the transition to food production, but some discussion of the expanding uses of domesticated animals during this period was useful for attempting to understand the complex nature of interaction of these human populations in each of the three regions. Zooarchaeological inferences were correlated when possible with sources such as Egyptian texts, literature and art of later (historical) periods to gain insight into the changing importance of different taxa to the social institutions by which Dynastic Egyptian society was characterized and maintained. This multi-stage analysis forms a necessary first step of future research for identifying the processes and ramifications of similar development in other early complex societies. The methods utilized and the success of the research is summarized below. While some indication is given for future research throughout, additional studies are also suggested in the final section of this chapter.

## Research Review and Contributions to the Field

The methods used in the present analysis to study the environmental and cultural bases of Egyptian society first required reconstruction of the habitat or natural environment at the time that domesticated species were introduced or brought under human control locally. The hydraulic and soil nutrient conditions—constituting the primary limiting factors of forage—of different regions of Egypt were presented (chapter 3), in order to locate areas of greatest resource potential and to determine the extent of seasonal variation. Not surprisingly, the harsh, hot and dry conditions in the desert regions resulted in highly variable, unpredictable and often sparse resources, and oases provided important stability and refuge. The Valley resources were considerably more abundant, but dependent upon seasonal flooding for nutrients and water. The particulars of the Valley floodplain resulted in fairly small catchment basins of varying quality land and containing a dense and predictable range of resources. Similarly, Delta resources were dependent upon the annual flood waters, but differences in topography allowed greater diversity and density of floral and faunal distributions.

It was assumed that the spread of domesticates was dependent not only on the ability of a taxon to survive in an area, but also whether it was sufficiently advantageous for the human population in that area to care for the species. An examination of the relative biological and physiological capacity of cattle, sheep, goat and pigs was fundamental to understanding the choices by humans for exploiting a particular species or its products in a given area. Comparison of some of the more distinctive attributes of these four herd species indicated that variations would have rendered each differently able to survive in each of the three geographic regions of Egypt (chapter 4). For example, both sheep and goat are versatile species, surviving on low quality foods and in hot, dry habitats, such as the Eastern and Western Desert regions. Attributes such as young breeding age and rapid maturation allow quick herd rebound from unexpected natural catastrophes. Goats are better able than sheep to survive in areas with lower quality food and under drier conditions. In contrast, cattle are adapted to survival in a wide range of habitats, but because this species requires absolutely greater amounts of food and water, it is not as well adapted as sheep or goats in marginal areas. Additionally, cattle require several more years to reach sexual and physical maturity, and as a result rebound much more slowly than either sheep or goats. This trait further limits its suitability to survive in the harsh and unpredictable conditions of the deserts. Finally, it was demonstrated that pigs, previously considered to be of only limited value because of Egypt's harsh conditions, are in fact well adapted to the habitats in the Valley and Delta regions. Through these comparisons, observed differences from expectations of natural abundances could more reliably be attributed to cultural factors.

The preceding demonstrated that the natural properties of the resources themselves were important in determining where or how densely the animals occurred. Fundamental to being defined as domesticates, however, is the control of these animal species by humans for their own purposes. A predictive model was therefore developed based on issues of economic and social production among modern societies utilizing these same domesticated taxa under similar environmental conditions (chapter 5). Five strategies were identified: nomadic pastoralism, semi-nomadic pastoralism, transhumant pastoralism, agro-pastoralism, and ranching. Each was found to possess certain diagnostic traits, of which many produced archaeologically recoverable evidence.

Nomadic pastoralists today occupy marginal habitats where agriculture is either not feasible or yields are very unpredictable. As a result, plant resources include gathered wild vegetables and fruits or domesticated grains obtained through barter with groups in other areas. In areas of sufficient water, cattle are raised, primarily for milk. This produces a diagnostic pattern in herd composition which is recognized archaeologically by a preponderance of males or castrates, since females are protected and die only of natural causes. Cattle also play important roles in marking status. Sheep or goats are often raised in greater numbers than cattle, and are utilized for meat, producing an archaeologically recognizable pattern in which the most abundant remains are those of adults. Population movements are determined by available pasture, and the decision to move is typically made by herd owners. In the essentially treeless grasslands, dung cakes subsitute for firewood in the nearly treeless grasslands. The highly mobile nature of these groups necessitates temporary structures of light construction; the archaeological debris is minimal.

Semi-nomadic pastoralists are involved to a slightly greater (albeit unquantified) degree with agriculture, planting some crops around seasonal water holes. Surpluses are rare, and storage facilities were minimal. Herd size and composition are similar to those of nomadic pastoralists. and it proved to be difficult to distinguish them archaeologically.

Transhumant pastoralists today occupy lands which can support large-scale agriculture, and animal husbandry contributes less to the diet and economy. Dung continues to be utilized for fuel to some degree, although it also becomes an item of exchange. Household gardens are maintained in settlements near wet season pastures, and small stock such as sheep and goat are raised for both milk and meat. The majority of large stock are pastured at some distance from the settlement in combined herds (i.e., belonging to several households). Sexual division of labor is such that women tend the household gardens while men carry out the majority of activities associated with animal husbandry. Clearly the zooarchaeological patterns of a large-stock camp and the more permanent settlement would be dramatically different. Both camps move seasonally.

In agro-pastoral societies, the majority of subsistence and economic production is obtained through agricultural pursuits; animal husbandry occurs only in a secondary or supplementary capacity. Resources have become more privatized, and competition for land dictates that animals are kept in pens or fenced pastures at some distance from the settlement. A small segment of the essentially sedentary population must relocate the herds on a seasonal basis, and in some areas fodder must be provided. Dung becomes an important economic item; it is exchanged for seasonal access to pastureland. Herd structure is largely unchanged from previous strategies, although the number of animals a given herder will own is considerably smaller. Cattle remain important as status and economic symbols. The greater population density and permanence of site occupation resutls in greater accumulation of debris, often in prescribed locations according to activity, and social stratification is more complex. This is manifested archaeologically most clearly in differential access to luxury items and in the treatment of burials.

Ranching strategies have received less scientific study, but two forms were recogizable. Free-range ranching was noted in marshlands and in areas where land was readily available. Cattle are raised for profit, with zooarchaeological profiles marked by the *absence* of prime-yield animals. Small numbers of suids or sheep are raised to supplement the diet of the ranchhands. The archaeological pattern of these remains should mimic the meat-based pattern recognized among other pastoral groups. As ranches move to more marginal lands, they become territorial in nature, fencing in the animals and controlling breeding to further improve the stock (and thus profits). Territorial ranches are characterized by the exploitation of a single product (whether meat, milk or in the case of sheep, wool). Selective breeding was expected to result in morphological and eventually osteological changes in the chosen taxa. The emphasis on the animals for profit corresponded to a decrease in religious/ritual uses of animals.

In addition, it was possible to arrange these strategies along a continuum representing increasing authority and/or control over animals and land. The continuum was not intended and should not be viewed as representing an unavoidable or unidirectional cultural evolution. Thus, equally important as the biological capacity for survival of these species were the human constraints placed on the reproduction and productivity of those animals. For example, because pigs provide only non-renewable resources (e.g., meat and hides), they represent a somewhat specialized alternative to the other taxa. Because the quantity and quality of renewable resources vary considerably seasonally, the structure of a herd had as much to do with the relative reliance on milk/milk products as on meat/skins (cf. Redding 1981; Russell 1988). The ability of sheep and goat herds to rebound from catastrophic losses render them more suitable than cattle to sustained offtake for human consumption. Not surprisingly, cattle are utilized most often for milk and blood products, and represent a fundamental means to mark social status.

Traits identified in each of the strategies were used to predict the nature and degree of reliance on domesticated taxa following their introduction and/or adoption in the Egyptian Desert, Valley and Delta regions. Tracing the development of the domesticated animal complex included surveying the literature devoted to the origins of domesticates, but the loci of origin were viewed as less important than the direction of spread and the changes in societies resulting from the adoption of those animals. The ethnographic-based model was readily shown to have some merit, particularly for the Predynastic (chapter 6). The adoption of domesticates appeared early in the desert regions, where wild resources were unpredictable and at least seasonally limited or unavailable. Nonetheless, the incorporation of domesticated animals (or plants) did not immediately result in a dramatic shift in either economy or social structure. Rather, these resources were added to the existing foraging strategy. For example, whereas wild plants occuring along lake margins had been collected seasonally, some domesticated plants were also grown. Similarly, hunted resources were not abandoned, but contributed less to the overall diet through time. Archaeological evidence of these seasonally mobile desert inhabitants is limited to a few simple storage and habitation structures, reminiscent of modern nomadic pastoralists.

The archaeological record in the Delta essentially begins at sites with domesticates. Agricultural pursuits were already more important than hunted and gathered resources. Cattle dominate the faunal assemblages, with pigs abundant at a site along a distributary channel but sheep/goats abundant at sites along desert wadis. These patterns were expected solely on the basis of habitat preferences and tolerances of the various species. Sites are larger, apparently occupied permanently, with abundant storage facilities, substantial structures, and evidence of social stratification. These traits are typical of the agro-pastoral strategy outlined by the ethnographic cases. However, there is no unequivocal evidence of stables or the provisioning of fodder, and it is possible that Predynastic Delta sites will eventually be shown to fit more precisely in the category of semi-sedentary or transhumant pastoralism.

The adoption of domesticates was either unnecessary in the resource-abundant Nile Valley for centuries, or the process of spread was slow up the Nile from the Delta. There is limited evidence of interaction of Valley-dwellers with desert inhabitants throughout the Predynastic, and it is likely that the Valley-dwellers were aware of domesticates long before they incorporated them into their own society and economy. Sites with reliable faunal data in the Nile Valley are few, but the two presented in this dissertation are indicative of a milk-based emphasis on cattle and a meat-based use of small stock. The remainder of evidence from the sites was limited, and it was not possible to definitively characterize the strategy at either site.

In my interpretation of ethnographic cases and archaeological data, I have relied heavily on biological concepts to prevent an overdependence on 'culture' as an explanation. Basically, an ecological approach acknowledges that the environment influences human society, but cultural mechanisms often develop which are not clearly 'adaptive' but serve to overcome environmental limitations. Thus, both culture and the environment were conceived as contributing, to some degree, to observed social practices, as well as for helping to explain diversity between cultures.

The methods for the investigation of alternatives of social and economic (subsistence) production and intensification were closely linked to zooarchaeological analysis. However, faunal inferences are limited for a number of reasons. Therefore, it was necessary to supplement them with other lines of evidence such as artistic depictions, ancient Egyptian governmental and private documents, and information from classical authors. This more challenging task of integrating different anthropological, archaeological and historical approaches was attempted to try to understand the intricate relationships between different segments of Dynastic Egyptian society (chapter 7). This phase of research relied on the qualitative, rather than quantitative, analysis of these sources. Some aspects of the record are still too incomplete for detailed interpretations, but the methodology was developed for applying evolutionary theory to a future understanding of why patterns of human food production took the form they did, and by what mechanisms they were maintained within the interacting pastoral and agrarian–urban societies.

Archaeological evidence in the deserts left by indigenous populations was inconclusive; these areas have not been systematically explored for occupations during the Dynastic and the absence of data is not interpreted as failure of the model. Exploitation of the areas by Dynastic Egyptian government-sponsored mining or quarrying suggests a domesticate-based strategy not considered by the present model, and represents a needed addition to this model. Further, faunal assemblages from settlements associated with mining and quarrying sites are expected to contribute to the general understanding of government control of subsistence, because of the apparent provisioning of such expeditions.

Data for the Valley region were somewhat better represented, and suggest that more than one strategy was utilized. Additionally, the data from sites in this area suggest that larger taxa may have been subject to greater governmental control and that pigs, for example, were emphasized as supplemental meat sources by lower social classes. This is an important point, considering that pigs have long been considered unimportant economically to the ancient Egyptians. That pigs were perhaps restricted to lower social ranks suggests some refinement is needed in the model itself through a finer-grained reconstruction of the ecological or habitat zones within such large areas. Future investigations should also focus on the degree of governmental control over subsistence in outlying areas.

Delta sites were perhaps the most thoroughly tested against expectations; this was possible through the availability of a comparatively greater number of published reports on large, diverse faunal assemblages. These data provided strong evidence at one site of a ranching-type strategy, apparently to fill government obligations such as taxation, and less likely, religious obligations (i.e., ritual sacrifice). Convincing support for this interpretation was noted among Egyptological sources, which also suggested that additional sites of this type would have been required to meet the ever increasing needs of the redistributive system. However, because the strategy is documented at only a single site thus far it is unwise to extend interpretations. Settlement research itself is a fairly new idea to Egyptian archaeology, and clearly more research and accumulated data are needed to substantiate the claims made here.

## Directions for Future Research

"While acknowledging that few questions have definitive answers, it is nevertheless incumbent on any scholar in this field to put forward the questions appropriate to the current state of knowledge, and then to provide tentative answers that will facilitate future research" [Bar-Yosef and Khazanov 1992:1-2]. Investigation of similarities and differences in trajectories of development depends upon accumulating sufficient data on ecological history, economy, and sociopolitical configurations within the various regions where prehistoric pastoralism evolved. These types of data may eventually answer questions of why some populations adopt agriculture and others pastoral lifeways, and how food production relates to social complexity. Gaps existing in the available faunal and historical records outlined above suggest several areas of future research.

Additionally, comparative studies may help expose the processes of cultural development that shaped the archaeological imprint of early livestock herding societies in each region. Clearly, for many regions of Africa, much data still remains to be gathered and analyzed before stronger inferences can be made regarding the factors behind the particular path of development in any given region. Continued refinement of the direction and mechanisms for the introduction of the four major (and other) domesticated species into Egypt is necessary. While it seems clear that at least sheep and goats were brought into Egypt in an already domesticated form, it was not possible in this thesis to identify specific cultural traits from the Near East transmitted concurrent with or resulting from the spread of the domesticated taxa. Similar but even larger voids remain in the present understanding of the origins of domesticated cattle and pigs. With the recent interest in determining patterns of the spread of domesticates, the accumulation of needed information will not be far in the future, and soon comparative studies more detailed than the present one will be possible. As has been briefly mentioned here, there is increasing evidence in many areas that the spread of domesticated animals accompanied—or even followed—the adoption of domesticated plants. The implications of this sequence have not been investigated here, but provide a fascinating avenue of future research.

Differences in the physical anatomy of camel and donkey feet render each better adapted to long-distance travel in different geographical area. For example, camels cannot negotiate the rocky terrain of the Eastern Desert highlands, but donkeys can easily do so (e.g., Hobbs 1989:37). Similarly, donkeys do not respond well to walking across sand, yet with their broad foot pads, camels are ideally suited to such conditions. The ability of each taxon to carry considerably heavier loads over distance than humans could manage would have dramatically increased the distance of trade in each direction. This raises several interesting questions. If donkeys were introduced first, is there evidence that they were replaced by camels in the Western Desert? If camels were utilized in the Eastern Deserts, is there evidence that particular portions of the human population were left behind with them, or were they abandoned (as is the case now [Hobbs 1989])? Human populations remaining at the base of the Red Sea mountains would need sufficient resources and cover until the travelers returned. This suggests perhaps that they briefly turned to hunting, that some of the food animals would also be left behind, that more durable storage and food preparation facilities were needed, and/or possibly that they made use of caves or rock shelters as temporary shelters or pens. The desert regions are virtually untapped archaeological resources; here, extensive systematic surveys of campsites and seasonal settlements are necessary.

The reconstruction of herding strategies based on the presence of a limited number of domesticated food animals, particularly if hunted species are also included, might result in a highly skewed interpretation of the subsistence base. The construction and longer use of animal pens, food preparation and storage facilities might, incorrectly, suggest a much more sedentary lifestyle than was actually practiced by a normally highly mobile population.

Parallel development of ideas and interpretations seems to be occurring more and more frequently between archaeologists and Egyptologists. I would argue that a rift of specialization is growing ever wider between the two specialties, primarily because of the impossibility in keeping up with incredible amounts of data accumulating in either specialty. Epigraphic and literary data are perhaps daunting to archaeologists who lack the detailed training to conduct such studies themselves, but as the present research shows, there are abundant journals and other publications which are readily accessible, understandable and cogent to research questions posed by the anthropological archaeologist. Also, several of the early interpretations based solely on Egyptological sources have been demonstrated false, and should serve as a reminder to scholars of ancient Egyptian language and art that material remains are an integral part of reconstructing and understanding the society. Interdisciplinary cooperation is essential for thorough and high-quality interpretations.

Other topics for future research lie more within the realm of expertise of ethnographers and ecologists. The centrality of cattle to indigenous African societies was perhaps overstated in the ethnographies examined for the present work. Even among human populations whose flocks of sheep and goat dramatically outnumber cattle, the emphasis on cattle for social status was, apparently, inadvertently replicated by ethnographers in an underreporting of details on the variety of uses of small taxa. In several of the societies with semi-nomadic and semi-sedentary patterns (see chapter 5), the bulk of meat (and possibly milk) comes from sheep and goat rather than cattle, and so these smaller animals play a much more frequent role in the daily lives of the herders than is generally recognized. Significant gaps exist in the data concerning caloric or nutritional content of various animal products; information concerning the amounts of meat and fat from African species are especially sketchy. Studies similar to those conducted by Dahl and Hjort (1976), Redding (1981) and Russell (1988) are needed for smaller domesticated taxa. In particular, studies of this type for (African) pigs are essentially lacking, although the present analysis clearly demonstrates that suids contributed regularly to the diet of a fairly large segment of the Egyptian population.

Similarly, although pigs were mentioned as a food resource in some societies in which agricultural produce is the dominant economic activity, the mechanisms for control or redistribution of this species were not noted. Considerable work on these sorts of biases needs to be conducted in order to better comprehend the human labor investments involved in raising this species in such societies. Also, the relative enrichment of soils (and yields) resulting from fertilization with the dung from the four domesticated taxa has not been systematically tested. Such assessments would permit refinement of the present model by improving the understanding of the relative values of various taxa.

The seasonal or gender-based variance in consumption of different resources has been largely ignored in the literature of modern pastoralists until relatively recently. Energetic or caloric studies of modern pastoral populations are time-consuming, labor-intensive and, consequently, expensive. They are also somewhat difficult because the necessity to weigh each morsel before it is consumed is not always easily accepted by the population under study. Nonetheless, valuable information results. Such studies suggest an aspect of the model that has been largely overlooked here—gender-based access to resources in ancient Egypt. The ethnographic data already presented certainly indicate seasonal variability in human diet, and differential access to resources by sex among their domesticated animals (i.e., women remain in villages tending gardens while men care for mobile herds), although quantified differences in diet were not recorded. Similarly, while it would not be possible to transfer actual caloric investment to the archaeological past (see Redding 1981), detailed studies of these issues might permit ranking of activities by energy expenditure. This would be valuable for determining more precisely when one strategy becomes too labor intensive and is likely to be replaced with a more efficient strategy. In this way, the evolution of strategies might become more clear.

While caloric/energetic studies may be useful for predicting or ranking behaviors among populations practicing certain strategies, they would need to be tested against the archaeological record. Isotopic analyses allow fairly fine-grained reconstruction of human diet, particularly the distinction between aquatic-, meat- and plant-dominated food consumption, which would be useful for calculating the dietary differences between the various sub-populations (e.g., nomadic pastoralist versus a rancher) as well as between social classes. Additionally, isotopic analyses of hair from Nubian mummies demonstrated seasonal dietary changes (Sandord et al. 1983; White 1993). These types of analyses also aid in more accurately interpreting pathologies and aberrations on osteological remains. Publications abound concerning a decline of the nutritional plane following the shift to agricultural-based subsistence (see Hassan 1981 and references cited therein), and there is tantalizing osteological evidence from human skeletal material in Egypt. Corroborating this line of evidence with isotopic analyses can only improve the interpretability and understanding of the effects of this dramatic social and economic shift. An further problem is that for human dietary analysis, small amounts of bone or hair must be destroyed, further reducing the likelihood of obtaining permission to test such remains presently curated in Egypt. However, numerous mummies (etc.) are housed in museums throughout the world and perhaps would not require such permission. Obviously, carrying out a project of this magnitude would necessitate strong ties of cooperation among a fairly large group of scientists.

Isotopic analyses also have the potential for much more refined reconstruction of past environments (e.g., Sikes 1995), which would be of immeasurable aid in determining more precisely both the nature of available resources in a particular habitat as well as subsequent floristic shifts resulting from overgrazing or clearing for agricultural endeavors. Unfortunately, it is extremely difficult to obtain governmental permits necessary to remove cultural samples from Egypt, and to my knowledge no facilities there exist to conduct such tests. Perhaps with additional training of Egyptian antiquity inspectors[1], the importance of soil testing will come to be recognized and the various national research institutes will be able to successfully negotiate for the exportation of archaeological soil samples.

## Conclusions

In summary, the multi-stage process of this research yielded valuable information concerning the interrelationship of developing human societies and domesticated animals. The thorough zooarchaeological analysis of both new and previously published data was needed in order to answer fundamental questions concerning geographic and temporal distributions of domesticated taxa. The site– and regional–level distributions which resulted from this synthesis permitted identification of potential breeding centers, restrictions of taxa to different social ranks, and other attributes of increasing social complexity.

The inferences suggested by the zooarchaeological patterns were strengthened through comparison with other lines of evidence in order to correctly decipher their cultural significance. In order to obtain information concerning the effects of domestication on Egyptian society in particular, models of ethnographic uses were tested using art historical, Egyptological and other sources of information. Comparison of the archaeological record to ethnographic data has been in common practice in many areas of the world, but surprisingly, had not been in Egypt. The model defined here—based on modern societies from Africa and the Near East—is important for this reason alone. The model should be broadly applicable to archaeological remains from other regions in these two broad areas, and perhaps even to other areas of the world with similar climatic and habitat conditions. In the future, it may be possible through comparative analyses to apply inferences based on these data to complex societies in general.

[1] For example, through archaeological field schools sponsored by the American Research Center in Egypt, the Supreme Council for Egyptian Antiquities, and the United States Agency for International Development.

# Appendix A: Recognizing Domesticated Animals from Archaeological Remains

## Introduction

Considerable effort has been devoted to defining accurately the terms used to recognize and measure domesticates archaeologically. Such definitions of the process have oscillated between purely biological and cultural, and the criteria for distinguishing wild and domestic have developed accordingly. By definition, biological criteria involve the genetic effects, whether quantifiable or entirely qualitative, resulting from human intervention (e.g. Bökönyi 1969; Reed 1969). Cultural criteria include behavioral, artifactual and architectural features expectedly associated with domesticated animals (e.g., Zeuner 1963; Flannery 1969; Smith 1969). The intermediate interdisciplinary approach emerging from recent investigations has broadened the foundation on which the analysis of the origins of domestic taxa is based, and is discussed in greater detail in the following section.

Briefly, purely biological models rely so heavily on morphological criteria that other considerations are ignored. Similarly, a strictly cultural approach may interpret anomalous criteria *possibly* due to domestication as 'proof' when in fact the phenomena are entirely unrelated to human intervention. An intermediate perspective, however, combines aspects of both extremes, and incorporates geologic and environmental stimuli as well (e.g., Banks 1984; Brewer et al. 1994). As archaeological and other techniques are tested and improved, the recovered data can be analyzed more completely. The resultant loci and chronologies for the 'earliest' domestic species naturally reflect these changes. In this Appendix, the development of the definitions and criteria used to identify domesticated animals will be presented.

In the early stages of research on domestication, measurable changes in the limb-bone and skull characteristics were essentially the only scientific techniques available to distinguish between wild and domestic breeds (cf. Bökönyi 1969; Amorosi 1989; Chaplin 1969; Clutton-Brock 1970; Grigson 1969, 1976, 1978, 1980; Prummel and Frisch 1986, von den Driesch 1976; Zeuner 1963); age/sex ratio criteria became more prevalent during and following the 1960s (Ducos 1969, 1978; Ducos and Helmer 1980, Flannery 1969; Noddle 1983; Reed 1961; Silver 1970). It was not until the early 1970s that internal structures of bones were investigated (Daly et al. 1973) and only more recently that genetic analyses have been applied (Bradley et al. 1996; Loftus et al. 1994; Manwell and Baker 1980a,b; Weiner and Bar-Yosef 1990) or the environmental implications of domesticated animal populations considered (Clason and Clutton-Brock 1982, Garrard 1982; Wetterstrom 1994).

## Definitions

A major issue concerning the studies of the origins of domestic species is that of the true meaning of the term 'species.' The simplest definition recognizes two unique species when individuals of the populations no longer produce viable offspring. However, examples of hybridization—when two species breed producing an intermediate form—are not excluded (Hardesty 1977). Terms such as 'breed,' or 'type' are more appropriately used to describe subspecies or regional variations within a species, although they have unfortunately been used interchangeably with 'species' (Hardesty 1977).

The term 'domestication' has been redefined numerous times in the several decades of its use. Bökönyi (1969:220) chose a highly cultural definition in which the most essential criterion is the overt control of breeding by humans. Two phases in the process are recognized: (1) animal keeping, and (2) animal breeding. In the former, animals are kept in pens or loose herds, but humans do not interfere with the breeding of the animals as a group, nor do they control the food on which the animals subsist. In the latter stage, however, humans deliberately prohibit or encourage reproductive behavior between particular animals with desired characteristics (e.g. size, strength, milk, etc.). Such a definition is reminiscent of Darwin's statements that:

> man, without any intention or thought of improving the breed, by preserving in each successive generation the individuals which he prizes most and by destroying the worthless individuals, slowly, though surely, induces great changes. As the will of man thus comes into play we can understand how it is that domestic races of animals and cultivated races of plants often exhibit an abnormal character as compared with natural species, for they have been modified not for their own benefit, but for that of man [1868:4, cited in Clutton-Brock 1994:27].

The distinction between the two stages of domestication has been largely ignored in investigations concerning the prehistoric origins of domesticates for the simple reasons that researchers considered the criteria used insufficient to distinguish kept from bred archaeological populations and/or the criteria were misapplied.

From both Bökönyi's and Darwin's definitions of domestication, the intention underlying the control of animals by humans is clear: to produce animals and plants which better meet the perceived needs of that human population. Similarly, Ducos believed that all the criteria used to distinguish domesticated from wild animals "stem not from the evolutionary dynamics of the animal but from those of human society. Therefore, that which is characteristic of domestication must be defined with reference to human society" (1978:54). However, there need be no recognizable intention on the part of the humans to produce *particular* results, in that it

> is not a prerequisite for the domestication of plants and, indeed, may be counterproductive. …[P]eople act and their actions may be motivated by immediate goals. People...will not choose an obviously inconvenient, difficult, or inefficient subsistence strategy. This is not to claim, however, that the strategy chosen need represent the 'best' or 'most efficient' one—it may only be judged given the perceptible options in any place and at any time [Rindos 1984:86].

Evolutionary biologists reject the importance of intentionality as a source of information about the evolution of behavior, because it is impossible to verify/falsify scientifically.

A final definition—and the one used here—argues that the genetic makeup of a domesticated species has been sufficiently altered "to satisfy the vital needs of humans that if the plant or animal is placed back into its natural environment, it will be at a selective disadvantage when competing against its wild counterparts" (Brewer et al. 1994:1). Thus, although a few domesticated individuals survive in the wild population, the majority are no longer competitive and die out; those surviving typically also begin to exhibit many of the physical and behavioral characteristics of their wild counterparts (such as feral horses, pigs and goats). In addition, this intermediate perspective addresses the issue of failed and successful attempts at domestication. More important, it allows for the possibility that only humans benefit from the association, whereas most other definitions imply a symbiotic relationship from which both parties benefit (e.g., Harris 1989; Rindos 1984; Zeuner 1963). Now that an acceptable definition has been provided, the criteria used to justify the assignment of archaeological remains to domestic or wild categories can be discussed.

## Criteria

Numerous methods have been published throughout the several decades of research on the process of domestication and still other researchers debate the criteria employed to distinguish domestic from wild forms (e.g. Bökönyi 1969; Clutton-Brock 1970; Grigson 1976, 1978; Jarman and Wilkinson 1972; Olsen 1979). Generally criteria from three types of data are used to identify examples of prehistoric domestication:

(1) Ecological criteria—Assessment of the demography, ecology and biogeography of exploited animal populations through comparisons of sex ratios, mortality and survivorship patterns between recovered archaeological materials and a documented wild population.

(2) Physical characteristics—such as size, morphology and color of the animals.

(3) Cultural evidence—Artistic data and the presence of material objects known ethnographically to be associated with domestic animals (e.g. halters, pens, etc.).

### *Ecological Criteria*

The presence of animals outside their ancestral range is often the first criterion used as a basic determinant of a domesticated animal. Unfortunately, the ancestry of most of these species is not well enough understood to determine their previous geographic distribution. To define the ancestral range, the principle of uniformitarianism is applied to the range of modern wild animals to identify those regions in which they might once have lived—with remains of animals occurring outside this range classified as domesticates. As geological, palynological and environmental studies are conducted, the paleoenvironment can be reconstructed in more detail, enabling finer distinction of suitable habitats.

Wild animals have very nearly equal sex ratios whereas domestic populations tend to have more females (Bökönyi 1969; Payne 1973). More females produce more offspring as well as greater amounts of secondary products; only a few males are needed for reproduction. In addition, this female-dominated composition enables the population to 'rebound' more quickly from a severe season in areas of unpredictable rainfall (Hardesty 1977). Because of the differing contributions of each sex, age profiles are necessarily tied to sex ratios. Wild populations tend to exhibit attritional mortality patterns regardless of sex—a peak in mortality at a young age with a steady decline of those which survive (see Figure A.1); domestic populations, however, have a much different profile which varies by sex (see Figure 5.13; Ducos 1969; Silver 1970). Therefore, a typical mortality pattern among male domesticates is the natural peak at a young age, a leveling off during growth, and then a second sharp decline in survival shortly after animals reach adult body size. Females, on the other hand, generally have an attritional pattern after the initial peak in mortality as newborns.

Ducos (1969) demonstrated that if sex is not accounted for, mortality patterns of domestic cattle and sheep/goat species may be indistinguishable from the pattern of wild populations. Males killed at a young age fit the wild population curve of expected high immature mortality, and because females are kept in higher numbers and generally exhibit attritional patterns, the combined curve resembles that of a wild population. The change in the age structure of a population as a measure of domestication has been applied since the early 1960s, although the measurements and reliability with which the determinations are made have changed. Tooth eruption patterns and occurrence of epiphyseal fusion were the first methods by which age was determined. Both eruption and fusion rates vary by species, and are highly dependent upon the environment in which the species occurs, and the quality of available forage (Hardesty

1977; Silver 1970). Increases in the quality of forage markedly reduce the length of time before eruption and fusion are complete. That is, bones of animals which had access to higher quality forage will be identified as older individuals than those of same–age animals in lower quality food areas.

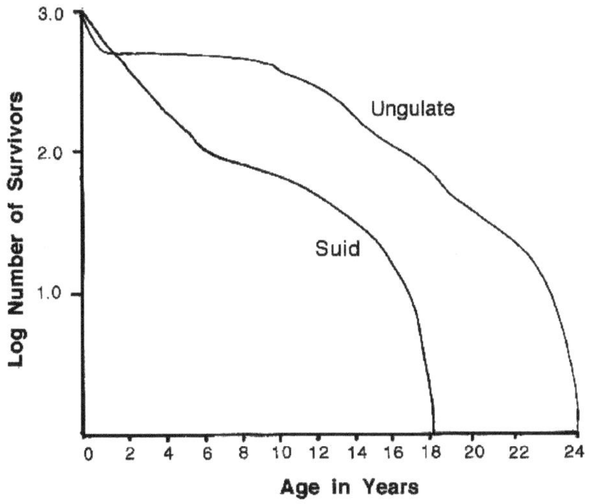


Figure A.1. Schematic of Generalized Mortality Profiles for Wild Animal Populations.

Subsequent studies (i.e., from the 1970s and later), identified general categories ages based on extent of tooth wear for each species, and bypassed the problems of specific age determination just mentioned. The use of cross-sectioning teeth for annual markers has become more common, and relies on more complex technology. The process of identifying ages based on tooth cementum has the same problems of missing or blurred outer edges of other seasonality studies, but has the added source of error of reabsorption or destruction of the inner markers (Klein et al. 1981; Payne 1985). As a result, this method has most typically been applied for determining season at death rather than overall age, although Klein et al. (1981) demonstrated that with computer image enhancement of the markers, highly accurate estimates were obtained from known-age specimens.

### *Physical Criteria*

Most of the reports from the late 1950s and into the middle 1960s concentrated on comparing sizes of recovered bones with modern specimens on the assumption that domesticates are generally smaller than their wild counterparts. However, since domestication typically reduces sexual dimorphism, while decreasing overall size; it should become harder to distinguish males from females on the basis of size alone. Figure A.2 depicts this graphically, using prehistoric and modern data of cattle from Britain. The specimens toward the upper right were of prehistoric age and were identified as aurochsen (wild cattle). The specimens toward the lower left were of modern domesticated cattle. Note not only the overall decrease in size from prehistoric to modern times, but also the closer clustering of both males and females among the modern specimens.

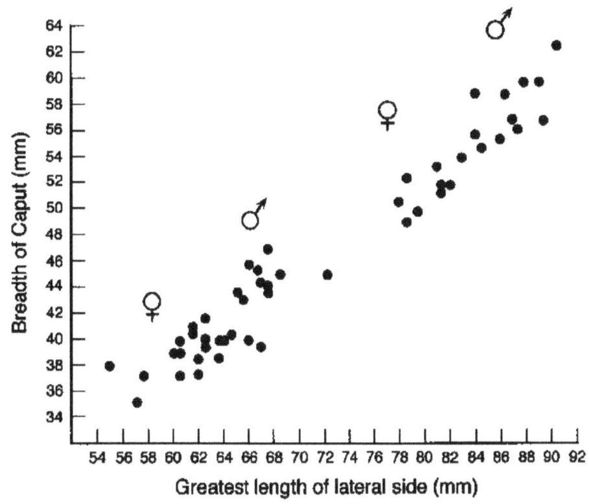


Figure A.2. Schematic Showing the Decrease in Sexual Dimorphism Following Domestication Using the Talus (after Boessneck and von den Driesch 1978:figure 4).

Additionally, the smaller size of domesticates can result from other causes: the lower quality of food provided by humans, protection from predators, or genetic isolation from the wild gene pool (Gautier 1984; Hardesty 1977). Archaeologically, it may also simply indicate females in a sexually dimorphic wild population. Enormous effort has been devoted to defining the size range of modern wild species in an area which eventually had domesticated remains, so that smaller remains can be classified as domesticates (Bökönyi 1973, 1974; Boessneck and von den Driesch 1978; Grigson 1969, 1970, 1980; Noddle 1983; Prummel and Frisch 1986; Stampfli 1983; Uerpmann 1978, 1979; Walker 1985).

Patricia Daly et al. (1973) tested an innovative technique in which the internal structures of bones were examined by thin–section for changes between wild and domestic populations. Three distinctions were noted which occurred *independent* of species or post-depositional processes and which did not show any overlap between wild and domestic specimens (1973:158). First, domestic animals have a much thinner cortical (exterior) portion of bone compared with wild individuals.[1] Second, the spaces in the trabecular (interior) portion are much larger and more numerous in domestic animals—both of which reduce the overall mass of domesticated animal bone. Finally, the orientation of crystalline minerals within the bones exhibits marked differences: wild specimens show

[1] Smith and Horowitz (1984:468) claimed this was evidence of osteoporosis as a result of "continued calcium drain through prolonged milking and repeated pregnancies." However, Chang and Koster (1986:110) noted that the sample sizes were "too small to be statistically significant..." and "[w]e still have too little control over the etiology of osteoporosis for Smith and Horowitz's findings to be accepted as definitive."

a random orientation of the minerals, with only a faint pattern of concentric rings appearing parallel to the shaft. Bones of domestic individuals, however, have a highly organized pattern of alternating layers of the minerals (each of which is perpendicular to neighboring layers). Although this appears to be an ideal method for identifying initial stages of domestication (because these changes begin to appear within the first generation), it has received little attention.

It is also possible to test the relative genetic diversity of herds in different areas to ascertain a relative measure of time since domestication, although so far this technique has been systematically applied for African materials only to bovids (e.g., Bradley et al. 1996; Loftus et al. 1994).

The change or loss of horns became a popular measure of domestication during the mid-to-late 1960s, and reached its peak with several studies by Caroline Grigson (e.g., 1969, 1976, 1978, 1980). When initially used, the loss of horns was stated to occur in females as a result of domestication (Armitage and Clutton-Brock 1976), although the only information available for sex determination was based on sexual dimorphism. Another method for demonstrating domestication involved the change in direction of horn core curvature. Wild modern ungulate species typically have fairly straight, outwardly curving horns. In archaeological samples, domestication was 'proven' by the presence of horn cores which turned inward or which twisted along their length (Bökönyi 1973; Zeuner 1955). Horns which turned inward were considered to be evidence of domestication because—in theory—animals had been selectively bred so that the tips of the horns no longer pointed outward to skewer handlers. Several authors questioned this trait on the basis of observed variability among wild populations (e.g., Chaplin 1969; Isaac 1962; Jarman and Wilkinson 1972). Using artistic representations, it became apparent that twisted horns had some aesthetic quality; horns were 'perverted' so that they both twisted in the same rather than opposing directions (Smith 1969; Zeuner 1963). While neither direction of horn curvature or twisting is a definitive character by itself, when used in conjunction with other traits, they probably are reasonable indicators of domestication.

As more studies accumulated, other variations in horn cores were observed, such that castrates were being identified based on indentations along the length of the horn core (Noddle 1983), although this has been shown to be incorrect. Recent cross-sectional analyses indicate these indentations are actually showing periods of nutritional stress, and occur more often in breeding females (Siegel 1976). Additional work using cross-sectioning of horn cores has been used to distinguish breeds of cattle and sheep/goat based on the shape of the cross-section. Wild animals tend to have thick–walled, ovoid–shaped horns, whereas domestic specimens are thinner and have a flatter cross–section (Bökönyi 1973).

While it is generally accepted that domestic animals as a rule display a much larger diversity of characteristics than the same wild species; comparatively little attention has been paid (by non-geneticists interested in domestication, at least) in the striking phenomenon of the great variety in their coat colors, wild species typically having much more uniform coats. A wild animal's coloring is usually well adapted to its natural environment; both in terms of absorbing or reflecting heat from the sun and enabling the animal to hide from predators. Animals with darker coat colors exhibit higher surface and skin temperatures, and thus may be somewhat more likely to suffer from heat stress than lighter colored animals (Macfarlane 1968a:168). The combined effect of three forms of selection—of the conspicuous by predators, of the deviant from the norm in a social group by predators, and of social aggression and isolation from conspecifics—leads to the perpetuation of a certain standardization of coloring among wild animals (cf. Hemmer 1990:19-21).

In domestic animals, the first two of these important selection factors are eliminated as defense from predators is taken over by humans (note: possible exception of ranching, see chapter five). Decreasing selection immediately allows diversity to increase; if selected breeding is added to the resulting enriched diversity, new, altered standards become possible. While it cannot be proven as a motivation for selective animal breeding by prehistoric humans, mammalian coat color has also been related to the basic level of its activity, its reaction intensity, and social bonding (cf. Hemmer 1990). Coat-coloring pigments are produced by the same biochemical pathways as those essential for information processing of environmental stimuli; thus selection of certain coat colors can produce a corresponding change towards (or away from) attenuated behavior and increased tolerance, more uniformity in daily and seasonal activities, and loosening of social bonds, complexity and differentiation (see for example, Keeler 1947, 1975; Pees and Hemmer 1980; Röhrs and Kruska 1969; H. Schwabe 1979a,b). The fragility of wool and hairs renders coat color essentially invisible archaeologically as a measure of domestication, but incorporation of textual and pictographic data—abundant in Egypt during the dynastic period—allows some consideration of the possibility of selective breeding. The resultant behavioral changes have thus far not been considered.

### *Cultural Criteria*

The next category is the presence of artistic or material evidence of domestication. As previously mentioned, Smith (1969) showed through artistic representations that a variety of animals were kept penned or tied together in Egypt, with some being force-fed. Worshipped animals such as male cattle were presumably force–fed to keep the animals (and thus the deities they represented) content and benevolent (see especially Brewer et al. 1994:84-86; C. Schwabe 1978:14-28). Animals which were not associated with any known animal cult were assumed to be force-fed to fatten them before slaughter. Smith was able to distinguish between forms of male cattle based on morphological characters of skeletal material and in art to conclude that the bull around which the cattle cult was based was a local wild species, and the representations of other force-fed bulls were domestics imported from the south for consumption (1969:312). This early method of determining domestication is obviously restricted to areas with detailed art styles and cannot be universally applied. That the wild animals still exist today demonstrates that the decision to domesticate was not entirely successful in all cases.

Halters, leads, yokes, bells, pens or other structures form a portion of the material culture found among modern peoples with domesticated animals. Mendoza (1986) refers to these items as only indirect evidence of domestication and argues that osteological evidence should provide the definitive assignment. Aside from suspected fenced areas and tethering stones (e.g., Pachur 1982), these items are not often preserved archaeologically. Regardless, they do not necessarily prove domestication—only that animals were being kept (i.e., they cannot show the relationship of breeding). When combined with other criteria, the validity of the case for domestication is certainly improved.

# APPENDIX B: Zooarchaeological Methods

## Introduction

While the research presented here was intended for a wider audience than only zooarchaeological specialists, familiarity with considerable amounts of methodology and theory has been assumed. Rather than interupt the flow of the argument regarding the role of the domesticated animal complex in Egyptian cultural development, discussion of the techniques and debates surrounding quantification, sample size, biases, etc., such issues will be presented here—available to those who wish to learn about the zooarchaeological framework on which the interpretations in this dissertation rest. The "traditional" presentation of site-specific faunal data in tables or graphic displays can be found in Appendix D.

*Zooarchaeological Methodology*

*Identification.* The first step in the analysis of faunal remains examined by this author was to sort each lot (unique provenience) by taxonomic class: Mammalia, Aves (birds), Pisces (fish), Reptilia (turtles, snakes, etc.), and Mollusca (fresh or marine shells). Then, each group of these remains was separated into "identifiable" and "unidentifiable" fragments. Identifiable bones were those which could be identified on firm morphological or metrical basis at least to the taxonomic level of family, and ideally to the level of genus or species. Each identifiable bone was initially treated as a separate entity, and up to a dozen different pieces of information were recorded about each fragment, including the taxon, skeletal element, fragmentation, fusion stage for long bones, eruption and wear stage for teeth, various types of human modification, and provenience. Certain key aspects of the processing of identifiable bones are discussed below.

Taxonomic identifications were accomplished primarily through reference to comparative specimens in Douglas Brewer's personal faunal collection of Egyptian taxa, curated by the American Research Center in Egypt. In instances in which a comparative specimen was lacking (e.g., *Alcelaphus bucelaphus*), published texts concerning anatomical characters and preferred habitats were used (e.g., Boessneck 1963; von den Driesch 1976; Schmid 1970; Walker 1985). The analysis of several Egyptian faunal assemblages was carried out over several field seasons, and every effort was made to assure consistency of identification criteria.

### Unidentifiable Bones

Bones remained classified as unidentifiable when they could not be assigned to a taxonomic level more specific than Order. The term "unidentifiable" is, in actuality, a misnomer as all of the material in this category could be identified to *some* level of specificity. Bone fragments were separated into categories pertaining to the size of the animal—large, medium or small—as well as to general skeletal region represented—cranial, axial, and limb.

Bones included in the large mammal category are probably of cattle, but could also conceivably be of horse, camel, etc.. And because hunting continued throughout Dynastic Egypt (at least as an elite sport), remains of hippopotamus and other wild animals may also be represented in recovered archaeological samples. Bone elements included in the medium mammal category are most likely sheep, goats, pigs or canids, and may also include similarly-sized wild animals. When no wild taxa were identified in assemblages, "large mammal" bones were reassigned to referred categories (i.e., designated "cf.") if they were identifiable to element (e.g., ribs). Small mammals include rabbits, various rodents, etc., which are present in most recovered samples in small numbers. Skeletal categories within these size groups were further divided into more specific regions. For example, whenever possible elements from the cranial region were divided into subcategories such as skull, horn core, mandible, teeth, etc.. Additionally, a category of unidentifiable element was included for each size group, and finally, a category of unidentifiable size/ unidentifiable element designated the most fragmentary and least identifiable bones.

Thus, the unidentifiable classification includes pieces of bones too fragmentary to be identified to element or size of mammal, let alone to genus or species; but also includes bones for which more specific identification was potentially possible but would not yield results that warranted the time spent recording all the information noted for identifiable bones. While large mammal vertebral, rib, limb, skull or mandibular fragments could in most instances be reasonably assumed to be of cattle, similar elements for the smaller size classes were nonetheless classified as unidentifiable because of the greater range of possible genera. As a result of this conservative process of identification, the assemblages examined by this author—the Derry Batrawi Collection from the Predynastic site of Merimde Beni-salâme, remains from Archaic levels at Mendes, the non-human remains from Graco-Roman levels at Memphis, and New Kindom faunal material from East Karnak—include a large amount of material in a general category such as "large mammal." Material in each of these categories was counted, and human modifications were noted. These categories are directly comparable to more generalized size and element categories recorded in the identifiable portion of the assemblage. This equivalence provides for the ability to combine data from both portions of the assemblage, derive counts by general size group or skeletal region for the whole assemblage, and increase the interpretability of each sample (see Yokell in prep, 1997, n.d.a,b,c). Thus, since the ability to identify remains varies between analysts (depending more on their relative amounts of experience than natural talent), a reanalysis of these assemblages may result in the identification of a few elements to more specific categories, but this will not affect the overall interpretations. It is also important to note that although material in the generalized categories was interpretively useful in site-specific reports, these data were *not* equated with specimens in other collections assigned by other analysts to more specific taxonomic categories.

### Age and Sex of Animals

Information concerning the age of various animal species was recorded with two separate types of data: longbone fusion and mandibular tooth eruption and wear. Sex determinations were rarely possible because of the highly fragmentary nature of the recovered remains, and sex ratios could not be systematically compared from all sites.

Longbone survivorship curves were calculated for each species using a method devised by Redding (1982:248) that computes "fusion scores" based on the proportion of bones recovered that are fused, unfused, and in the process of fusing for each age class. Bones with the same *latest* age at fusion were combined into single age classes. The fusion score was then computed for each class, representing the precentage of animals surviving beyond this latest possible age. Even though the calibration of ages at which bones fuse (or teeth erupt and wear) may not be exact, the *sequence* of fusion (or eruption and subsequent wear) is postulated to be similar across taxa.

A major limitation of longbone fusion curves is the restricted age represented. The bones used here are all fully fused by approximately 6 years (depending on the species in question). In contrast, though the age classes become broader in older animals, mandibles can be used to age animals throughout their entire life span. Tooth eruption patterns also have greater resolution in age determination for animals less than ten months of age (see Zeder 1991:93). The computation of survivorship curves using mandibular teeth is based on Payne's system (1973; see Appendix A).

### Quantification

Preservational factors further affect each assemblage in unique ways. To assure consistency, metrical analyses based on von den Dreisch (1976) were used to distinguish species of similar size (eg. sheep and goat). In many instances, however, a more conservative generalized sheep/goat category was used. This portion of the analysis resulted in nominal-level data from which the geographic distribution of domesticated taxa was discerned. Recognition of changes in distribution through time was possible through the examination of faunal data from temporally varied sites.

Following Grayson's (1988:62-3) coding procedures, fracture patterns, the size and placement of butchering marks and other taphonomic modifications were then recorded on inventory sheets. Rarely were sufficient numbers of culturally modified bones recovered to permit statistical analysis of patterns. Several assemblages (eg. Merimde Beni-Salâme and Ma'adi) were reported before many taphonomic and statistical biases were understood; these were reevaluated here using current techniques of analysis of ordinal level data (e.g., Lyman 1984, 1985; Grayson 1984, 1988). The remains from each site were tabulated to determine the distribution of relative abundances (rather than simply presence/absence) of various taxa, and the results were compared geographically. The potential for breeding centers, restrictions of taxa to particular social classes, etc., could then be tentatively identified through quantitative analysis.

The zooarchaeological record is not a perfect one, and the organic nature of bone renders it susceptible to many destructive processes (see Figure B.1). Effects of preparation (such as smashing or boiling of longbones), carnivore and rodent gnawing, surface weathering and soil leaching are only a few of the sources of biases which a faunal analyst must consider before attempting to interpret the identified sample. Still a young field, much of the faunal research has concerned the development and evaluation of methods to quantify and overcome these and other biases.

Initially, the raw count of identified specimens (NISP) was used to calculate relative abundances of various species (see Appendix D for NISP values from specific sites). However, there are several factors which affect the NISP. For example, not all animals have the same number of bones; thus a complete skeleton of one species—such as pigs—may yield a higher NISP than a complete skeleton of another species with fewer bones, giving a false sense of relative abundance. Similarly, bones of smaller animals are more fragile and tend to break easily. Assuming all were recovered, this could also lead to an erroneous conclusion of abundances. The problem is essentially one of interdependence; a fundamental assumption of NISP is that each bone fragment represents a unique individual.

In order to overcome problems of NISP, a more complex measure was borrowed from paleontology: the **M**inimum **N**umber of **I**ndividuals (or MNI). Although used by Stock in 1929 to interpret the Pleistocene fauna of Rancho La Brea, the method first gained popularity in archaeology following a series of articles by White (1952, 1953a, 1953b, 1954, 1955). With this technique, the elements of each species are analyzed separately, and summed according to anatomical side. The most abundant element or portion (eg. right distal femur) is determined for each species, and used in comparisons of abundance. Because this is truly the minimum number of animals, it had been interpreted as an absolute measure of

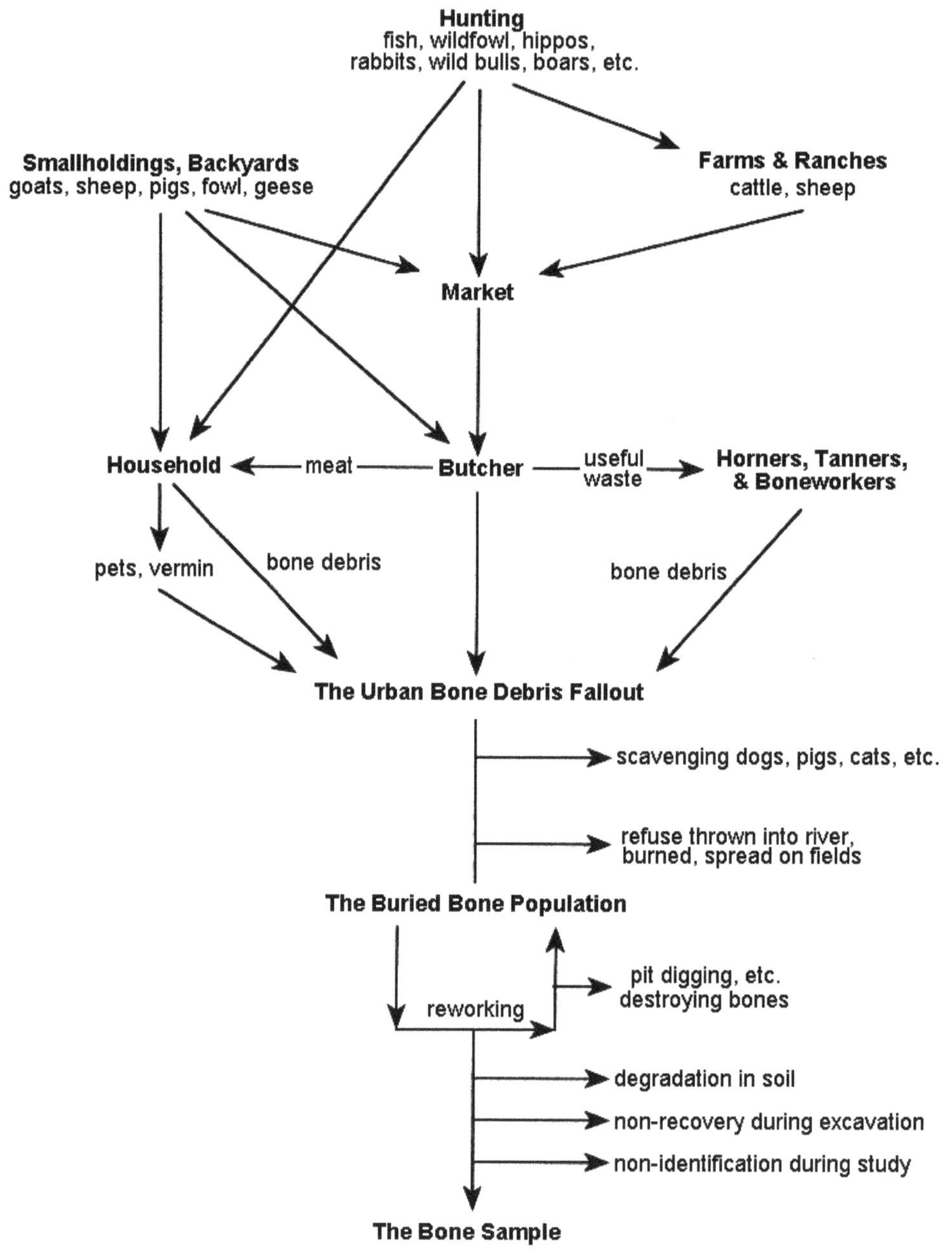


Figure B.1. Simplified flow diagram from livestock to the zooarchaeological sample.

abundance. As such, it had been used in more statistically complex calculations in order to ascertain values of meat, calories, the prehistoric living population of utilized species, etc. Unfortunately, although MNI eliminates problems of interdependence, new sources of bias are introduced.

The size of the aggregate unit used significantly affects MNI values (Grayson 1978, 1979, 1984). Archaeological sites are excavated in levels, whether artifical, stratigraphic or cultural. For interpretative purposes, faunal remains recovered by cultural layers are preferred. However, in many instances the stratigraphic or cultural layers cannot be discerned during the excavation process, and artificial levels must be used. These levels often cross culturally significant boundaries, resulting in the mixing of temporally distinct assemblages of artifacts. The MNI for each species often changes when grouped by artificial and cultural levels. This phenomenon is particularly important in attempts to quantify body-part representation (see Marshall and Pilgram 1993).

Both NISP and MNI are affected by sample size, although it is particularly evident in MNI. With further excavations, NISP values for each species will continue to increase. When relying on MNI, there is a positive relationship between the number of aggregate units and the MNI value. That is, as the number of aggregate units (levels) increases (decreasing sample sizes within each), the MNI also increases. Thus, NISP and MNI are opposite extremes.

More recently, researchers have reduced the level of analysis from an interval or ratio scale to an ordinal level. Grayson (1984) demonstrated that the relationship between NISP and MNI is not constant. By returning to an ordinal level and using the two measures together, it is possible to increase the robusticity of the conclusions. Species are arranged in rank order of abundance by both measures; if the rankings are statistically equivalent, then the accuracy of the orders can be assumed (Grayson 1984:106). Unfortunately, MNI data for several of the Egyptian sites were not published or otherwise available, and as a consequence, it was necessary to compare sites using only NISP and its derivatives.

Previous research has successfully demonstrated the increasing bias against smaller bones with larger screen sizes (Casteel 1972; Clason and Prummel 1977; Grayson 1984; Payne 1972; Schafer 1992; Thomas 1969). Grayson's commentary on Thomas' analysis reinforced that more than 95% of small mammals are lost with ¼" (6.35 mm) screen. Thus, a reliance on a large screen size may produce a taxonomic list which is strongly skewed toward larger species, and result in erroneous interpretations of species utilization and abundance.

Watson (1972) successfully demonstrated a less obvious benefit to smaller screen mesh. Her reexamination of several Near Eastern faunal assemblages resulted in the identification of a 'critical' length for several species below which fragments are unlikely to retain identifiable characteristics. The recovery and identification of specimens above that length can have significant results on the relative abundances of species. The proportions (or ranks) of species recovered with a large screen mesh in part are a reflection of the size of the fragments recovered. Clearly, the fragments of a medium-sized animal will be smaller on average than the fragments of a larger animal if the two are processed in the same way. With a large screen, this would result in the larger species appearing more abundant, a figure that might not reflect true frequencies. With a smaller screen, however, more of the bones of both species would be recovered and a closer approximation of actual relative abundances could be achieved. Screening is becoming a more common excavation practice in Egypt, but mesh sizes are typically at least ½" (12.7mm); smaller screen sizes are often used only to process selected soil samples for archaeobotanical remains. Thus, it is possible that all of the Egyptian faunal samples here are biased toward large animals to an unknown degree. However, the ubiquity of even extremely fragmented remains of fish in all collections examined argues that the bias is minimal.

# APPENDIX C: Key for Standardized Zooarchaeological Anatomical Nomenclature

For improved accessibility of the data herein by non-English speaking zooarchaeologists, and indeed for non-specialists in general, anatomical terminology follows *Nomina Anatomica Veterinaria* (1983), the standard recommended by the International Conferences on Archaeozoology (see Peters 1987). Note, however, that this key is applicable only to limited mammal species[1], and should not be used to describe avian (bird) or piscine (fish) remains. The terms given here denote bones (or taxonomic features thereof) which occur frequently archaeologically; this list is not exhaustive.

| Latin Terms | English Terms |
|---|---|
| ***SKELETON AXIALE*** | ***AXIAL SKELETON*** |
| *OSSA CRANII* | BONES OF THE SKULL |
| *Os Occipitale* | Occipital |
| *Foramen mangum* | Foramen magnum |
| *Condylus occipitalis* | Occipital condyle |
| *Canalis hypoglossi* | Hypoglossal canal |
| *Squama occipitalis* | Squamus region |
| *Os basisphenoidale* | Basisphenoid |
| *Os temporale* | Temporal |
| *Meatus acusticus externus* | External auditory meatus |
| *Bulla tympanica* | Auditory bulla(e) |
| *Os parietal* | Parietal |
| *Os interparietale* | Interparietal |
| *Os frontale* | Frontal |
| *OSSA FACIEI* | BONES OF THE FACE |
| *Os nasale* | Nasal |
| *Os lacrimale* | Lacrimal |
| *Maxilla* | Maxilla |
| *Os conchae nasalis ventralis* | Nasal concha(e) |
| *Os palatinum* | Palatine |
| *Os zygomaticum* | Zygomatic, Jugal or Malar |
| *Mandibula* | Mandible |
| *Corpus mandibulae* | Body of the mandible |
| *Margo alveolaris* | Alveolar border |
| *Foramen Mentale* | Mental foramen |
| *Facies labialis* | Labial surface[2] |
| *Facies buccalis* | Buccal surface[3] |
| *Facies lingualis* | Lingual surface[4] |
| *Ramus mandibulae* | Ramus |
| *Fossa masseterica* | Masseteric fossa |
| *Foramen mandibulae* | Mandibular foramen |
| *Processus coronoideus* | Coronoid process |
| *Processus condylaris* | Condylar process |
| *Os hyoideum* | Hyoid |
| *COLUMNA VERTEBRALIS* | VERTEBRAL COLUMN |
| *Corpus verebrae* | Vertebral body |
| *Arcus vertebrae* | Vertebral arch |
| *Pediculus arcus vertebrae* | Pedicle |
| *Lamina arcus vertebrae* | Lamina |
| *Foramen vertebrale* | Vertebral foramen |
| *Foramen intervertebrale* | Intervertebral foramen |
| *Processus spinalis* | Dorsal spinal process |
| *Processus transversus* | Transverse process |
| *Processus mamillaris* | Mamillar process |
| *Vertebrae cervicalis* | Cervical vertebra |
| *Atlas* | Atlas, or $C_1$ |
| *Ala* | Ala |
| *Axis* | Axis, or $C_2$ |
| *Dens* | Dens |
| *Vertebrae thoracicae* | Thoracic vertebra |
| *Fovea costalis cranialis* | Costal facet (anterior) |
| *Fovea costalis caudalis* | Costal facet (posterior) |
| *Vertebrae lumbales* | Lumbar vertebra |
| *Os sacrum (Vertebrae sacrales)* | Sacral vertebra, or Sacrum |
| *Ala sacralis* | Ala |
| *Facies auricularis* | Auricular surface |
| *Tuberositas sacralis* | Sacral tuberosity |
| *Foramina sacralia (dorsalia/ventralia)* | Sacral foramina |
| *Vertebrae caucales (coccygeae)* | Caudal vertebra |
| *SKELETON THORACIS* | THORACIC CAGE |
| *Cartilago costalis* | Costal cartilege |
| *Os Costale* | Ribs |
| *Caput costae* | Head |
| *Facies articularis capitis costae* | Articular surface |
| *Tuberculum costae* | Tubercle |
| *Sternum* | Sternum |
| *Manubrium* | Manubrium |
| *Sternabrae* | Sternabrae |
| *Processus xiphoideus* | Xiphistern/xiphoid process |
| ***SKELETON APPENDICULARE*** | ***APPENDICULAR SKELETON*** |
| ***CINGULUM MEMBRI THORACICI*** | |
| *Scapula* | Scapula |
| *Facies costalis* | Medial surface |
| *Facies lateralis* | Lateral surface |
| *Spina scapulae* | Spine |
| *Fossa supraspinata* | Suprascapular fossa |
| *Fossa infraspinata* | Subscapular fossa |
| *Acromion* | Acromion process |
| *Margo dorsalis* | Dorsal / Superior margin |
| *Margo caudalis* | Caudal / Inferior border |
| *Cavitas glenoidalis* | Glenoid or Glenoid fossa |
| *Tuberculum supraglenoidale* | Supraglenoid tubercle |
| *Processus coracoideus* | Coracoid process |
| *Clavicula* | Clavicle |
| *SKELETON BRACHII* | UPPER FORE LIMB SKELETON |
| *Humerus* | Humerus |
| *Caput humeri* | Head |
| *Collum humeri* | Shaft |
| *Tuberculum majus* | Greater tuberosity |
| *Tuberculum minus* | Lesser tuberosity |
| *Sulcus intertubercularis* | Bicepital groove |
| *Tuberositas deltoidea* | Deltoid crest |
| *Crista supracondularis lateralis* | Supracondylar ridge |
| *Condylus humeri* | (distal epiphysis) |
| *Capitulum humeri* | Capitulum |
| *Trochlea humeri* | Trochlea |
| *Epicondylus medialis* | Medial Epicondyle |
| *Eipcondylus lateralis* | Lateral Epicondyle |
| *SKELETON ANTEBRACHII* | LOWER FORE LIMB SKELETON |
| *Radius* | Radius |
| *Caput radii* | Head |
| *Fovea capitis radii* | Fovea |
| *Circumferentia articularis* | Articular surface for radial notch |
| *Collum radii* | Shaft |
| *Tuberositas radii* | Radial tuberosity |
| *Trochlea radii* | (distal epiphysis) |
| *Facies articular carpea* | Carpal articulations |
| *Processus styoideus* | Styloid process |
| *Incisura ulnaris* | Ulnar notch |
| *Ulna* | Ulna |

[1] This nomenclature is applicable to:

| | | | |
|---|---|---|---|
| Ruminantia (Ru) | Ruminants | Carnivora (Car) | Carnivores |
| *Bos taurus* (bo) | cattle | *Felis catus* (fe) | cat |
| *Ovis aries* (ov) | sheep | *Canis familiaris* (ca) | dog |
| *Capra hircus* (cap) | goat | Ungulata (Un) | Ungulates |
| *Equus caballus* (eq) | horse | *Sus scrofa domestica* (su) | pig |

[2] I.e., toward the lips

[3] I.e., toward the cheek

[4] I.e., toward the tongue

|  |  |
|---|---|
| *Olecranon* | Olecranon process |
| *Processus coronoideus medialis* | Coranoid process |
| *Margo interosseus* | Interosseus crest |
| *Caput ulnae* | (distal epiphysis) |
| *Processus styloideus* | Styloid process |
| *SKELETON MANUS* | BONES OF THE 'HAND' |
| *Ossa carpi* | Carpals |
| *Os carpi radiale* | Scaphoid, or Navicular |
| *Os carpi intermedium* | Lunar, or Semi-lunar |
| *Os carpi ulnare* | Cuneiform, Triquetrum, or Pyramidal |
| *Os carpi accessorium* | Pisiform |
| *Os carpale I* | Trapezium |
| *Os carpale II* | Trapezoid |
| *Os carpale III* | Magnum, or Capitate |
| *Os carpale IV* | Unciform, or Hamate |
| *Os carpi intermedioradiale* | Scapholunate? |
| *Os carpale II et III* | ? |
| *Ossa metacarpalia I - IV* | Metacarpals I - IV |
| *Osssa digitorum manus* | Phalanges |
| *Os compedale* | Proximal phalanx, or Ph. I |
| *Os coronale* | Medial phalanx, or Ph. II |
| *Os ungulare, Os unguiculare* | Distal (Terminal)phalanx, or Ph. III |
| *Ossa sesamoideae* | Sesamoids |
| *OSSA MEMBRI PELVINI* | BONES OF THE PELVIS |
| *Cingulum membri pelvini* | |
| *Os coxae* | Innominate or Pelvis |
| *Fossa acetabuli* | Acetabulum |
| *Facies lunata* | Lunate surface |
| *Spina ischiadica* | Ischial spine |
| *Foramen obturatum* | Obturator foramen |
| *Os ilium* | Ilium |
| *Ala ossis ilii* | Ala |
| *Os ischii* | Ischium |
| *Ramus ossis ischii* | Ramus |
| *Tuber ischiadicum* | Ischial tuberosity |
| *Os pubis* | Pubis |
| *SKELETON FEMORIS* | UPPER HIND LIMB SKELETON |
| *Os femoris* | Femur |
| *Caput ossis femoris* | Head |
| *Fovea capitis* | Fovea |
| *Trochanter major* | Greater trochanter |
| *Fossa trochanterica* | Trochanteric fossa |
| *Trochanter minor* | Lesser trochanter |
| *Trochanter tertius* | Third Trochanter |
| *Crista intertrochanterica* | Intertrochanteric crest |
| *Linea intertrochanterica, Facies aspera* | Linea aspera |
| *Condylus medialis* | Medial condyle |
| *Condylus lateralis* | Lateral condyle |
| *Fossa interconylaris* | Intercondylar fossa |
| *Patella* | Patella |
| Facies articularis | Articular surface |
| *SKELETON CRURIS* | LOWER HIND LIMB SKELETON |
| *Tibia* | Tibia |
| *Facies articularis proximalis* | Proximal articular surface |
| *Condylus medialis* | Medial condyle |
| *Condylus lateralis* | Lateral condyle |
| *Facies articularis fibularis* | Fibular articulation |
| *Eminentia interconylaris* | Intercondylar eminence |
| *Tuberositas tibiae* | Tibial tuberosity |
| *Corpus tibiae* | Shaft |
| *Linea m. poplitei* | Popliteal lines |
| *Margo lateralis* | Interosseus border |
| *Malleolus medialis* | Medial malleolus |
| *Fibula* | Fibula |
| *Caput fibulae* | Head |
| *Facies articularis capitis fibulae* | Articular surface |
| *Corpus fibulae* | Shaft |
| *Margo interosseus* | Interosseus border |
| *Malleolus lateralis* | Lateral malleolus |
| *Facies articulares malleoli* | Articular surface |
| *SKELETON FEDIS* | BONES OF THE (HIND) FEET |
| *Ossa tarsi* | Tarsals |
| *Talus* | Talus or Astragalus |
| *Caput tali* | Head |
| *Callum tali* | Neck |
| *Corpus tali* | Body |
| *Calcaneus* | Calcaneus |
| *Sustentaculum tali* | Sustentaculum |
| *Os tarsi centrale* | Navicular (su) |
| *Os tarsale I* | Internal Cuneiform |
| *Os tarsale II* | Middle Cuneiform |
| *Os tarsale III* | External Cuneiform |
| *Os tarsale IV* | Cuboid |
| *Os tarsale I et II* | Naviculocuboid |
| *Os tarsale II et III* | External&Mid Cuneiform |
| *Os centroquartale* | ? |
| *Ossa metatarsalia I - V* | Metatarsals |
| *Os metatarsale III et IV (Ru)* | Cannon Bones |
| *Ossa digitorum pedis* | Phalanges |
| | Proximal phalanx, or Ph. I |
| | Medial phalanx, or Ph. II |
| | Distal phalanx, Terminal Phalanx, or III |

# APPENDIX D: "Raw" Faunal Data for Sites Presented in the Text

Table D.1. Osteometrics of Mammalian Remains in the Derry Batrawi Collection from Merimde-Benisalâme (after von den Driesch 1976; Walker 1985). English equivalents of Latin terminology can be found in Appendix C.

| Taxon | Unit | Element | Measurements (mm) |
|---|---|---|---|
| *Bos* | 1.513.02 | *Radius* | GL=29.1 cm; Sd=4.5 |
| *Bos* | 1.513.03 | *Talus* | DM=2.93; GLm=5.67;Gll=6.14;Bd=3.8;Dl=3.47 |
| *Bos* | 1.513.03 | *Talus* | GLm=5.89;Gll=6.3;Bd=4.07;Dl=3.46 |
| *Bos* | 1.513.03 | *Talus* | GLl=6.05; Dl=3.44 |
| *Bos* | 1.513.03 | *Talus* | DM=3.46; GLm=5.73; GLl=6.18; Bd=3.90; Dl=3.68 |
| *Bos* | 1.513.03 | *Talus* | BD=4.10 |
| *Bos* | 1.513.03 | *Talus* | GLm=6.19; GLl=6.87; BD=4.85; DL=4.47 |
| *Bos* | 1.513.03 | *Talus* | GLl=6.90; Dl=4.06 |
| *Bos* | 1.513.03 | *Talus* | GLm=6.03; GLl=6.50 |
| *Bos* | 1.513.04 | *Os compedale* | length =36.5 |
| *Bos* | 1.513.04 | *Os digitorum pedis II* | L=34.2; W=21 (hindfoot?) |
| *Bos* | 1.513.04 | *Os coronale* | L=34.9; W=37.0 |
| *Bos* | 1.513.04 | *Os coronale* | L=36.0 |
| *Bos* | 1.513.09 | *Os digitorum pedis I* | GLPe=62.9; (hindfoot?) |
| *Bos* | 1.513.09 | *Tibia* | BD=54.0; Dd=45.6 |
| *Bos* | 1.513.10 | *Humerus* | BD=88.0; BT=76.38 |
| *Bos* | 1.513.10 | *Os metacarpalia* | BP=6.05 |
| *Bos* | 1.513.10 | *Os metacarpalia* | BP=60.0 |
| *Bos* | 1.513.10 | *Scapula* | BG=57.0; LG=69.0; GLP=80.82; SLC=68.0 |
| *Bos* | 1.513.10 | *Tibia* | Bd=5.96; Dd=4.77 |
| *Bos*, sm | 1.513.10 | *Scapula* | BG=46.79; LG=54.90; GLP=63.0 |
| *Bos* | 1.513.10 S01-150 | *Radius* | BFp=81.00; Bp=86.73 |
| *Bos* | 1.514.23.1 | $M_1$ | L=2.96; B=1.55; heavy wear |
| *Bos* | 1.514.23.1 | $M_1$ | L=2.67; B=1.58; heavy wear |
| *Bos* | 1.514.23.1 | $M_1$ | no L; B=1.89; moderate/heavy wear |
| *Bos* | 1.514.23.1 | $M_1$ | L=2.10; B=1.85, extr wear..<1cm enamel |
| *Bos* | 1.514.23.1 | $M_2$ | L=2.46; B=2.03; heavy wear |
| *Bos* | 1.514.23.1 | $M_2$ | L=2.60; B=1.95; light wear |
| *Bos* | 1.514.23.1 | $M^1$ | L=2.60; B=1.95 heavy wear |
| *Bos* | 1.514.23.1 | $M^2$ | L=2.80; B=1.86; heavy wear |
| *Bos* | 1.514.23.1 | $M^3$ | L=3.60; B=2.07 |
| *Bos* | 1.514.23.1 | $M^3$ | L=2.91; B=2.26; heavy wear |
| *Bos* | 1.514.23.1 | *Mandibula* | $M_3$.. erupting; L=3.0; B=1.97. |
| *Bos* | 1.390, crate 25 | *Radius* | BFp=70.7; Bp=77.5 |
| *Bos*/Beisa Oryx? | 1.513.04 | *Os compedale* | W=58.0 |
| *Bos*/Beisa Oryx? | 1.513.04 | *Os compedale* | W=58.7 |
| *Bos*/Beisa Oryx? | 1.513.04 | *Os compedale* | W=60.0 |
| *Bos*/Beisa Oryx? | 1.513.04 | *Os compedale* | W=59.0 |
| *Bos*/Beisa Oryx? | 1.513.04 | *Os compedale* | W=52.5 |
| *Bos*/Beisa Oryx? | 1.513.04 | *Os compedale* | W=51.0 (immature, not fully fused) |
| *Bos*/Beisa Oryx? | 1.513.04 | *Os compedale* | W=54.6 |

Table D.1 (continued)

| Taxon | Unit | Element | Measurements (mm) |
|---|---|---|---|
| *Alcelaphus bucelaphus* ? | 1.513.04 | *Os compedale* | L=76.5 |
| *Hippopotamus* | 1.390, crate 25 | *Humerus* | Bd=140.0, no Bt |
| *Hippopotamus* | 1.390, crate 25 | *Humerus* | BP=155.0 |
| *Hippopotamus* | 1.390, crate 25 | *Tibia* | Bd=98.6; Dd=75.5 (immature, not fully fused) |
| *Hippopotamus* | CW, crate 25 | *Tibia* | BD=83.0; Dd=68.0. (immature, not fully fused) |
| *Hippopotamus* | 1.512A34 | *Talus* | GLl=10.36; GLm=9.33; Dl=6.40; Dm=6.70 |
| Canid ? | 1.513.01 | *Scapula* | A=26.2; B=18.0 |
| *Gazella dama*? | 1.513.01 | *Scapula* | A=21.3; B=21.1; C=25.4 |
| *Gazella thompsoni*? | 1.513.08 | *Tibia* | A=25.5; B=15.0 |
| *Gazella thompsoni*? | 1.513.08 | *Tibia* | A=24.4; B=14 |
| *Ovis/Capra* | 1.513.01 | *Scapula* | A=19.2; B=19.0; B=26.0 |
| *Ovis/Capra* | 1.511A125 | *Os Femoris* | max breadth 2.05 |
| *Ovis/Capra* | 1.513.01 | *Scapula* | A=23.2; B=24.5;C=25.5 |
| *Ovis/Capra* | 1.513.01 | *Scapula* | A=24.2; B=23.0; C=26.6 |
| *Ovis/Capra*? | 1.513.01 | *Scapula* | A=14.0; B=12.8; C=17.5 (immature, not fully fused) |
| *Ovis/Capra*? | 1.513.01 | *Scapula* | A=15.5; B=13.1; C=19.4 |
| *Ovis/Capra* | 1.514.23.4 | *Mandibula* | GOC=4.30;M3-L=2.54;B=.80. $M_3$ newly erupted |
| *Sus* | 1.511A91 | *Radius* | max width 23.0 |
| *Sus*, sm? | 1.513.01 | *Scapula* | A=20.5; B=20.0; C=24.0 |
| *Sus* | 1.514.23.1 | $M_2$ | L=1.86; B=1.14; light wear |
| *Sus* | 1.514.23.1 | $M_3$ | L=3.03; B=1.78; light/moderate wear |
| *Sus* | 1.514.23.3 | *Mandibula*$P_{1-4}$, $M_{1-2}$. | $M_2$..L=2.14; B=1.42. moderate wear. $M_3$ visible, but not erupted. |
| *Sus* (Wild?) | 1.514.23.4 | *Mandibula* | $M_3$ erupting; L=3.21; B=1.75 |
| Waterbuck? | 1.513.04 | *Os coronale* | BP=38.7 |
| Waterbuck? | 1.513.09 | *Os metacarpalia* | BP=39.6 |
| Waterbuck? | 1.513.09 | *Os metacarpalia* | BP=42.8 |

Table D.2. Cutmarks and Other Modifications of Faunal Remains from Merimde-Benisalâme in the Derry Batrawi Collection.

| Taxon | Unit | Element | Nature of Modification |
|---|---|---|---|
| Bos | 1.513.03 | *Talus* | carnivore puncture |
| Bos | 1.513.03 | *Talus* | possible cutmarks on inferior surface |
| Bos | 1.513.03 | *Talus* | possible cutmarks on inferior surface |
| Bos | 1.513.03 | *Talus* | possible cutmarks on inferior surface |
| Bos | 1.513.10 | *Humerus* | cutmarks perpendicular to length; carnivore gnawed |
| Bos | 1.513.10 S01-150 | *Humerus* | smashed (occurred when fresh bone?) |
| Bos | 1.513.03 | Magnum | heavily rodent gnawed |
| Bos | 1.514.23.6 | *Mandibula* | rodent gnawed |
| Bos | 1.513.01 | *Os coxae* | carnivore gnawed |
| Bos | 1.513.10 S01-150 | *Os coxae* | weathering cracks obscure possible cutmarks on *Ala ossis ilii* diagonal to *Os ilium* height |
| Bos | 1.513.04 | *Os digitalis pedis II* | rodent gnawed |
| Bos | 1.513.10 S01-150 | *Radius* | cutmarks on anterior surface |
| Bos | 1.513.10 S01-150 | *Radius* (imm.) | smashed (occurred when fresh bone?) |
| Bos | 1.513.09 | *Tibia* | drill holes through lateral groove |
| Bos | 1.513.10 | *Tibia* | cutmarks on posterior & medial edge |
| Bos | 1.514.23.15 | *Vertebra thoracica* | possible cutmarks on spine, ant. to postzygopophysis |
| Bos (?) | **1.514.23.14** | *Os costale* | cut- and rodent marks |
| Bos (?) | **1.514.23.14** | *Os costale* | cut- and rodent marks |
| Bos (?) | 1.514.23.15 | *Os costale* (imm.) | faint cutmarks |
| Bos (?) | 1.514.23.09 | *Tibia* (imm.) | drill holes through lateral groove |
| Bovidae | 1.513.06 | *Femur* | heavily rodent gnawed |
| Bovidae | 1.513.09 | Metapodial (imm.) | carnivore gnawing |
| Canis | **1.514.23.4** | *Mandibula* | rodent (and carnivore?) gnawed |
| Canis | 1.513.08 | *Ulna* | 2 cuts perpendicular to length, just below proximal tip |
| Canis | **1.514.23.4** | *Mandibula* | cutmarks |
| Canis | 1.514.23.13 | *Os craniale* (fragment) | rodent gnawed condylus occipitalis |
| *Gazella dama*? | 1.513.01 | *Scapula* | cutmarks laterally, parallel to glenoid |
| *Gazella* spp. | 1.513.01 | *Scapula* | rodent gnawed |
| Gazelle/smgoat | 1.513.01 | *Scapula* | carnivore gnawed center of glenoid |
| Gazelle/smgoat | 1.513.01 | *Scapula* | possible cutmarks inferior border below spina scapula |
| *Homo* | 1.511 A.91/92? | *Os coronale* | split lengthwise into lateral/medial halves |
| *Hippo*? | no prov. noted | *Os costale* | possible carnivore punctures |
| Mammal, lg | 1.513.01 | *Scapula* | cutmarks diagonal to length, on facies costalis |
| Mammal, lg | 1.513.01 | *Scapula* | carnivore gnawing |
| Mammal, lg | 1.514.8 S01 | Metapodial | heavily rodent gnawed |
| Mammal, lg | 1.511 A145,brn paper | *Os costale* | cutmarks perpendicular to length |
| Mammal, lg | 1.514.15 | *Os costale* | cutmarks medially |
| Mammal, lg | **crate 25 S03-1.0** | *Scapula*? | polished edge |
| *Ovis*, prob. | 1.513.09 | *Humerus* | rodent & carnivore gnawed |
| *Ovis*, prob. | 1.513.09 | *Humerus* | rodent & carnivore gnawed |
| *Ovis/Capra* | 1.511 A139 (orP) | *Femur* (imm.) | smashed (occurred when fresh bone?) |
| *Ovis/Capra* | 1.514.23.4 | *Mandibula* | rodent gnawed |
| *Ovis/Capra* | 1.514.4 S01 | *Mandibula* | heavily rodent gnawed |
| *Ovis/Capra* | 1.514.23.6 | *Mandibula* | possible cutmarks on facies buccalis, parallel to ramus, & below/lateral to processus condylaris |
| *Ovis/Capra* | 1.514.23.6 | *Mandibula* | possible cutmarks on lateral surf, parallel to ramus, & below/lateral to processus condylaris |
| *Ovis/Capra* | 1.514.23.15 | *Os coxae* | rodent gnawed fossa acetabuli |

Table D.2: (continued)

| Taxon | Unit | Element | Nature of Modification |
|---|---|---|---|
| *Ovis/Capra* | 1.511 (A139/P) | *Radius* | smashed (occurred when fresh bone?) |
| *Ovis/Capra* | 1.513.08 | *Scapula* | Cutmarks present on blade |
| *Ovis/Capra?* | 1.513.01 | *Scapula* | possible cutmarks on facies costalis parallel to glenoid |
| *Ovis/Capra?* | 1.513.08 | Metapodial (m-carpal?) | carnivore gnawed |
| Mammal, md | 1.511 A.91/92? | Phalanx I | split lenthwise into lateral/medial halves |
| Mammal, md | 1.514.23.12 | *Vertebra Lumbale* (1st) | rodent gnawed corpus vertebra |
| *Sus* | 1.511 (A91/92?) | *Humerus* (imm) | rodent-gnawed cutmarks above tuberuculum minus |
| *Sus* | 1.514.23.2 | Mandibular symphysis | perpendicular and parallel cutmarks along inferior border, and dozens of short cutmarks on both sides |
| *Sus* | 1.514.23.2 | Mandibular symphysis | perpendicular and parallel cutmarks below premolar |
| *Sus* | 1.514.23.8 | Mandibular symphysis | rodent gnawed |
| *Sus* | **1.514.23.3** | *Mandibula* | cutmarks |
| *Sus* | 1.514.23.4 | *Mandibula* | possible cutmarks on lateral surface perpendicular to ramus, posterior to M1 |
| *Sus* | 1.514.23.8 | *Maxilla* | possible rodent gnawing on edges |
| *Sus* | 1.513.06 | *Os metacarapalia III* | probable cutmarks on anterior and lateral surfaces |
| *Sus* | 1.513.08 | *Ulna* | heavy rodent gnawmarks, cutmarks perpendicular to length above trochlear notch |
| *Sus* | 1.513.08 | *Ulna* | 2 short/deep cuts on lateral edge by trochlear notch perpendicular to length |
| *Sus?* | 1.513.08 | *Humerus* | carnivore punctures and rodent gnawmarks |
| *Alcelaphus bucelaphus* | 1.513.09 | *Os metatarsalia* | cutmarks perpendicular to length on lateral shaft and condyle |
| FISHES: | | | |
| *Clarias* | 1.514.4 S01 | Dentary | heavily rodent gnawed |
| *Lates* | 1.514.23.20 | Vertebra, trunk | cutmarks medio-laterally |
| *Lates* | 1.514.23.20 | Vertebra, trunk | rodent marks |
| *Lates* | 1.514.22 | Vertebra, trunk | rodent marks |
| *Synodontis* | 1.514.22 | Pectoral spine | polished at terminal end |

Table D.3. Number of Identified Specimens of Taxa Recovered from Selected Dynastic Delta Sites.

| | Tell Ibrahim Awad[1] | Mendes[2] | Memphis New Kingdom[3] | Memphis Greco-Roman[4] | Kom el-Hisn |
|---|---|---|---|---|---|
| Mammals: | | | | | |
| *Bos* | 76 | 35 | | 88 | 14 |
| *Ovis* | 13 | - | | 4 | - |
| *Capra* | 1 | - | | 2 | - |
| *Ovis/Capra* | 7 | 31 | | 39 | 311 |
| *Sus* | 112 | 102 | | 18 | 397 |
| *Alcelaphus bucalephus* | 4 | - | | 7(?) | 16 |
| Hippopotamus | 14 | 1 | | - | - |
| Donkey | 10 | - | | - | 41 |
| other | 1 | 3 | | 16 | 12 |
| Fishes: | | | | | |
| Catfish (*Clarias* or *Heterobranchus*) | 50 | 71 | | 183 | 6 |
| *Synodontis* | 3 | 31 | | 173 | 83 |
| *Lates* | 10 | 1 | | 59 | - |
| other | 12 | 12 | | 45 | 236 |
| Totals | 313 | 287 | | 634 | 1116 |

[1] Data from Boessneck and von den Driesch 1986:Tables 1,2.
[2] Data combined from Brewer and Wenke 1992:Table 1; Yokell n.d.a.
[3] Data from Hecker 1984.
[4] Data from Yokell n.d.b.

Table D.4. Number of Identified Specimens from Hierakonpolis. (Data from McArdle 1982:Table V.1).

| | Locality 29 | Locality 11 | Totals |
|---|---|---|---|
| *Bos* | 299 | 76 | 375 |
| *Ovis* | 14 | 14 | 28 |
| *Capra* | 37 | 18 | 55 |
| *Ovis/Capra* | 157 | 211 | 368 |
| *Sus* | 52 | 14 | 66 |
| *Canis* | 5 | 2 | 7 |
| other mammals | 4 | 1 | 5 |

# REFERENCES


Abdalla, Alid Jamaa
1981 Sudan Pastoronomads in transition: Problems of evolution and adjustment. *Die Nomaden im Geschichte und Gegewart*, pp. 203–211. Veroffentlichen des Museums für Völkerkunde zu Leipzig, Heft 33.

AERA (Ancient Egyptian Research Associates)
1996 The 1995 field season: A massive fish processing center discovered amidst enigmatic, long low plastered benches. *AERAgram* 1(1):8–9.

Alexander, Richard D.
1978a Biology, determinism, and human behavior: A reply to Slobodkin. *Michigan Discussions in Anthropology* 3:154–166.
1978b Natural selection and societal laws. In *The Foundations of Ethics and Its Relationship to Science*, vol. 3: *Morals, Science and Society*, edited by T.E. Engelhardt and D. Callahan, pp. 249–290. New York: Hastings on Hudson.
1979 Evolution and culture. In *Evolutionary Biology and Human Social Behavior: An anthropological perspective*, edited by N.A. Chagnon and W. Irons, pp. 59–78. New York: Doubleday.

Allchin, R.
1963 Cattle and economy in neolithic South India. In *Man and Cattle*, edited by F. Zeuner, pp. 36–50. Occasional Paper 18. London: Royal Anthropological Institute.

Ambrose, Stanley H.
1982 Archaeology and linguistic reconstructions of history in East Africa. In *The Archaeological and Linguistic Reconstructions of African History*, edited by C. Ehret and M. Posnansky, pp. 104–158. Berkeley: University of California Press.
1984 The introduction of pastoral adaptations to the highlands of East Africa. In *From Hunters to Farmers: The causes and consequences of food production in Africa*, edited by J.D. Clark and S.A. Brandt, pp. 212–239. Berkeley: University of California Press.
1996 The African Neolithic. In *Encyclopedia of Precolonial Africa: Archaeology, History, Languages, Cultures and Environments*, edited by Joseph O. Vogel, pp.281–283. New York: Altamira Press.

Ambrose, Stanley H. and Karl Lorenz
1987 *Origins and Dispersal of Modern Humans: Behavioral and biological perspectives.* Cambridge: University Press.

Amorosi, Thomas
1989 *A Post-cranial Guide to Domestic Neo-Natal and Juvenile Mammals. The identification and aging of Old World species.*Oxford: B.A.R. International Series 533.

Andrews, F.W.
1948 The vegetation of the Sudan. In *Agriculture of the Sudan*, edited by J.D. Tothill, pp. 32–61. Oxford: University Press.

Angress, Shimon
1962 *An Annotated Bibliography on the Origin and Descent of Domestic Mammals, 1900–1955. Fieldiana* 54(1):1–88. Chicago: Field Museum of Natural History.

Arkell, A.J. and P. Ucko
1965 Review of predynastic development in the Nile Valley. *Current Anthropology* 2:145–166.

Armitage, P.L. and Juliet Clutton-Brock
1976 A system for classification and description of the horn cores of cattle from archaeological sites. *Journal of Archaeological Science* 3:329–348.

Armstrong, R.G.
1964 *The Study of West African Languages*. Ibadan: Ibadan University Press.

Attia, M.I.
1953 *Deposits in the Nile Valley and the Delta.* Cairo: Papers of the Geological Survey of Egypt.

Avni, Gideon
1989 Survey of deserted Bedouin campsites in the Negev highlands and its implications for archaeological research. In *Pastoralism in the Levant: Archaeo-logical methods in anthropological perspectives*, edited by O. Bar-Yosef and A. Khazanov, pp. 241–254. Monographs in World Prehistory 10. Madison, Wisconsin: Prehistory Press.

Ayrout, Henry Habib, S.J.
1963 *The Egyptian Peasant*, translated from French by John Alden Wiliams. Boston, Massachussetts: Beacon Press.

Ayyad, Mohamed and Samir I. Ghabbhour
1986 Hot Deserts of Egypt and the Sudan. In *Ecosytems of the World,* vol 12B: *Hot Deserts and Arid Shrublands*. edited by Goodall, pp. 149–202. Amsterdam: Elsevier Publishing.

Baer, K.
1960 *Rank and Title in the Old Kingdom*. Chicago: University of Chicago Press.
1962 The low price of land in ancient Egypt. *Journal of the American Research Center in Egypt* 1:25–45.

Bagnold, R.A., O.H. Myers, R.F. Peel and H.A. Winkler
1939 An expedition to the Gilf Kebir and 'Uweinat, 1938. *Geographical Journal* 93:283–313.

Baîburtcjan, A.A.
1963 A new method of increasing the productivity of livestock (partial castration). *Animal Breeding Abstracts* 31:2.

Baines, John
1987 Practical religion and piety. *Journal of Egyptian Archaeology* 73:79–98.

Baines, John and Jaromír Málek
1980 *Altas of Ancient Egypt*. Oxford: Phaidon Press.

Baker, -
1974 incompletely cited in Wetterstrom (1993).
Banks, Kimball M.
1984 *Cimates, Cultures and Cattle: The Holocene archaeology of the eastern Sahara*. Dallas: Southern Methodist University.
Banning, E.B. and I. Köhler-Rollefson
1986 Ethnoarchaeological survey in the Beda area, Southern Jordan. *Zeitschrift des Deutschen Palästine-Vereins* 102:152–170.
1989 Ethnographic lessons for the pastoral past: Camp locations and material remains near Beidha, southern Jordan. In *Pastoralism in the Levant: Archaeological methods in anthropological perspectives*, edited by O. Bar-Yosef, and A. Khazanov, pp. 181–204. Monographs in World Prehistory 10. Madison, Wisconsin: Prehistory Press.
Barbour, K.M.
1961 *The Republic of the Sudan: A regional geography*. London: University of London Press.
Bar-Yosef, O. and A. Khazanov
1992 Introduction. In *Pastoralism in the Levant: Archaeological materials in anthropological perspectives*, edited by O. Bar-Yosef and A. Khazanov, pp. 1–10. Monographs in World Prehistory 10. Madison, Wisconsin: Prehistory Press.
Bard, Kathryn A.
1987 The geography of excavated predynastic sites and the rise of complex society. *Journal of the American Research Center in Egypt* XXIV:81–93.
1994 *From Farmers to Pharaohs: Mortuary evidence for the rise of complex society in Egypt*. Sheffield, England: Sheffield Academic Press.
Barfield, Thomas J.
1993 *The Nomadic Alternative*. Englewood Cliffs, New Jersey: Prentice Hall.
Barker, Graeme
1985 *Prehistoric Farming in Europe*. Cambridge: University Press.
Barker, Graeme and Claudia Chang
1988 On the origins of milk and wool production in the Old World. *Current Anthropology* 29(5):743–748.
Barker, Graeme and Clive Gamble
1985 Beyond domestication: A strategy for investigating the process and consequence of social complexity. In *Beyond Domestication in Prehistoric Europe. Investigations in subsistence archaeology and social complexity*, edited by G. Barker and C. Gamble, pp. 1–32. London: Academic Press.
Barker, G. and D. Gilbertson
1996 Farming the desert: Retrospect and prospect. In *Farming the Desert. The* UNESCO *Libyan valleys archaeological surveys*, Volume one: *Synthesis*, edited by G. Barker, D. Gilbertson, B. Jones and D. Mattingly, pp. 343–364. A joint publication of Tripoli:UNESCO Publishing and Department of Antiquities, & London:Society for Libyan Studies.
Barker, G., D. Gilbertson with C.O. Hunt and D. Mattingly
1996 Romano-Libyan agriculture: Integrated models. In *Farming the Desert. The* UNESCO *Libyan valleys archaeological surveys*, Volume one: *Synthesis*, edited by G. Barker, D. Gilbertson, B. Jones and D. Mattingly, pp. 265–290. A joint publication of Tripoli: UNESCO Publishing and Department of Antiquities, & London:Society for Libyan Studies.
Barker, G., D. Gilbertson, B. Jones and D. Mattingly (editors)
1996 *Farming the Desert. The UNESCO Libyan valleys archaeological surveys*, Volume one: *Synthesis*. A joint publication of Tripoli:UNESCO Publishing and Department of Antiquities, & London:Society for Libyan Studies.
Barth, F.
1956 Ecologic relationships of ethnic groups in Swat, North Pakistan. *American Anthropologist* 58(5):1079–1089.
1962 Nomadism in the mountain and plateau areas of southwest Asia. In *The Problems of the Arid Zone*, pp. 341–355. Paris: Unesco.
1964 Competition and symbiosis in north-east Baluchistan. *Folk* 6(1):15–22.
1969 (editor) *Ethnic Groups and Boundaries: The social organization of culture difference*. Boston: Little, Brown and Co.
1976 Socio-economic changes and social problems in pastoral lands: Some concrete factors. In *Proceedings of an International Meeting on Ecological Guidelines for the Use of Natural Resources in the Middle East and South West Asia Held at Persepolis, Iran*, pp. 74–80. International Union for Conservation of Nature and Natural Resources (IUCN) Publications, New Series, No. 34. Morges, Switzerland: IUCN.
Barthelme, J.W.
1975 *Fisher-Hunters and Neolithic Pastoralists in East Turkana, Kenya*. Cambridge Monographs in African Archaeology 13. Oxford: B.A.R. Internat-ional Series 254.
Bate, D.M.A.
1953 The Vertebrate Fauna. In *Es Shaheinab*, edited by A.J. Arkell, pp. 11–19. London: Oxford University Press.
1955 Vertebrate faunas of Quaternary deposits in Cyrenaics. In *Prehistory and Pleistocene Geology in Cyrenaican Libya*, edited by C.B.M. McBurney and R.W. Hey, pp. 274–291. Cambridge: Cambridge University Press.

Baumgartel, E.
1947 *The Cultures of Prehistoric Egypt, I.* London: Oxford University Press.
Beattie, W.A.
1980 *Beef Cattle Breeding and Management.* Sydney: University Press.
Bell, Barbara
1970 The oldest records of the Nile Floods. *Geographical Journal* 136:169–173.
Bennett, John W.
1984 Ecosystems, environmentalism, resource conservation, and anthropological research. In *The Ecosystem Concept in Anthropology*, edited by E. Mora, pp. 289–310. American Association for the Advancement of Science, Selected Symposia Series 92. Boulder, Colorado: Westview Press.
1993 *Human Ecology as Human Behavior. Essays in environmental and development anthropology.* London: Transaction Publishers.
Berger, Rainer and Reiner Protsch
1973 The domestication of plants and animals in Europe and the Near East. *Orientalia* 10:12–29.
Berntsen, J.L.
1979 Economic variations among Maa-speaking peoples. *Hadith* 7:108–127. Cited in P. Robertshaw (1989).
Berton, G.W., F.E. Knox, D.W. Beardsley
1964 Effect of age on the chemical composition, palatability and digestibility of grass leaves. *Agronomy Journal* 56:160–161.
Binford, L., and S. Binford
1968 *New Perspectives in Archaeology.* Chicago: Aldine.
Bleiberg, Edward
1988 The redistributive economy in New Kingdom Egypt: An examination of *B3kw(t)*. *Journal of the American Research Center in Egypt* XXV:157–168.
Blumenschine, R.J.
1986 Carcass consumption sequences and the archaeo-logical distinction of scavenging and hunting. *Journal of Human Evolution* 15:639–659.
Blumenschine, R.J. and T.M. Caro
1986 Unit flesh weights of some East African bovids. *African Journal of Ecology* 24:273–286.
Blumler, Mark A. and Roger Byrne
1991 The ecological genetics of domestication and the origins of agriculture. *Current Anthropology* 13(1):23–54.
Boas, Franz
1940 *Race, Language and Culture.* New York: Macmillan
Boessneck, Joachim
1963 Osteologische Unterscheidungsmerkmal zwischen Schaf (*Ovis aries* Linné) und Ziege (*Capra hircus* Linné). *Kuhn Archiv* 78:1–129.
Boessneck, Joachim and Angela von den Driesch
1976 *Tell el-Dab'a III: Die Tierknochenfunde 1966–1969.* Vienna: Osterreichische Akademie der Wissenschaftem Denschriften der Gesamtakademie, Band V.
1978 The significance of measuring animal bones from archaeological sites. In *Approaches to Faunal Analysis in the Middle East.* edited by R. H. Meadow and M.A. Zeder, pp. 25–39. Peabody Museum Bulletin, No. 2. Cambridge, Massachusetts: Harvard University.
1988 Tierknochenfunde vom Tell Ibrahim Awad im östlichen Nildelta. In *The Archeology of the Nile Delta: Problems and Priorities*, edited by E.C.M.van den Brink, pp. 117–122. Amersterdam: Netherlands Foundation for Archaeological Research.
1990 Appendix III: Tierreste aus der vorgeschichtlichen Siedlung von el-Omari bei Heluan/unterägypten. In *El-Omari: A neolithic settlement and other sites in the vicinity of Wadi Hof, Helwan*, edited by F. Debono and B. Mortensen, pp. 99–108. Archäologische Veroffenlichungen, Deutsches Archaologisches Institut, Abteilung Kairo 82.
1993 Eine außergewöhnliche Tierknochendeponie in einem Gebäude der 25./26. Dynastie im Stadtgebiet nordwestlich des späten Chnumtempels auf Elephantine. *Mitteilungen des Deutsches Archäo-logisches Institut Abteilung Kairo* 49:189–201.
Boessneck, Joachim, A. von den Driesch and R. Ziegler
1989 Die Tierreste von Maadi und Wadi Digla. *In Maadi III: The non-lithic small finds and the structural remains of the Predynastic settlement*, edited by I. Rizkana and J. Seeher, pp. 87–128. Rhein: Verlag Philipp von Zabern.
Bohrer, -
1975 incompletely cited in Wetterstrom (1993).
Bökönyi, S.
1969 Archaeological problems and methods of recognizing animal domestication. In *The Domestication and Exploitation of Plants and Animals*, edited by P. Ucko and G.W. Dimbleby, pp. 219–230. London: Duckworth.
1973 Some problems of animals domestication in the Middle East. In *Domestikationsforschung und Geschichte der Haustierre*, edited by J. Matolsçi, pp. 69–76. Budapest: Akademiai Kaido.
1974 *A History of the Domesticated Animals in Eastern Europe.* Budapest: Akademiai Kaido.
1976 Development of early stock rearing in the Near East. *Nature* 264(5581):19–23.
1985 The animal remains of Maadi, Egypt: A preliminary report. *Studi di Palethnolgia in onore di S.M. Puglisi.* Rome: Universita di Roma "La Sapienza".
1987 Animal domestication and early animal husbandry in Central, East and South Europe. In *The Neolithic Revolution.* Oxford: B.A.R. International Series 349:163–8.

Bomann, Ann and Robert Young
1994 Preliminary survey in the Wadi Abu Had, Eastern Desert, 1992. *Journal of Egyptian Archaeology* 80:23–44.

Bonaparte, Napoléon
1994 *Description de l'Egypte*.Köln, Germany: Benedikt Taschen Verlag. (reprint of the original 1809 version published by l'Imprimerie Impériale, Paris.)

Bontkes, Tjark Struif
1991 *On Dinka, Cattle and Grain: An interdisciplinary simulation study of a rural area in Southern Sudan.* Wageningen Agricultural University Papers 91/3.

Boserup, Esther
1965 *The Condition of Agricultural Growth: The economics of agrarian change under population pressure*. Chicago: Aldine Publishers.

Bourriau, Janine
1981 *Umm el-Ga'ab: Pottery from the Nile Valley before the Arab conquest.* Cambridge: University Press.

Bower, John
1988 Evolution of stone age food-producing cultures in East Africa. In *Prehistoric Cultures and Environ-ments in the Late Quaternary of Africa*.Cambridge Monographs in African Archaeology 26. Oxford: B.A.R. International Series 405:91–113.
1991 The pastoral neolithic of East Africa. *Journal of World Prehistory* 5(1):49–81.

Bower, J. and T.J. Chadderdon
1986 Further excavations of pastoral neolithic sites in Serengeti. *Azania* 21:129–133.

Bower, J. and C.M. Nelson
1978 Early pottery and pastoral cultures of the central rift valley, Kenya.*Man* 13:554–566.

Bradley, Daniel G., David E. MacHugh, Patrick Cunningham, and Ronan T. Loftus
1996 Mitochondrial diversity and the origins of African and European cattle. *Proceedings of the National Academy of Science* 93:5131–5135.

Bradley, R.
1978 Prehistoric field systems in Britain and northwest Europe. A review of some recent work. *World Archaeology* 9:265–280.

Brandt, S.A.
1984 New perspectives on the origins of food production in Ethiopia. In *From Hunters to Farmers: The causes and consequences of food production in Africa*, edited by J.D. Clark and S.A. Brandt, pp. 173–190. Berkeley: University of California Press.

Brandt, S.A. and N. Cardner
1987 Pastoral rock art in the Horn of Africa: Making sense of udder chaos. World Archaeology 19:194–213.

Brandt, S.A. and Rodolfo Fattovich
1990 Late Quaternary research in the Horn of Africa. In *History of African Archaeology*, edited by P. Robertshaw, pp. 95–108. London: James Curry, Ltd.

Breasted, James Henry
1906 *Ancient Records of Egypt. Historical Documents from the Earliest times to the Persian Conquest*, 4 vols. Chicago, Illinois: University of Chicago Press.

Breman, H. and C.T. de Wit
1983 Rangeland productivity and exploitation in the Sahel. *Science* 221:1341–47.

Breuil, H.
1934 Peintures rupestres préhistoriques du Harrar (Abyssinie). *L'Anthropologie* VLIV:23–55.

Breutz, P.L.
1991 *The Social and Political System of the Sotho-Tswana. Four generations of traditional culture change*. Ramsgate: Breutz.

Brewer, Douglas J.
1986 *Cultural and Environmental Change in the Fayum, Egypt: An investigation based on faunal remains*. PhD dissertation, University of Tennessee.
1987 Seasonality in the prehistoric Faiyum baised on the incremental growth structures of the Nile Catfish (Pisces: *Clarias*). *Journal of Archaeological Science* 14:459–472.
1989a *Fishermen, Hunters and Herders. Zooarchaeology in the Fayum, Egypt (ca. 8200—5000 bp).* Oxford: B.A.R. International Series 478.
1989b Analysis of Omari faunal skeletal remains at Cairo Medical School, October 16–18th, 1989. Unpublished manuscript.
1991a Fishing in prehistoric Egypt: inferences from faunal femains. In *Perspectives in Zooarchaeological Research: Essays in honor of Paul W. Parmalee*, edited by B. Styles, J. Purdue, W. Klippel, pp. 333–340. Illinois State Museum Scientific Papers, vol. 23, Springfield.
1991b A Reply to Van Neer. *Sahara* 4:165.
1991c Temperatures in Predynastic Egypt inferred from the remains of the Nile Perch. *World Archaeology* 22(3):288–303.
1992 University of Illinois Research Board Proposal.

Brewer, Douglas J. and R.F. Friedman
1989 *Fish and Fishing in Ancient Egypt.* Warminster: Aris and Phillips.

Brewer, Douglas J., Donald B. Redford and Susan Redford
1994 *Domestic Plants and Animals: The Egyptian origins*. Warminster: Aris and Phillips.

Brewer, Douglas J. and Robert J. Wenke
1992 Transitional late predynastic—early dynastic occupations at Mendes: a preliminary report. In *The Nile Delta in Transition: 4th–3rd millennium* B.C., edited by E.C.M. van den Brink, pp. 191–198. Amsterdam: Netherlands Foundation for Archaeological Research.

Brewer, Douglas and Carol A. Yokell
1996 The Role of Fishing in Ancient Egypt. In Prehistoric *Hunter-Gatherer Fishing Strategies*, edited by M. Plew, pp. 180–207. Boise: University of Idaho Press.

van den Brink, E.C.M.
1988 Das Vermessen fon Tierknochenfunde vom Tell Ibrahim Awad im ostichen Nildelta. In *The Archaeology of the Nile Delta, Egypt: Problems and priorities*, edited by E.C.M. van den Brink, pp. 117–112. Amsterdam: Netherlands Foundation for Archaeological Research.
1992 (editor) *The Nile Delta in Transition: 4th–3rd millennium* B.C. Amsterdam: Netherlands Foundation for Archaeological Research.

Brooks, P.M., J. Hanks, J.V. Ludbrook
1977 Bone marrow as an index of condition in African ungulates. *Southern African Journal of Wildlife Research* 7:61–66.

Brown, Maj. Robert H.
1892 *The Fayûm and Lake Mœris*. London: Edward Stanford.

Brunton, M.N.
1979 The breeding biology and early development of *Clarias gariepinus* (Pisces: Clariidae). *Transactions of the Zoological Society of London* 35:1–45.

Brunton, G. and G. Caton-Thompson
1928 *The Badarian Civilization and Predynastic Remains near Badari*. British School of Archaeology in Egypt, Publication 46. London: Bernard Quaritch.

Butterworth, Martyn
1985 *Beef Cattle Nutrition and Tropical Pastures*. London: Longman.

Butzer, Karl
1959 Environment and human ecology in Egypt during Predynastic and early Dynastic times. *Bulletin de la Société de Géographie d'Égypt* XXXII:43–87.
1960 Archaeology and Geology in Ancient Egypt. *Science* 132:1617–1624.
1971 *Environment and Archaeology: An ecological approach to prehistory*. Chicago:Aldine Publishers.
1975 Patterns of environmental change in the Near East during Late Pleistocene and early Holocene times. In *Problems in Prehistory: North Africa and the Levant*, edited by F.Wendorf and A. Marks, pp. 389–410. Dallas: Southern Methodist University Press.
1976 *Early Hydraulic Civilization of Egypt*. Chicago: Aldine Publishers.
1980 Pleistocene history of the Nile Valley in Egypt and lower Nubia. In *The Sahara and The Nile: Quaternary environments and prehistoric occupation in northern Africa*, edited by A.J. Martin, W. Faure, and H. Faure, pp. 253–280. Rotterdam: Balkema.

Butzer, K., G. Isaac, J. Richardson, C. Washbourne-Kamay
1972 Radiocarbon dating of East African lake levels. *Science* 175:1069–1076.

Carr, C.J.
1977 *Pastoralism in Crisis. The Dasanetch and their Ethiopian lands*. Department of Geography Research Paper No. 180. Chicago: University of Chicago.

Carter, P.C. and J.D. Clark
1976 Adrar Bous and African cattle. In*Panafrican Congress on Prehistory and Quaternary Studies, 7th session (1971)*, edited by B. Ababe, J. Chavaillon and J.E.G. Sutton, pp. 487–493. Addis Ababa: Provisional Military Government of Socialist Ethiopia, Ministry of Culture.

Chang, C. and H.A. Koster
1986 Beyond bones: Toward an archaeology of pastoralism. In *Advances in Archaeological Method and Theory 9*, edited by M.J. Schiffer, pp. 97–148. New York: Academic Press.

Chaplin, Raymond E.
1969 The use of non-morphological criteria in the study of animal domestication from bones found on archaeolgoical sites. In *The Domestication and Exploitation of Plants and Animals*, edited by P. Ucko and G. Dimbleby, pp. 231–245. London: Duckworth.

Caton-Thompson, G.
1952 *Kharga Oasis in Prehistory*. London: Althone Press.

Caton-Thompson, G. and E. Gardner
1934 *The Desert Fayum*. London: The Royal Anthropological Institute of Great Britain and Ireland.

Cerny, J.
1954 Prices and Wages in Egypt in the Ramesside Period. *Journal of World Prehistory* 1:903–922.

Cheesman, R.E.
1936 *Lake Tana and the Blue Nile: An Abyssinian quest.* London: Macmillan and Co, Ltd.

Childe, V. Gordon
1936 *Man Makes Himself*. London: C.A. Watts and Co.

Chowdhury, K.A. and G.M. Buth
1970 4500-year-old seeds suggest that true cotton is indigenous to Nubia. *Nature* 227:85–86.

Christaller, W.
1966 *Central Places in Southern Germany* (translated by C.W. Baskin). Englewood Cliffs, New Jersey: Prentice Hall.

Christenson, Andrew
1980 Change in the human niche in response to population growth. In *Modeling Change in Prehistoric Subsistence Economies*, edited by T. Earle and A. Christenson, pp.31–72. New York: Academic Press.

Clark, J.G.D.
1952 *Prehistoric Europe: The economic basis*. London: Methuen.

1957 *Archaeology and Society*, 3rd edition. London: Methuen.

Clark, J.D.

1954 *Prehistoric Cultures of the Horn of Africa.* Cambridge: University Press.

1962 The spread of food production in sub-saharan Africa. *Journal of African History* 3:211–228.

1976 Prehistoric populations and pressures favoring plant domestication in Africa. In *Origins of African Plant Domestication*, edited by J.R. Harlan, J.M. de Wet, and A.B.L. Stemler, pp. 67–105. Paris: Mouton, the Hague.

1984 Prehistoric cultural continuity and economic change in the central Sudan in the Early Holocene. In *From Hunters to Farmers: The causes and consequences of food production in Africa*, edited by J.D. Clark and S.A. Brandt, pp. 113–126. Berkeley: University of California Press.

Clark, J.D. and S.A. Brandt (editors)

1984 *From Hunters to Farmers: The causes and consequences of food production in Africa.* Berkeley: University of California Press.

Clason, A.T. and Juliet Clutton-Brock

1982 The impact of domestic animals on the vegetation during the first phases of animal husbandry in the Mediterranean and the Near East. In *Palaeoclimates, Palaeoenvironments and Human Communities in the Eastern Mediterranean in Later Prehistory*, edited by J.L. Bintliff and W. van Zeist. Oxford: B.A.R. International Series 139:145–88.

Close, Angela

1990 Living on the edge: Neolithic herders in the eastern Sahara. *Antiquity* 64:70–96.

Clutton-Brock, Juliet

1970 The origin of the dog. In *Science in Archaeology,* 2nd edition, edited by J. Brothwell and E.S. Higgs, pp. 303–309. New York: Praeger.

1984 *Animals and Archaeology: Early herders and their flocks*. Oxford: B.A.R. International Series 202.

1987 *A Natural History of Domesticated Animals.* Cambridge: University Press.

1989 Introduction to pastoralism. In *The Walking Larder: Patterns of domestication, pastoralism, and predation*, edited by J.Clutton-Brock, pp. 115–118. One World Archaeology Series 2. London: Unwin Hyman.

1993 The spread of domestic animals in Africa. In *The Archaeology of Africa: Food, metals and towns*, edited by T. Shaw, P. Sinclair, B. Andah, and A. Okpoko, pp. 61–70. One World Archaeology Series 20. London: Routledge.

1994 The Unnatural World: Behavioral Aspects of Humans and Animals in the Process of Domestication. In *Animals and Human Society: Changing perspectives*, edited by A. Manning and J. Serpell, pp. 23–35. London: Routledge.

Coetzee, J.A.

1964 Evidence for a considerable depression of the vegetation belts during the Upper Pleistocene on East African mountains. *Nature* 204(4958):564–566.

Cohen, Y.

1974 *Man in Adaptation: The cultural present*, 2nd edition. New Haven, Connecticut: Yale University Press.

Cohen, Mark

1977 *The Food Crisis in Prehistory: Overpopulation and the origins of agriculture.* New Haven, Connecticut: Yale University Press.

Cook, -

1973 Production, ecology and economic anthropology: Notes towards an integrated reference. *Social Science Information* 12(1):25–52.

Cory,V.L.

1927 Activities of livestock on the range. *Bulletin of the Texas Agricultural Experiment Station* 367.

Cranstone, B.A.L.

1969 Animal husbandry: the evidence from ethnography. In *The Domestication and Exploita-tion of Plants and Animals*, edited by P. Ucko and G.W. Dimbleby, pp. 248–263. London: Duckworth.

Crazzolara, J.P.

1934 Die Bedeutung des Rindes bei den Nuer. *Africa* 7:300–320.

Cruz-Uribe, Eugene

1985 A Saïte request for payment. *Journal of Egyptian Archaeology* 71:129–133.

Dahl, G.

1979 *Suffering Grass: Subsistence and society of Waso Borana.* Stockholm: Stockholm Studies in Social Anthropology 5. Stockholm: University Press.

Dahl, G. and Anders Hjort

1976 *Having Herds: Pastoral herd growth and household economy.* Stockholm Studies in Social Anthropology 2. Stockholm: University Press.

Daly, Patricia

1969 Approaches to faunal analysis in archaeology. *American Antiquity* 34(1):146–153.

Daly, Patricia, D. Perkins, Jr., and I.M. Drew

1973 Effects of domestication on the structure of animal bone. In *Domestikationsforschung und Geschichte der Haustiere*, edited by J. Matolsçi, pp.157–161. Budapest: Akademiai Kaido.

Darby, W.J., P. Ghalioungui, and L. Grivetti

1977 *Food: The gift of Osiris*, 2 vols. New York: Academic Press.

Dardaillon, M.

1987 Seasonal feeding habits of the wild boar in a Mediterranean Wetland, the Camargue (Southern France). *Acta Theriologica* 32(23):389–401.

Darwin, Charles
1868 *The Variation of Animals and Plants Under Domestication*, 2 vols. London: Joan Murray.
David, Nicholas
1976 History of crops and peoples in north Cameroun to AD 1900. In *Origins of African Plant Domestication*, edited by J. Harlan, J. DeWet and A. Stemler, pp. 223–267. The Hague: Mouton.
1982 Prehistory and historical linguistics in Central Africa: Points of contact. In *Archaeological and Linguisitic Reconstruction of African History*, edited by C. Ehret and M. Posnansky, pp. 78–95. Berkeley: University of California Press.
Davis, Whitney
1990 The study of rock art in Africa. In *A History of African Archaeology*, edited by P. Robertshaw, pp. 271–295. London: James Curry, Ltd.
Dawson, W.R.
1928 The pig in ancient Egypt. A commentary on two passages of Herodotus. *Journal of the Royal Asiatic Society of Great Britain and Ireland* (1928):597–608.
Debono, Fernand
1948 El-Omari (près d'Hélouan). Exposé sommaire sur les campagnes des fouilles 1943–1944 et 1948. *Annales du Service* XLVIII:36–569.
Dekeyser, P.L.
1955 Les mammifières de l'Afrique Noire Française. *Institute Français d'Afrique Noire, Initiations Africaines I*. (cited in Banks 1984)
Deng, F.M.
1972 *The Dinka of the Sudan*. New York: Holt, Reinhart and Winston.
Deshler, W.W.
1964 The Dodos: A cattle-keeping tribe in East Africa. In *Focus on Geographic Activity: A collection of original studies*, edited by R.S. Thoman and D.J. Patton, pp. 7–11. New York: McGraw-Hill.
1965 Native cattle keeping in eastern Africa. In *Man, Culture and Animals. The role of animals in human ecological adjustments*, edited by A. Leeds and A.D. Vayda, pp. 153–168. Washington, D.C.: American Association for the Advancement of Science, Publication 78.
Devendra, C. and M.F. Fuller
1979 *Pig Production in the Tropics*. Oxford: University Press.
Dombrowski, J.C.
1971 *Excavations in Ethiopia: Lalibela and Natchabiet caves, Begemeder Province*. Unpublished PhD thesis, Boston University.
Donald, C.R.
1984 Examination of the archaeological samples provided by Barry J. Kemp from the Tell el-'Amarna site. In *Amarna Reports I*, edited by B.J.Kemp, pp. 56–58. London: Egypt Exploration Society.
Dreyer, Günter, with contributions by J. Boessneck, A. von den Driesch and Stefan Klug
1990 Umm el-Qaab. Nachuntersuchungen im frühzeitlichen Königsfriedhof 3./4. Vorbericht. *Mitteilungen des Deutsches Archäologisches Institut Abteilung Cairo* 46:53–90.
Ducos, P.
1969 Methodology and results of the study of the earliest domesticated animals in the Near East (Palestine). In *The Domestication and Exploitation of Plants and Animals*, edited by P. Ucko and G. Dimbleby, pp. 265–275. London: Duckworth.
1978 'Domestication' defined and methodological approaches to its recognzition in faunal assemblages. In *Approaches to Faunal Analysis in the Middle East*, edited by R.H. Meadow and M.A. Zeder, pp. 53–56. Peabody Museum Bulletin 2. Cambridge, Massachusetts: Harvard University.
Ducos, P. and D. Helmer
1980 Le point actuel sur l'apparition de la domestication dans le Levant. In *Préhistoire du Levant*, edited by J. Cauvin and P. Sanlaville, pp. 523–528. Paris: Centre National de la Recherche Scientifique, No. 598.
Dunnell, R.
1980 Evolutionary theory and archaeology. In *Advances in Archaeological Method and Theory*, vol. 3, edited by M. B. Schiffer, pp. 35–99. New York: Academic Press.
Dyson-Hudson, N.
1966 *Karimojong Politics*. Oxford: University Press.
1972 The study of nomads. *Journal of Asian and African Studies* 7(1–2):2–29.
1985 Pastoral production systems and livestock develop-ment projects: An East African perspective. In *Putting People First*, edited by M.M. Cernea, pp. 157–186. Oxford: University Press.
Dyson-Hudson, R. and N. Dyson-Hudson
1969 Subsistence herding in Uganda. *Scientific American* 220(1–2):30–47.
1970 The food production system of a semi-nomadic society: The Karimojong, Uganda. In *African Food Production Systems: Cases and Theory*, edited by Peter F.M. McLoughlin, pp. 91–123. Baltimore: The Johns Hopkins Press.
1980 Nomadic pastoralism. *Annual Review of Anthropology* 9:15–61.
Dyson-Hudson, R. and J.T. McCabe (editors)
1985 *South Turkana Nomadism: Coping with an unpredictably varying environment*. New Haven, Connecticut: Human Relations Area Files.
Dyson-Hudson, R. and E.A. Smith
1978 Human territoriality: an ecological assessment. *American Anthropologist* 80:21–41.
Earle, Timothy
1989 The evolution of chiefdoms. *Current Anthropology* 30(1):84–88.

Earle, Timothy and Robert W. Preucel
1987 Processual archaeology and the radical critique. *Current Anthropology* 28(4):501–537.
Ehret, Christopher
1974 *Ethiopians and East Africa: The problems of contacts*. Nairobi: East African Publishing House.
1979 On the antiquity of agriculture in Ethiopia.*Journal of African History* 20:161–177.
1982a The first spread of food production to southern Africa. In *Archaeological and Linguisitic Reconstruction of African History*, edited by C. Ehret and M. Posnansky, pp. 151–181. Berkeley: University of California Press.
1982b Linguistic inferences about early Bantu history. In *Archaeological and Linguistic Reconstruction of African History*, edited by C. Ehret and M. Posnansky, pp. 57–65. Berkeley: University of California Press.
Ehret, C. and M. Posnansky
1982 *Archaeological and Linguistic Reconstruction of African History*. Berkeley: University of California Press.
Eiwanger, Joseph
1978 Erste Vorbericht über die Wiederaufnahme der Grabungen in der neolithischen Siedlung Merimde- Benisalâme. *Mitteilungen des Deutschen Archäo-logischen Institut, Abteilung Kairo* 34:33–42.
1979 Zweiter Vorbeicht über die Wiederaufnahme der Grabungen in der neolithischen Siedlung Merimde- Benisalâme. *Mitteilungen des Deutschen Archäo-logischen Institut, Abteilung Kairo* 35:23–57.
1980 Dritter Vorbeicht über die Wiederaufnahme der Grabungen in der neolithischen Siedlung Merimde- Benisalâme. *Mitteilungen des Deutschen Archäo-logischen Institut, Abteilung Kairo* 36:61–70.
1982 Die neolithische Siedlung von Merimde-Benisalâme: Vierter Bericht. *Mitteilungen des Deutschen Archäologischen Institut, Abteilung Kairo* 38:67–82.
1984 *Merimde-Benisalâme I: Die Funde der Urschicht*. Mainz: Philipp von Zabern.
1988 *Merimde-Benisalâme II: Die Funde der mittleren Merimdekultur*. Mainz: Philipp von Zabern.
Eldar, Iris, N. Yaacov, and Dov Nahlieli
1989 The Bedouin and their campsites in the Dimona region of the Negev: Comparative model for the study of ancient desert settlements. In *Pastoralism in the Levant: Archaeological methods in anthro-pological perspectives*, edited by O. Bar-Yosef, and A. Khazanov, pp. 205–218. Monographs in World Pre-history 10. Madison, Wisconsin: Prehistory Press.
Ellen, Roy
1989 *Environment, Subsistence and System. The ecology of small-scale social formations*. Cambridge: Cambridge University Press.
ElMahi, Ali Tigani
1988 *Zooarchaeology of the Middle Nile Valley: A study of four Neolithic sites near Khartoum*. Cambridge Monographs in African Archaeology 27. Oxford: B.A.R. International Series 418.
Elphick, R.
1977 *Kraal and Castle*. Miscellany No. 116. New Haven, Connecticut: Yale Historical Publications.
Epstein, H.
1971 *The Origins of the Domestic Animals of Africa*. New York: Academic Press.
Epstein, H. and I.L. Mason
1984 Cattle. In *Evolution of Domestic Animals*, vol. 1, edited by I.L. Mason, pp. 6–27. London: Longman.
Evans-Pritchard, E.E.
1940 *The Nuer: A Description of the Modes of Livelihood of a Nilotic People.* Oxford: Clarendon Press.
1951 Some forms and features of Nuer sacrifice. *Africa* 21:112–121.
1953 The sacrificial role of cattle among the Nuer. *Africa* 23:181–198.
1956 *Nuer Religion*. Oxford: Clarendon Press.
Eyre, C.J.
1987 Work and the organization of work in the Old Kingdom. In *Labor in the Ancient Near East*, edited by M.A. Powell, pp. 5–47. New Haven, Connecticut: American Oriental Society.
1994 The water regime for orchards and plantations in pharaonic Egypt. *Journal of Egyptian Archaeology* 80:57–80.
FAO
1978 *FAO Production Yearbook*, No. 32.
Faure, H., E. Manguin, R. Nydal
1963 Formations lacustres du Quaternaire supérieur du Niger oriental. *Bulletin du Bureau de Recherche Geologie et Minerologie* 3:41–63.
Fernea, Elizabeth Warnock and Robert A. Fernea
1991 *Nubian Ethnographies*. Prospect Heights, Illinois: Waveland Press, Inc.
Finegan, Jack
1979 *Archaeological history of the ancient Middle East.* New York: Dorset Press.
Firth, R.
1964 Capital, saving and credit in peasant socieites: a viewpoint from economic anthropology. In *Capital, Saving and Credit in Peasant Societies. Studies from Asia, Oceania, the Caribbean and Middle America*, edited by R. Firth and B.S. Yamey, pp. 15–34. London: Allen and Unwin.
Fischer, H.G.
1959 Some notes on the easternmost nomes of the Delta in the Old and Middle Kingdoms. *Journal of Near Eastern Studies* 18:129–142.
1966 In *Le Tombeau de Ti*. Cairo: L'Institut Français d'Archéologie Orientale.
1976 *Varia, Egyptological Studies*.

Flannery, Kent
1968 The Olmec and and the valley of Oaxaca: A model for interregional interaction in Formative times. In *Dumbarton Oaks Conference on the Olmec*, edited by E. Benson, pp. 79–110. Washington, D.C.: Dumbarton Oaks.
1969 Origins and ecological effects of early domestication in Iran and the Near East. In *The Domestication and Exploitation of Plants and Animals,* edited by P. Ucko and G. Dimbleby, pp. 73–100. London: Duckworth.
1973 The origins of agriculture. *Annual Review of Anthropology* 2:271–310.
Fleming, A.
1979 *The Darmoor Reaves: Boundary Patterns and Behaviour Patterns in the 2nd millenium b.c.*, edited by V.A. Maxfield, pp. 115–131. Exeter: Devon Archaeological Society. Cited in Noddle (1989).
Forde, C. D.
1963 *Habitat, Economy, and Society*, revised edition. London: Methuen and Co.
Forster, E.S. and E. Hefner (translators)
1968 *Columella de ru rustica*. Vol II. London: Loeb Classical Library Hienemann. Cited in Noddle (1989).
French, M.H.
1970 Observations on the goat. *F.A.O. Agricultural Studies* 80.
Friedman, J.
1974 Marxism, structuralism, and vulgar materialism. *Man* (N.S.) 9:444–69.
Gaillard, Cl.
1934 Contribution à l'étude de la faune préhistorique de l'Egypte. *Extrait des Archives du Museum d'Histoire Naturelle de Lyon* 14.
Galán, José
1994 Bullfight scenes in ancient Egyptian tombs. *Journal of Egyptian Archaeology* 80:81–96.
Gabriel, B.
1977 Early and Mid-Holocene climate in the eastern central Sahara. In *Drought in Africa 2*, edited by D. Dalby, R.J. Harrison-Church, and F. Bezzaz, pp. 65–67. Oxford: International African Institute.
Galaty, John G.
1989 Cattle and cognition: Aspects of Maasai practical reasoning. In *The Walking Larder: Patterns of domestication, pastoralism, and predation*, edited by J. Clutton-Brock, pp. 215–230. One World Archaeology Series 2. London: Unwin Hyman.
Galvin, Marianne
1984 The hereditary status of the titles of the cult of Hathor. *Journal of Egyptian Archaeology* 70:42–49.
Gamble, Clive S.
1981 Social control of the economy. In *Economic Anthro-pology*, edited by A. Sheridan and G.N. Bailey, pp. 215–229. Oxford: B.A.R. International Series 96.
Gamer-Wallert, I.
1970 *Fische und Fischkulte im alten Ägypten.* Agyptologische Abhandlungen, 21. Weisbaden.
Gardiner, A., T.E. Peet, and J. Cerny
1955 *Inscriptions of Sinai*, volume 2. London: Egypt Exploration Society.
Garrard, Andrew N.
1982 The environmental implications of a re-analysis of the large mammal faunal from the Wadi el-Mughara caves, Palestine. In *Palaeoclimates, Palaeo-environments and human communities in the eastern Mediterranean in later prehistory,* edited by J.L. Bintliff and W. van Zeist. Oxford: B.A.R. International Series 139:145–88.
1984 The selection of southwest Asian animal domesticates. In *Animals and Archaeology: Early herders and their flocks*, edited by J. Clutton-Brock and G. Grigson, pp. 117–202. Oxford: B.A.R. International Series 202.
Garwood, P., D. Jennings, R. Skeates and J. Toms (editors)
1991 *Sacred and Profane: Proceedings of a conference on archaeology, ritual and religion, Oxford 1989.* Monograph No. 32. Oxford: University Committee on Archaeology.
Gautier, A.
1976a Freshwater mollusks and mammals from upper Palæolithic sites near Idfu and Isna. In *Prehistory of Nubia*, vol. 1, edited by F. Wendorf, pp. 80–99. Dallas: Fort Burgwin Research Center and Southern Methodist University Press.
1976b Animal remains from localities near Dishna. In *Prehistory of the Nile Valley*, edited by F. Wendorf and R. Schild, pp. 365–367. New York: Academic Press.
1976c Animal remains from archaeological sites of the terminal Palaeolithic to Old Kingdom age in the Fayum. In *Prehistory of the Nile Valley*, edited by F. Wendorf and R. Schild, pp. 369–381. New York: Academic Press.
1980 Contributions to the archæozoology of Egypt. In *The Prehistory of the Eastern Sahara*, edited by F. Wendorf and R. Schild, pp. 317–344. New York: Academic Press.
1984 Archaeozoology of Bir Kiseiba region of Eastern Sahara. In *Cattle-Keepers of the Eastern Sahara*, edited by F. Wendorf, R. Schild and A. Close, pp. 49–72. Dallas: Fort Burgwin Research Center and Southern Methodist University Press.
1987 Fishing, fowling and hunting in Late Palaeolithic times in the Nile Valley in Upper Egypt. *Palaeoecology of Africa* 18:429–440.
1988 The final demise of *Bos ibericus*. *Sahara* 1:37–48.
Ghosh, P.K. and R.K. Abichandani
1981 *Water in the Eco-Physiology of Desert Sheep.*

Central Arid Zone Research Institute Monograph No. 17. Jodhpur: Harvard Press.

Ghosh, P.K. and M.S. Khan
1980 *The Goat in the Desert Environment*. Central and Arid Zone Research Institute Monograph 12. Jodhpur: Harvard Press.

Gifford-Gonzalez, D.P. and J. Kimengich
1984 Implications of a faunal assemblage from a pastoral neolithic site in Kenya: Findings and a perspective on research. In *From Hunters to Farmers: The causes and consequences of food production in Africa*, edited by J.D. Clark and S.A. Brandt, pp. 240–251. Berkeley: University of California Press.

Gilbert, Allan S.
1988 Zooarchaeological observations on the slaughter-house of Meketre. *Journal of Egyptian Archaeology* 74:69–89.

Gillam, Robyn
1995 Preistesses of Hathor: Their function, decline and disappearance. *Journal of the American Research Center in Egypt* XXXII:211:237.

Goedicke, H.
1967 Königiiche Dokumente aus dem altern Reich. Ägyptologische Abhandlungen 14:1–256.
1988 The northeastern Delta and the Mediterranean. In *The Archaeology of the Nile Delta: Problems and Priorities*, edited by E.C.M. van den Brink, pp. 165–175. Amsterdam: Netherlands Foundation for Archaeological Research.
1994 A cult inventory of the eighth dynasty from Coptos (Cairo JE 43290). *Mitteilungen des Deutsches Archäologisches Institut Abteilung Cairo* 50:71–84.

Goodall, D. D. (editor)
1986 *Ecosystems of the World*, volume 12B: *Hot Deserts and Arid Shrublands*. Amsterdam: Elsevier Press.

Gordon, A. and A.W. Sampson
1939 Composition of common California foothill plants as a factor in range management. *Bulletin of the University of California College of Agriculture Experimental Station* 627.

Gordon, Andrew H. and Calvin W. Schwabe
1995 The Egyptian *w3s* -scepter and its modern analogues: Uses as symbols of divine power or authority. *Journal of the American Research Center in Egypt* XXXII:185–196.

Gouin, P.
1990 Rapes, jarres, et faisselles. La production et l'exploration des produits laitiers dans l'Indus du 3e millenaire. *Paléorient* 16(2):37–54.

Grayson, Donald K.
1984 *Quantitative Zooarchaeology: Topics in the analysis of archaeological faunas*. Orlando: Academic Press.
1988 *Danger Cave, Last Supper Cave, Hanging Rock Shelter: The faunas*. Anthropological Papers of the American Museum of Natural History, vol. 66, part I. New York.

Greenfield, Haskel
1988 The origins of milk and wool production in the Old World. *Current Anthropology* 29(4):573–593.

Grigson, Caroline
1969 The uses and limitations of differences in absolute size in the distinction between bones of aurochs (*Bos primigenius*) and domestic cattle (*Bos taurus*). In *The Domestication and Exploitation of Plants and Animals*, edited by P. Ucko and G. Dimbleby, pp. 272–294. London: Duckworth.
1976 The craniology and relationships of four species of *Bos*. 3. Basic craniology: *Bos taurus L.* saggital profiles and other non-measurable characters. *Journal of Archaeological Science* 3:115–136.
1978 The craniology and relationships of four species of *Bos*. 4. *Journal of Archaeological Science* 5:123–152.
1980 The craniology and relationships of four species of *Bos*. 5. *Bos indicus* Linné. *Journal of Archaeological Science* 7:3–32.
1982 Porridge and pannage: Pig husbandry in Neolithic England. In *Archaeological Aspects of Woodland Ecology*, edited by M. Bell and S. Limbrey, pp. 297–333. Oxford: B.A.R. International Series 146.

Guilday, John E., Paul Parmalee and Donald Tanner
1962 Aboriginal butchering techniques at the Eschelman site (36LA12). *Pennsylvania Archaeologist* 32(2):59–63.

Gulliver, P.H.
1951 *A Preliminary Survey of the Turkana*. University of Cape Town, School of African Studies, New Series no. 26.
1955 *The Family Herds: A study of two pastoral tribes in East Africa, the Jie and the Turkana*. London: Routledge and Kegan Paul.

Gulliver, P.H. and P. Gulliver
1953 *The Central Nilo-Hamites*. London: International African Institute.

Haaland, Gunnar
1969 Economic determinants in ethnic processes. In *Ethnic groups and Boundaries: The social organization of culture difference*, edited by F. Barth, pp. 58–73. Boston, Massachusetts: Brown, Little and Company.

el-Hadidi, M.N. and L. Boulos
1988 *The Street Trees of Egypt*, revised edition. Cairo: The American University in Cairo Press.

el-Hadidi, M.N. and I. Springuel
1978 Plant life in Nubia (Egypt), vol. I. Introduction: plant communities in the Nile islands at Aswan. *Täckholmia* 9:103–109.
1989 The natural vegetation of the Nile valley at Wadi Kubbaniya. In *Prehistory of the Wadi Kubbaniya, Volume 2: Stratigraphy, paleoeconomy, and environment*, edited by F. Wendorf, R. Schild, and A.E. Close, pp. 243–

251. Dallas: Southern Methodist University Press.

Hafez, E.S.E.

1968a Behavioral adaptation. In *Adaptation of Domestic Animals*, edited by E. Hafez, pp. 202–214. Philadelphia: Lea and Febiger.

1968b Environmental effects on animal productivity. In *Adaptation of Domestic Animals*, edited by E. Hafez, pp. 74–93. Philadelphia: Lea and Febiger.

1968b Principles of animal adaptation. In *Adaptation of Domestic Animals*, edited by E. Hafez, pp. 3–17. Philadelphia: Lea and Febiger.

Haiman, Mordechai and Yuval Goren

1992 "Negbite" Pottery: New aspects and interpretations and the role of pastoralism in designating ceramic technology. In *Pastoralism in the Levant: Archaeo-logical methods in anthropological perspective*, edited by O. Bar-Yosef and A. Khazanov, pp. 143–152. Monographs in World Archaelogy 10. Madison, Wisconsin: Prehistory Press.

Hakanen, R.

1984 *Preliminary Study of Suitability of Ureaphosphate Treatment in Fodder Conservation in Tropical Developing Countries.* Research report to Emil Aaltonen Foundation, Tampere, Finland. (Cited in Muthuri and Kinyamario 1989.)

Hale, E.B.

1962 Domestication and the evolution of behavior. In *The Behavior of Domestic Animals*, edited by E. Hafez, 21–53. London: Baillière, Tindall and Cox.

Halverson, J.

1976 Animal categories and terms of abuse. *Man* (N.S.) 11(4):505–516.

Hardesty, Donald L.

1977 *Ecological Anthropology*. New York: Wiley.

Hardin, Garret

1968 The tragedy of the commons. *Science* 162:1243–1248.

Harlan, Jack R.

1975 *Crops and Man.* Madison, Wisconsin: American Society of Agronomy.

1982 The origins of indigenous African agriculture. In *Cambridge History of Africa,* vol. 1, edited by J.D. Clark, pp.624–654. New York: Cambridge University Press.

Harlan, J., J. deWet, and A. Stemler

1976 *Origins of African Plant Domestication.* The Hague: Mouton Publishers.

Harrell, James A. and Thomas A. Brown

1995 An Old Kingdom basalt quarry at Widan el-Faras and the quarry road to Lake Mœris. *Journal of the American Research Center in Egypt* XXXII:71–92.

Harris, D.

1977 Alternative pathways toward agriculture. In *Origins of Agriculture*, edited by C. A. Reed, pp. 179–243. The Hague: Mouton Publishers.

1989 An evolutionary continuum of people-plant interaction. In *Foraging and Farming: The evolution of plant exploitation*, edited by D. Harris and G. Gilman, pp. 11–26. One World Archaeology Series 13. London: Unwin Hyman.

Harris, D.R. and G.C. Gilman (editors)

1989 *Foraging and Farming: The evolution of plant exploitation.* One World Archaeology Series 13. London: Unwin Hyman.

Harris, Marvin

1974 *Cows, Pigs, Wars and Witches. The riddles of culture.* New York: Random House.

1985 *Good to Eat: Riddles of food and culture.* New York: Random House.

Hartmann, Fernande

1923 L'Agriculture dans l'ancienne Egypte. Paris: Imprimeries Réunies.

Hassan, F.A.

1973 Discussion and criticism on mechanics of population growth during the Neolithic. *Current Anthropology* 14(5):535–540.

1978 Archaeological explorations of the Siwa Oasis region, Egypt. *Current Anthropology* 19(1):146–148.

1980 Prehistoric settlement along the main Nile. In *The Sahara and the Nile: Quaternary environments and prehistoric occupation in northern Africa*, edited by M.A.J. Williams and H. Faure, pp. 421–450. Rotterdam: Balkema.

1981a *Demographic Archaeology.* New York: Academic Press.

1981b Historical Nile floods and their implications for climatic change. *Science* 212:1142–45.

1984a Environment and subsistence in predynastic Egypt. In *From Hunters to Herders: The causes and consequences of food production in Africa*, edited by J.D. Clark and S.A. Brandt, pp. 57–64. Berkeley: University of California Press.

1984b Mid-Holocene desertification and human responses in the Western Desert of Egypt. Paper presented at the 17th annual Chacmool Conference, Calgary, Alberta, Canada.

1986a Holocene lakes and prehistoric settlement of the Western Fayum. *Journal of Archaeological Science* 13:483–501.

1986b Desert environment and origins of agriculture in Egypt. *Norwegian Archaeological Review* 19:63–76.

1988 The Predynastic of Egypt. *Journal of World Prehistory* 2(2):125–185.

1993 Town and village in ancient Egypt: Ecology, society and urbanization. In *The Archaeology of Africa: Food, metals and towns*, edited by T. Shaw, P. Sinclair, B. Andah, and A. Okpoko, pp. 551–569. One World Archaeology Series 20. London: Routledge.

Hassan, F.A. and G.T. Gross

1987 Resources and subsistence during the early Holocene at Siwa Oasis, northern Egypt. In

*Prehistory of Arid North Africa: Essays in honor of Fred Wendorf,* edited by A. Close, pp. 85–103. Dallas: Southern Methodist University Press.

Hastorf, Christine A.
1980 Changing resource use in subsistence agricultural groups of the prehistoric Mimbres River Valley, New Mexico. In *Modeling Change in Prehistoric Subsistence Economies*, edited by T.K. Earle and A.L. Christenson, pp. 79–120. New York: Academic Press.

Hawass, Zahi, Fekri A. Hassan, and Achilles Gautier
1988 Chronology, sediments, and subsistence at Merimda Beni-salâma. *Journal of Egyptian Archaeology* 74:31–38.

Haynes, K.E., and S.M. el-Hakim
1979 Appropriate technology and public policy: The urban-waste management system in Cairo. *Geographical Review* 69:102.

Hayes, W.C.
1964 Most ancient Egypt. *Journal of Near Eastern Studies* 23:217–274.
1965 *Most Ancient Egypt*. Chicago: University Press.

Hecker, H.M.
1982 A zooarchaeological inquiry into pork consumption in Egypt from prehistoric to New Kingdom times. *Journal of the American Research Center in Egypt* XIX:59–71.
1984 Preliminary report on the faunal remains from the Workmen's Village. In *Amarna Reports I*, edited by B. Kemp, pp.154–164. London: Egypt Exploration Society.

Heiser, Charles B., Jr.
1990 *Seed to Civilization: The story of food.* Cambridge, Massachussetts: Harvard University Press.

de Heinzelin, J., P. Haesaerts and F. Van Noten
1969 Geologie recente et prehistoire au Jebel 'Uweinat. *Africa-Tervuren* XV(4):120–126. (Cited in Banks 1984)

Helck, W.
1974 *Die altägyptischen Gaue.* Wiesbaden: Reichert Verlag.

Hemmer, Helmut
1990 *Domestication: The decline of environmental appreciation.* Translated by Neil Beckhaus. Cambridge: University Press.

Herre, Wolf
1969 The science and history of domesticated animals. In *Science in Archaeology*, edited by D. Brothwell and E. Higgs, pp. 257–272. London: Duckworth.

Herskovits, M.J.
1926 The cattle complex in East Africa. *American Anthropologist* 28:230–72, 361–380, 494–528, 633–664.

Hester, J.J. and P.M. Hobler
1969 Prehistoric settlement patterns in Libyan Desert. *University of Utah Anthropological Papers*, No. 92. (incompletely cited in Banks 1984)

Hilliard, Sam
1972 *Hog Meat and Hoe Cake: Food supply in the Old South: 1840–1860*. Carbondale, Illinois: University Press.

Hillman, Gordon C. and M. Stuart Davies
1990 Measured domestication rates in wild wheats and barley under primitive cultivation, and their archaeological implications. *Journal of World Prehistory* 4(2):157–222.

Hobbs, Joseph J.
1989 *Bedouin Life in the Egyptian Wilderness*. Austin: University of Texas Press.

Hoffman, Michael A.
1982 *The Predynastic of Hierakonpolis —An interim report*. Egyptian Studies Association 1, Cairo.
1987 *A Final Report to the National Endowment for the Humanities of Predynastic Research at Hierakonpolis, 1985–1986*. University of South Carolina: Earth Sciences and Resources Institute.
1991 *Egypt Before the Pharaohs: The predynastic foundations of Egyptian civilization*, revised edition. Austin: University of Texas Press.

Hole, Frank
1984 A Reassessment of the Neolithic Revolution. *Paléorient* 10(2):49–60.
1989 A two-part, two-stage model of domestication. In *The Walking Larder: Patterns of domestication, pastoralism, and predation*, edited by J. Clutton-Brock, pp. 97–104. One World Archaeology Series 2. London: Unwin Hyman.

Holmes, D. L.
1993 Rise of the Nile delta. *Nature* 363(June):402–403.

Houlihan, Patrick F.
1986 *The Birds of Ancient Egypt*. Warminster, England: Aris and Phillips.
1996 *The Animal World of the Pharaohs*. Cairo: The American University in Cairo Press.

Howell, P., M. Lock and S. Cobb
1988 *The Jonglei Canal, impact and opportunity*. Cambridge Studies in Applied Ecology and Resource Management. Cambridge: University Press.

Hume, W. F.
1925 *Geology of Egypt*, volume 1: *The Surface Features of Egypt, Their Determining Causes and Relation to Geological Structure*. Cairo: Government Press.

Huntingford, G.W.B.
1953 *The Nandi of Kenya: Tribal control in a pastoral society*. London: Routledge and Kegan Paul.

Hussel, Lothar
1981 Sahel-ranching in Westafrika. *Die Nomaden im Geschichte und Gegewart*, pp. 141–150. Veroffent-lichen des Museums für Völkerkunde zu Leipzig, Heft 33.

Huston, J.E.
1978 Forage utilization and nutrient requirements of

the goat. *Journal of Dairy Sciences* 61:988–993.

Ingham, Bruce

1986 *Bedouin of Northern Arabia: Traditions of the Al-Dhafir*. London: KPI.

Ingold, T.

1980 *Hunters, Pastoralists and Ranchers: Reindeer economies and their transformations*. Cambridge Studies in Social Anthropology 28. Cambridge: Cambridge University Press.

1984 Time, social relationships and the exploitation of animals: anthropological reflections on prehistory. In *Animals and Archaeology, vol 3: Early herders and their flocks*, edited by J. Clutton-Brock and C. Grigson, pp. 3–12. Oxford: B.A.R. International Series 202.

1987 *The Appropriation of Nature: Essays on human ecology and social relations*. Iowa City, Iowa: University Press.

1988a (editor) *What is an Animal?* One World Archaeology Series 1. London: Unwin Hyman.

1988b Introduction. In *What is an Animal?*, edited by T. Ingold, pp. 1–16. One World Archaeology Series 1. London: Unwin Hyman.

1994 From trust to domination: An alternative history of human-animal relations. In *Animals and Human Society: Changing perspectives*, edited by A. Manning and J. Serpell, pp. 1–22. London: Routlege.

Inskeep, R.R.

1969 The archaeological background. In *The Oxford History of South Africa*, vol. 1, edited by M. Wilson and L. Thompson, pp. 451–470. Oxford: University of Oxford Press.

Irons, W.

1979 Political stratification among pastoral nomads. In *Pastoral Production and Society*, edited by L'Équipe Écologie et Anthropologie des Sociétés Pastorales, pp. 361–374. Cambridge: University Press.

Isaac, E.

1962 On the domestication of cattle. *Science* 137:195–204.

1971 On the domestication of cattle. In *Prehistoric Agriculture*, edited by S. Streuver, pp. 451–470. New York: American Museum of Natural History.

Jacquet, J.

1987 Excavations at Karnak-North: Observations and interpretations. In *Problems and Priorities in Egyptian Archaeology*, edited by J. Assmann, G. Burkard and V. Davies, pp. 105–107. London: KPI.

Jac J. Janssen

1975 *Commodity Prices from the Ramessid Period: An economic study of the village of the necropolis workmen at Thebes*. Leiden: E.J. Brill.

1982 Gift-giving in ancient Egypt as an economic feature. *Journal of Egyptian Archaeology* 68:253–258.

1991 Requisitions from Upper Egyptian temples (P. BM 10401). *Journal of Egyptian Archaeology* 77:79–94.

1994 Debts and credit in N.K. *Journal of Egyptian Archaeology* 80:19–136.

Jarman, M.R.

1969 The prehistory of upper Pleistocene and Recent cattle. *Proceedings of the Prehistoric Society* 35.

Jarman, M.R. and P.F. Wilkinson

1972 Criteria of animal domestication. In *Papers in Economic Prehistory*, edited by E. Higgs, pp. 83–96. Cambridge: Cambridge University Press.

Jeffreys, D.G., J. Malek and H.S. Smith

1982 Memphis 1984. *Journal of Egyptian Archaeology* 71:1–14.

Johnson, A. and C.A. Behrens

1982 Nutritional criteria in Machiguenga food production decisions: A linear-programming analysis. *Human Ecology* 10:179–189.

Johnson, Douglas H.

1993 *Governing the Nuer. Documents by Percy Coriat on Nuer History and Ethnography 1922–1931*. JASO Occasional Papers, No. 9. Oxford.

Johnson, G.A.

1983 Decision-making organization and pastoral nomad camp size. *Human Ecology* 11(2):173–197.

Johnson, Janet H.

1987 Ptolemaic bureaucracy from an Egyptian point of view. In *The Organization of Power. Aspects of Bureaucracy in the Ancient Near East*, edited by McG. Gibson and R. Biggs, pp. 141–150. Studies in Ancient Oriental Civilization 46. Chicago: Oriental Institute.

Jones, Michael

1990 The temple of Apis in Memphis. *Journal of Egyptian Archaeology* 76:141–147.

Jordan, Terry G.

1993 *North American Cattle-Ranching Frontiers: Origins, diffusion and differentiation*. Albuquerque: University of New Mexico.

Junker, Hermann

1928 Bericht über die von der Akademie der Wissenschaften in Wien nach dem Westdelta Entsendete Expedition. *Denkschrift Akademie Wissenschaft Philosophische-Historische Klasse* 28:14–24.

1929 Vorbericht über die Grabungen auf der neolithischen Siedlung von Merimde-Benisalâme. *Anzeiger der Akademie der Wissenschaften in Wien, Philosophische-Historische Klasse* 66:156–250.

1930 Vorbericht über die Grabungen auf der neolithischen Siedlung von Merimde-Benisalâme. *Anzeiger der Akademie Wissenschaften in Wien, Philosophische-Historische Klasse* 67:21–83.

1932 Vorbericht über die Grabungen auf der neolithischen Siedlung von Merimde-Benisalâme 1931/32. *Anzeiger der Akademie der Wissenschaften in Wien, Philosophische-Historische*

*Klasse* 69:36–52.
1933 Vorlaufiger Bericht über die Grabungen auf der neolithischen Siedlung von Merimde-Benisalâme 1933. *Anzeiger der Akademie der Wissenschaften* in Wien, *Philosophische-Historische Klasse* 70:54–82.
1934 Vorbericht über die funfte von der Akademie der Wissenschaften in Wien und dem Egyptiska Museet in Stockholm unternommene Grabung auf der neolithischen Siedlung Merimde-Benisalâme von 13. Februar bis 26 Marz 1934. *Anzeiger der Akademie der Wissenschaften in Wien, Philosophische-Historische Klasse* 71:118–132.
1940 Vorbeicht über die siebente Grabung der Akademie der Wissenschaften in Wien auf der vorgeschicht-lichen Siedlung Merimde-Benisalâme vom 25. Januar bis 4. April 1939. *Anzeiger der Akademie der Wissenschaften in Wien, Philoso-phische-Historische Klasse* 77:1–17.

Kadish, Gerald E.
1988 Seasonality and the name of the Nile. *Journal of the American Research Center in Egypt XXV:185–194.*

Kantor, H.
1952 Further evidence for early Mesopotamian relations with Egypt. *Journal of Near Eastern Studies* XI:239–250.

Kaplony, P.
1963 Der Inschriften der ägyptischen Frühzeit. Weisbaden: Ägyptologische Abhandlungen.

Kassas, M.
1952 Habitat and plant communities in the Egyptian Desert, I: Introduction. *Journal of Zoology* 40:342–351.

Kassas, M. and Zhran
1967 incompletely cited in Goodall (1986).

Keegan, William F.
1986 The optimal foraging analysis of horticultural production. *American Anthropologist* 88:92–107.

Keeler, C.E.
1947 Coat colour, physique and temperament. *Journal of Heredity* 38:271–277.
1975 Genetics of behavior patterns in color phases of the red fox. In *The Wild Canids*, edited by M. Fox, pp.399–413. New York: Van Nostrand Reinhold.

Keenan, Jeremy
1977 *The Tuareg. People* of *Ahaggar*. London: Allen Lane.

Kees, Hermann
1961 *Ancient Egypt: A cultural topography*. London: Faber and Faber.

Kemp, B.J.
1984–7 *Amarna Reports I, II, III, IV.*London: Egypt Exploration Society.
1989 *Ancient Egypt: Anatomy of a Civilization.* London: Routledge.

Kendall, R.L.
1969 *An Ecological History of Lake Victoria Basin.* PhD Dissertation, Duke University.

Khazanov, A.M.
1978 Characteristic features of nomadic communities in the Eurasian steppes. In *The Nomadic Alternative*, edited by W. Weissleder, pp. 119–126. The Hague: Mouton Publishers.
1984 *Nomads and the Outside World.* Translated by J. Crookenden. Cambridge Studies in Social Anthropology 44. Cambridge: University Press.

Klein, Richard
1984 The prehistory of stone age herders in South Africa. In *From Hunters to Farmers: The causes and consequences of food production in Africa*, edited by J.D. Clark and S.A. Brandt, pp. 281–290. Berkeley: University of California Press.
1986 The prehistory of stone age herders in the Cape province of South Africa. In *Prehistoric Pastoralism in Southern Africa*, edited by M. Hall and A.B. Smith, pp. 5–12. South African Archaeological Society, Goodwin Series, 5.

Klein, Richard and Katherine Cruz-Uribe
1989 *The Analysis of Animal Bones from Archaeological Sites*. Chicago: University of Chicago Press.

Klein, Richard G., Cornelia Wolf, Leslie G. Freeman, and Katheryn Allwarden
1981 The use of dental crown heights for constructing age profiles of Red Deer and similar species in archaeological samples. *Journal of Archaeological Science* 8:1–31.

Klitzsch, Eberhard, Rushdi Said, and Eckart Shrank (editors)
1984 *Research in Egypt and Sudan. Sonderorschung-bereich 69: Results of the Special Project Arid Areas, Period 1981–1984*. Berliner Geowissen-schaftliche Abhandlungen, Reihe A/Band 50. Berlin: Dietrich Reimer.

Köhler-Rollefson, Ilse
1988 The aftermath of the Levantine neolithic revolution in the light of ecological and ethnographic evidence. *Paléorient* 14(1):87–93.
1992 A model for the development of nomadic pastoralism on the Transjordanian Plateau. In *Pastoralism in the Levant: Archaeological methods in anthropological perspective*, edited by O. Bar-Yosef and A. Khazanov, pp. 11–18. Monographs in World Prehistory 10. Madison, Wisconsin: Prehistory Press.

Kokabi, von Mostefa
1980 Tierknochenfunde aus Giseh/Ägypten. *Annalen des Naturhistorischen Museums in Wien, Series B: Botanik und Zoologie* 83:519–537.

Kozlowski, J.K. and B. Ginter
1989 The Fayum Neolithic in the light of new discoveries. In *Late Prehistory of the Nile Basin and the Sahara*, edited by L. Krzyzaniak and M. Kobusiewicz, pp. 158–179. Poznan: Muzeum Archeologiczne w Poznaniu.

Kroeper, Karla
1989 *Settlement in the Nile Delta to the end of the Old Kingdom.* Ph.D. dissertation. Warsaw: Uniwersytet Warszawski Wydzial Historcyczny.

Krzyzaniak, Lech
1978 New light on early food production in the Central Sudan. *Journal of African History* 19:159–172.

Krzyzaniak, Lech, and M. Kobusiewicz (editors)
1984 *Origin and Early Development of Food-Producing Cultures in North Eastern Africa.* Poznan: Polish Academy of Sciences.

LaBianca, Øystein Sakala
1990 *Sedentarization and Nomadization: Food system cycles at Hesban and vicinity in Transjordan.* Berrien Springs, Michigan: Institute of Archaeology and Andrews University Press.

Larson, Daniel, Hector Neff, Donald Graybill, Joel Michaelsen, and Elizabeth Ambos
1996 Risk, climatic variability, and the study of southwestern prehistory: An evolutionary perspective. *American Antiquity* 61(2):217–241.

Lee, R.B.
1968 What hunters do for a living, or, how to make out on scarce resources. In *Man the Hunter*, edited by R.B. Lee and I. DeVore, pp. 30–48. Chicago: Aldine.
1969 !Kung Bushman subsistence: An input—output analysis. In *Environment and Cultural Behavior*, edited by A.P. Vayda, pp, 47–70. Garden City: Natural History Press.

Lee, R.B. and I. DeVore (editors)
1968 *Man the Hunter*. Chicago:Aldine.

Leeds, Anthony and Andrew P. Vayda (editors)
1965 *Man, Culture, and Animals. The role of animals in human ecological adjustments.* Washington, D.C.: American Association for the Advancement of Science, Publication 78.

van Lepp, Jonathan
1995 Evidence for irrigation in Amration art. *Journal of the American Research Center in Egypt* XXXII: 197–209.

Levy, Thomas E.
1989 Transhumance, subsistence and social evolution. In *Pastoralism in the Levant: Archaeological methods in anthropological perspectives*, edited by O. Bar-Yosef and A. Khazanov, pp. 65–82. Monographs in World Prehistory 10. Madison, Wisconsin: Prehistory Press.

Lewthwaite, James
1981 Plains tails from the hills: transhumance in Mediterranean archaeology. In *Economic Archaeology: Towards an intergration of ecological and social approaches*, edited by A. Sheridan and G. Bailey, pp. 57–66. Oxford: B.A.R. International Series 98.

Lhote, H.
1966 Les peintures parietales d'époque bovidienne du Tassili. *Journal de la Societe des Africanistes* 36(1):7–27.

Lichtheim, Miriam
1973 *Ancient Egyptian Literature: A Book of Readings. Volume I: The Old and Middle Kingdoms.* Berkeley: University of California Press.
1976 *Ancient Egyptian Literature: A Book of Readings. Volume II: The New Kingdom.* Berkeley: University of California Press.
1980 *Ancient Egyptian Literature: A Book of Readings. Volume III: The Late Periods.* Berkeley: University of California Press.

Lincoln, Bruce
1981 *Priests, Warriors, and Cattle: A study in the ecology of religions.* Berkeley: University Press.

Livingstone, D.A.
1967 Postglacial vegetation of the Ruwenzori Mountains in equatorial Africa. *Ecological Monographs* 37:25–52.
1975 Late Quaternary climatic change in Africa. *Annual Reviews of Ecology and Systematics* 6:249–356.

Loftus, R.T., D.E. MacHugh, D.G. Bradley, P.M. Sharp, and P. Cunningham
1994 Evidence for two independent domestications of cattle. *Proceedings of the National Academy of Science U.S.A.* 91:2757–2761.

van Loon, Dick
1978 *Small-scale Pig Raising.* Charlotte, Vermont: Garden Way Publishing.

Lortet, L. and C. Gaillard
1907 *La Faune Momifiée de l'Ancienne Egypt* (série 4). Lyon: Archives du Musée d'Histoire Naturelle de Lyon.

Lorton, D.
1974 *The Juridical Terminology of the International Relations in Egyptian Texts through Dynasty XVIII.* Baltimore, Maryland.

Lösche, A.
1954 *The Economics of Location.* New Haven, Connecticut: Yale University Press.

Lyman, R. Lee
1979 Available meat from faunal remains: A consideration of techniques. *American Antiquity* 44(3):536–545.
1984 Bone density and differential survivorship of fossil classes. *Journal of Anthropological Archaeology* 3:259–299.
1985 Bone frequencies: Differential transport, *in situ* destruction, and the MGUI. *Journal of Archaeological Science* 12:221–236.

Mace, Ruth
1993 Transitions between cultivation and pastoralism in Sub-Saharan Africa. *Current Anthropology* 34(4):363–382.

Macfarlane, W.V.
1968a Adaptation of ruminants to tropics and desesrts. In *Adaptation of Domestic Animals*, edited by E. Hafez, pp. 164–182. Philadelphia: Lea and Febiger.
1968b Comparative functions of ruminants in hot

environments. In *Adaptation of Domestic Animals*, edited by E. Hafez, pp. 264–276. Philadelphia: Lea and Febiger.

Mackenzie, D.
1971 *Goat Husbandry*. London: Faber and Faber.

Maitima, J.M.
1991 Ecological changes in the central rift valley, Kenya and their impact on food resources. In *Origins and Development of Agriculture in East Africa: The ethnosystems approach to the study of early food production in Kenya*, edited by R.E. Leakey and L.J. Slikkerveer, pp. 43–48. Ames, Iowa: Iowa State University.

Manwell, C. and C.M. Baker
1980a Chemical classification of cattle. I. Breed groups. *Animal Blood Groups and Biochemical Genetics* 11:127–150.
1980b Chemical classification of cattle. II. Phylogenetic tree and specific status of the zebu. *Animal Blood Groups and Biochemical Genetics* 11:151–162.

Marshall, Fiona
1986 *Aspects of the Advent of Pastoral Economies in East Africa.*. PhD dissertation, University of California, Berkeley.
1989 Rethinking the role of *Bos indicus* in Sub-Saharan Africa. *Current Anthropology* 30(2):235–241.
1990 Cattle herds and caprine flocks: Early pastoral strategies in south-western Kenya. In *Early Pastoralists of South-western Kenya*, edited by P.T. Robertshaw, pp. 205–260. Nairobi: British Institute in Eastern Africa.

Marshall, F.B. and Tom Pilgram
1993 NISP vs. MNI in quantification of body-part repre-sentation. *American Antiquity* 58(2):261–269.

Marshall, F.B., K. Stewart and J. Barthelme
1984 Early domestic stock at Dongodien in North Kenya. *Azania* 19:120–127.

Martin, Cary J.
1986 A Demotic land lease from Philadelphia: P. Bm 10560. *Journal of Egyptian Archaeology* 72:159–173.

Marx, Emanuel
1964 *Pre-capitalist Economic Formations*. London: Lawrence and Wishart.
1978 The ecology and politics of nomadic pastoralists in the Middle East. In *The Nomadic Alternative: Modes and models of interaction in the African-Asian deserts and steppes*, edited by W. Weissleder, pp. 71–74. The Hague: Mouton Publishers.

Matolsçi, J. (editor)
1976 *Domestikationsforschung und Geschichte der Haustierre*. Budapest: Akademiai Kaido.

Mauny, R.
1957 Répartition de la grand 'faune éthiopienne' du Nord-Ouest Africain du Paléolithique à nos jours. *Proceedings of the 3rd Panafrican Congress on Prehistory, Livingstone*, pp. 102–105. (incompletely cited in Banks 1984)

Maxwell, T.A.
1980 Journey to the Gilf Kebir and Uweinat, Southwest Egypt, 1978, Chapter VII: Geomorphology of the Gilf Kebir. *Geographical Journal 146:51–93.*

McArdle, John
1982 Preliminary report on the Predynastic fauna of the Hierakonpolis project. In *The Predynastic Site of Hierakonpolis—An interim report*, edited by M. Hoffman, pp. 116–121. Egyptian Studies Association Publication 1, Cairo University Herbarium and Department of Sociology and Anthropology, Western Illinois University. Oxford: Alden Press.

McCabe, J.T.
1984 *Livestock Management among the Turkana: A social and ecological analysis of herding in an East African pastoral population.* Unpublished Ph.D dissertation, Department of Anthropology. Binghamton, NewYork: State University.

McDowell, Andrea
1992 Agricultural activity by the workmen of Deir el-Medina. *Journal of Egyptian Archaeology* 78:195–206.

McHugh, W.P.
1974 Late prehistoric cultural adaptation in Southwest Egypt and the problem of the Nilotic origins of Saharn cattle pastoralism. *Journal of the American Research Center in Egypt.* 11:2–29.
1990 Implications of a decorated predynastic terracotta model for Saharan Neolithic influence in the Nile Valley. *Journal of Near Eastern Studies* 49(3):265–280.

McHugh, W.P., G.G. Schaber, C.S. Breed, and J.F. McCauley
1989 Neolithic adaptation and the Holocene functioning of tertiary drainages in southern Egypt and northern Sudan. *Antiquity* 63:320–326.

McLoughlin, Peter F.M. (editor)
1970 *African Food Production Systems: Cases and theory*. Baltimore: The Johns Hopkins Press.

Meadow, R.H.
1975 Mammal Remains from Hajji Firuz: A study in methodology. In *Archaeozoological Studies,* edited by A.T. Clason, pp. 265–283. Amsterdam: North-Holland Publishers.
1992 Inconclusive remarks on pastoralism, nomadism, and other animal-related matters. In *Pastoralism in the Levant: Archaeological materials in anthropo-logical perspectives*, edited by O. Bar-Yosef and A. Khazanov, pp. 261–269. Monographs in World Arch-aeology 10. Madison, Wisconsin: Prehistory Press.

Mendoza, Ruben
1986 Plant and animal domesticatio: Direct versus indirect evidence. *Antiquity* 60:7–14.

Menghin, O. and M. Amer
1932 Excavations of the Egyptian University in the Neolithic Site at Maadi, First Preliminary Report (Season of 1930–1931). Cairo: University Press.
Miller, N.F.
1984 The use of dung as fuel: An ethnographic example and an archaeological application. *Paléorient* 10:71–79.
Miller, Noami F. and Wilma Wetterstrom
in press Food and Drink in the Ancient Near East and North Africa. In *Cambridge History of Food.* (1996)
Miller, Robert L.
1990 Hogs and Hygiene. *Journal of Egyptian Archaeology* 76:125–140.
Millet, N.B., G.D. Hart, T.A. Reyman, M.R. Zimmerman, and P.K. Lewin
1980 Rom I: Mummification for the Common People. In *Mummies, Disease and Ancient Cultures*, edited by A. and E. Cockburn, pp. 71–84. New York: Cambridge University Press.
Mills, A.
1984 Research in the Dakhleh Oasis. In *Origin and Early Development of Food-Producing Cultures in North-Eastern Africa*, edited by L. Kryzaniak and M. Kobusiewicz, pp. 203–210. Poznan: Archaeological Museum.
Mithen, Steven J.
1990 *Thoughtful Foragers: A study of prehistoric decision making.* New Studies in Anthropology. Cambridge: Cambridge University Press.
Moens, Marie-Francine and Wilma Wetterstrom
1988 The agricultural economy of an Old Kingdom town in Egypt's west delta: Insights from the plant remains. *Journal of Near Eastern Studies* 47(3):159–173.
Monastersky, Richard
1996 The Case of the global jitters. Even in seemingly stable times, climate can take an abrupt turn. *Science News* 149:140–141.
Mond, Sir Robert and Oliver H. Meyers
1937 *Cemeteries of Armart*, 2 vols. London: Egypt Exploration Society.
Montet, P.
1925 *Scènes de la Vie Privée dans les Tombeaux Égyptiens de l'Ancien Empire.* Strasbourg.
1958 *Géographie de l'Egypte Ancienne*, 2 vols. Paris: Klincksieck.
Moran, Emilio (editor)
1984a *The Ecosystem Concept in Anthropology.* American Association for the Advancement of Science Selected Symposia Series 92. Boulder, Colorado: Westview Press.
1984b Limitations and advances in ecosystems research. In *The Ecosystem Concept in Anthropology*, edited by E.Moran, pp. 3–32. American Association for the Advancement of Science Selected Symposia Series 92. Boulder, Colorado: Westview Press.
Mount, L.E.
1968 Adaptation of Swine. In *Adaptation of Domestic Animals*, edited by E. Hafez, pp. 277–291. Philadelphia: Lea and Febiger.
Murdock, G.P.
1967 *Ethnographic Atlas.* Pittsburg, Pennsylvania: University Press. (for Human Relations Area Files)
Murnane, William J.
1983 *The Penguin Guide to Ancient Egypt.* New York: Penguin Books.
Murphy, Edwin
1990 *The Antiquities of Egypt. A translation with Notes on Book I of the Library of History of Diodorus Siculus*, revised edition. London: Transaction Publishers.
Murray, George W.
1935 *Sons of Ishamel: A study of the Egyptian Bedouin.* NY: Humanities Press.
Muthuri, F. and J. Kinyamario
1989 Nutritive value of papyrus (*Cyperus papyrus*): A tropical emergent macrophyte. *Economic Botany* 43:23–30.
Muzzolini, A.
1983 *L'art rupestre du Sahara Central: Classification et chronologie. Le boeuf dans la préhistoire africaine.* Thèse 3ème cycle. Université de Provence, Aix-en-Provence.
1986 *L'Art Rupestre Préhistorique des Massifs Centraux Sahariens.* Oxford: B.A.R. International Series 318. Also published as Cambridge Mono-graphs in African Archaeology 16.
1992 Dating the earliest central Saharan rock art: archaeological and linguistic data. In *Followers of Horus: Studies dedicated to Michael Allan Hoffman*, edited by R. Friedman and B. Adams, pp. 147–155. Egyptian Studies Association Publication No. 2, Oxbow Monograph 20. Oxford: Oxbow Books and Bloomington, Indiana: David Brown Book Co.
1993 The emergence of food-producing economy in the Sahara. In *The Archaeology of Africa: Food, metals and towns*, edited by T. Shaw, P. Sinclair, B. Andah, A. Okpoko, pp. 227–239. One World Archaeology Series 20. London: Routledge.
Neiman, Fraser D.
1995 Stylistic variation in evolutionary perspective: Inferences from decorative diversity and inter-assemblage distance in Illinois Woodland ceramic assemblages. *American Antiquity* 60(1):7–36.
Neumann, K.
1987 Middle Holocene vegetation of the Gilf Kebir, S.W. Egypt: a reconstruction. *Palaeoecology of Africa* 18:179–188.
Newberry, P.
1893–4 *el-Bersheh: The Tomb of Tehuti-hetep*, 2 vols. London: Egypt Exploration Fund.
1928 The pig and the cult animal of Set. *Journal of*

*Egyptian Archaeology* 14:211–225.
Nicholaisen, J.
1963 *Ecology and culture of the Pastoral Tuareg.* Copen-hagen: Nationalmuseets Skrifter Ethnografisk Raekke IX.
Noddle, B.A.
1983 Size and shape, time and place: Skeletal variations in cattle and sheep. In *Integrating the Subsistence Economy*, edited by Marten Jones, pp. 211–223. Oxford: B.A.R. International Series 181.
1989 Flesh on the bones. Some notes on animal husbandry of the past. *Archaeozoologia* III(1,2):25–50.
O'Connor, David
1972a The geography of settlement in ancient Egypt. In *Man, Settlement and Urbanism*, edited by P. Ucko, R. Tringham, and G. Dimbleby, pp. 681–698. London: Duckworth.
1972b A regional population in Egypt to *circa* 600 B.C. In *Population Growth: Anthropological implications*, edited by B. Spooner, pp. 78–100. Cambridge: Massachusetts Institute of Technology Press.
1990 Egyptology and archaeology: an African perspective. In *A History of African Archaeology*, edited by P. Robertshaw, pp. 236–251. London: James Curry, Ltd.
1993 Urbanism in bronze age Egypt and northeast Africa. In *The Archaeology of AFrica: Food, metals and towns*, edited by T. Shaw, P. Sinclair, B. Andah, and A. Okpoko, pp. 570–586. One World Archaeology Series 20. London: Routledge.
Olsen, Stanley J.
1979 Archaeologically, what constitutes an early domestic animal? *Advances in Archaeological Method and Theory*, Volume 2, edited by M. Schiffer, pp. 175–97. New York: Academic Press.
Owen, R.
1982 Palaeolimnology and archaeology of Holocene deposits northeast of Lake Turkana, Kenya. *Nature* 298:523–529.
Pachur, H.J.
1982 Das Abflussystem des Djebel Dalmar— eine Singularität? *Würzburger Geographische Arbeiten* 56:93–110. Cited in Muzzolini (1993).
Pachur, H.J. and H.P. Roper
1984 The Libyan (Western) Desert and northern Sudan during the Late Pleistocene and Holocene. In *Berliner Geowissenschaftliche Abhandlungen. Raihe A/Band 50: Research in Egypt and Sudan. Sonderforschungsbereich 69: Results of the special research project arid areas period 1981—1984,* edited by E. Klitzsch, R. Said, and E. Schrank, pp. 249–284. Berlin: Dietrich Reimer.
Parvaneh, V.
1972 The physical and chemical characteristics of sheep tail fat (*Donbeh*). *Tropical Science* 14:179–171.
Paulissen, E. and P.M. Vermeersch
1987 Earth, man and climate in the Egyptian Nile Valley during the Pleistocene. In *Prehistory of Arid North Africa*, edited by A.E. Close, pp. 29–67. Dallas: Southern Methodist Univeristy Press.
Pavitt, Nigel
1991 *Samburu.* New York: Henry Holt and Co.
Payne, Sebastian
1969 A metrical distinction between sheep and goat metacarpals. In *The Domestication and Exploitation of Plants and Animals*, edited by P. Ucko and G. Dimbleby, pp. 295–305. London: Duckworth.
1973 Kill-off patterns in sheep and goats: The mandibles from Asvan Kale. *Anatolian Studies* 23:281–304.
1985 Morphological distinction between the mandibular teeth of young sheep, *Ovis*, and goats, *Capra*. *Journal of Archaeological Science* 12:139–147.
Pees, W. and H. Hemmer
1980 Hirngröße und Aktivität bei Wildschafen und Hausschafen (Gattung *Ovis*) *Saugetierkundliche Mitteilungen* 28:39–45.
Pennington, Renee and Henry Harpending
1993 *The Strucutre of an African Pastoralist Community. Demography, history and ecology of the Ngamiland Herero.* Oxford: Clarendon Press.
Perlov, Diane Catherine
1987 *Trading for influence: The social and cultural economics of livestock marketing among the highland Samburu of northern Kenya.* PhD dissertation, University of California, Los Angeles.
Phillipson, David
1977 *The Later Prehistory of Eastern and Southern Africa.* New York:Africana.
1984 Early food production in sub-saharan Africa. In *From Hunters to Farmers: The causes and consequences of food production in Africa,* edited by J.D. Clark and S.A. Brandt, pp. 272–280. Berkeley: University of California Press.
1985 *African Archaeology.* Cambridge: Univeristy Press.
Pimentel, D., and M. Pimentel.
1979 *Food, Energy, and Society.* London: Edward Arnold.
Podzorski, Patricia V.
1990 *Their Bones Shall Not Perish: An examination of predynastic human skeletal remains from Naga-ed-Dêr in Egypt.* New Malden Surry, England: SIA Publishing.
Polanyi, K.
1957 The economy as an instituted process. In *Trade and Markets in the Early Empires*, edited by K. Polanyi, C. Arensberg and H. Pearson. Glenco: Free Press.

Posener, George
1962 *Dictionary of Egyptian Civilization.* New York: Tudor.
Pratt, D.J. and M.D. Gwynne
1977 *Rangeland Management and Ecology in East Africa.* Huntington, New York: Robert E. Krieger Publishing.
Preucel, Robert W.
1995 The postprocessual condition. *Journal of Archaeological Research* 3(2):147–175.
Price, E.O. and J.A. King
1968 Domestication and adaptation. In *Adaptation of Domestic Animals* , edited by E. Hafez, pp. 34–45. Philadelphia: Lea and Febiger.
Protsch, Rainer and Rainer Berger
1973 Earliest radiocarbon dates for domesticated animals. *Science* 179:235–239.
Prummel, Wietske and Hans-Jorg Frisch
1986 A guide to the distinction of species, sex and body side in bones of sheep and goat. *Journal of Archaeological Science* 13:567–577.
Purohit, G.R.
1972 *Water Metabolism in Desert Sheep.* Ph.D dissertation. Jodhpur: University of Jodhpur.
Purohit, G.R., P.K. Gosh, and G.C. Taneja
1976 Effect of water restriction on dry matter intact and digestibility of nutrients in pure and cross-bred Marwari sheep. *Annals of the Arid Zone* 15(1–2):95–101.
Pyke, Graham J.
1984 Optimal foraging theory: A critical review. *Annual Review of Ecology and Systematics* 15:523–575.
Quirke, Stephen
1992 *Ancient Egyptian Religion.* London: British Museum Press.
Raish, Carol
1992 *Domestic Animals and Stability in Pre-State Farming Societies.* Oxford: B.A.R. International Series 579.
Redding, Richard
1981 *Decision making in subsistence herding of sheep and goats in the Middle East.* PhD dissertation, University of Michigan.
1984a The faunal remains. In *Archaeological Investigations at El-Hibeh 1980: Preliminary report,* edited by R.J. Wenke, pp. 39–49. Malibu: Undena.
1984b Theoretical determinants of a herd's decisions: modeling variation in the sheep/goat ratio. In *Animals and Archaeology 3: Early Herders and their Flocks*, edited by J. Clutton-Brock and C. Grigson, pp. 161–170. Oxford: B.A.R. International Series 202.
1988 A general explanation of subsistence change: from hunting and gathering to food production. *Journal of Anthropological Archaeology* 7:56–97.
1991 The role of the pig in the subsistence system of ancient Egypt: A parable on the potential of faunal data. In *Animal Use and Culture Change,* edited by P.J. Crabtree and K. Ryan, pp. 20–30. MASCA Research Papers in Science and Archaeology 8, Supplement.
1992 Egyptian Old Kingdom patterns of animal use and the value of faunal data in modeling socioeconomic systems. *Paléorient* 18(2):99–107.
Redford, Donald
1986 Egypt and western Asia in the Old Kingdom. *Journal of the American Research Center in Egypt* XXIII:125–143.
Redford, Donald, Sara Orel, Susan Redford, and Steven Schubert
1991 East Karnak Excavations, 1987–1989. *Journal of the American Research Center in Egypt* XXVIII:75–106.
Reed, Ch.
1961 Osteological evidence for prehistoric domestication in southwestern Asia. *Zeitschrift fur Tierzuchtungs und Zuchtungsbiologie* 76(1):31–38.
1969 Pattern of animal domestication in the prehistoric Near East. In *The Domestication and Exploitation of Plants and Animals*, edited by P. Ucko and G. Dimbleby, pp. 361–388. London: Duckworth.
1977 *Origin of Agriculture*. The Hague: Mouton.
Reining, Priscilla
1970 *African Food Production Systems: Cases and theory*, edited by P. McLoughlin, pp. 41–90. Baltimore: The Johns Hopkins Press.
Renfrew, Colin
1973 *The Explanation of Culture Change.* London: Duckworth.
1977 Space, time and polity. In *The Evolution of Social Systems*, edited by J. Friedman and M.J. Rowlands, pp. 89–112. London: Duckworth.
Renfrew, Colin and Stephen Shennan (editors)
1982 *Ranking, Resource and Exchange. Aspects of the archaeology of early European Society.* Cambridge: University Press.
Richardson, J.L. and A.E. Richardson
1972 History of an African rift lake and its climatic implications. *Ecological Monographs* 42:449–534.
Rigby, P.
1985 *Persistent Pastoralists: Nomadic Societies in Transition.* London: Zed Books.
Rindos, David
1984 *The Origins of Agriculture: An evolutionary perspective.* New York: Academic Press.
1985 Darwinian selection, symbolic variation, and the evolution of culture. *Current Anthropology* 26(1):65–88.
1989 Darwinism and its role in the explanation of domestication. In *Foraging and Farming: The evolution of plant exploitation*, edited by D. Harris and G. Hillman, pp. 27–41. One World Archaeology Series 13. London: Unwin Hyman.

Ripinsky, Michael
1985 The camel in dynastic Egypt. *Journal of Egyptian Archaeology* 71:134–141.
Ritchie, C.
1987 *The Political Economy of Resource Tenure in the Kalahari: San survival in Namibia and Botswana.* M.A. thesis. Boston: Boston University.
Ritner, Robert
1986 The site of the wild bull-hunt of Amenophis III. *Journal of Egyptian Archaeology*(Brief communications) 72:193–194.
Rizkana, I. and J. Seeher (editors)
1989 *Ma'adi III. The non-lithic small finds and the structural remains of the Predynastic settlement.* Mainz am Rhein: Verlag Philipp von Zabern.
Robertshaw, Peter
1989 Development of pastoralism in East Africa. In *The Walking Larder: Patterns of domestication, pastoralism, and predation*, edited by J. Clutton-Brock, pp. 207–214. One World Archaeology Series 2. London: Unwin Hyman.
1990 (editor)*A History of African Archaeology.* London: James Curry, Ltd.
1991 On agricultural beginnings in Kenya: Retrospect and prospects. In *Origins and Development of Agriculture in East Africa: The ethnosystems approach to the study of early food production in Kenya*, edited by R. Leakey and Slikkerveer, pp. 7–16. Ames, Iowa: Iowa State University.
Robertshaw, P. and D.P. Collett
1983 The identification of pastoral peoples in the archaeological record: An example from East Africa. *World Archaeology* 15:67–78.
Röhrs, M. and D. Kruska
1969 Der Einfluß der Domestikation auf das Zentralnervensystem und Verhalten von Schweinen. *Deutsche tierärztlische Wissenschaft* 76:514–518.
Rosen, Steven A.
1988 Notes on the origins of pastoral nomadism: A case study from the Negev Desert and Sinai. *Current Anthropology* 29:498–506.
Roth, Ann Macy
1987 The organization and functioning of the royal mortuary cults of the Old Kingdom in Egypt. In *The Organization of Power. Aspects of bureaucracy in the ancient Near East*, edited by McG. Gibson and R. Biggs, pp. 133–140. Studies in Ancient Oriental Civilization 46. Chicago: Oriental Intitute.
Rothe, Russell D., George Rapp Jr., and William K. Miller
1996 New hieroglyphic evidence for pharaonic activity in the Eastern Desert of Egypt. *Journal of the American Research Center in Egypt* XXXIII:77–104.
Rowley-Conwy, Peter
1991 Sorghum from Qasr Ibrim, Egyptian Nubia, c. 800 B.C.–A.D. 1811: A preliminary study. In *New Light on Early Farming: Recent developments in palaeo-ethnobotany*, edited by J.M. Renfrew, pp. 191–212. Edinburgh: University Press.
Ruffer, M.A.
1919 *Food in Egypt.* Mémoire presenté à l'Institut Egyptien 1. Cairo.
Russell, Kenneth W.
1988 *After Eden: The behavioral ecology of early food production in the Near East and North Africa.* Oxford: B.A.R. International Series 391.
Ryder, Michael L.
1964 The origin of spinning. *Antiquity* 38:293–294.
1965 Report on textiles from Çatal Hüyük. *Anatolian Studies* 15:175–176.
1969 Changes in the fleece of sheep following domestication (with a note on the coat of cattle). In *The Domestication and Exploitation of Plants and Animals*, edited by P. Ucko and G. Dimbleby, pp. 495–521. London: Duckworth.
1983 *Sheep and Man.* London: Duckworth.
Sadr, Karim
1991 *The development of nomadism in ancient north-east Africa.* Philadelphia: University of Pennsylvania Press.
Sahlins, M.D.
1976 *Culture and Practical Reason.* Chicago: University Press.
Sahlins, M.D. and E.R. Service
1960 *Evolution and Culture.* Ann Arbor, Michigan: University Press.
Said, Rushdi
1962 *The Geology of Egypt.* Amsterdam: Elsevier.
1981 *The Geological Evolution of the River Nile.* New York: Springer-Verlag.
1990 (editor)*The Geology of Egypt.* Rotterdam: Balkema Press.
1993 *The River Nile: Geology, Hydrology and Utilization.* New York: Pergamon Press.
Salzman, P.C.
1967 Political organization among nomadic peoples. *Proceedings of the American Philosophical Society* 111(2):115–31.
1971 Movement and resource extraction among pastoral nomads: the case of the Shah Nawazi Baluch. *Anthropological Quarterly* 4(3):185–197.
Samuel, Delwen
1996 Investigation of ancient Egyptian baking and brewing methods by correlative microscopy. *Science* 273:488–490.
Sandford, K.S.
1934 *Paleolithic Man and the Nile Valley in Upper and Middle Egypt. A Study of the Region during Pliocene and Pleistocene Times. Part 3.* Oriental Institute Publication 18. Chicago: University Press.
Sandford, M.K., D.P. Van Gerven and R.R. Meglen.
1983 Elemental hair analyses: New evidence on the etiology of *cribia orbitalia* in Sudanese Nubia.

*Human Biology* 55:831–844.
Sato, Shun
1980 Pastoral movements and the subsistence unit of the Rendille of northern Kenya with special reference to camel ecology. *Senri Ethnological Studies* 6:1–78.
Schapera, I.
1953 *The Tswana*. London: Routledge and Kegan Paul.
Schild, R. and F. Wendorf
1989 The late Pleistocene Nile in Wadi Kubbaniya. In *The Prehistory of Wadi Kubbaniya, Vol 2: Stratigraphy, Paleoeconomy, and Environment*. Dallas: Fort Burgwin Research Center and Southern Methodist University Press.
Schmidt-Nielsen, Knut
1964 *Desert Animals*. Oxford: University Press.
1979 *Desert Animals: Physiological Problems of Heat and Water*. New York: Dover.
Schneider, Harold
1957 The subsistence role of cattle among the Pokot and in East Africa. *American Anthropologist* 59:278–300.
1979 *Livestock and Equality in East Africa: The economic basis for social structure*. Bloomington: Indiana University Press.
Schwabe, Calvin W.
1978 *Cattle, Priests, and Progress in Medicine*. Fourth Wesley W. Spink Lectures in Comparative Medicine. Minneapolis: University of Minnesota Press.
1994 Animals in the ancient world. In *Animals and Human Society: Changing Perspectives*, edited by A. Manning and J. Serpell, pp. 36–58. London: Routledge.
Schwabe, C.W., J. Adams and C. Hodge
1982 Egyptian beliefs about the bull's spine: An anatomical origin for Ankh. *Anthropological Linguistics* 24:445–79.
Schwabe, H.W.
1979a Öko-ethologische Studien zur Ausbreitungspotenz der Hausratte (*Rattus rattus* L.). *Zoologisches Jahrbuch, Systematik* 106:124–168.
1979b Pigmentationskorrelierte Verhaltensunterschiede bei Hausratten (*Rattus rattus* L.). *Zoologisches Jahrbuch, Systematik* 106:406–426.
Sealy, Judith and Royden Yates
1994 The chronology of the introduction of pastoralism to the Cape, South Africa. *Antiquity* 68:58–67.
Servant, M. and S. Servant
1970 Les formations lacustures et les diatomées du Quaternaire récent du fond de la cuvette tchadienne. *Revue Géographique, Physiographique et Géologique* 12(1):63–67.
1972 Nouvelles données pour une interprétation paléoclimatique de séries continentales du Bassin Tchadien (Pléistocene récent, Holocène). *Palaeolecology of Africa* 6:87–92.
Sethe, K.
1906–09 *Urkunden der 18. Dynastie*. Leipzig: Hinrichs. Cited in Newberry (1928:211).
Shaw, Ian
1994 Pharoanic quarrying and mining: settlement and procurement in Egypt's marginal regions. *Antiquity* 68:108–119.
Shaw, Thurston
1973 The origins and devlopment of food production in Africa. In*Panafrican Congress on Prehistory and Quaternary Studies, 7th session (1971)*, edited by B. Ababe, J. Chavaillon and J.E.G. Sutton, pp.259–264. Addis Ababa: Provisional Military Government of Socialist Ethiopia, Ministry of Culture.
1977 Hunters, gatherers and first farmers in West Africa. In *Hunters, Gatherers and First Farmers Beyond Europe*, edited by J.V.S. Megaw, pp. 69–126. Leicester: Leicester University Press.
1984 Archaeological evidence and effects of food-producing in Nigeria. In *From Hunters to Farmers: The causes and consequences of food production in Africa*, edited by J.D. Clark and S.A. Brandt, *pp. 152–157*. Berkeley: University of California Press.
Shaw, Thurston, Paul Sinclair, Bassey Andah and Alex Okpoko (editors)
1993 *The Archaeology of Africa: Food, metals and towns*. London: Routlege.
Sheridan, Alison and Geoff Bailey (editors)
1981 *Economic Archaeology: Towards an integration of ecological and social approaches*. Oxford: B.A.R. International Series 96.
Sherratt, A.
1981 Plough and pastoralism: aspects of the second products revolution. In *Studies in Honor of David Clarke*, edited by I. Hodder, G. Isaac, and N. Hammond, pp. 261–305. Cambridge: University Press.
1983 The secondary exploitation of animals in the Old World. *World Archaeology* 15:90–104.
Shinnie, P.L.
1996 *Ancient Nubia*. London: Kegan Paul.
Sidney, J.
1965 The past and present distribution of some African ungulates. *Transactions of the Zoological Society of London*, Vol. 30.
Siegel, Jane
1976 Animal paleopathology: possibilities and problems. *Journal of Archaeological Science* 3(4):349–384.
Sikes, Nancy
1995 *Early Hominid Habitat Preferences in East Africa: Stable Isotopic Evidence from Paleosols*. PhD dissertation, Department of Anthropology, University of Illinois, Urbana-Champgain.
Silberbauer, George B.
1981 *Hunter and Habitat in the Central Kalahari Desert*. Cambridge: University Press.

Silver, I.A.
1970 The ageing of domestic animals. In *Science in Archaeology*, 2nd edition, edited by J. Brothwell and E. Higgs, pp. 283–302. New York: Praeger.
Simms, Steven R.
1988 The archaeological structure of a bedouin camp. In *Journal of Archaeological Science* 15:197–211.
Simoons, Frederick J.
1971 The antiquity of dairying in Asia and Africa. *Geographical Review* 61(3):431–439.
1979 Dairying, milk use and lactose malabsorption in Eurasia: A problem in culture history. *Anthropos* 74:61–80.
Smith, Andrew B.
1980 Domesticated cattle in the Sahara and their introduction into W. Africa. In *The Sahara and the Nile*, edited by M.A.J. Williams and H. Faure, pp. 489–501. Rotterdam: Balkema.
1984 Origins of the Neolithic in the Sahara. In *From Hunters to Farmers: The causes and consequences of food production in Africa*, edited by J.D. Clark and S.A. Brandt, pp. 84–92. Berkeley: University of California Press.
1986 Cattle domestication in North Africa. *African Archaeological Review* 4:197–203.
1987 Seasonal exploitation of resources on the Vredenberg Peninsula after 2000 BP. In *Papers in the Prehistory of the Western Cape, South Africa*, edited by J. Parkington and M. Hall, pp. 393–402. Oxford: B.A.R. International Series 332.
1992a Origins and spread of pastoralism in Africa. *Annual Review of Anthropology* 21:125–141.
1992b *Pastoralism in Africa. Origins and development ecology*. London: Hurst and Co.
Smith, Bruce
1975 Toward a more accurate estimation of the meat yield of animal species at archaeological sites. In *Archaeozoological Studies*, edited by A.T. Clason, pp.99–106. Amsterdam, North Holland Press.
Smith, H.S.
1969 Animal domestication and animal cult in dynastic Egypt. In *The Domestication and Exploitation of Plants and Animals*, edited by P. Ucko and G. Dimbleby, pp. 307–314. London: Duckworth.
Smith, Michael
1984 The ecosystem concept in anthropology. In *The Ecosystem Concept in Anthropology*, edited by E. Moran, pp. 87–102. American Association for the Advancement of Science Selected Symposia Series 92. Boulder, Colorado: Westview Press.
Smith, P. and L.K. Horowitz
1984 Radiographic evidence for changing patterns of animal exploitation in the southern Levant. *Journal of Archaeological Science* 11:467–475.
Smith, Susan
1980 The environmental adaptation of nomads in the West African Sahel: A key to understanding prehistoric pastoralists. In *The Sahara and the Nile: Quaternary environments and prehistoric occupation in northern Africa*, edited by M.A.J. Williams and H. Faure, pp. 467–487. Rotterdam: Balkema.
Solecki, R.L.
1981 *An Early Village Site at Zawi Chemi Shanidar*. Malibu: Undena.
Spalinger, Anthony
1991 Some revisions of temple endowments in the New Kingdom. *Journal of the American Research Center in Egypt* XXVIII:21–40.
Spaulding, Jay and J.L. Spaulding
1989 *Pigs: The democratic philosophers of Medieval Sudan*. Working Papers in African Studies No. 134. Boston: Boston University African Studies Center.
Spear, Thomas and Richard Waller (editors)
1993 *Being Maasai: Ethnicity and Identity in East Africa*. London: James Currey, Ltd.
Spencer, Paul
1965 *The Samburu: A study of gerontacracy in a nomadic tribe*. Berkeley: University of California Press.
1973 *Nomads in Alliance: Symbiosis and growth among the Rendille and Samburu of Kenya*. London: Oxford University Press.
Spooner, B.
1971 Towards a generative model of nomadism. *Anthropological Quarterly* 44(3):198–210.
1973 *Nomads in Alliance: Symbiosis and growth among the Rendille and Samburu of Kenya*. London: Oxford University Press.
Springuel, I.
1981 *Studies on the natural vegetation of the islands of the First Cataract at Aswan, Egypt*. Unpublished PhD thesis, Aswan Faculty of Science. Asyut, Egypt.
Stahl, Ann
1984 A history and critique of investigations into early African agriculture. In *From Hunters to Farmers: The causes and consequences of food production in Africa*, edited by J.D. Clark and S.A. Brandt, pp. 9–22. Berkeley: University of California Press.
Stampfli, H.R.
1983 The fauna of Jarmo with notes on animal bones from Matarrah, the Amuq, and Karim Shahir. In *Prehistoric Archaeology along the Zagros Flanks*, edited by L.S. Braidwood, R.J. Braidwood, B. Howe, C.A. Reed, and P.J. Watson, pp.431–483. Oriental Institute Publications 105. Chicago: Oriental Institute of the University of Chicago.
Stanley, Daniel J. and Andrew G. Warne
1993a Nile Delta: Recent geological evolution and human impact. *Science* 260(April): 628–634.
1993b Sea level and initiation of Predynastic culture in the Nile delta. *Nature* 363(June):435–438.

Stein, Gil
1987 Regional economic integration in early state societies: Third millennium B.C. pastoral production at Grittile, southeast Turkey. *Paléorient* 13(2):101–111.

Stemler, Ann
1984 The transition from food collecting to food production in Northern Africa. In *From Hunters to Farmers: The causes and consequences of food production in Africa*, edited by J.D. Clark and S.A. Brandt, pp. 126–131. Berkeley: University of California Press.

Stenning, D.J.
1959 *Savanna Nomads*. London: Oxford University Press.
1960 Transhumance, migratory drift, migration: Patterns of pastoral Fulani nomadism. In *Cultures and Societies of Africa*, edited by S. and P. Ottenburg, pp. 135–159. New York: Random House.

Stewart, Frances L. and Peter W. Stahl
1977 Cautionary note on edible meat poundage figures. *American Antiquity* 42(2):267–270.

Stiles, D.
1981 Hunters of the northern East African coast: Origins and historical processes. *Africa* 51(4):848–862.

Strickon, A.
1965 The Euro-American ranching complex. In *Man, Culture and Animals. The role of animals in human ecological adjustments,* edited by A. Leeds and A. Vayda, pp. 229–258. Washington, D.C.: American Association for the Advancement of Science, Publication 78.

Stutt, Arthur and Stephen Shennan
1990 The nature of archaeological arguments. *Antiquity* 64:766–777.

Tapper, Richard L.
1988 Animality, humanity, morality, society. In *What is an Animal?*, edited by T. Ingold, pp. 47–60. One World Archaeology Series 1. London: Unwin Hyman.

Terrill, C.E.
1968 Adaptation of sheep and goats. In *Adaptation of Domestic Animals*, edited by E. Hafez, pp. 246–263. Philadelphia: Lea and Febiger.

Thalen, D.C.P.
1974 *Ecology and utilization of desert shrub rangelands in Iraq*. The Hague: W. Junk.

Tobin, Vincent Arieh
1988 Mytho-theology in ancient Egypt. *Journal of the American Research Center in Egypt* XXV:169–183.

Tomlin, D.C., R.R. Johnson, and B.A. Dehority
1965 Relationship of lignification to *in vitro* cellulose digestibility of grasses and legumes. *Journal of Animal Sciences* 24:161–165.

Topps, J.H.
1977 Adaptation of cattle to drought conditions and their requirements for food and water. In *Drought in Africa*, edited by D. Dalby, R.J. Harrison Church and F. Bezzaz, pp. 101–104. London: International African Istitute.

Torry, William I.
1973 *Susbistence Ecology Among the Gabra: Nomads of the Kenya/Ethiopian frontier*. PhD dissertation, Columbia University.

Trigger, Bruce G.
1993 *Early Civilizations. Ancient Egypt in context.* Cairo: American University in Cairo Press.

Trigger, B., B.J. Kemp, D. O'Connor, A. Lloyd
1983 *Ancient Egypt. A Social History*. Cambridge: Cambridge University Press.

Turner, -
1960 incompletely cited in Macfarlane 1968a.

Turton, J.D.
1962 The effect of castration on meat production and quality in cattle, sheep and pigs. *Animal Breeding Abstracts* 30:447.

Ucko, P. and G.W. Dimbleby (editors)
1969 *Domestication of Plants and Animals*. London: Duckworth.

Uerpmann, H.P.
1978 Metrical analysis of faunal remains from the Middle East. In *Approaches to Faunal Analysis in the Middle East*, edited by R.H. Meadow and M.A. Zeder, pp. 41–45. Peabody Museum Bulletin, No. 2. Cambridge, Massachusetts: Harvard University.
1979 *Probleme der Neolithisierung des Mittelmeer-raumes*. Beihefte zum Tübinger Atlas des Vorderen Orients, Reihe B, 28. Weisbaden: Dr. Ludwig Reichert.

Valbelle, D.
1985 Les Ouvriers de la Tombe. In *Deir el-Médineh à l'époque ramesside*, pp.148–157. Cairo.

Van Neer, Wim
1986 Pectoral spines of Clariidae as indicators of season of death: An example from the Byzantino-Islamic site of Apamea (Syria; 6th–7th century A.D.). In *Fish and Archaeology: Studies in osteometry, taphonomy, seasonality and fishing methods*, edited by D.C. Brinkhuizen and A.T. Clason, pp. 1–18. Oxford: B.A.R. International Series 294.

Van Noten, Francis
1978 *Rock Art of the Jebel Uweinat*. Graz, Austria: Akademische Druck- und Verlagsanstalt.

Vandier, J.
1955 *Manuel d'archéologie égyptienne. II: Les Grands Époques: L'architecture religieuse et civile.* Paris: A. and J. Picard.
1969 *Manuel d'archéologie égyptienne V.* Paris: A. and J. Picard.

Vayda, A.P.
1967 On the anthropological study of economics. *Journal of Economic Issues* 1:86–90.

van der Veen, M., A. Grant and G. Barker
1996 Romano-Libyan agriculture: Crops and animals. In*Farming the Desert. The* UNESCO *Libyan*

*valleys archaeological surveys*, Volume one: *Synthesis*, edited by G. Barker, D. Gilbertson, B. Jones and D. Mattingly, pp. 227–264. A joint publication of Tripoli:UNESCO Publishing and Department of Antiquities, & London:Society for Libyan Studies.

Vermeersch
1978 *ElKab II*. Leuven: University Press.

Verner, M.
1986 A slaughterhouse from the Old Kingdom. *Mitteilungen des Deutsches Archäologisches Insitut, Abteilung Kairo* 42:181–189.

Voigt, E.A.
1977 The subsistence economy of a sixth millennium village in the Ushnu-Solduz Valley. In *Mountains and Lowlands: Essays in the archaeology of greater Mesopotamia*, edited by L.D. Levine and T.C. Young, pp.307–346. Bibliotheca Mesopotamica 7.

Voigt, E.A. and I. Plug
1984 Happy rest: the earliest iron age fauna from the S--pansberg. *Sud Afrikanse Tydskrif vir Wetenskap* 80:221–227. Cited in Noddle (1989).

von den Driesch, A.
1976 *A Guide to the Measurement of Animal Bones from Archaeological Sites*. Peabody Museum Bulletin #1. Cambridge, Massachusetts: Harvard University Press.
1986a Tierknochenfunde aus Qasr el-Sagha/Fayum (Neolithicum Mittleres Reiche). *Mitteilungen des Deutsches Archäologisches Insitut, Abteilung Kairo* 42:1–8.
1986b Fische im alten Äegpten—eine osteoarchäologische Untersuchung. *Documenta Naturae* 34:1–33.

von den Driesch, A. and J. Boessneck
1985 *Die Tierknochenfunde aus der neolitischen Siedlung von Merimde-Benisalâme am westlichen Nildelta*. Munich: Institut für Palaeoanatomie, Domestikationsforschung und Geschichtre der Tiermedizin.

Von Thünen, Johann Heinrich
1966 *Von Thünen's Isolated State*, translated by Carla Wartenberg and edited by Peter Hall. London: Pergamon.

Walker, Rikki
1985 *A Guide to Post-Cranial Bones of East African Mammals*. Palo Alto: Hylochoerus Press.

Waller, R.
1976 The Maasai and the British 1895–1905. *Journal of African History* 17:529–553.

Wapnish, Paula and Brian Hesse
1988 Urbanization and the organization of animal production at Tell Jemmeh in the Middle Bronze Age Levant. *Journal of Near Eastern Studies* 47(2):81–94.

Wasylokowa, K., J.R. Harlan, J. Evans, F. Wendorf, R. Schild, A.E. Close, H. Krolik, and R.A. Housley
1993 Examination of botanical remains from early neolithic houses at Nabta Playa, Western Desert, Egypt, with special reference to sorghum grains. In *The Archaeology of Africa: Food, metals and towns*, edited by T. Shaw, P. Sinclair, B. Anhah, and A. Okpoko, pp. 154–164. One World Archaeology Series 20. London: Routledge.

Watson, Patty Jo
1979 *Archaeological Ethnography in Western Iran*. Viking Fund Publications in Anthropology, No. 57. Tuscon: University of Arizona.

Wattenmaker, Patricia
1982 Analysis of the faunal remains. In *Quseir al-Qadim 1980: Preliminary report*, edited by D. Whitcomb and J. Johnson, pp. 347–353. Malibu: Undena.
1987 Town and village economics in an early state society. *Paléorient* 13(2):113–122.

Wegner, Josef
1995 The history and function of the settlement at Areika. *Journal of the American Research Center in Egypt* XXXII:127–160.

Weiner, J.
1973 Dressing percentage, gross body composition and caloric value of the roe deer. *Acta Theriologica* 18:209–222.

Weiner, S. and O. Bar-Yosef.
1990 States of preservation of bones from prehistoric sites in the Near East: A survey. *Journal of Archaeological Science* 17(2):187–96.

Weissleder, Wolfgang (editor)
1978 *The Nomadic Alternative: Modes and models of interaction in the African-Asian deserts and steppes*. The Hague: Mouton Publishers.

Wendorf, F. and R. Schild
1976 *ThePrehistory of the Nile Valley*. New York: Academic Press.
1980 *The Prehistory of the Eastern Sahara*. Dallas: Southern Methodist University Press.
1986 *The Prehistory of Wadi Kubbaniya*. Dallas: Southern Methodist University Press.
1994 Are the early Holocene cattle in the Eastern Sahara domestic or wild? *Evolutionary Anthropology* 3(4):118–128.

Wendorf, F. R. Schild and A. Close
1984 *Cattle-Keepers of the Eastern Sahara: The Neolithic of Bir Kiseiba*. Dallas: Department of Anthropology, Institute for the Study of Earth and Man, Southern Methodist University.

Wendorf, F., A. Close, R. Schild, K. Wasylikowa, R. Housley, J. Harlan, and H. Królik
1992 Saharan exploitation of plants 8000 BP. *Nature* 359:721–724.

Wenke, Robert J.
1986 Old Kingdom community organization in the western delta. *Norwegian Archeological Review*, 19:15–33.
1989 Egypt: Origins of complex societies.*Annual Review of Anthropology* 18:129–55.
1991 The evolution of early Egyptian civilization: Issues and evidence. *Journal of World Prehistory* 5(3):279–329.

Wenke, Robert J. and Douglas J. Brewer
1991 Research Proposal submitted to the National Endowment for the Humanities.
1992 The Neolithic—Predynastic transition in the Fayyum depression. In *Followers of Horus: Studies dedicated to Michael Allan Hoffman*, edited by R. Friedman and B. Adams, pp. 175–184. Egyptian Studies Association Publication No. 2, Oxbow Monograph 20. Oxford: Oxbow Books and Bloomington, Indiana: David Brown Book Co.
1996 The Archaic and Old Kingdom Delta: The evidence from Mendes and Kom el-Hisn. In *House and Palace in Ancient Egypt*, edited by Manfred Bietak. Vienna: Austrian Archaeological Institute.

Wenke, R., P. Buck, H. Hamroush, M. Kobusiewicz, K. Kroeper, R. Redding
1988 Kom el–Hisn: Excavation of an Old Kingdom settlement in the Egyptian delta. *Journal of the American Research Center in Egypt* XXV:5–34.

Wenke, R., P. Buck, J. Hanley, M. Lane, J. Long, and R. Redding
1983 The Fayyum archaeological project: Preliminary report of the 1981 season. *American Research in Egypt Newsletter* 122:25–40.

Wenke, R., J. Long, and P. Buck
1980 Epipaleolithic and neolithic subsistence and settlement in the Fayyum Oasis of Egypt. *Journal of Field Archaeology* 15:29–51.

Wenke, R. and Richard Redding
1985 Excavations at Kom el-Hisn, 1984. *American Research Center in Egypt Newsletter* 129:1–11.

Wente, Edward
1990 *Letters from Ancient Egypt*, vol. 1. Atlanta, Georgia: Scholars Press.

Wetterstrom, Wilma
1993 Foraging and farming in Egypt: The transition from hunting and gathering to horticulture in the Nile valley. In *The Archaeology of Africa: Food, metals and towns,* edited by T. Shaw, P. Sinclair, B. Andah, and A. Okpoko, pp. 165–226. One World Archaeology Series, 20. London: Routledge.
1994 Ecology and agriculture in ancient Egypt: The relationship between the land and the people. Paper presented at the 6th annual symposium of the American Research Center in Egypt, New York.

White, Christine D.
1993 Isotopic determination of seasonality in diet and death from Nubian mummy hair. *Journal of Archaeological Science* 20:657–666.

Wild, H.
1966 *Tombeau de Ti.* Cairo: L'Institut Français d'Archéologie Orientale.

Wilk, Richard R. and William L. Rathje
1982 Household archaeology. *American Behavioral Scientist* 2596):617–639.

Wilkinson, Sir J. Gardner
1988 *The Ancient Egyptians. Their life and customs*, 2 vols. New York: Bonanza Books. (reprint by John Murray of the 1854 publication)

Wilkinson, P.F.
1972 Current experimental domestication and its relevance to prehistory. In *Papers in Economic Prehistory*, edited by E.S. Higgs, pp. 107–118. Cambridge University Press.

Willcocks, W. and J.I. Craig
1913 *Egyptian Irrigation*, 2 vols, 3rd edition. London: Spon.

Williams, M.A.J.
1971 Geomorphology and Quaternary ecology of Adrar Bous. *Geographical Journal* 137:450–455.
1984 Late Quaternary prehistoric environments in the Sahara. In *From Hunters to Farmers: The causes and consequences of food production in Africa*, edited by J.D. Clark and S.A. Brandt, pp. 74–83. Berkeley: University of California Press.

Williamson, G. and W.J.A. Payne
1978 *An Introduction to Animal Husbandry in the Tropics*, 3rd edition. London: Longman.

Wilmsen, E.N.
1973 Interaction, spacing behavior and the oraganization of hunting bands. *Journal of Anthropological Research* 29:1–31.
1982 Studies in diet, nutrtion and fertility among a group of Kalahari bushmen in Botswana. *Social Science Information* 21:95–125.

Winkler, H. A.
1938 *Rock-Drawings of Southern Upper Egypt, I.* London: Egypt Exploration Society.
1939 *Rock-Drawings of Southern Upper Egypt, II (including 'Uweinat).* London: Egypt Exploration Society.

Winlock, H.E.
1955 *Models of Daily Life in Ancient Egypt from the Tomb of Meket-Ré at Thebes.* Cambridge: University Press.

Winterhalder, B. and E.A. Smith
1981 *Hunter-Gatherer Forgaging Strategies: Ethnographic and archaeological analyses.* Chicago: University Press.

Wittfogel, Karl
1957 *Oriental Despotism: A comparative study of total power.* New Haven, Connecticut: Yale University Press.

WOVA (World Association of Veterinary Anatomists)
1983 *Nomina Anatomica Verterinaria*, third edition. Ithaca, New York: International Committee on Veterinary Gross Anatomical Nomenclature.

Wright, H. E., Jr.
1968 Natural environment of early food production north of Mesopotamia. *Science* 161:334–339.
1976 The environmental setting for plant domestication in the Near East. *Science* 194:385–389.
1977 Environmental change and the origins of agriculture in the Old and New Worlds. In

*Origins of Agriculture*, edited by C.A. Reed, pp. 281–318. The Hague: Mouton Publishers.

Wright, H.T.
1969 *The Administration of Rural Production in an Early Mesopotamian Town.* Museum of Anthropology, Anthropological Papers 38. Ann Arbor: University of Michigan Press.

Yokell, Carol A.
in prep A The faunal remains from Hermann Junker's expedition to the predynastic site of Merimde Beni-Salâme in Egypt's western delta.
in prep B Idealized depictions or historical records of offerings? Inferences from faunal remains from a decade of excavations at Karnak. Ms on file with the University of Illinois Graduate College Fellowships and Grants Office.
1997 Pigs are edible, too! How untested assumptions complicated interpretations of Egyptian archaeology. Paper presented at the 2nd Annual Midwest Graduate Student Conference in African studies, Urbana-Champaign, Illinois.
n.d.a Notes on the faunal remains from Archaic levels at Mendes, 1992 and 1993 seasons. Ms on file with the University of Illinois Graduate College Fellowships and Grants Office.
n.d.b Preliminary analysis of the faunal remains from the 1995 season of the ARCE-USAID field school at Memphis. Ms on file with the American Research Center in Egypt, Cairo.

Youatt, William
1837 *Sheep: Their breeds, management and diseases.* London: Baldwin and Cradock.
1847 *The Pig: A treatise on the breeds, management, feeding, and medical treatment of swine; with directions for salting pork, and curing bacon and hams.* Philadelphia: Lea and Blanchard.

Yousef, M.K., L. Hahn and H.D. Johnson
1968 Adaptation of cattle. In *Adaptations of Domestic Animals*, edited by E. Hafez, pp. 233–245. Philadelphia: Lea and Febiger.

Zeder, Melinda
1988 Understanding urban process through the study of specialized subsistence economy in the Near East. *Journal of Anthropological Archaeology* 7:1–55.
1991 *Feeding Cities: Specialized animal economy in the ancient Near East.* Smithsonian Series in Archaeo-logical Inquiry. Washington, D.C.: Smithsonian Institution Press.
1994 Of kings and shepherds: Specialized animal economy in Ur III Mesopotamia. In *Chiefdoms and Early States in the Near East: The organizational dynamics of cultural complexity*, edited by G. Stein and M. Rothman, pp. 175–192. Monographs in World Prehistory 18. Madison, Wisconsin: Prehistory Press.

Zeuner, F.E.
1955 The goats of early Jericho. *Palestine Exploration Quarterly* 86:70-86.
1963 *A History of Domesticated Animals.* New York: Hutchinson.

van Zinderen Bakker, E.
1976 Paleoecological background of the origin of agriculture in Africa. In *Origins of African Plant Domestication*, edited by J. Harlan, pp. 43–63. The Hague: Mouton Publishers.

Zohary, D. and M. Hopf
1988 *Domestication of Plants in the Old World.* Oxford: University Press.

www.ingramcontent.com/pod-product-compliance
Lightning Source LLC
LaVergne TN
LVHW071218210926
848482LV00015B/837